Auto Repair

for dummies®
A Wiley Brand

Auto Repair

3rd Edition

by Desiree White, SheMechanic® and CEO of Crown's Corner Mechanics, and Deanna Sclar

for dummies®
A Wiley Brand

Auto Repair For Dummies®, 3rd Edition

Published by: **John Wiley & Sons, Inc.,** 111 River Street, Hoboken, NJ 07030-5774, www.wiley.com

For general information on our other products and services, please contact our Customer Care Department within the U.S. at 877-762-2974, outside the U.S. at 317-572-3993, or fax 317-572-4002. For technical support, please visit https://hub.wiley.com/community/support/dummies.

Wiley publishes in a variety of print and electronic formats and by print-on-demand. Some material included with standard print versions of this book may not be included in e-books or in print-on-demand. If this book refers to media that is not included in the version you purchased, you may download this material at http://booksupport.wiley.com. For more information about Wiley products, visit www.wiley.com.

Library of Congress Control Number is available from the publisher.

ISBN 978-1-394-40820-7 (pbk); ISBN 978-1-394-40821-4 (ePUB); ISBN 978-1-394-40822-1 (ePDF)

SKY10163711_072826

Contents at a Glance

Table of Contents

Introduction

For a lot of people, getting a driver's license feels like freedom. Then the freedom machine starts making a noise, flashing a light, leaking on the driveway, or demanding a repair bill with enough zeros to ruin your week. Suddenly, the open road feels a little less poetic.

The problem usually isn't that cars are impossible. It's that most of us were handed the keys long before anyone explained what the machine was trying to tell us. We learn how to steer, brake, signal, and park, but not how to tell a harmless noise from a dangerous one, how to do the boring maintenance that saves real money, or how to talk to a repair shop without feeling like we just wandered into an expensive guessing game.

That's what this book is for. We're not trying to turn you into a master technician with a lift, a wall of specialty tools, and a hobby that requires nitrile gloves by the box. Our goal is to help you become the kind of driver who understands the basics, handles the simple stuff, spots trouble early, knows when a job is safely DIY, and knows when it's time to put the tools down and call a pro.

About This Book

This edition of *Auto Repair For Dummies* is about much more than old-school wrenching. Yes, it covers the hands-on basics: opening the hood, checking fluids, changing a tire, using a jack safely, building a toolbox, and doing the preventive maintenance that keeps a vehicle from getting dramatic at the worst possible time. But it also lives in the world your car lives in now.

That means you'll find help with modern electrical systems, scan tools, computer-controlled ignition and fuel systems, direct injection, turbocharging, emissions hardware, advanced safety systems, hybrid technology, EV charging basics, battery thermal management, and the reality that sometimes the smartest repair move is not "do it yourself," but "diagnose it correctly and choose the right help."

We explain what the major systems do, how they work together, what they need from you, what warning signs matter, and what you can often check before you start buying parts out of frustration. We keep the jargon on a leash, the step-by-step stuff practical, and the safety lines bright and obvious — especially around brakes, lifting, and high-voltage hybrid/EV hardware.

Foolish Assumptions

When we say "foolish assumptions," we don't mean you're foolish. We mean we're making a few guesses about why you picked up this book. We're assuming one or more of these sounds like you:

- You're smart, capable, and perfectly able to learn this stuff, but cars have never exactly been your favorite language.
- You want to understand your vehicle without turning auto repair into a second career.
- You'd like to stop nodding politely at mysterious repair-shop jargon while wondering whether you actually need the thing that costs $1,200.
- You want to do the simple maintenance and easy fixes yourself, both to save money and to know the job was done right.
- You want clear guidance on which jobs are reasonable for a driveway DIYer and which jobs belong to a professional with better equipment and more liability insurance.
- You drive an older vehicle, a newer computer-controlled vehicle, or something in between — gas, diesel, hybrid, or EV — and you want advice that fits the systems your vehicle actually has.
- You'd like to catch little problems while they're still cheap, manageable, and mildly annoying instead of waiting until they become smoke, tow trucks, and emotional damage.

If that sounds like you, you're in the right place.

Icons Used in This Book

Throughout this book, I use a few icons to flag the information you'll probably want to notice before you charge ahead with a wrench or a little too much confidence.

TIP

The Tip icon points out shortcuts, smart habits, and small moves that make life easier and save time or money.

REMEMBER

A Remember icon flags the kind of information worth keeping in your head, your notes, or your glove box because it comes up again and again.

WARNING

The Warning icon marks the stuff that can hurt you, damage the vehicle, or turn a manageable job into an expensive one if you ignore it.

TECHNICAL STUFF

The Technical Stuff icon gives you the deeper why behind the system. It's there when you want the extra layer of understanding, but you won't be lost if you skim past it or never read it.

Beyond the Book

In addition to what's in these pages, this book also comes with a Cheat Sheet that gives you quick-reference reminders, checklists, and other "tell me the important part fast" help. It's the kind of thing you'll appreciate when you don't feel like rereading a whole chapter just to confirm a pressure check, a maintenance habit, or a roadside sanity check. Just go to `www.dummies.com` and search for "Auto Repair For Dummies Cheat Sheet."

Where to Go from Here

You can read this book straight through, or you can treat it like the automotive emergency contact you keep nearby and use only when the car starts acting up. Both approaches work.

If you've never opened the hood without moral support, start at the beginning with Part 1. If your car is already making drama, head straight to Part 5 and let the symptoms guide you. If you drive a hybrid or EV — or you're thinking about one — Chapter 10 and the hybrid/EV sections throughout the book can help you separate the familiar stuff from the high-voltage "nope, not today" stuff. If you want to get better at routine maintenance before anything goes wrong, Chapter 2 is one of the highest-value stops in the whole book.

Most of all, start with one small win. Check the oil. Check the tire pressure. Read the battery label. Use a scan tool instead of guessing. Learn where the jack points are before you need them on the side of the road in bad shoes. Small wins build confidence fast, and confidence is what turns "I can't do this" into "Okay, I can do this part."

And if a job turns out to be too complicated, too risky, or too far into orange-cable territory, that doesn't mean you failed. It means you understood the job well enough to make a smart decision, which is exactly the point.

1 Getting to Know Your Vehicle

IN THIS PART . . .

Learn essential skills to stay safe and confident around your car.

Perform quick monthly checks to catch problems early.

Build a toolbox with the tools you actually need.

Understand how your car starts, runs, and moves.

IN THIS CHAPTER

» Staying safe before you start

» Identifying key parts and opening the hood with confidence

» Fueling or charging your car the right way

» Jacking and lifting the car safely

» Changing a tire and understanding TPMS alerts

» Handling roadside safety and emergencies

Chapter 1

Introducing Essential Skills for Every Driver

Most people feel at least a little nervous about doing their own car maintenance. Maybe you've never popped the hood. Maybe you've heard horror stories about cars falling off jacks or mysterious dashboard lights that never go away. Relax — this chapter is here to show you that with the right gear, a little knowledge, and a healthy dose of common sense, you can take control of your car instead of the other way around.

This chapter gives you a no-nonsense foundation you can use right away. You start with safety and getting oriented to the parts and info every driver should know, including how to fuel or charge properly. Then you pop the hood with confidence, jack and lift the car safely, swap a tire, and understand TPMS. Finally, you can practice how to keep calm and safe if something goes wrong on the roadside.

HOW I GOT HERE — AND WHY I KNOW YOU CAN DO THIS, TOO

Before I was The SheMechanic®, I was a single mom working in healthcare, trying to hold everything together while working long shifts and spending hours every day in Atlanta traffic. I was exhausted, I was missing time with my kids, and I knew I needed to find another way. What started as a way to earn extra money became something much bigger when I began buying cars, fixing them, and selling them right out of my carport. That side hustle didn't just help me survive a hard season of life — it helped me discover what I was truly built to do.

I did not come into this business with years of formal shop experience. I taught myself. I started with Google and YouTube, then got more serious and pulled the curriculum from a local college program, ordered the books, and taught myself the material at home. I learned the same way a lot of people do when they are determined: by reading, studying, testing myself, getting my hands dirty, making mistakes, and refusing to quit. I started with smaller repairs, moved into deeper diagnostics, and eventually got to the point where I was tearing down engines, understanding every part, and building them back up. Along the way, I learned the programs, the tools, the software, and the business side, too.

As my skills grew, my kids were right there with me. We learned together. What began with flipping cars at home grew into a mobile mechanic business, with my tools in the trunk and me going wherever the work was. I recorded everything — the wins, the hard days, the setbacks, the breakthroughs, the happy moments, the frustrating moments, and the growth — because this journey changed my life in real time. Over time, that mobile business became Crown's Corner Mechanics, a thriving repair shop where we fix cars, build engines, serve our community, and keep breaking barriers in an industry that does not always expect to see women leading from the front.

This is exactly why I am so happy to write this book. I know what it feels like to start with no roadmap, no shop background, and no one handing you permission. I also know what can happen when you are willing to learn anyway. I am living proof that you do not have to come from the automotive world to understand it. You can learn this. You can do this. And I hope this book helps every reader feel more confident, more capable, and more connected to their vehicle — because if I could build this life one lesson at a time, I truly believe they can, too.

Getting Started Right

Picture this chapter as your starter kit for everything we're going to build on. We're kicking things off with the basics — like how to safely jack up your car and remove a wheel — because once you're comfy doing that, you'll breeze through the more advanced stuff. It's like learning to walk before you run — except with a lot more grease and a lot more laughs.

We picked these starting points because they're the building blocks for everything else. For example, once you've got a handle on the basics of wheel removal, checking your brakes or rotating your tires will be second nature. And when we dive into bigger repairs in later chapters, you'll be so glad you've got these fundamentals down.

Why did we choose these specific topics for this chapter? Because they're the core skills that will make every future task easier. Whether it's diagnosing a noise or tackling a bigger engine fix, these basics will keep you grounded and confident.

Using Personal Protective Gear

Before you so much as reach for a wrench, dress the part. You wouldn't fry bacon in the nude (at least we hope not), so don't go poking around under the hood without basic protection. This section walks you through the personal gear that helps you stay protected.

Even simple jobs can fling grit, drip fluids, or create sharp edges. Gear up with the basics:

- **Safety glasses:** Shield eyes from rust, grit, and splashes. Keep a clear pair in the garage and a tinted pair for outdoor work.
- **Mechanic's gloves:** Unlike fabric garden gloves, mechanic's gloves combine a snug fit, good dexterity, and palm materials that resist cuts and heat. Choose light-duty gloves for general work and heavier cut-resistant gloves when handling sharp metal.
- **High-visibility vest:** Neon fabric with reflective tape makes you obvious at night or in rain. This visibility is essential for roadside work.

- **Hearing protection:** Use industrial hearing protectors — not winter ear warmers. Wear them whenever you're using impact tools, grinding, or hammering. You'll use hearing protection during tire changes and again during wheel/brake and wheel-service work (see Chapters 16 and 18).
- **Respiratory protection (N95–P100):** A disposable N95 filters most dust; a P100 filters finer particles (ideal for brake dust and rust).
- **Fire extinguisher (ABC):** Multipurpose A-B-C extinguishers (see Figure 1-1) handle ordinary combustibles, flammable liquids, and electrical fires. Keep a small, charged unit in the garage (and a second in the trunk, if you do roadside work).

WARNING

Never blow brake dust with compressed air. Instead of removing the dust safely, compressed air just spreads it everywhere — onto nearby components, your clothing, tools, and into the shop air, making cleanup harder, not easier. Wipe or use a vacuum with a HEPA filter.

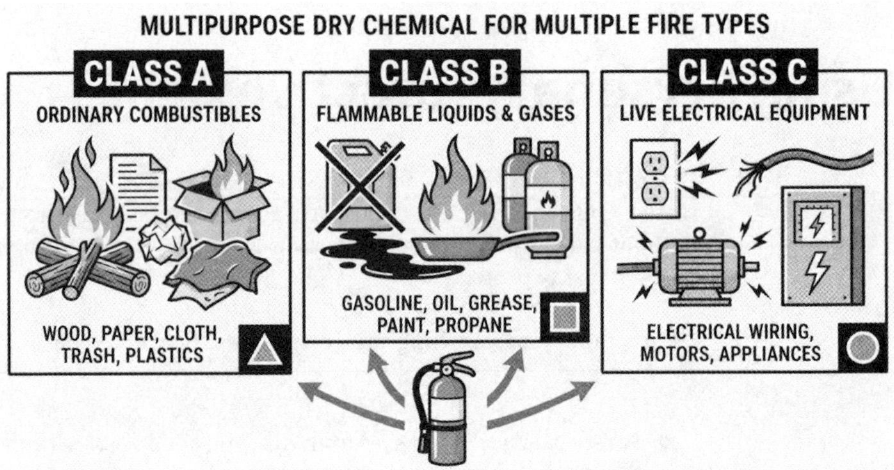

Generated with AI using OpenAI

FIGURE 1-1: Fire extinguisher (ABC): What it means.

- **Work lighting:** A headlamp or LED shop light frees both hands and helps you see leaks, fasteners, and alignment marks.
- **First-aid kit:** Stock adhesive bandages (including fingertip/knuckle sizes), antiseptic wipes, burn cream/gel, tweezers, saline eye wash, and nitrile gloves — items you'll actually use in a garage.

- **Clothing:** Wear close-fitting sleeves, avoid dangling jewelry, and tie back long hair.
- **Footwear:** Wear closed-toe, grippy shoes or boots; steel toes are a plus when handling wheels or brake rotors.

Auto parts stores, hardware/big-box stores, and online retailers carry all of these items. If you're on a budget, start with glasses, gloves, and a vest; add the rest as you go.

Practicing Roadside Safety

If your car breaks down, your first job isn't playing mechanic — it's making yourself visible and staying out of traffic. Safety comes first; the fix can wait.

This short list of gear keeps you safe and seen while doing roadside repairs (see "Using Personal Protective Gear" earlier in the chapter, for more):

- **Reflective triangles:** Don't park one triangle right behind the bumper. Place triangles 100 to 200 feet back; if you have three, stagger them — one near the car, one farther back, and one offset if the road curves — to warn drivers early.
- **Portable roadside lights:** LED beacons or electronic flares are bright, compact, reusable, and far safer than old-school burn-type flares.
- **Phone power:** Keep a charged power bank in the glove box so that your phone doesn't die when you need to call for help.

If you have to stop on the roadside, follow these steps to stay safe:

1. **Pull over to the safest spot you can find.**

   Aim for a wide shoulder or exit ramp; avoid blind curves. Keep wheels turned away from traffic.

2. **Turn on your hazards and stay belted.**

   If traffic is heavy or visibility is poor, stay in the vehicle until it's safe to get out.

3. **Put on a hi-vis vest before exiting.**

   Step out on the passenger-side if possible. Face traffic when walking near the roadway and never turn your back on moving cars — even for a second.

4. **Set reflective triangles.**

   Walk facing traffic, place them back from the car as described in the preceding list, and add LED beacons if you have them.

5. **Call for help and share your location.**

   Use your app/roadside number; drop a map pin if needed.

6. **Re-enter traffic carefully.**

   When help arrives or you're ready to leave, pack up triangles and merge when it's clearly safe.

TIP

Practice using your triangle kit and LED beacons at home in daylight so deployment is automatic when it's dark or raining.

WARNING

If you're on a high-speed road with a narrow shoulder or poor visibility, stay in the vehicle with your seatbelt on and call for help rather than standing outside.

Review the information in the "Using Jacks and Stands to Lift Safely" section, later in this chapter, before attempting any roadside tire work.

Unlocking Vehicle Info with Your VIN

Every car has a story — and your *Vehicle Identification Number* (VIN) is the 17-character decoder ring that tells it. Think of the VIN like your car's birth certificate, medical chart, and driver's license all rolled into one. The VIN tells you what engine you've got, what kind of transmission it's rockin', what emissions system it uses — all the stuff parts people care about, but you probably don't (yet).

Finding your VIN

You can usually find your VIN in one of these places:

- **On the dashboard:** Stand outside the car and peek through the windshield on the driver's side, near where the glass meets the dash. There's usually a little metal plate tucked in there. Found it? You just leveled up.
- **On the door jamb:** Open the driver's door and look where the door latches. There's often a white or silver sticker with a barcode and your VIN. It might look boring, but it's VIP info.

- **On your paperwork:** Your VIN is also printed on your registration and insurance card. If your glove box looks like a receipt explosion, this is a good time to organize it.

TIP

If the dashboard VIN doesn't match the title or registration, stop and investigate. If only the door-jamb label differs, ask whether the vehicle had collision repair or a replacement label and verify the history before buying parts or trusting the paperwork.

Getting car-specific information

Running your VIN means entering the 17 characters into a trusted lookup so you get car-specific information. Think of it like scanning a product barcode to pull up the exact model and options — no guesswork. The VIN is public vehicle data tied to the car, not your personal info.

Use free lookups for safety recalls (for example, the federal recall portal) and Search by VIN on manufacturer/parts sites to confirm that a part matches your exact year, make, model, engine, and trim. For history reports (accidents, title issues), services like Carfax and AutoCheck are paid. Your owner portal or dealer can also use the VIN to retrieve build info and service bulletins.

TIP

If any parts site offers a Search by VIN option, always use it. It's like telling a barista your coffee order in your exact voice instead of letting them guess based on your hair color and vibe.

Getting the most out of your VIN

With your VIN in hand, you're able to do the following things:

- **Order the right parts.** Your VIN locks in the exact combo of engine, trim, transmission, and emissions package so that you don't buy the radiator that fits only the obscure export variant.
- **Check for recalls.** A quick VIN search shows whether your car needs a free safety fix, or a *recall* — don't skip them.
- **Verify the vehicle's history (used-car shopping).** History reports surface accidents, title problems, and odometer issues.
- **Pull exact specs.** Fluid types and service information vary by build, and the VIN points you to the right data so that you avoid using the wrong fluid or following the wrong procedure.

Wanting to go deeper?

See Chapter 3 for tools like torque wrenches, plus how to use them, and Chapter 14 for the full breakdown on oil types, viscosity, and fluid know-how.

Keeping Your Car Running with the Right Fuel (or Charge)

Back in the day, your only concern was picking the right pump handle — black for regular and green for diesel, and you didn't mix them up. One modern gotcha: Pump nozzles are different sizes. The diesel nozzle is larger, which usually prevents you from jamming diesel into a gas car — but the smaller gasoline nozzle fits many diesel fillers, so it's possible to misfuel a diesel with gas. We see it all the time, and it causes a big (and expensive) issue. Today, you may be juggling gas stations, charging stations, or both, depending on what's parked in your driveway.

Gasoline: The old classic

Gas stations are still the most common fueling stop, but there are some rules of the road:

TIP

- **Don't top off after the nozzle clicks.** All you're doing is overfilling the charcoal canister in your *EVAP system* — basically drowning the part of your car that filters fuel vapors. You'll be rewarded with a glowing Check Engine Light and maybe a lecture from your mechanic.
- **Tighten the cap.** A loose gas cap is the No. 1 cause of mystery check engine lights. If your car tattles on you, check the cap before you panic.
- **Watch the octane.** Premium isn't better unless your engine calls for it. Feeding your Corolla 93-octane is like buying filet mignon for a goldfish.

TECHNICAL STUFF

Octane isn't a power booster — it's a resistance rating. It measures how well gasoline can handle heat and pressure without spontaneously igniting inside your engine. The higher the octane, the more heat and compression it can take before it says, "I'm gonna blow."

EV charging: Welcome to the future

Electric cars don't sip gas — they gulp electricity. Here's what that means in day-to-day driving:

- **Level 1 (110 to 120 volts):** A plain wall outlet. Adds about three to five miles of range per hour. This level is fine for short hops; otherwise it's like filling a swimming pool with a coffee straw.
- **Level 2 (240 volts):** A home charger or public station. Adds 20 to 30 miles per hour. This level is the overnight sweet spot: Plug in before bed, wake up full.
- **DC fast charging:** The espresso shot of EV fueling. Adds 60 to 100-plus miles in 20 to 30 minutes. Perfect for trips, but not a daily diet — frequent fast charging can age a battery faster than Level 2.

REMEMBER

If you install Level 2 at home, check your panel capacity first and ask the electrician about rebates. On road trips, precondition the battery (via the car's settings/app) on the way to a fast charger — it shortens charge time and saves you dollars at pay-by-the-minute stations.

Hybrids: The overachievers

Hybrids burn gas, store electricity, and switch between the two without asking your permission. Some even plug in for bonus range. Translation:

- **Yes, you still need gas.** The charge port won't save you when the tank is empty.
- **Sometimes you need both.** Monday: gas station. Tuesday: charging station. Wednesday: explaining why it sounds like a lawnmower one minute and a spaceship the next.

Opening the Hood

For some folks, popping the hood feels like trying to break into Fort Knox. The lever hides like it's playing peek-a-boo, the latch never wants to cooperate, and when you finally get it open, you're staring into what looks like the engine room of the Millennium Falcon. Relax — opening the hood is easier than it looks.

Just follow these steps:

1. **Pull the release lever to unlock the hood.**

   Most cars keep the release lever by the driver's left knee, but some hide it down by the pedals. Pull it, and you'll hear a faint clunk as the hood unlatches. Congratulations — you've just beaten level one.

2. **Slide your hand under the hood's front edge to release the latch and lift the hood.**

   Find the little metal lever in there — push, pull, or wiggle it (depending on your car) while lifting the hood. Don't worry if you look awkward; every mechanic does the hood shuffle at least once a day.

3. **Prop it up.**

   Older cars come with a *prop rod* — a skinny metal stick that you must fit into a hole like you're assembling IKEA furniture. Newer cars usually have hydraulic struts that hold the hood up for you. If yours has struts, give thanks; if it has a rod, welcome to arm-day training. Before you work under the hood, make sure the prop rod is fully seated or the struts are holding the hood securely.

WARNING

A hood can fall if the prop rod isn't seated properly or if weak hood struts stop holding. Before you put your head or hands under the hood, make sure the prop rod is fully seated in the correct hole or that the struts are holding the hood securely. If the hood sags, shifts, or won't stay up, stop and fix the support before you continue.

Once the hood is up, take a minute to get familiar with the basics. You don't need to know how to rebuild an engine (yet), but spotting these parts (see Figure 1-2) makes you look 10 percent more confident instantly:

- **Battery:** Usually a black box with two cables. Pro tip: Don't touch both posts at once unless you enjoy being a human fuse.
- **Oil dipstick:** A little handle (often yellow or orange) that lets you check oil level. Think of the dipstick as your car's version of a bathroom scale.
- **Coolant reservoir:** A translucent plastic jug with MAX and MIN lines. If the jug is empty, your car's basically dehydrated.
- **Brake fluid reservoir:** A small container near the back of the engine bay. Keeping this reservoir topped up means your brakes will stop you instead of just suggesting it.
- **Fuse box:** A black plastic box full of tiny fuses. Blow one, and your headlights or radio may go on strike.

TIP

Take a quick picture of the engine bay with your phone. Later, when you're asking, "What's that thing again?" you'll have your own cheat sheet.

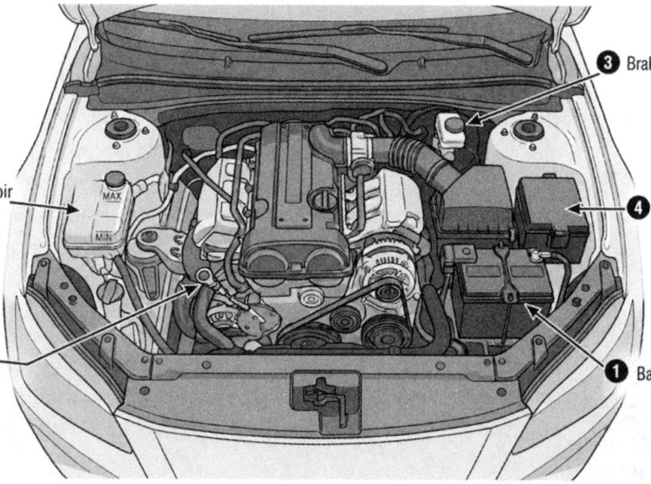

FIGURE 1-2: Where to find parts under the hood.

Generated with AI using OpenAI

Taking Things Apart

The biggest rookie mistake? Not recording how something came apart. Losing or mixing up fasteners can derail a repair, and moving a ground wire to the wrong spot can keep the car from starting. Avoid that headache with three habits that take seconds and save hours later.

Before you even loosen the first bolt:

1. **Take clear before photos.**

   Snap close-ups from a few angles. Get the routing of hoses and the order of washers/spacers in the frame. One photo can save a lot of head-scratching later — and it's satisfying to compare the before/after when you're done.

2. **Bag and label hardware.**

   Think of each small part or group of parts as a little *sub-assembly* — basically a mini-unit of the bigger puzzle. When you take something apart, you want to keep all the nuts, bolts, and screws from each sub-assembly together in a labeled bag. That way, when you're putting it all back, you know exactly which little group of hardware goes where. It makes re-assembly way easier and a lot less of a guessing game.

3. **Tag wires and connectors.**

   Wrap a small strip of color-coded electrical tape and add a quick note (A-A, B-B, or short words). You'll avoid a late-night wiring-diagram rabbit hole.

FIRST TEARDOWN CONFIDENCE

The first engine I took apart was with my 16-year-old son, right in the front yard. We bagged every bolt (labeled to its part) and stuck matching labeled tape on each piece laid out on the dining table in disassembly order. When it was time to put it back together, those bags and labels turned two first-timers into a team with a plan — and the engine ran. Use that approach for any job, big or small.

WARNING

Before unplugging electrical connectors (12-volt systems), disconnect the negative battery cable to prevent shorts. Never touch or open anything with orange-sheathed high-voltage cables — hybrid/EV work is for trained pros.

Here's a quick re-assembly checklist:

- Match your tags (A-A, B-B) and confirm grounds are back on clean metal.
- Hand-start all bolts and then torque in sequence to spec.
- Do a final photo compare with your before shots.

REMEMBER

Grounds matter. A *ground* is the wire or strap that connects an electrical part to the car's metal body or frame so that electricity can return to the battery. Put each ground wire back on bare, clean metal in the exact location it came from. If the engine won't start after re-assembly, recheck your grounds and your photos/tags first. For a deeper dive into grounding, wiring, and other electrical troubleshooting, see Chapter 6.

Using Jacks and Stands to Lift Safely

Whether you're checking fluids or lifting a vehicle, a few simple safety steps can make the difference between a quick fix and a serious injury.

WARNING

Lifting a car is where safety gear really matters. Do it right, and the job feels routine; do it wrong, and you risk damage or injury.

Gathering big safety tools

Think of big safety tools like this: The *jack* is like a strong friend who can lift the car but can't hold it forever. That's what *jack stands* are for: They step in and do the heavy holding while you work safely underneath. And wheel chocks? They're like parking boots for your tires; they keep the car from rolling away mid-job. Anytime you're lifting a car, you need all three: Lift it, lock it, and block it. No exceptions.

Here's a more in-depth explanation of each one:

- **Hydraulic floor jack:** This tool lifts the vehicle off the ground. It rolls on wheels and uses a long handle to pump fluid through a metal plunger called a *piston,* giving you the power to raise even a heavy car with minimal effort. You place the flat pad under a designated *jack point.* (Check your owner's manual — the jack point is usually a reinforced pinch weld or metal cross-member.) Don't just pick a random spot; the wrong placement can crush parts or crack the body.
- **Jack stands (rated in tons):** Jack stands are your real support system. Once the car is lifted, you slide them under the vehicle at proper jack points and adjust them to equal height. Then you lower the jack slightly so that the full weight rests on the stands, not the jack. Make sure the ground is hard and level — no gravel, no slanted driveways. Also, check the weight rating — a pair rated 2 tons means it can support 4,000 pounds total when used correctly (but that's split across both stands, not one).
- **Wheel chocks:** You tuck these solid wedges in front of or behind the tires that stay on the ground — usually the opposite end of where you're lifting. So if you're raising the front of the car, chock both rear wheels. *Wheel chocks* stop the car from rolling or shifting while you work, even if it's in Park or gear. Think of wheel chocks as a cheap insurance policy that keeps gravity from becoming your enemy.

WARNING

Never crawl under a car supported by a jack — jacks can slip or leak. Set rated jack stands on a solid, level surface. Chock the wheels and do a quick shake test before going under. If the vehicle rocks, shifts, wobbles, or a stand or chock moves, do not go under it. Lower the vehicle, reset the jack stands and wheel chocks, and test again until the vehicle feels rock-solid.

Lifting an auto

Follow these steps — every time — in this order to safely lift an auto:

1. **Park, prep, and secure the vehicle.**

   Work on level, solid ground. Put the transmission in Park (or in gear for a manual), set the parking brake, and place wheel chocks on the opposite end of the car from where you'll lift.

2. **Find the jack points.**

   Use the owner's manual to identify reinforced lift points (often notches/ridges at the pinch welds or reinforced pads on trucks/SUVs). Only lift at these spots to avoid crushing bodywork or components.

3. **Position the jack and raise the car slowly.**

   Center the jack pad on the lift point and raise the vehicle just high enough to place your jack stands at their support points. Pause if anything shifts or creaks.

4. **Set jack stands and lower onto them.**

   Place rated stands under the correct support points at equal height. Lower the car onto the stands and remove light pressure from the jack.

5. **Do a shake test.**

   Give the vehicle a firm push at a safe body point. If it wobbles, reset your stands and chocks until it's rock-solid.

6. **Lower safely when finished.**

   Raise the car slightly, remove the stands, and lower slowly. Remove chocks last.

WARNING

A word of caution for EV & hybrid cars: Many vehicles have a battery pack under the floor. Don't place a jack under the battery. Use the EV/hybrid-specific lift points shown in the owner's manual; some models require adapter pucks.

WARNING

Check weight ratings on your jack and stands and be sure they meet or exceed your vehicle's weight. Some stand ratings are per pair, others per stand — confirm the manufacturer's convention.

TIP

As an additional backup (not a substitute for stands), you can slide a removed wheel under a sturdy rocker area away from your work zone. It won't hold the car, but it adds a margin of protection if something slips.

Dealing with Tire Changes

Flat tires never schedule themselves around your convenience. They show up in the rain, in the dark, or when you're already late. Knowing how to handle one — and having the right gear — keeps a hassle from becoming a hazard.

TIP

Even if you have roadside assistance, practice a tire change at home once. A sunny-driveway rehearsal beats learning on the shoulder while traffic blasts by. Also, familiarize yourself with these items:

- **Wheel lock key:** Some cars use locking lug nuts to discourage thieves. The key looks like a funky socket and usually lives in the glove box or with the spare/jack kit. No key equals no wheel off, so confirm you have it before a trip.
- **Torque wrench basics:** A *torque wrench* is a tool that lets you tighten bolts to a specific amount of force so that you hit that just-right zone — neither too tight nor too loose. There's a Goldilocks zone for lug nuts: Too tight can warp rotors or strip studs, and too loose risks a wobbly wheel. Use a torque wrench to tighten in a star pattern to the specified torque in your owner's manual or service info. For more on using a torque wrench and other essential tools, see Chapter 3.
- **Modern alloys versus hubcaps:** Many newer cars have exposed lug nuts and no hubcaps. If your car has a center cap over the lugs, pop it off gently per the manual.
- **Portable tire inflators:** A compact 12-volt or battery-powered inflator can top up a slow leak long enough to reach a shop. It's a temporary assist, not a repair.
- **Plug kits:** For small tread punctures (think nails, not sidewalls), a simple plug kit can get you rolling. Treat plugs as temporary and have a pro inspect or repair the tire internally.
- **Work lights:** A rechargeable LED work light or headlamp makes you visible and turns a roadside scramble into an organized task.
- **Gloves and mats:** A pair of work gloves and a folding kneeling pad or mat save your hands and knees — especially on gravel, snow, or mud.
- **Spare tire reality check:** Know what your car carries: full-size spare, space-saver ("donut"), or a *sealant/compressor kit* only. Your plan changes depending on what's in the trunk.

REMEMBER

After installing the wheel, torque the lugs in a star pattern to spec. Recheck the torque after a short drive if your manual recommends it.

WARNING

Never work under a vehicle supported only by a jack. Review the previous section in this chapter, set wheel chocks, and use rated jack stands on level ground before you do anything that puts you beside or under the car.

TIP

Lug hardware varies: Some wheels use conical (tapered) seats, others ball seats. Match the hardware to the wheel design and always follow the manufacturer's torque specification rather than a generic number.

For the full step-by-step tire change procedure (with diagrams), jump to Chapter 16.

Checking Out the Tire Pressure Monitoring System

That little glowing horseshoe on your dash isn't a good-luck charm — it's your car's way of saying check your tire pressures. The Tire Pressure Monitoring System (TPMS) warns you when pressure is low, but like any tech, it has quirks.

Here are a few important things to know:

- **Automatic reset:** On many cars, once you inflate the low tire(s) to the door-jamb spec, the light turns off after a short drive.
- **Manual reset:** Some systems need a Reset via a dash button or infotainment menu to tell the car pressures are set.
- **Sensor issues:** Wheel-mounted sensors age and can fail. If the light stays on even with correct pressures (or flashes and then stays on), you may have a sensor or system fault, not a flat.
- **Cold-weather effect:** A big outdoor temperature drop lowers pressure and can trigger the light in the morning. Inflate to spec and recheck after a short drive.
- **Limits of older systems:** On cars made before 2008 — before the federal TPMS mandate kicked in — the system may not identify which tire is low or show the exact pressure. You'll just get a general warning, so you may need to check all four tires manually. For cars from 2008 onward, thanks to that mandate, the TPMS typically tells you exactly which tire is low and what the pressure is.

If the TPMS light comes on, follow these steps to make some checks:

1. **Pull over safely and inspect.**

   If a tire looks obviously low or damaged, address that tire first. Keep a digital gauge and portable inflator in the trunk. When the light pops on, you can verify pressure and top up in minutes without hunting for a gas-station air pump.

2. **Measure all four tires with a digital gauge.**

   Use the recommended pressure listed on the door jamb as your target, not the number on the tire's sidewall. The *door jamb* is the area inside the driver's door frame where you'll find a sticker with the correct tire pressures for your vehicle. The *sidewall* is simply the side of the tire, where you'll often see the tire brand and maximum pressure rating. That number on the sidewall is the maximum the tire can hold, not the recommended pressure for everyday driving — always go with the door jamb info for a safe and comfy ride.

3. **Inflate to spec and recheck.**

   A compact inflator can top up a slow leak enough to reach a shop. Don't drive any distance on a severely underinflated tire — you can overheat and destroy the tire (and possibly the wheel). If in doubt, inflate first or call roadside assistance.

4. **Drive a few miles or perform the reset.**

   Many systems clear automatically after driving; others require a Reset per your owner's manual.

5. **Schedule service if the light persists.**

   A weak/faulty sensor or system fault needs a shop to test and replace/program.

REMEMBER

Think of TPMS as a backup — helpful, but you still check pressures monthly and before trips. (The monthly maintenance checklist in Chapter 2 reinforces manual pressure checks.)

TECHNICAL STUFF

Some vehicles use direct TPMS (sensors in each wheel); others use indirect systems that infer pressure from wheel speeds. After tire rotation or sensor replacement, some cars need a relearn/reset procedure; see the owner's manual.

Handling Lockouts

Nothing stings quite like staring at your keys through the window. The good news: Lockouts happen to everyone (you aren't alone!), and you have safe ways to deal with them.

Here are a few tips for cars manufactured 2005 and onward:

- **Dead key-fob batteries:** Fobs are great . . . until they aren't. Keep a spare fob battery in the glove box or wallet and swap it when range gets wonky.

- **Digital keys:** Many newer cars let you unlock with a smartphone app. It only helps if your phone's charged and you have service. Some models offer Bluetooth/NFC (Near Field Communication) unlock that works offline — check your manual.
- **Hidden key inside the fob:** Many key fobs have a small mechanical key blade tucked inside. Look for a slider, latch, or release button on the fob, remove the key, and use it to unlock the driver's door if the fob battery dies. On some cars, the key cylinder is hidden behind a small cap on the door handle, so check your owner's manual before you actually need it.
- **When all else fails:** Skip the coat hanger. DIY lock-picking ruins weatherstripping, scratches paint, and can trigger airbags. Call roadside help or a locksmith.

When you're locked out of an older car

This list provides tips for old-school lockouts (older cars, before the year 2005):

- **Spare keys:** Skip the old magnetic box under the bumper (thieves know it). Leave a spare at home or with a trusted friend.
- **Manual locks:** If a window's cracked, you might finagle the button — but pros have the slim tools; you have a wire hanger. See the problem?
- **AAA/roadside assistance:** It's usually faster and safer than improvising — and often included in basic coverage.

What to do right now if you're locked out

If you're locked out right now, follow these steps:

1. **Check all doors and the hatch.**

   Sometimes one lock or handle behaves differently.

2. **Try your manufacturer's app or digital key.**

   Many newer cars have an app from the automaker (like the GMC app) that can unlock the doors.

3. **Open the manufacturer's app and follow the unlock prompt; move to an area with a better signal, if needed.**

4. **Use the hidden key in the fob.**

   Most fobs have a slide-release key blade. Pop the small cover on the driver's door handle to reveal the cylinder and unlock manually.

5. **If the fob won't start the car once inside, hold the fob against the start button (or the steering column sweet spot) to start.**

   This step lets a weak-battery fob be recognized.

6. **Call roadside help if the preceding steps don't work.**

   It's cheaper than replacing a bent door frame or airbag module.

THE MOST EXPENSIVE TWO MINUTES OF MY WEEK

We lock every car in the shop. It's a good policy — it keeps keys from walking away and makes sure cars don't get tampered with. But that policy turned into a problem one afternoon when we went to move a customer's vehicle . . . and the 12-volt battery had died.

No power meant the key fob didn't work. And even though we had the actual key, it couldn't unlock the door — the lock mechanism was completely electronic. So there we were, staring at a car we couldn't open, couldn't jump, and definitely couldn't move.

Now, I'm a mechanic — not a magician. I knew I could try to slide a tool in through the door seal to pop it manually, but that's also a great way to scratch the tint, bend the trim, or worse, trigger the side curtain airbags — none of which I wanted to explain to a customer.

So I called a locksmith. He showed up, did his thing, and had the door open in less than two minutes. And I swear that door clicked open smoother than anything I've ever touched.

The bill, on the other hand? That stung.

Lesson learned: Sometimes the smartest tool in the shop isn't a pry bar or scan tool — it's a professional with the right skills, and a credit card that can handle the damage.

IN THIS CHAPTER

» Getting your bearings under the hood and on digital dashboards

» Swapping filters and airflow

» Spotting belt and hose issues

» Checking the fluids that matter

» Caring for tires

Chapter 2 Conducting Preventive Maintenance

Think of this chapter as your car's monthly wellness visit — your easy routine to keep things running smoothly all year long. In this chapter, we walk you through all the little checkups that, when done regularly, can save you from big headaches down the road. We cover everything from filters and fluids to tires and tech checks, all in a friendly, easy-to-follow way.

Staying Ahead: Why These Monthly Checks Matter (and Pay Off Later)

Ten minutes here can prevent the uh-oh later. We front-load Chapter 2 with simple routines because they unlock confidence for bigger wins in later chapters, such as diagnosing electrical gremlins (Chapters 5 and 6), chasing cooling issues (Chapters 12 and 13), or picking the right oil and interval (Chapter 14).

REMEMBER

These quick checks complement — not replace — the deeper maintenance we talk about in later chapters.

Getting Your Bearings under the Hood

Even if you've popped the hood once or twice, taking a moment to really get familiar with what's under it is going to make everything else a whole lot easier. Think of the process like finding your comfort zone so that you can move around confidently. In this section, we show you how to get oriented, recognize the key components, and feel at home under the hood so that you know exactly where everything lives and are ready to tackle your monthly routine with confidence.

REMEMBER

A car that gets regular mini-checkups is safer, quieter, and cheaper to own, and the Appendix provides a monthly maintenance checklist to make sure you're not missing anything. Keep this checklist on your phone and treat it like brushing your teeth: quick, easy, and worth it.

If you're by the car, think of this section as a calm, one-minute tour — not a test. If you're not sure how to pop the hood, Chapter 1 walks through the steps.

Once the hood is open, you're just putting names to five landmarks:

- **Battery:** The rectangular box with two thick cables (red + and black –) that stores and delivers power to start the engine and run lights, locks, and infotainment. Clean, snug terminals help prevent slow starts and odd electrical hiccups.
- **Oil dipstick:** A small colored handle (often yellow or orange) attached to a thin metal strip you pull out to read the oil level. A simple, reliable way to confirm the engine has enough oil (and that it isn't unusually dark or gritty), which protects the engine from wear.
- **Coolant reservoir:** A translucent plastic tank with MIN/MAX marks, connected to the radiator. This reservoir allows the cooling system to expand and contract as the engine heats and cools, keeping temperature in the safe zone. The level should sit between the lines when the engine is cold.
- **Brake-fluid reservoir:** A small, usually semi-clear container near the back of the engine bay (cap may say DOT 3/4/5.1). This container holds the hydraulic fluid that transmits your foot's force to the brakes. A slowly dropping level can hint at pad wear; very low fluid can signal a leak that needs attention.
- **Serpentine belt:** The long, ribbed belt snaking around several pulleys at the front of the engine. Belts drive critical accessories, such as the alternator (charging), water pump (cooling on many cars), power steering pump (on some), and A/C compressor. A quick look for fraying, missing ribs, or shiny glazing helps you catch wear early.

If anything looks a little different under your car's hood, no stress — locations vary, but the labels and purpose are the same. Snap a quick photo of what you see, if you'd like; it becomes a handy cheat sheet for the checks you can do in this chapter.

Deciphering Digital Dashboards and Service Apps

This section takes a friendly, low-pressure look at the messages your car gives you. Start by glancing at the instrument cluster for maintenance reminders (things like Service due or an oil-life percentage). Then, if your automaker has a phone app, open it to see any vehicle health notes in one place. Think of these as gentle nudges, not emergencies. If the message is time/mileage-based (a routine reminder), you'll clear/reset it after you finish the task. We show you when and how in the relevant sections (oil life and service intervals in Chapter 14, warning lights and basic diagnostics in Chapters 5 and 6, and no-start triage in Chapter 22).

Here's how to tell what your car's message means:

- **Maintenance reminders (routine):** Words like Maintenance required, Service due, or an oil-life number are scheduling prompts. Do the task and then reset the reminder. (You can find the reset steps where they apply, especially in Chapter 14.)
- **Fault or warning lights (problem):** Icons like Check Engine, ABS, Airbag, or Charging System mean a system has flagged an issue. Those lights aren't reset-and-forget — they call for a quick check or scan. (See the basics in Chapters 5 and 6 and what to do if the car won't start in Chapter 22.)
- **Manufacturer's app:** Many brands show oil-life, tire pressures, or open recalls in their app's Vehicle Health section. Use it as a dashboard for reminders and then confirm details in the owner's manual or Chapter 14.

WARNING

If a light is red, flashing, or the car drives poorly, skip the reset and jump to Chapters 5 and 6, which cover electrical and diagnostics, or Chapter 22, which offers a breakdown guide. Clearing a fault without fixing the cause just hides the clue you need.

Changing Filters

Changing filters might sound a bit technical, but think of it as giving your car a fresh breath of air. We walk you through changing two main filters: the engine air filter and the cabin air filter. Both of these filters are quick and easy to check, and doing so helps your engine run smoothly and your car's interior stay fresh.

Engine air filter

Your engine air filter keeps dust and debris out of your engine's air supply, helping it run smoothly and efficiently. Checking and replacing the engine air filter is easy, and it keeps your engine breathing clean. To change the engine air filter, follow these steps:

1. **Locate the airbox.**

   The *airbox* is usually a black box with clips or screws and a big hose connected to the engine's intake. The airbox is usually located near the front or side of the engine bay, often on top or to the side. The intake is basically the air pathway for your engine. (For more about the engine's intake, see Chapter 7.)

2. **Open and inspect the filter.**

   Once you open the airbox, hold the filter element up to the light. If you can't see light through it or it's full of dirt, it's time for a new one.

3. **Seat the gasket.**

   Make sure the rubber edge sits flat before you close the airbox.

TIP

If you need a new filter, you can find engine and cabin filters at any auto parts store or online. Bring your car's VIN with you to ensure you get the exact filter for your vehicle. Knowing your car's VIN is an easy way to make sure you're buying the right part. (For more on your car's VIN, see Chapter 1.)

Cabin air filter

Your cabin air filter is like a breath of fresh air for your car's interior. It helps keep the air that flows through your HVAC system (that's your car's heating, ventilation, and air-conditioning) nice and clean. When the cabin filter is clogged, your heater and A/C won't blow as strongly, and it can even affect how quickly your windows defog. You can find out more about the HVAC system in Chapter 19, but the following steps guide you through checking your filter.

1. **Locate the cabin air filter.**

   In many cars, the cabin air filter is behind the glove box. You may need to lower the glove box door to see the filter housing. In some models, it may be under the dashboard or under the hood near the *cowl,* the area at the base of your windshield. Your owner's manual will point you right to it.

2. **Check the airflow direction.**

   When replacing the filter, follow the arrow on the new filter so that it's installed in the correct airflow direction.

WARNING

If an ADAS camera is behind the windshield near the mirror, keep that area clean and free of rain-repellent overspray. ADAS stands for Advanced Driver Assistance System, and an ADAS camera helps with things like lane-keeping or emergency braking. We cover ADAS calibration in Chapter 18 when we talk about tires and alignment.

Checking Belts and Hoses

Checking your belts and hoses may sound like a small thing, but it's a great way to catch little issues before they become big ones.

The serpentine belt is a long, winding belt that snakes around various pulleys at the front of your engine. Its job is to drive multiple accessories, such as the alternator, power steering pump, and air-conditioning compressor. When you're checking this belt, look for *glazing* (a shiny appearance), cracks, or missing ribs. If the serpentine belt is worn out, it can't do its job properly.

In addition, many different types of hoses are under the hood, including coolant hoses and heater hoses. These hoses carry coolant to keep your engine at the right temperature. Check them for swelling, soft spots, cracks, or any crusty areas around the clamps.

REMEMBER

If you smell coolant or see any leaks or your temperature gauge is acting weird, see Chapters 12 and 13 immediately. Ignoring these signs may lead to overheating, which risks serious engine damage. Acting quickly can prevent costly repairs and keep you safe on the road.

TECHNICAL STUFF

Many modern belts are made of EPDM, which stands for ethylene propylene diene monomer. EPDM is a durable type of rubber that doesn't crack as easily as older materials, so you might feel for wear or check if the ribs are worn down. When in doubt, check your service info or ask a shop.

Checking Your Battery

Your car's 12-volt battery may be small, but it's mighty important. Here's how to give it a quick checkup to keep everything running smoothly:

- **Check for corrosion.** Take a look at the battery *terminals* (those metal posts on top of the battery). If you see any white or greenish corrosion, you can clean it off with a proper battery cleaner or a baking soda solution. Just remember to rinse and dry it. Then tighten the terminals and add a little protection (like dielectric grease) to keep the corrosion from coming back.
- **Check the charge.** If your car is starting slowly or the accessories (like the radio or lights) seem weak, you can check the battery's state of charge with a simple tester. We go deeper into battery diagnostics in Chapters 5 and 6.

WARNING

If you have a hybrid or EV, remember that your 12-volt battery can still leave you stranded even though you have a high-voltage pack. Never mess with any orange-cabled components — those are high voltage. We cover high-voltage safety in Chapter 6.

TIP

If your car sits for weeks at a time, a smart battery maintainer can help keep the 12-volt battery healthy. You can check out Chapter 3 for tool options.

Monitoring and Topping Off Fluids

The quick checks we describe in this section are your car's monthly wellness visit. We keep it simple and point you to the right chapter when you want the deeper dive.

TIP

Keep a small rag, a funnel, and paper towels in the trunk. A two-minute peek is easier when you're not hunting for supplies.

Engine oil

You can check your engine oil with a dipstick or digitally. If you have a dipstick, park on level ground, shut the engine off for a few minutes, then pull the dipstick, wipe, re-insert, and read. Oil should sit between the marks. If it's near low, add the exact type of oil your car calls for. (We unpack specs and the oil life monitor in Chapter 14.)

Many newer cars don't have a dipstick and instead use a digital oil-level display in the cluster or infotainment. Look for an Oil Level screen in vehicle settings or maintenance menus. Follow the on-screen prompts. You may need to have the engine warm and be parked level. We explain digital oil monitoring and service intervals in Chapter 14.

REMEMBER

Change oil or low oil level messages are different from the Oil Life Monitor's percentage. One is about how much oil; the other is about when to change it — see Chapter 14 for the full story.

Coolant

The coolant is for engine temperature control. The coolant reservoir is a translucent tank with MIN/MAX lines. Check when the engine is cold — the level should be between the marks.

If the coolant is low, don't just top it off blindly. Low coolant can mean a leak or the wrong mix. Head to Chapters 12 and 13 to find out what to use and what to check next.

WARNING

Never open a hot radiator cap because pressure plus heat equals scalding. Use only the reservoir level for quick checks. (To find out how the system works and how to service it, see Chapters 12 and 13.)

Brake fluid

The brake fluid provides hydraulic stopping power. The small reservoir near the back of the engine bay should sit near the "MAX" line.

A gradual drop in brake fluid can simply track pad wear; very low or dirty fluid needs attention. Deep-dive into types (DOT 3/4/5.1), intervals, and safe handling in Chapters 15 and 16.

Transmission fluid

Some cars have a transmission dipstick you can read; many newer ones are sealed or require checking from underneath with the vehicle level and the fluid at a specific temperature. That's not a monthly driveway task.

If you do have a dipstick, your owner's manual will show the exact procedure (often engine running, shifter in Park).

Want the full how-to and service guidance? See Chapter 19 for fluid types (ATF, CVT, DCT), service intervals, and correct check and refill procedures.

WARNING

Don't open transmission fill/level plugs at random. The wrong procedure can over- or under-fill and harm the unit. Save the full check for Chapter 19 or a pro.

Power steering

Some cars have power steering fluid, but some don't. If your car has a power-steering fluid reservoir, check that level and condition like other fluids.

Many modern cars use electric power steering (EPS), which means no fluid to check. We explain steering types and care in Chapter 17.

Taking Care of Tires and TPMS

Your tires are the only part of the car that actually touch the road, so a quick check here pays off in safety, handling, and fuel economy. Treat the TPMS as your early-warning system and a handheld gauge as your truth check. Set pressures to the door-jamb numbers when the tires are cold and then let TPMS keep watch while you drive.

Pressures

Set the pressures to the door-jamb numbers. Use the sticker on the driver's door jamb — those PSI numbers are what your suspension, handling, and tire life are tuned for. The big number on the tire sidewall is a maximum, not a target (Chapter 1 explains this distinction).

The sticker gives the number based on the car being cold. In this case, *cold* means the car has been parked for three-plus hours or driven less than a mile. Temperature and driving heat change pressure.

Some cars list different pressures for front and rear. Follow the sticker exactly, especially when towing or fully loaded.

REMEMBER

A cold snap can drop pressures overnight and trigger a TPMS light. Fill to door-jamb spec and drive a few miles. Many systems clear themselves, while others need a menu/button Reset (covered in Chapter 1).

WHAT YOUR MEASUREMENTS MEAN

As a general wear, here's what those measurements mean:

- **~10/32 in (varies by model):** New tires
- **4/32 in or less:** Hydroplaning resistance falls off. Replace soon for rain.
- **5/32 in or less:** Packed snow needs more bite. Replace sooner for snow.
- **2/32 in:** Below this measurement is unsafe (and often illegal). Legal bare minimum United States.

Tread

Tread refers to the pattern of grooves and raised rubber on the surface of your tire that grips the road. Your *tread* isn't just rubber left — it's your rain-and-grip insurance. Deeper grooves move water and slush out from under the tire so that you keep steering, braking, and accelerating when roads are ugly.

To measure and read the wear story, use a tread-depth gauge. Press the probe into a main groove and read the number. Check three spots across the tire (inner edge, center, and outer edge) and two or three places around the tire. Write down the readings; that pattern tells a story.

Look across the grooves for little raised bridges, or *wear bars*. When the surrounding tread is flush with those bars, the tire is at the built-in minimum (about 2/32 in on most passenger tires). If you're getting close, start planning for replacement.

You can also use a gauge to measure the grooves. If you don't have one handy, you can use a coin as a backup. The quarter test assesses wet-road safety. If Washington's head isn't covered (≈ 4/32 in), wet stopping distances jump. Plan to replace your tires soon. To test for the legal minimum, use a penny. If you can see all of Lincoln's head (≈ 2/32 in), the tire is worn out and needs to be replaced now.

Wear pattern

You can read the wear pattern to figure out what to fix, not just replace. Table 2-1 gives you the scoop on what to do.

TABLE 2-1 **Wear Pattern**

What you see	What it means	What to do
Center worn more than edges	Over-inflated	Drop to the door-jamb pressures. (See the section "Pressures," earlier in this chapter.)
Both edges worn	Under-inflated	Bring pressure up to spec.
One edge worn	Alignment/camber issue	Chapter 18 links tire wear to alignment and even ADAS camera calibration after some suspension work.
Feathering/cupping (scalloped feel)	Balance, shocks/ struts, or toe	Ask for a balance check and an inspection of suspension parts; see Chapter 18 for the deeper dive.

Rotations

For tire rotations, you'll want to follow your manual and don't hide a problem. Rotate on the schedule in your owner's manual; it keeps wear even. If you see feathering/cupping, address balance/alignment rather than rotating it away. For rotation patterns and alignment basics, see Chapter 18.

TIP

Keep a compact inflator and a quality gauge in the trunk. A TPMS light becomes a five-minute top-up, not a detour (see Chapter 3).

TECHNICAL STUFF

Some cars use direct TPMS (a sensor in each wheel), others indirect TPMS (it infers a low tire from wheel speed). After rotations or sensor swaps, some models need a relearn/reset. Your owner's manual shows the steps, and Chapter 1 gives you the quick behavior overview.

Keeping an Eye on Wipers and Washers

Clear vision is half of safe driving. This quick monthly check keeps the glass clean, the blades doing their job, and your car's driver-assist "eyes" from getting confused:

- **Blades:** If they chatter, streak, skip, or leave missed arcs, it's time to replace them. Lift the arm gently, press the small release tab, and note the adapter style your car uses (hook, pinch-tab, or bayonet) so the new blades click right in. *Hook adapters* look like a curved hook at the end of the wiper arm, *pinch-tabs* have two small side tabs you press, and *bayonets* have a straight, narrow metal arm. Replace both blades at the same time for an even wipe.

- **Washer fluid:** Use a ready-to-pour all-season fluid; in winter, pick one rated for subfreezing temps. Avoid plain water (it freezes, streaks, and can grow algae). Fill the reservoir with the windshield-spray icon on the cap; a small funnel keeps spills off paint.
- **Cameras and sensors:** Gently wipe the windshield area in front of the ADAS camera (near the rear-view mirror) and the radar cover in the grille. Grime here can blind safety systems. Skip heavy rain-repellent near the camera's view.

After alignment/suspension work or a windshield replacement, some cars require ADAS calibration. You can see how this ties into alignment in Chapter 18.

TIP

In winter, leave wipers down when parked and de-ice the glass, not the rubber. Don't chip ice off the blades — spray de-icer on the windshield and let the defroster do the work.

Conducting Tech Checks

A tiny bit of tech goes a long way. This section shows you how to use a simple scan tool and your car's own screens to understand what the dashboard is trying to tell you — without turning you into a full-time technician. When you're ready for the deeper dive, go to Chapters 3, 5, and 6.

- **OBD-II at home (scanner plus phone app):** Plug a basic Bluetooth scanner into the OBD-II port (usually under the dash) and open the app. You can read trouble codes, see live data (like coolant temp or O_2 sensor activity), and confirm whether a fix worked. Don't clear codes before you write them down — they're clues. You discover what common lights mean in Chapter 5 and how to test with meters in Chapters 3 and 6.
- **Built-in diagnostics (vehicle health screens and the manufacturer's app):** Many cars show maintenance reminders, oil-life percentage, TPMS readings, or Vehicle Health reports right in the cluster/infotainment or the automaker's phone app. Treat those diagnostics as starting points and then confirm with a handheld gauge or scan tool where it matters (tires, fluids, and codes). Cross-refs for the details live in Chapter 1 (TPMS basics) and Chapters 5 and 6 (electrical/diagnostics).

TIP

If a Check Engine light appears, snap a photo of the dash and save the code from your scanner/app. A steady light means schedule a check soon; a flashing light means misfire — park it to protect the catalytic converter and jump to Chapter 22 for triage.

Getting Two Quick Wins with EV/Hybrids

Even with a big high-voltage battery on board, your monthly EV/hybrid check is mostly simple, visual stuff. These two fast habits keep charging safe and thermal systems happy, while anything orange-cabled stays strictly hands-off. For deeper know-how, we point you to Chapters 6, 10, and 13 as you grow your skills.

Charging cable care

Before you plug in, glance at the connector for bent/discolored pins, a sticky or damaged latch button, and nicks or chew-marks along the jacket. If anything looks off, don't use it. Seat the connector until it clicks and keep caps on when stored.

Avoid puddles; coil and store the cable clean and dry so grit doesn't grind into the contacts next time. (Charging basics and best practices live in Chapter 10.)

TIP

If a home outlet or plug feels hot after Level-1 charging, stop and have the receptacle checked. Heat means resistance. Chapter 10 covers safer home-charging setups.

Inverter/battery coolant

Many hybrids/EVs use separate coolant loops for the inverter, battery, and cabin. Look for reservoirs labeled for those systems and check MIN/MAX when the car is cold. If any loop is low, don't top off with a random coolant; different chemistries don't mix. Flag it and flip to Chapter 13 for the right coolant and next steps, with Chapter 6 for what's safe to touch.

REMEMBER

Your EV/hybrid still has a 12-volt battery; the quick health check from the earlier "Checking Your Battery" section applies here, too. See Chapter 6 for testing basics.

WARNING

Never open, probe, or tighten anything on orange-sheathed high-voltage components. That's pro-only territory. Review Chapter 6 before doing more than a visual check.

IN THIS CHAPTER

» Gearing up with essential safety equipment

» Building your core hand tool collection

» Embracing digital tools for modern cars

» Organizing and building your toolbox smartly

Chapter 3

Stocking the Modern Toolbox

Walking into the tool aisle at the hardware store can feel like stepping into Hogwarts for the first time — overwhelming, magical, and slightly terrifying. You're surrounded by shiny chrome, mysterious gadgets, and enough options to make your head spin. Do you need a 12-point socket or a 6-point? What's the difference between a combination wrench and an adjustable wrench? And why does everyone keep talking about the 10mm socket like it's the Bermuda Triangle of the tool world?

Here's the good news: You don't need to buy everything at once, and you definitely don't need the most expensive tools to get started. What you do need is a solid foundation of quality basics that'll handle 90 percent of the jobs you'll tackle on your car. This chapter walks you through exactly what to buy, why you need it, and how to avoid wasting money on tools that'll just collect dust.

Whether you're changing your first air filter or diving into your first brake job, the right tools make the difference between "I did it!" and "I give up." Let's build your toolbox the smart way — one essential tool at a time.

Safety First: Personal Protective Equipment

Before you buy a single wrench, let's talk about the most important tools in your arsenal: the ones that keep you safe. Working on cars exposes you to sharp edges, hot surfaces, toxic fluids, flying debris, and heavy parts that can crush fingers faster than you can say "ouch."

In Chapter 1, we cover all the essential personal protective equipment (PPE) you need — safety glasses, mechanic's gloves, proper work clothing, hearing protection, respirators, and fire extinguishers. If you don't already have these items, flip to Chapter 1 and make that your first shopping list. No exceptions.

REMEMBER

Your safety gear is just as important as your wrenches and sockets. Don't skip it, don't cheap out on it, and always use it. Every. Single. Time.

Core Hand Tools: The Foundation of Your Toolbox

Hand tools are exactly what they sound like: tools you hold and operate by hand, without electricity, batteries, air pressure, or any other power source. Hand tools are the backbone of any repair job. They don't need charging, they don't break down easily, and if you buy quality, they'll outlast your car (and maybe you). Start with these essentials, and you'll be able to tackle most basic maintenance and repairs.

Combination wrenches (metric and SAE)

A *combination wrench* is a wrench that has an open-end on one side and a box-end (closed loop) on the other as shown in Figure 3-1. The open-end is great for quick adjustments; the box-end grips bolts more securely and is less likely to slip and round off the corners. You'll need both metric sizes, which are measured in millimeters, and *SAE* sizes. SAE stands for Society of Automotive Engineers, and in tool sizing, it usually refers to inch-based or fractional sizes. Cars love to mix and match, so having both sets saves you from staring at one stubborn bolt like it personally betrayed you.

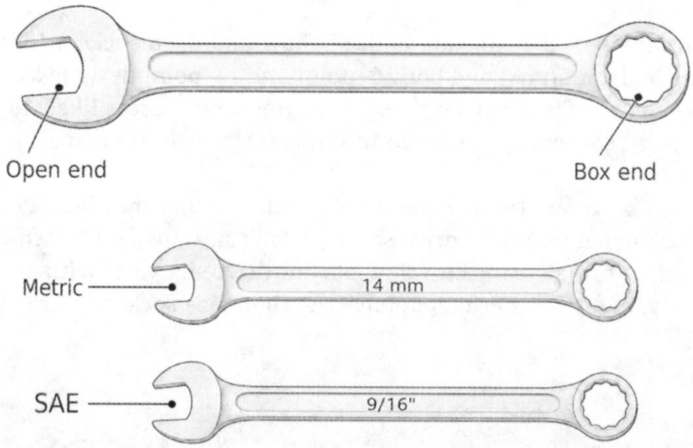

FIGURE 3-1: Combination wrench anatomy.

Generated with AI using OpenAI

Common sizes to start with:

- **Metric:** 8mm, 10mm, 12mm, 13mm, 14mm, 15mm, 17mm, 19mm
- **SAE:** 1/4", 5/16", 3/8", 7/16", 1/2", 9/16", 5/8", 3/4"

TIP

The 10mm wrench (and socket) has a supernatural ability to disappear. Buy extras. Seriously. You'll thank me later.

Socket set with ratchet

A *ratchet* is a handle with a built-in mechanism that lets you tighten or loosen a fastener in one direction and then swing the handle back without removing it. A *socket* is a removable, cylinder-shaped tool that snaps onto the ratchet and fits over a nut or bolt head.

You can buy them alone or as a set, but socket sets are your best friend. A ratchet lets you turn bolts without lifting the tool off the fastener — way faster than a wrench.

Sockets come in three common *drive sizes* (the square hole that fits the ratchet):

- **1/4" drive:** Small sockets for tight spaces and delicate work
- **3/8" drive:** The workhorse — handles most everyday jobs
- **1/2" drive:** Big sockets for heavy-duty fasteners (lug nuts, suspension bolts)

Look for sets that include both shallow and deep sockets (deep sockets fit over long bolts or studs) and both 6-point and 12-point designs as seen in Figure 3-2. Six-point sockets grip bolts more securely and are less likely to round off corners; 12-point sockets are easier to fit onto fasteners in tight spaces.

Drive size refers to the square nub on the ratchet that fits into the socket. A 3/8" drive ratchet uses 3/8" drive sockets. You can't mix and match without an *adapter*, which is a small connector that lets one drive size work with another. Adapters are handy, but it's easier to just have the right size socket and ratchet for the job.

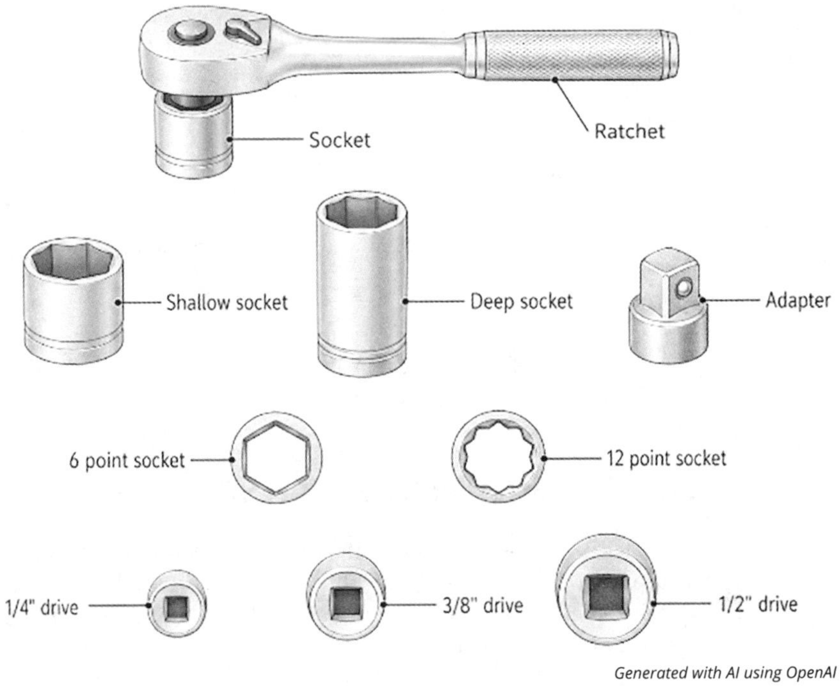

FIGURE 3-2: Socket set components.

Extension bars and universal joints

Extension bars let you reach bolts buried deep in the engine bay or hidden behind other parts. *Universal joints* (U-joints) let you turn bolts at an angle when you can't get the ratchet lined up straight. A set of short, medium, and long extensions, plus a U-joint or two, will save you hours of frustration.

Adjustable wrench

An *adjustable wrench* (sometimes called a crescent wrench, after the brand) has a movable jaw that fits multiple sizes of nuts and bolts. It's not as secure as a combination wrench or socket, but it's a lifesaver when you need a size you don't have or when you're working with oddball fasteners.

WARNING

Always pull toward the adjustable side of the wrench (the side with the movable jaw). Pushing away can cause the jaw to slip and round off the bolt — or smash your knuckles into something sharp.

Pliers (needle-nose, slip-joint, and locking)

Pliers are the Swiss Army knife of the toolbox. You'll use them to grip, twist, pull, hold, and occasionally swear at stubborn parts.

Start with these three types:

- **Needle-nose pliers:** Long, skinny jaws for reaching into tight spaces and gripping small parts
- **Slip-joint pliers:** Adjustable jaws for general gripping and turning
- **Locking pliers (vise grips):** Lock onto a part and hold it tight, freeing up your hands

Screwdrivers (Phillips, flat-blade, and Torx)

You'd think screwdrivers would be simple, but cars use a ridiculous variety of screw heads. At minimum, you need

- **Phillips (cross-head):** The most common type
- **Flat-blade (slotted):** For old-school screws and prying (carefully)
- **Torx (star-shaped):** Increasingly common on modern cars

Get a set with multiple sizes of each type, as shown in Figure 3-3. Magnetic tips are a bonus — they help you hold onto tiny screws in tight spaces.

REMEMBER

Use the right size and type of screwdriver for the job. A too-small or wrong-type driver will strip the screw head, turning a simple job into a nightmare extraction project.

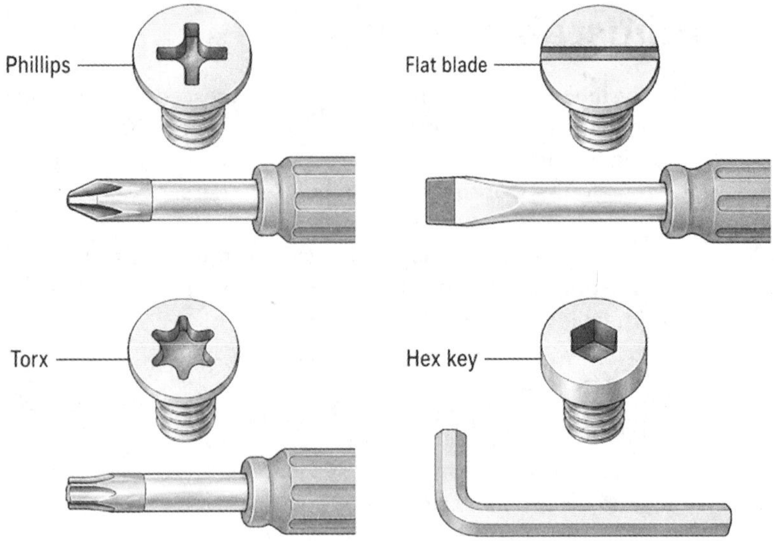

Generated with AI using OpenAI

FIGURE 3-3: Common fastener types and their matching drivers.

Hex keys (Allen wrenches)

Hex keys (also called Allen wrenches) fit into hexagonal sockets in bolts and screws. They're common on brake calipers, interior trim, and aftermarket parts. Get a set in both metric and SAE sizes.

Pry bars and trim tools

Sometimes you need to gently (or not so gently) persuade parts to come apart. *Pry bars* help separate stuck components; *plastic trim tools* let you pop off interior panels and clips without scratching or breaking them.

Lifting and Supporting Your Vehicle Safely

In Chapter 1, we walk through the complete safety procedure for jacking and lifting your vehicle — where to place the jack, how to position jack stands, the importance of wheel chocks, and all the critical steps that keep you safe while working under a car. If you skipped that section, go back and read it now. Seriously.

After you know how to lift safely, we can talk about the actual equipment you need and what to look for when you're shopping. Think of this section as your buying guide for the tools that literally hold your life in their hands (or stands).

Hydraulic floor jack

A *hydraulic floor jack* is your primary lifting tool. It rolls on wheels and uses a long handle to pump hydraulic fluid through a piston, giving you the mechanical advantage to raise even a heavy vehicle with minimal effort.

Here's what to look for when purchasing a jack:

- **Weight rating:** Choose a jack rated for at least 1.5 times your vehicle's weight. Check your owner's manual or the sticker inside the driver's door for your car's weight.
- **Lift height:** Low-profile jacks (2 to 4 inches) work better for sports cars and lowered vehicles; SUVs and trucks need jacks with a higher lift capacity (often 6-plus inches).
- **Saddle pad:** The *saddle pad* is the top contact surface of the jack — the part that touches the vehicle's lift point. Look for a wide, rubber-coated saddle that won't slip or damage the lift point.
- **Build quality:** Steel construction beats aluminum for durability, though aluminum is lighter if you need portability.

WARNING

Never — NEVER — crawl under a car supported only by a jack. Jacks are for lifting, not supporting. Hydraulic seals can fail, handles can shift, and jacks can tip. Use jack stands every single time.

Jack stands (rated for your vehicle's weight)

Jack stands are non-negotiable. Jack stands are the tools that actually hold the weight of your car while you work underneath. A jack is only for lifting the car; jack stands are what keep it safely supported.

Here's what to look for:

- **Weight rating:** Always check the rating carefully. Some manufacturers rate stands per pair (for example, 2 tons per pair = 4,000 lbs total across both stands), while others rate per stand (for example, "2 tons each" = 4,000 lbs per stand). Confirm the manufacturer's convention and make sure the total capacity exceeds your vehicle's weight.
- **Adjustability:** *Ratcheting stands* let you pull the center support post upward until it clicks into place, giving you multiple height settings. *Pin-style stands* lock at fixed intervals. Both work — just make sure you can match the height on both sides.

- **Base width:** A wider base is more stable, especially on slightly uneven surfaces.
- **Saddle design:** Look for a wide, flat top with a V-notch or rubber pad to cradle frame rails securely.

TIP

Always use stands in pairs, set them at equal height, and place them under designated support points (not random parts of the undercarriage).

Wheel chocks

Wheel chocks are simple wedges that prevent your car from rolling while it's lifted, as shown in Figure 3-4. They're cheap, unglamorous, and absolutely essential.

Here's what to look for:

- **Material:** Rubber chocks grip better and won't scratch garage floors; hard plastic is lighter but can slide on smooth concrete.
- **Size:** Larger chocks work for trucks and SUVs; compact chocks are fine for sedans and coupes.
- **Pair them up:** Always use at least two chocks — one in front of and one behind the tire (or both behind, if space is tight).

WARNING

In my shop, I've seen mechanics with 20, 30, even 40 years of experience get hurt — or killed — because they got comfortable and skipped a step. "Just this once" turns into "just one more time," and that's when gravity wins.

Jacks lift. Stands support. Chocks prevent rolling. It's not complicated, but it's critical.

Creeper (optional but highly recommended)

A *creeper* is a low, wheeled platform that lets you roll under the car instead of lying on the cold, hard ground wondering what you did to deserve this situation.

TIP

If you have long hair, tie it back before you get on the creeper. I learned this one the hard way. Picture this: You're rolling confidently under the car, feeling like a pro, and then — YANK — your hair gets caught under a wheel and suddenly you're stuck, scalp screaming, inventing profanity that would make a sailor blush. Tie. It. Back.

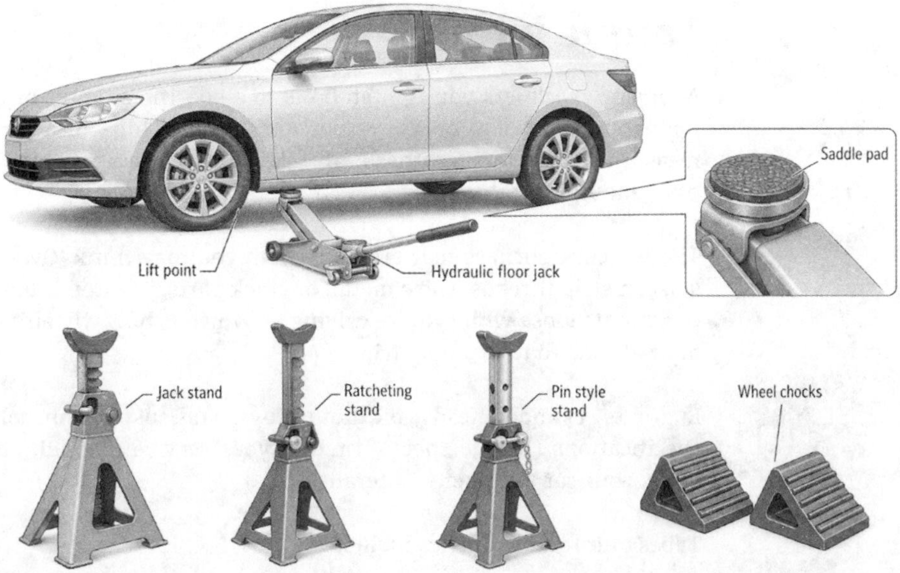

FIGURE 3-4: Proper safe lifting setup.

Generated with AI using OpenAI

Here's what to look for:

- **Padding:** A padded headrest and cushioned surface save your back and skull.
- **Wheels:** *Casters* are the small swivel wheels mounted underneath the tool or creeper. Look for smooth-rolling casters (at least four, ideally six) that glide on concrete without sticking.
- **Weight capacity:** Most creepers support 300 to 400 lbs; check the rating if you're carrying tools or a tool tray.
- **Size:** Standard creepers are about 40 inches long; *low-rider* models are shorter for tight spaces.

Your knees and spine will thank you. Trust me.

Measuring and Diagnostic Tools

Guessing is not a strategy when you're working on your car. *Measuring tools* help you work with precision, and *diagnostic tools* help you figure out what's actually wrong before you start throwing parts at the problem.

Torque wrench

A *torque wrench* lets you tighten bolts to a specific amount of force, measured in foot-pounds (ft-lbs) or Newton-meters (Nm). Think of a torque wrench like a measuring cup for tightness: It takes the guesswork out of "how tight is tight enough?"

The correct tightness matters more than you may think. Overtighten a bolt, and you can strip threads, warp metal, or crack parts. Tighten it too little, and the bolt can vibrate loose while you're driving — which is how wheels fall off and oil drain plugs decide to take a road trip.

REMEMBER

Lug nuts, cylinder heads, oil drain plugs, and suspension bolts all have torque specifications (torque specs) listed in your service manual, and following them keeps your car together — literally.

Types of torque wrenches include

- **Click-type:** The most common and affordable option. You set the desired torque on the handle, and the wrench makes a satisfying click when you hit it. It's like a kitchen timer for bolts: audible, reliable, and hard to miss.
- **Beam-type:** The budget-friendly choice. A needle on a scale shows you the torque as you pull. They're accurate, but require you to watch the gauge while tightening, which can be awkward in tight spaces.
- **Digital:** The fancy option. You set the torque on a screen, and it beeps or flashes when you reach it. They're more expensive, but super precise and easier to read — especially if your eyes aren't what they used to be.

TIP

Every torque wrench comes with instructions, but let's be honest — most people learn better by watching. If the manual feels like it's written in ancient Greek, hop on YouTube and search for your specific wrench model. Thousands of how-to videos show you exactly how to set a torque wrench, use it, and store it properly. Five minutes of video beats an hour of frustration.

Tire pressure gauge

Proper tire pressure improves fuel economy, handling, and tire life. It's one of those invisible things that actually matters, like flossing or remembering your anniversary.

Here's the problem: The gauge built into the gas station air pump is about as trustworthy as a weather forecast three weeks out. Those things have been beaten, frozen, and abused by thousands of drivers, and their idea of accurate is more like "in the general ballpark, maybe."

Do yourself a favor and buy a quality digital or dial-type gauge. Check your tires monthly and before any road trip. Digital gauges are easier to read (especially if you're working in the dark or forgot your glasses). Dial gauges are old-school reliable and never need batteries. Either way, $10 to $30 buys you peace of mind and better gas mileage.

TIP

Always check tire pressure when the tires are cold — before you've driven more than a mile or two. Driving heats up the tires and increases pressure, so if you check right after a trip, you'll get a reading that's higher than reality. It's like weighing yourself after Thanksgiving dinner — technically accurate, but not helpful.

Feeler gauges

Feeler gauges are thin metal strips used to measure teeny-tiny gaps: spark plug gaps, valve clearances, and other tolerances so small you'd need a microscope to see them clearly. They look like a little metal fan, the kind you'd use to cool off a very tiny, very hot bug.

Here's how they work: You slide different thickness blades into the gap until you find the one that fits snugly — not rattling around loose, but not forcing it like you're trying to jam a suitcase shut. Boom. You've just measured a gap to within a few thousandths of an inch, and you didn't even need to squint.

They're cheap, nearly indestructible, and weirdly satisfying to use. Plus, they make you feel like a precision engineer, even if you're just standing in your driveway in sweatpants.

TECHNICAL STUFF

Feeler gauges are labeled in thousandths of an inch (like 0.020") or millimeters. Keep them clean and rust-free. A corroded or bent blade won't slide smoothly, and your measurements will be off.

Calipers and micrometers (for advanced work)

If you're getting into engine building, machining, or any project where eyeballing it isn't an acceptable measurement technique, digital calipers and micrometers are about to become your new obsession. They let you measure parts down to thousandths of an inch — piston diameters, bearing clearances, brake rotor thickness, and other dimensions that matter way more than you'd think.

Most DIYers won't need these tools right away. If you're just changing oil and swapping brake pads, you're fine without them. But the moment you catch yourself wondering, "Is this cylinder bore still within spec?" or "How worn is this crankshaft journal," you've leveled up. Time to buy calipers.

TIP

Digital calipers are the easier option. Press a button, and they switch between inches and millimeters. They're easy to read, no squinting required. Micrometers are even more precise and are the go-to for measuring round parts like crankshaft journals or piston skirts. They take a little practice to use (there's a technique to getting consistent readings), but once you've got it, you'll feel like a machinist.

Digital Tools: Welcome to the 21st Century

Modern cars are rolling computers, and fixing them means speaking their language. Digital tools let you read trouble codes, monitor sensors, and diagnose problems that would've left mechanics scratching their heads 20 years ago. Think of these tools as your car's translator. They turn Check Engine Light panic into actual useful information.

OBD-II scanners and Bluetooth dongles

Most drivers today are working with a 1996 or newer vehicle, which means they probably have an OBD-II (On-Board Diagnostics) port — usually tucked under the dashboard near the steering column, like it's playing hide-and-seek. Plug in a scanner or Bluetooth dongle, and you can read diagnostic trouble codes (DTCs), which are your car's way of tattling on itself. If you drive an older, pre-1996 vehicle, it may use an OBD-I system instead, and those ports and readers weren't standardized the same way.

TIP

Translation: Check your vehicle's year, make, and model before buying a scan tool. For more on diagnostics, trouble codes, freeze-frame data, and how to research what those codes actually mean, see Chapter 5. Here's the breakdown:

- **Basic code readers:** The no-frills option. They spit out a code (like P0171), and you look it up online to figure out what it means. They're simple, cheap, and get the job done.
- **Bluetooth dongles:** The app-based option. These plug into the OBD-II port, as shown in Figure 3-5 and connect to your smartphone via free or paid apps (like Torque, BlueDriver, or OBD Fusion). You get live sensor data, *freeze*

frames (a snapshot of what was happening when the code triggered), and way more detail than a basic reader. It's like upgrading from a flip phone to a smartphone with pricing ranging from \$50 to \$150.

- **Professional-grade scanners:** The fancy ones. They do everything the cheaper tools do, plus *bidirectional controls* (you can command parts to turn on/off for testing), module programming, and manufacturer-specific codes. They're overkill for most DIYers, but if you're serious about diagnostics, they're worth it if you don't mind spending a few thousand dollars in most cases.

TECHNICAL STUFF

A trouble code tells you where to start looking, not what to replace. A P0171 code (System Too Lean) could mean a vacuum leak, a dirty mass airflow sensor, a failing fuel pump, or a dozen other things. Use the code as a clue, not a conviction. Don't just start throwing parts at the problem and hoping one sticks.

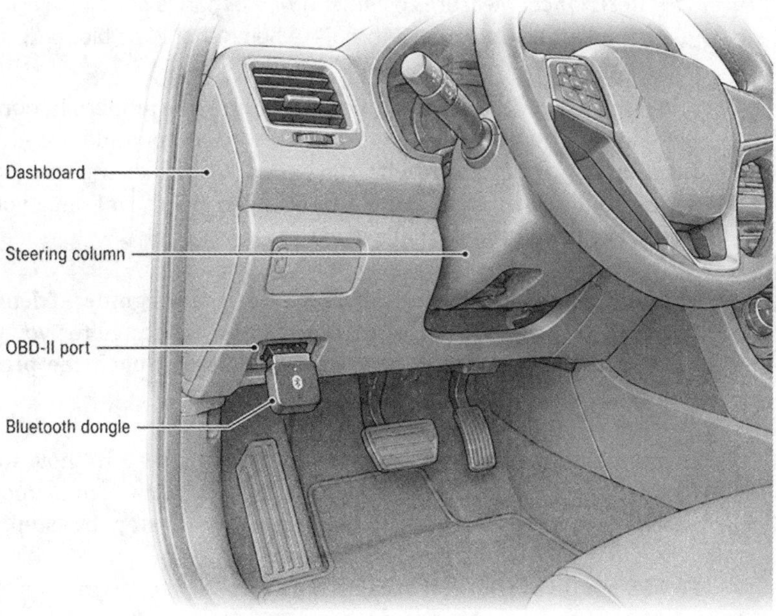

FIGURE 3-5: Locate your OBD-II.

Generated with AI using OpenAI

WARNING

Clearing a trouble code without fixing the problem is like turning off a smoke alarm without putting out the fire. The code will come back — usually angrier — and ignoring it can lead to bigger (and way more expensive) damage. Fix the issue first and then clear the code.

Digital multimeter

A *multimeter* is a handheld tool that helps you test electrical stuff in your car. Think of a multimeter as a detective gadget that answers questions like "Is my battery actually dead, or is something else broken?" or "Did this fuse blow, or is it fine?"

Here's what a multimeter does in plain English:

- **Voltage:** Measures electrical pressure. You use a multimeter to check whether your battery has enough juice or whether power is getting to a part that needs it.
- **Current:** Measures how much electricity is flowing through a wire. (Most beginners won't use this feature right away, and that's okay.)
- **Resistance:** Measures whether a wire or part is blocking electricity when it shouldn't be (or letting it through when it should be blocked).

If voltage, current, and resistance still sound like gibberish, don't worry — you're not alone. The good news? You don't need to understand every multimeter function in one day. Start with the basics: testing your battery voltage. That's the easiest and most useful thing a multimeter does, and once you've done it a few times, the rest starts to make sense.

TIP

Auto-ranging digital multimeters are the beginner-friendly option. They automatically figure out the right measurement range for you, so you don't have to twist a dial and guess. Just set it to Voltage, touch the probes to the battery terminals, and read the number. Done.

If you're still feeling lost, hop on YouTube and search "how to use a multimeter for beginners" or "how to test a car battery with a multimeter." Hundreds of short, clear videos walk you through the process step-by-step.

For deeper dives into electrical diagnostics — like testing sensors, tracing wiring problems, or checking grounds — see Chapter 6. We walk you through the whole process with pictures, examples, and way more hand-holding.

Battery tester

A *battery tester* checks your battery's voltage, cold-cranking amps (CCA — basically, how much oomph it has to start your car in freezing weather), and overall health. It's like a doctor's checkup for your battery. A battery test can tell you whether your battery is on its last legs before it leaves you stranded in a parking lot at 11 p.m. on a Tuesday.

Some advanced testers also check your *alternator* (the thing that recharges the battery while you drive) and your *starter* (the thing that cranks the engine). If you've ever wondered, "Is it the battery, the alternator, or am I just cursed?", this tool has answers.

Inspection camera (borescope)

An inspection camera, or *borescope,* is a tiny camera on a long, flexible cable that lets you see into places your eyeballs can't reach. Think inside engines, behind dashboards, under seats, or into that mystery hole where you dropped a bolt three minutes ago and now it's gone forever.

While not essential, a borescope is incredibly handy for diagnosing leaks, checking for hidden damage, finding lost hardware, or confirming that yes, something is definitely broken back there, and you're not imagining it.

Most modern borescopes connect to your smartphone, so you can take pictures or videos of whatever nightmare you've discovered. It's like giving your phone X-ray vision, except way more useful and slightly less cool.

Supplies and Organization

Tools last forever (if you treat them right), but supplies? Those disappear faster than snacks at a family reunion. Stock up on these essentials so that you're not making emergency runs to the auto parts store in the middle of a job — or worse, realizing you're out of gloves after you've already touched something greasy.

Shop rags and paper towels

You'll blow through shop rags and paper towels faster than you think. Oil spills, grease smudges, dirty hands, wiping down tools — it all adds up. Buy a big pack of reusable shop rags (the red or blue ones mechanics use) and keep a roll of heavy-duty paper towels handy for quick cleanups.

TIP

Wash shop rags separately from your regular laundry unless you want your bath towels to smell like a transmission.

WARNING

Keep a separate bin for used, oily rags. Don't toss them in with clean ones and definitely don't leave oil-soaked rags in a pile — they can spontaneously combust. (Yes, really. It's a thing. Google it if you don't believe me.)

Disposable nitrile gloves

Your hands aren't invincible, no matter how tough you think you are. Nitrile gloves protect your skin from chemicals, grease, and grime, and they make cleanup about a thousand times easier. Buy them in bulk (a box of 100) because you'll go through them like crazy.

TIP

Nitrile is better than latex (fewer allergies, better chemical resistance) and way better than bare hands (which will end up stained, cracked, and smelling like a refinery).

Degreaser, brake cleaner, and penetrating oil

Degreaser, brake cleaner, and penetrating oil are the holy trinity of automotive problem-solving:

- **Degreaser:** Cuts through grease, oil, and grime on engine parts, tools, and your workbench. Spray it on, let it sit, wipe it off. Magic.
- **Brake cleaner:** Evaporates almost instantly and leaves zero residue, which makes it perfect for cleaning brake parts, sensors, and electrical connectors. It's also great for degreasing small parts in a pinch.
- **Penetrating oil (like PB Blaster, Liquid Wrench, or WD-40 Specialist):** Known as the miracle worker for rusty, seized, or stubborn bolts. Spray it on, let it soak for 10 to 15 minutes (or overnight for really stuck fasteners), and watch the magic happen. Patience beats brute force every time and saves you from snapping bolts.

WARNING

When using brake cleaner, work in a well-ventilated area and keep it away from hot surfaces. It's flammable and evaporates fast, which means the fumes can ignite if you're not careful. Also, don't spray brake cleaner on painted surfaces — it'll strip the paint right off.

Zip ties, electrical tape, and duct tape

Zip ties, electrical tape, and duct tape are the "fix it until you can really fix it" essentials. Zip ties hold wiring harnesses, hoses, and random bits in place. Electrical tape insulates and protects wires. Duct tape . . . well, duct tape does everything except actual ductwork (ironically).

Keep a variety pack of zip ties (different lengths and strengths), a roll of black electrical tape, and a roll of quality duct tape (not the cheap stuff that falls apart in five minutes). You'll use them more than you expect.

REMEMBER

Zip ties are one-time-use fasteners. Once you cut them off, they're done. Buy them in bulk so you're never stuck reusing a sketchy, half-cut zip tie because you ran out.

Funnels (multiple sizes)

Funnels keep you from spilling oil, coolant, or other fluids all over the engine bay (and yourself). Get a few different sizes: a wide-mouth funnel for oil, a narrow one for topping off smaller reservoirs, and maybe a flexible one for tight spaces.

TIP

Label them or color-code them so that you're not using your oil funnel for windshield washer fluid and vice versa. Cross-contamination is a real thing, and it's annoying.

Drip pans and oil drain pans

If you're changing oil, coolant, or any other fluid, you need something to catch it. Oil drain pans come in all shapes and sizes. Some have spouts for easy pouring, while others have lids to keep the mess contained until you can dispose of it properly.

Get one that's big enough for your car's oil capacity (check your owner's manual) and easy to carry without sloshing. Your garage floor will thank you.

WARNING

Never dump used oil, coolant, or other fluids down the drain or into the trash. Take them to an auto parts store or recycling center that accepts used fluids. It's free, it's easy, and it's the law in most places.

Organizing Your Tools

The best tools in the world are useless if you can't find them. A little organization saves time, frustration, and money because you won't keep buying duplicates of tools you already own but can't locate. (We've all done it. No judgment.)

Toolboxes, bags, and organizers

Start with a portable toolbox or tool bag for basic jobs — something with a handle, compartments, and enough room for your most-used tools. As your collection grows, upgrade to a rolling tool chest with drawers, like the kind you see in professional garages with multiple drawers, smooth glides, and maybe a top compartment for small parts.

TIP

Organize by type (all wrenches together, all sockets together) or by frequency of use (everyday tools in the top drawer, specialty tools lower down). Whatever system works for your brain, stick with it.

Magnetic trays and parts organizers

Magnetic trays are small metal dishes that hold bolts, nuts, and washers while you work. Stick one to the side of your car or a metal workbench, and you'll never lose a fastener in the grass or down the engine bay again. (If you've ever spent 20 minutes searching for a dropped bolt with a flashlight, you know exactly why these trays are essential.)

Parts organizers with divided compartments keep fasteners sorted by size and type. Some have removable bins; others have adjustable dividers. Either way, they beat the "throw everything in a coffee can and hope for the best" method.

Pegboards and wall storage

If you have a dedicated workspace — garage, shed, corner of the basement — pegboards and wall-mounted tool holders are a game-changer. Hang wrenches, pliers, screwdrivers, and other frequently used tools so that you can see them at a glance and grab what you need without digging through drawers.

TIP

Bonus: Pegboards look cool and give off very "I know what I'm doing" vibes, even if you're still figuring it out.

Tool foam inserts (for serious organizers)

Tool foam — also called *shadow foam* — is custom-cut foam that fits in your toolbox drawers. Each tool has its own cutout, so you can see at a glance if something's missing. It's like a puzzle, except the pieces are wrenches, and the reward is never losing your 10mm socket again.

Is it overkill for beginners? Absolutely. Do professional mechanics swear by it? Also, yes. If you're the type of person who color-codes their closet or alphabetizes their spice rack, tool foam is your happy place.

TIP

You can buy pre-cut foam inserts for common tool sets, or you can buy blank foam sheets and cut your own. DIY foam cutting is weirdly satisfying — like arts and crafts, but greasier.

Building Your Digital Toolbox

Physical tools fix the car; digital tools fix the "I have no idea what I'm doing" problem. Twenty years ago, if you didn't know how to do something, you either found a repair manual the size of a phone book or called your uncle who "knows about cars." Now? You've got YouTube tutorials, diagnostic apps, online forums, and repair databases at your fingertips. The internet has democratized car repair, and you'd be foolish not to take advantage of it.

Repair manuals and online databases

Think of repair manuals as your car's instruction book, except way more detailed than the owner's manual that came in your glove box. These guides walk you through repairs step-by-step, with diagrams, torque specs, and troubleshooting tips. They're worth their weight in gold when you're staring at an engine bay wondering, "Where do I even start?"

Haynes and Chilton manuals

Haynes and Chilton manuals are the DIY classics. These manuals are written specifically for your car's make, model, and year, and they break down repairs into manageable steps with photos and illustrations. They cover everything from oil changes to engine rebuilds, and they're designed for regular people, not just professional mechanics.

You can buy these manuals as printed books (great for the garage — no dead batteries or greasy screens) or as digital downloads (searchable and easy to reference on your phone or tablet). They're affordable, beginner-friendly, and have been helping DIYers for decades.

They're best for home mechanics who want clear, visual instructions without paying a fortune.

TIP

Buy the manual for your specific year and model. A 2015 Honda Civic manual won't help you much if you're working on a 2022 Civic — parts, procedures, and specs change more than you'd think.

Factory service manuals (FSM)

Factory service manuals (FSM) are the official repair guides written by the car manufacturer and used by dealership technicians. They're incredibly detailed — sometimes too detailed — with every torque spec, wiring diagram, diagnostic procedure, and assembly note you could ever want.

The downside? They're expensive (often $100 to $300-plus), and they assume you already know a lot about car repair. They don't hold your hand the way a Haynes or Chilton manual does. But if you're serious about working on your car and want the most accurate, comprehensive information available, factory manuals are the gold standard.

TIP

Some manufacturers offer digital subscriptions (like Toyota's TIS or Honda's service info site) where you can pay for short-term access instead of buying the full manual outright. If you're only doing one big job, a day or week subscription can be a smart move.

These manuals are best for experienced DIYers, serious hobbyists, or anyone tackling complex repairs where precision matters.

AllData, Mitchell1, and other subscription services

AllData, Mitchell1, and other subscription services are professional-grade online databases used by independent repair shops and serious DIYers. They give you access to:

- Repair procedures with step-by-step instructions
- Wiring diagrams (essential for electrical diagnostics)

- Official notices from manufacturers about known issues, updated repair procedures, or recalls, known as *Technical Service Bulletins* (TSBs)
- Maintenance schedules, fluid specs, and torque values
- Diagnostic trouble code definitions and troubleshooting flowcharts

AllData and Mitchell1 are subscription-based (usually $20 to $50 per year for a single vehicle or more for multi-vehicle access). They're not as beginner-friendly as Haynes manuals — there's a learning curve — but the depth of information is unmatched.

These subscription services are best for DIYers who work on their cars regularly and want the same resources professional mechanics use.

TIP

Many public libraries offer free access to online repair databases like Chilton Library or AllData through their websites. Check your library's digital resources. You may be able to access thousands of dollars' worth of repair info for free with just a library card.

Free online resources

Before you spend money on manuals or subscriptions, take advantage of the massive amount of free information available online. The internet is packed with forums, manufacturer sites, and communities where mechanics and DIYers share real-world solutions to problems you're probably dealing with right now. These free resources won't replace a proper repair manual, but they're incredibly useful for quick questions, troubleshooting weird noises, getting second opinions, or confirming that yes, that sound is definitely not normal.

Here are some of the best free resources:

- **iATN (International Automotive Technicians' Network):** A forum where professional techs share real-world fixes, diagnostic tips, and solutions to tricky problems. It's like eavesdropping on a conversation between experienced mechanics — and they're happy to help.
- **Manufacturer websites:** Basic service info straight from the source. Some brands (like Toyota, Honda, and Ford) offer free access to basic service info, recalls, and TSBs. You won't get the full factory manual, but you can often find maintenance schedules, fluid specs, and recall information without paying a dime.

» **Reddit communities (r/MechanicAdvice, r/Cartalk, r/Justrolledintotheshop):** Real people sharing advice, photos, and "here's what worked for me" stories. Post a question with pictures, and you'll often get multiple responses from DIYers and pros alike. Just remember: Not all advice is good advice.

WARNING

Not all online advice is good advice. Cross-check information from multiple sources, and if something sounds sketchy or too good to be true ("just pour dish soap in your gas tank!"), it probably is. Stick to reputable sites, official manuals, and forums with active, knowledgeable communities.

IN THIS CHAPTER

» Understanding engines as energy converters

» Walking through the four-stroke cycle

» Exploring fuel delivery from carburetors to direct injection

» Demystifying ignition systems old and new

» Discovering modern power tricks: turbos, superchargers, and variable valve timing

Chapter 4

From Start to Roar: How Your Car Springs to Life

You turn the key (or push the button), and your car roars to life. But what actually happens in that split second between start and vroom? If you've ever wondered how a few gallons of liquid in a tank turn into forward motion, this chapter is your backstage pass to the greatest mechanical magic trick ever invented: the internal combustion engine.

Don't worry: We don't drown you in engineering jargon or expect you to rebuild an engine by the end of this chapter. Instead, we walk through the basics in plain English, with a few laughs along the way. This chapter helps you understand how air, fuel, and fire work together to make your car move and why modern engines are smarter, cleaner, and more powerful than ever before.

Whether you're driving a gas-powered sedan, a turbocharged hot hatch, a hybrid, or a full EV, this chapter gives you the foundation to understand what's happening under the hood — and sets you up for the deeper dives in later chapters.

The Engine: The Heart of the Machine

Under all the plastic covers and wiring, your car is basically a very controlled explosion machine — or, if it's electric, a very sophisticated spinning-magnet machine. Either way, the job is the same: Take stored energy and turn it into forward motion.

In the big picture, your engine is an *energy converter*. It takes chemical energy stored in fuel (gasoline, diesel, or even electricity in a battery) and turns it into *mechanical energy* — the kind that spins wheels and moves you down the road.

In other words, fuel is potential energy, like a coiled spring or a drawn bow. The engine's job is to release that energy in a controlled way, capture it, and use it to do work.

Electric vehicles skip the combustion part entirely. Instead of burning fuel, they use electricity stored in a battery to power electric motors that spin the wheels directly. No explosions, no exhaust, no oil changes — just electrons doing their thing.

Hybrids split the difference, combining a gas engine with electric motors and a battery pack that work together (or independently), depending on driving conditions.

We give hybrids and EVs their own spotlight in the section "Hybrids and EVs: When Combustion Meets Electricity (or Disappears Entirely)," later in this chapter, and a full deep dive in Chapter 10. For now, just think of the engine — whether it burns fuel or uses electricity — as a very sturdy, very picky machine that converts stored energy into rotation.

REMEMBER

Whether it's gas, diesel, or electric, every engine's job is the same: Convert stored energy into motion. The method changes, but the goal doesn't.

Turning Fuel into Motion

In a gas or diesel engine, turning fuel into motion means burning it inside a sealed chamber (a *cylinder*) to create a tiny explosion that pushes a piston down. A *piston* is a snug-fitting metal part that slides up and down inside the cylinder, kind of like a plunger. That piston is connected to a *crankshaft*, which spins and eventually turns your wheels. It's a beautifully orchestrated dance of physics, chemistry, and engineering — and it happens thousands of times per minute while you're cruising down the highway.

Here's the basic flow in a combustion engine:

1. **Fuel stores chemical energy in the form of gasoline, diesel, or alternative fuels.**
2. **The engine mixes that fuel with air in precise ratios.**

   You can find out more on this process in the section "Fuel Delivery: From Carburetors to Computers," later in this chapter.
3. **Ignition lights the mixture, creating a controlled explosion inside the cylinder.**
4. **The expanding hot gases push pistons down, which turn the crankshaft.**
5. **The crankshaft spins the transmission and drive wheels, moving you forward.**

   The *transmission* is the part that changes engine power into usable gear ratios. The *drive wheels* are the wheels that actually receive power and push the car forward.

   You can dig deeper into that power flow in Chapter 19.

The Four-Stroke Dance: How Combustion Engines Breathe

Most gas engines (and many diesels) use a four-stroke cycle to turn fuel into power. It's called *four-stroke* because each cycle involves four distinct movements of the piston inside the cylinder (see Figure 4-1). Think of this cycle like a choreographed dance routine: Each step has to happen in the right order, at the right time, or the whole thing falls apart.

Here's how the four-stroke cycle works:

1. **Intake stroke: Breathe in.**

   The piston starts at the top of the cylinder and moves down, creating a vacuum. At the same time, the intake valve opens, and the engine sucks in a mixture of air and fuel or just air, in the case of direct injection engines, which we cover in "Fuel Delivery: From Carburetors to Computers," later in this chapter. Think of this step like taking a deep breath before you blow out birthday candles.

2. **Compression stroke: Squeeze it tight.**

   Both valves close, and the piston moves back up, compressing the air-fuel mixture into a tiny space at the top of the cylinder. Compression is key: It makes the mixture more volatile and ready to explode. It's like squeezing a balloon until it's about to pop.

3. **Power stroke: Boom!**

   Right when the piston reaches the top and the mixture is fully compressed, the spark plug fires (in a gas engine) or the heat from compression ignites the fuel (in a diesel engine). The mixture explodes, driving the piston down with tremendous force. This stroke actually does the work: It's the one that turns the crankshaft and makes your car move. Everything else is just setup for this moment.

4. **Exhaust stroke: Breathe out.**

   The piston moves back up, the exhaust valve opens, and the burnt gases are pushed out of the cylinder and into the exhaust system. Then the cycle starts all over again. Intake, compression, power, exhaust. Repeat. Thousands of times per minute.

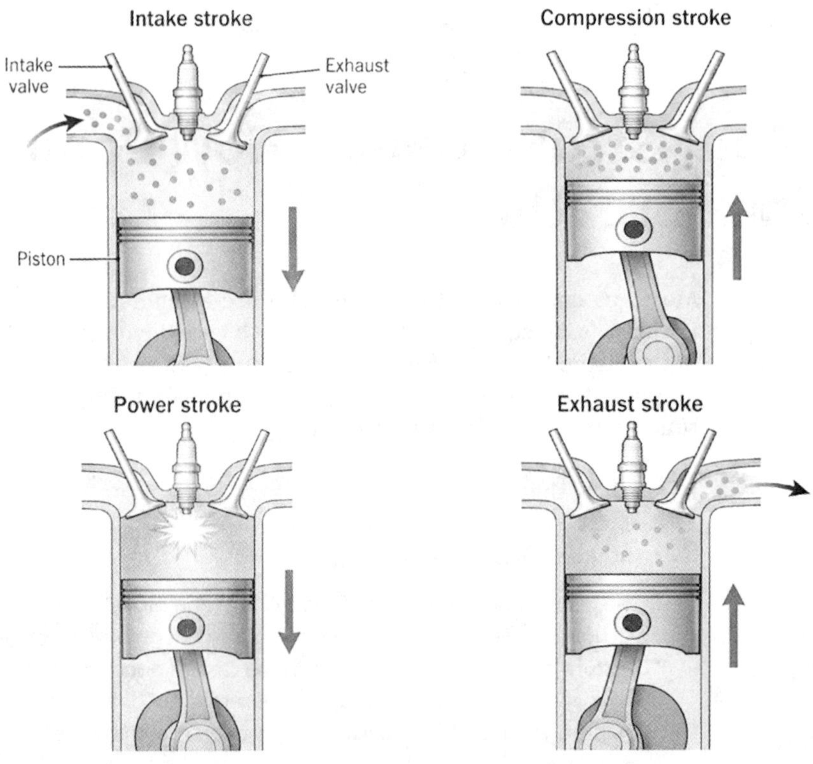

FIGURE 4-1: The four-stroke cycle: Intake, compression, power, exhaust.

Generated with AI using OpenAI

Most car engines have four, six, or eight cylinders, and they're all firing at different times in a carefully timed sequence. That's why your engine sounds smooth instead of like a jackhammer — the power strokes overlap, keeping things balanced.

Fuel Delivery: From Carburetors to Computers

Your engine needs fuel to burn, but how does that fuel get from the tank to the cylinders? The answer has evolved dramatically over the past few decades.

Carburetors: The old-school way

If you've ever worked on a classic car (or watched someone struggle with one), you've probably heard of carburetors. A *carburetor* is a mechanical device that mixes air and fuel in the right proportions and sends that mixture into the engine. It uses vacuum pressure and a series of jets, needles, and floats to do its job — no computers, no sensors, just physics and a lot of finicky adjustments.

Carburetors worked, but they had problems. They were sensitive to altitude, temperature, and humidity. They required constant tuning. And they weren't great at fuel economy or emissions. By the 1990s, carburetors were basically extinct in new cars, replaced by something much smarter: fuel injection. Figure 4-2 shows how a carburetor works.

Fuel injection: The modern standard

Fuel injection uses electrically controlled injectors to spray fuel directly into the *intake manifold*, the set of passages that carries incoming air to the engine's cylinders, or, in newer systems, directly into the cylinder. The engine's computer (the ECU, or Engine Control Unit) monitors dozens of sensors (air temperature, throttle position, oxygen levels in the exhaust, engine speed, and more) and calculates exactly how much fuel to inject and when. The result? Better fuel economy, more power, cleaner emissions, and no more choke knobs or carburetor tuning.

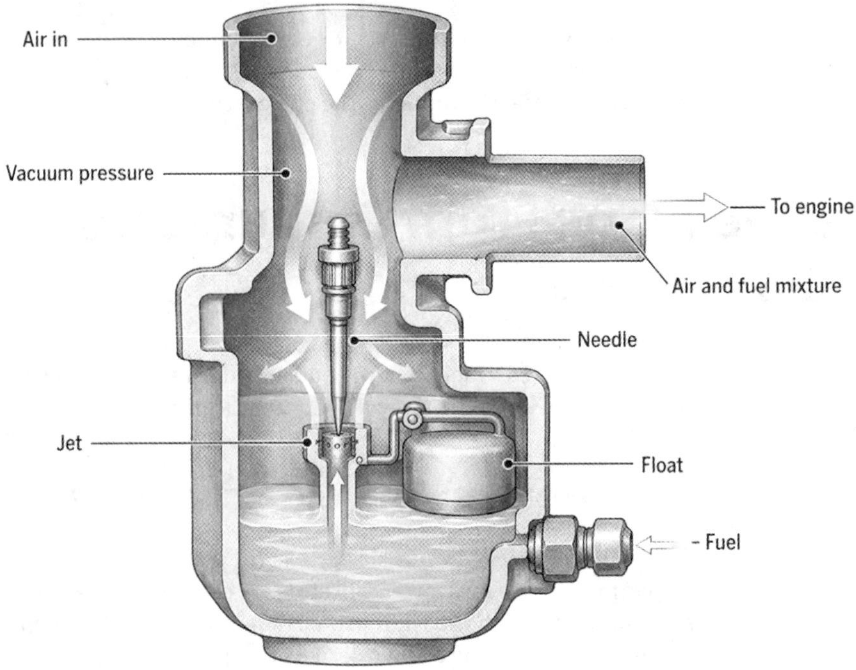

Generated with AI using OpenAI

FIGURE 4-2: The fuel mixing occurs outside the cylinder in the carburetor.

Today, you see two main types of fuel injection, which are shown in Figure 4-3:

- **Port fuel injection (PFI):** Injectors spray fuel into the intake manifold, just before the intake valve. The air and fuel mix in the manifold and then get sucked into the cylinder during the intake stroke. This type of fuel injection is the most common and has been the standard for decades.
- **Direct injection (DI):** Injectors spray fuel directly into the combustion chamber, bypassing the intake manifold entirely. Direct injection allows for more precise control, higher compression ratios, and better efficiency. It's becoming more common in modern engines, especially turbocharged ones.

Some engines use *dual injection*, which simply means that it uses both port and direct injection. The ECU can choose which system to use (or use both at once), depending on driving conditions. Dual injection is like having two chefs in the kitchen, each handling different parts of the meal.

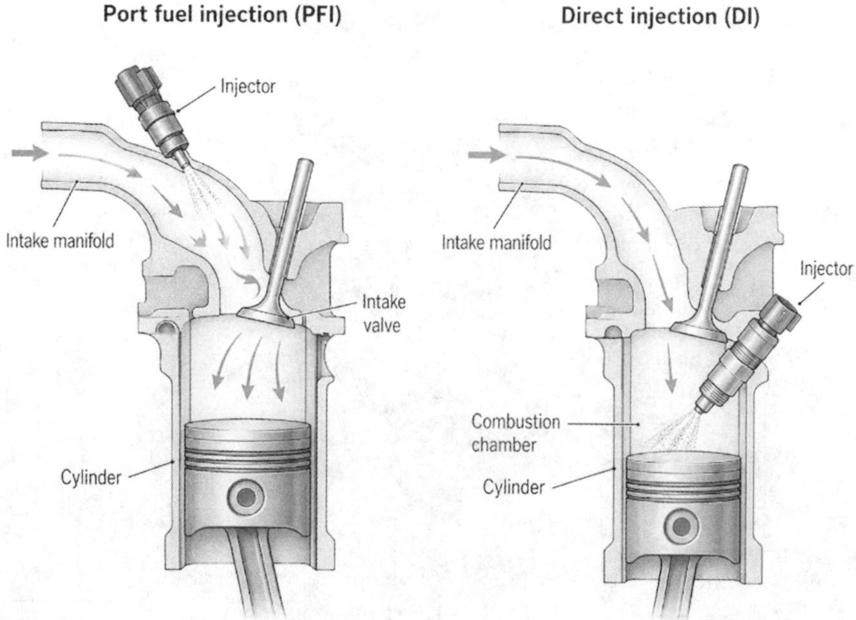

FIGURE 4-3: Port fuel injection versus direct injection.

Generated with AI using OpenAI

Ignition Systems: Lighting the Fire

Once the air-fuel mixture is compressed and ready to burn, something has to light it. That's the job of the *ignition system* — basically, a very precise way to create a spark at exactly the right moment.

Think of the process like lighting a gas grill: You need a spark to ignite the fuel. Your engine does the same thing, but thousands of times per minute, with perfect timing. Miss the timing by even a millisecond, and you lose power, waste fuel, or damage the engine.

The old days: Distributors and points

Older engines (think 1970s and earlier) used a mechanical *distributor* — a spinning shaft with a rotor inside that sent high-voltage electricity to each spark plug in turn, like a rotating sprinkler watering different parts of the lawn (see Figure 4-4). It worked, but it had problems:

- The mechanical points inside wore out and needed regular replacement.
- Timing had to be adjusted manually with a wrench and a timing light.
- Moisture, corrosion, and worn parts caused misfires and hard starts.

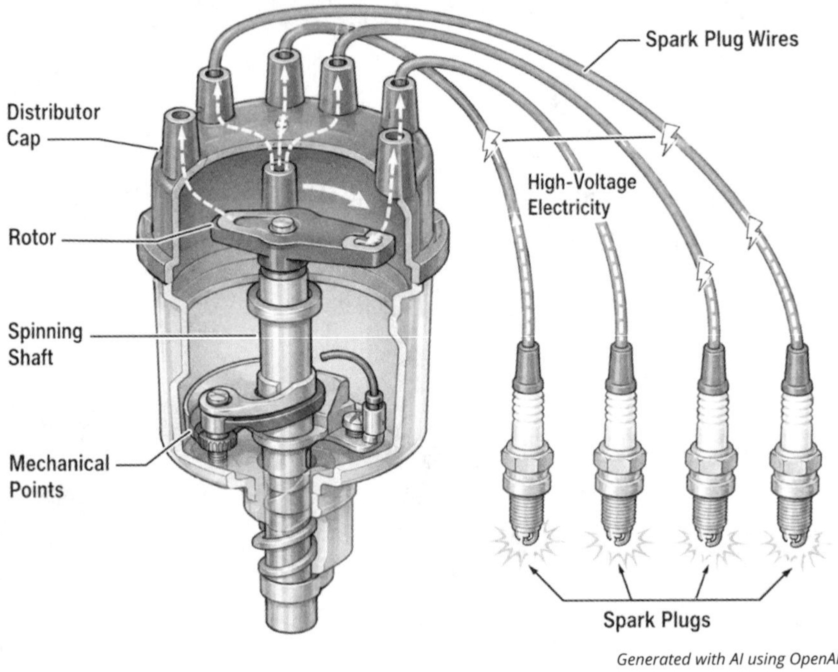

FIGURE 4-4: Distributors at a glance.

If you've ever heard someone say *tune-up*, they're talking about the days when distributors needed constant babysitting.

Electronic ignition: A big leap forward

In the 1980s and 1990s, cars started using *electronic ignition systems*. Instead of mechanical points that wore out, a sensor (usually a Hall effect sensor or optical pickup) told the computer when to fire the spark plugs. The distributor was still there, but the system was more reliable, required less maintenance, and delivered a stronger, more consistent spark.

Electronic ignitions were a huge improvement — fewer tune-ups, better fuel economy, and engines that actually started on cold mornings.

Coil-on-plug: The modern way

Today, most engines use *coil-on-plug (COP) ignition systems*, and it's beautifully simple: Each spark plug has its own ignition coil sitting directly on top of it. No distributor. No spark plug wires snaking around the engine. No moving parts (see Figure 4-5). The ECU controls each coil individually, firing the spark plugs with millisecond precision.

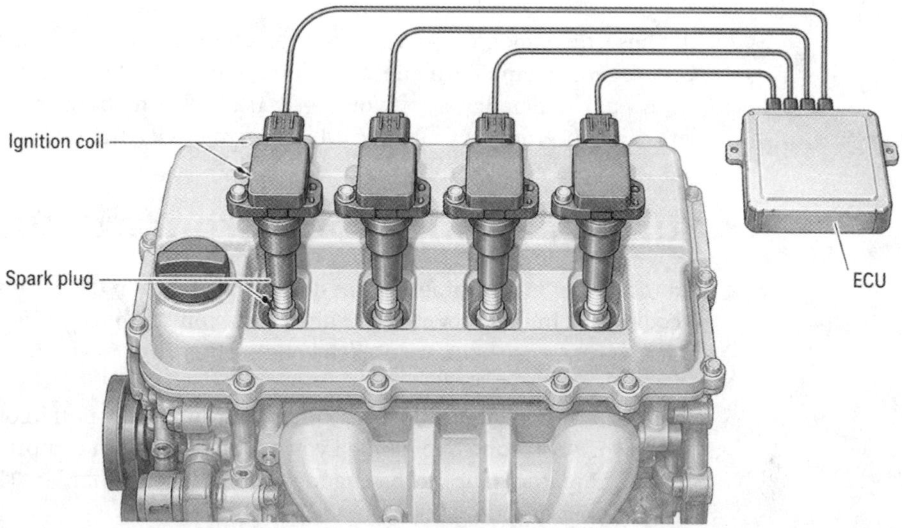

FIGURE 4-5: Coil-on-plug ignition systems.

Generated with AI using OpenAI

The result? Better fuel economy, more power, cleaner emissions, and almost zero maintenance — until a coil fails, which they all do eventually. The good news? Modern ignition systems are incredibly reliable, and when a coil does fail, you'll know it immediately: misfires, rough idle, loss of power, and a flashing check engine light that's basically screaming "FIX ME NOW!"

Replacing a failed coil is usually a quick, straightforward job — unplug the old one, pop in the new one, and you're back on the road. See Chapter 6 for more on ignition system maintenance and diagnostics.

WARNING

If your check engine light is flashing (not just on, but flashing), pull over and shut off the engine as soon as it's safe. A flashing light means the engine is misfiring badly enough to damage the catalytic converter, which is expensive to replace. A $50 coil replacement beats a $1,500 cat replacement every time.

Modern Power Tricks

Modern engines are smaller, lighter, and more efficient than ever, but they're also more powerful. How? Engineers have developed a toolkit of technologies that let engines breathe better, burn fuel more efficiently, and adapt to driving conditions in real time. It's like going from a flip phone to a smartphone — same basic job, but way smarter about how it gets done.

The following sections look at the big ones.

REMEMBER

All these technologies — turbos, superchargers, VVT, cylinder deactivation — work together in modern engines to give you the best of both worlds: Power when you need it, efficiency when you don't. It's why a modern four-cylinder can outperform a V8 from 20 years ago while getting twice the fuel economy.

Turbocharging: Boost from exhaust

A *turbocharger* is a turbine-driven device that forces more air into the engine than it could suck in on its own. More air means you can burn more fuel, which means more power — without making the engine bigger or heavier.

Think of a turbocharger like breathing: Your lungs can pull in only so much air on their own. But if someone handed you a scuba tank with compressed air, you could suddenly breathe a lot more oxygen without working harder. That's what a turbo does for your engine.

Here's how a turbocharger works: Exhaust gases, which would normally just blow out the tailpipe and disappear, spin a turbine as they exit the engine. That turbine is connected to a compressor on the intake side, which compresses incoming air and rams it into the cylinders. It's like giving your engine a shot of espresso — suddenly, a small four-cylinder can make as much power as a V6, with better fuel economy to boot.

The downside? *Turbo lag* — the brief delay between when you hit the gas and when the turbo spools up and delivers boost. It's like waiting for your computer to wake up from sleep mode. Modern turbos are much better at minimizing lag, and some engines use twin turbos (one small for quick response at low RPM, one large for high-end power) to eliminate it almost entirely. Turbocharged engines can be very reliable, but they're less forgiving of neglected oil changes, wrong oil specs, or poor maintenance because the turbo runs extremely hot and spins at very high speeds.

Figure 4-6 shows a turbocharger's airflow path.

TIP

Turbocharged engines run hotter and work harder, so they're more sensitive to oil quality and maintenance intervals. Stick to the manufacturer's recommended oil spec and change intervals — your turbo will thank you. See Chapter 14 for more on oil and why it matters.

Supercharging: Instant boost, no lag

A *supercharger* does the same job as a turbo — cramming more air into the engine — but it's driven directly by the engine's crankshaft via a belt, not by exhaust gases (see Figure 4-7). The result? Instant boost with zero lag. Hit the gas, and the power is right there, no waiting. It's like the difference between a microwave (instant) and an oven (gotta preheat).

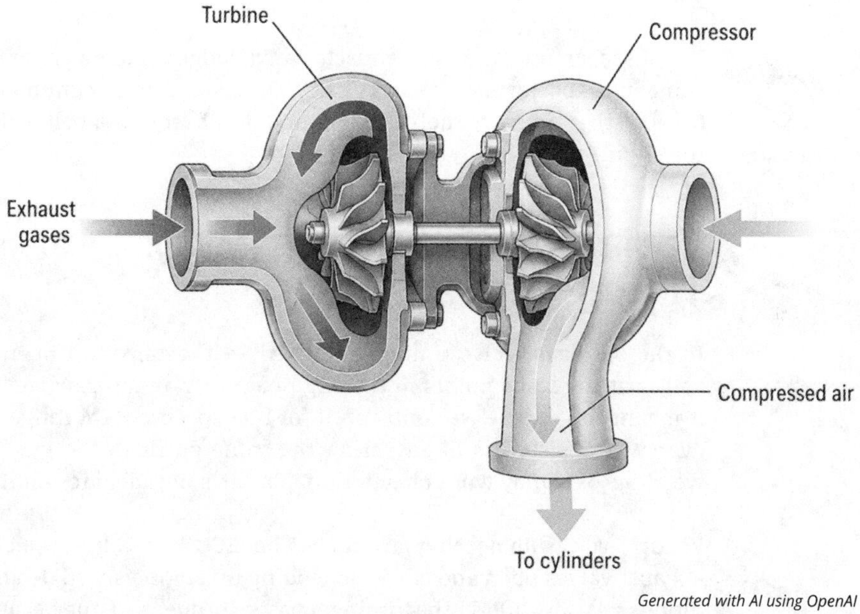

FIGURE 4-6: Turbocharger airflow path.

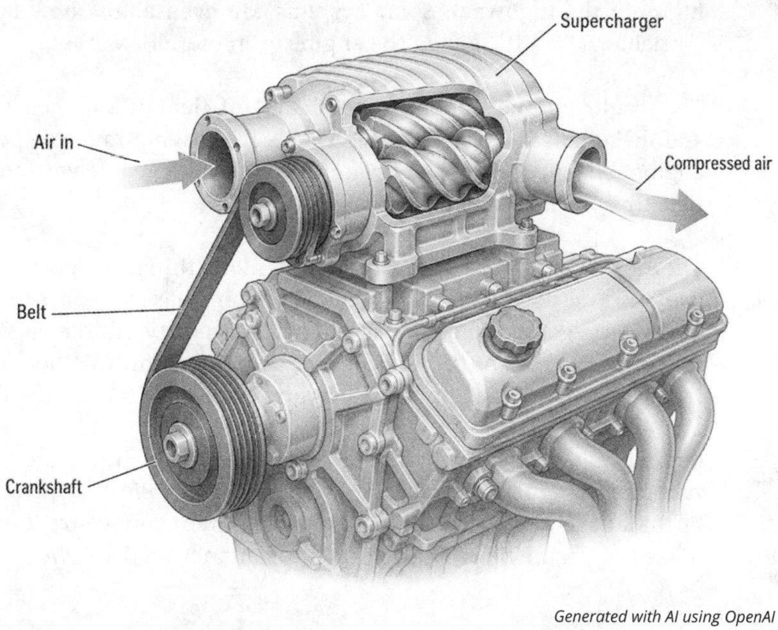

FIGURE 4-7: Supercharger belt drive.

The trade-off? Superchargers steal a little power from the engine to run (because they're belt-driven), so they're slightly less efficient than turbos. But for drivers who want instant throttle response and that glorious supercharger whine under hard acceleration, they're hard to beat. Plus, they sound awesome — like a jet engine spooling up.

TECHNICAL STUFF

You'll see superchargers on muscle cars (Dodge Challenger Hellcat, anyone?) and some high-performance sports cars. Turbos are more common on everyday cars because they're more fuel-efficient and don't require a belt-driven connection to the engine.

Variable valve timing (VVT): Timing that adapts

In the old days, valve timing was fixed — the camshaft opened and closed the valves at the same points in the engine cycle, no matter what. That was fine, but it meant the engine was optimized for one specific RPM range and compromised everywhere else. It's like wearing the same outfit to the gym, the office, and a wedding — it may work okay for one, but it's not ideal for all three.

Variable valve timing changes that. The ECU can adjust when the intake and exhaust valves open and close, depending on engine speed, load, and driving conditions. At low RPM, the timing favors torque and fuel economy (perfect for cruising). At high RPM, it shifts to maximize power (perfect for passing or merging onto the highway). Some systems can even adjust how far the valves open (variable valve lift), giving the engine even more flexibility.

The result? Engines that are smooth and efficient at low speeds, but still rev high and make power when you need it. It's like having multiple personalities in one engine, all controlled by software — and unlike people with multiple personalities, this one is totally normal and desirable.

The downside? More complexity and more things to go wrong. VVT systems use extra parts — such as solenoids, cam phasers, and sensors — and when those parts get worn, sticky, or clogged with dirty oil, the engine can run rough, lose power, rattle, or turn on the check engine light. In other words, VVT is awesome when it works, but it really appreciates clean oil and regular maintenance.

TECHNICAL STUFF

Common VVT systems include Honda's VTEC (which became a meme in car culture for its dramatic power kick), Toyota's VVT-i, BMW's VANOS, and GM's Active Fuel Management. They all do slightly different things, but the goal is the same: Make the engine more flexible and efficient across the RPM range.

Cylinder deactivation: Turning off cylinders you don't need

If you're cruising down the highway at a steady speed, you don't need all your engine's cylinders firing. *Cylinder deactivation* shuts down half the cylinders when you don't need them, turning a V8 into a V4 or a V6 into a V3. When you need power again — say, to pass or climb a hill — the system reactivates the cylinders instantly.

Think of cylinder deactivation like turning off lights in rooms you're not using. Why waste energy lighting up the whole house when you're just sitting in the living room?

The result? Better fuel economy without sacrificing power when you need it. The transitions are so smooth that most drivers never notice when cylinders shut off or come back online. Your truck still feels like a truck, but it sips fuel like a sedan when you're not towing or hauling.

The downside? More complexity. Cylinder deactivation systems rely on special hardware and oil control to switch cylinders on and off. On some engines, those parts have been known to cause problems, such as lifter wear, oil consumption, vibration, or expensive repairs. That doesn't mean every cylinder-deactivation system is bad, but it does mean oil quality, maintenance intervals, and using the correct oil spec matter a lot.

Hybrids and EVs: When Combustion Meets Electricity (or Disappears Entirely)

Not all engines burn fuel. Some use electricity. Some use both. Hybrids and electric vehicles are becoming more common every year, and they work very differently from traditional gas engines.

Hybrid vehicles: The best of both worlds

A *hybrid* combines a gasoline engine with one or more electric motors and a battery pack. The gas engine and electric motor can work together (for maximum power) or independently (for maximum efficiency). The battery recharges itself through *regenerative braking* — capturing energy that would normally be wasted as heat when you slow down and using it to recharge the battery (see Figure 4-8).

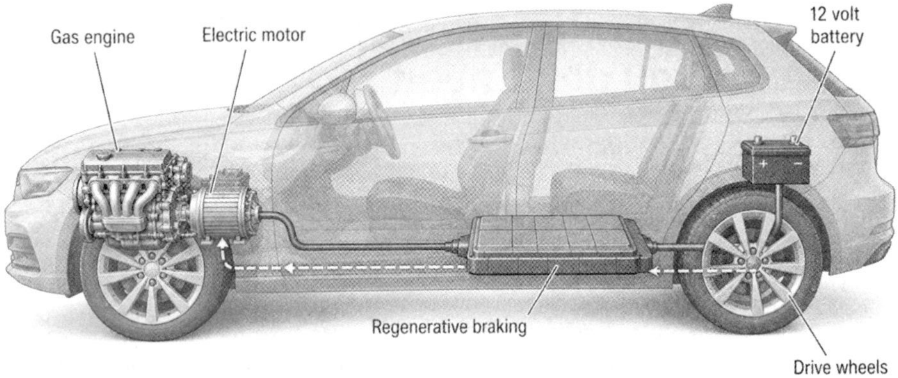

FIGURE 4-8: Hybrid powertrain layout.

Generated with AI using OpenAI

Hybrids and EVs come in a few main flavors:

- **Parallel or series-parallel hybrids:** Both the gas engine and electric motor can drive the wheels. Familiar examples include the Toyota Prius, Toyota Camry Hybrid, and Ford Escape Hybrid.
- **Series hybrids:** The gas engine never drives the wheels directly. Instead, it acts as a generator to recharge the battery, and the electric motor does all the driving. This setup is less common in everyday U.S. passenger cars, but examples include the BMW i3 with range extender and Nissan e-Power models in markets where they're sold. Think of it like a diesel-electric locomotive.
- **Plug-in hybrids (PHEVs):** These have larger batteries that you can recharge by plugging into an outlet. They can drive on electric power alone for 20 to 50 miles before the gas engine kicks in. Examples include the Toyota Prius Prime, Toyota RAV4 Prime, and Chrysler Pacifica Plug-in Hybrid. They're perfect for short commutes on electricity, long trips on gas.
- **Electric vehicles (EVs):** No combustion, no compromise — electric vehicles ditch the gas engine entirely. Examples include the Tesla Model 3, Nissan Leaf, Chevrolet Bolt EV, and Hyundai Ioniq 5. They use large battery packs (usually lithium-ion) to store electricity, and one or more electric motors to drive the wheels. No pistons, no spark plugs, no exhaust, no oil changes. Just instant torque, silent operation, and zero tailpipe emissions.

EVs are incredibly simple mechanically — far fewer moving parts than a gas car. But they come with their own challenges: charging infrastructure, range anxiety, and battery degradation over time. That said, the technology is improving fast, and EVs are becoming more practical (and affordable) every year.

Regenerative braking: Getting energy back

One of the coolest features of hybrids and EVs is regenerative braking. When you lift off the gas or hit the brakes, the electric motor reverses and acts as a generator, converting the car's kinetic energy back into electricity and storing it in the battery. It's like getting a refund every time you slow down.

Regen braking also reduces wear on your traditional friction brakes, which means brake pads and rotors last much longer on hybrids and EVs. Some EV drivers go years without needing new brakes.

Hybrids and EVs still have a 12-volt battery (just like a gas car) that powers the computers, lights, and accessories. If that 12-volt battery dies, the car won't start — even if the main battery pack is fully charged. See Chapter 2 for how to check and maintain the 12-volt battery.

Sensors and Software: The Brain behind the Brawn

Modern engines aren't just mechanical — they're digital. Every engine built in the last 25 years is controlled by an ECU, a powerful computer that monitors dozens of sensors and makes thousands of decisions per second to keep the engine running smoothly, efficiently, and cleanly.

The ECU: Your engine's brain

The ECU is the mastermind. It reads data from sensors all over the engine and vehicle, calculates the optimal fuel injection timing, ignition timing, valve timing, and more, and sends commands to actuators (fuel injectors, ignition coils, VVT solenoids, and so on) to make it happen. It does all of these activities in real time, adapting to driving conditions, temperature, altitude, and even fuel quality.

Think of the ECU like the conductor of an orchestra: It doesn't play any instruments itself, but it makes sure everyone plays together in perfect harmony.

Here are some of the most important sensors feeding data to the ECU:

- **Mass airflow sensor (MAF):** Measures how much air is entering the engine. The ECU uses this number to calculate how much fuel to inject.
- **Oxygen sensors (O2 sensors):** Measure the oxygen content in the exhaust. The ECU uses this data to fine-tune the air-fuel ratio for maximum efficiency and minimum emissions.
- **Throttle position sensor (TPS):** Tells the ECU how far you've pressed the gas pedal so that it knows how much power you're asking for.
- **Crankshaft position sensor:** Tells the ECU exactly where each piston is in its stroke so that it can fire the spark plugs and injectors at precisely the right moment.
- **Knock sensor:** Listens for engine knock (pre-ignition or detonation) and tells the ECU to retard ignition timing if it detects a problem, which protects the engine from damage.
- **Coolant temperature sensor:** Tells the ECU how hot the engine is so that it can adjust fuel delivery and idle speed accordingly (cold engines need more fuel).

Adaptive control: The engine that learns

Modern ECUs, especially on computer-controlled vehicles from the 1990s onward and most OBD-II vehicles from 1996 on, don't just follow a fixed program — they learn and adapt. If you drive aggressively, the ECU adjusts shift points and throttle response to match. If you drive gently, it optimizes for fuel economy. If you fill up with lower-octane fuel than the engine prefers, the ECU detects knock and adjusts ignition timing to prevent damage.

This ability is why two identical cars can feel different to drive — the ECU adapts to recent driving habits, fuel quality, temperature, altitude, and the conditions it encounters.

The ECU stores learned values in its memory, including fuel trims, which are corrections to the base fuel map, and idle speed adjustments. If you disconnect the battery, the ECU loses these values and has to relearn them, which is why the car may idle rough or feel sluggish for the first few miles after a battery replacement. If you buy a used car, those learned values aren't permanent personality traits from the previous owner. As you drive, the ECU gradually relearns your habits and local conditions, so the car can adjust to you over time.

Efficiency and Emissions: Cleaner, Greener, and Required by Law

Modern engines aren't just more powerful — they're also cleaner and more efficient than ever before. That's partly because engineers are brilliant, but it's also because governments around the world have imposed strict emissions and fuel economy standards that automakers have to meet.

Catalytic converters: Cleaning up the exhaust

A *catalytic converter* is a device in the exhaust system that uses precious metals (platinum, palladium, and rhodium) to convert harmful pollutants into less harmful substances, specifically

- Carbon monoxide (CO) → Carbon dioxide (CO_2)
- Hydrocarbons (unburned fuel) → CO_2 and water
- Nitrogen oxides (NO_x) → Nitrogen and oxygen

Catalytic converters have been mandatory on cars in the United States since 1975, and they've dramatically reduced air pollution. Modern converters are incredibly efficient — often converting 90 percent or more of harmful emissions. Imported enthusiast cars can be a little trickier: A car built for another country isn't automatically exempt from U.S. emissions rules. In general, it has to meet the applicable EPA requirements for its model year or qualify for a specific exemption, such as certain older vehicles imported in their original configuration.

WARNING

Catalytic converters contain valuable metals, which is why they're a popular target for thieves. If your car is parked outside, consider parking in a well-lit area or installing a cat shield. Replacing a stolen cat is expensive.

Fuel economy standards: Miles per gallon (and beyond)

Governments set Corporate Average Fuel Economy (CAFE) standards that require automakers to meet minimum average fuel economy across their entire fleet. These standards have gotten stricter over time, pushing automakers to develop more efficient engines, lighter vehicles, and hybrid/EV technology.

The result? The average new car today gets better fuel economy than ever before even as it's also faster, safer, and more comfortable.

Alternative fuels: Ethanol, biodiesel, and beyond

Gasoline and diesel aren't the only fuel options. Many cars can run on *ethanol blends* (E10, E15, or E85), which are made from renewable sources like corn or sugarcane. Diesel engines can run on *biodiesel*, made from vegetable oils or animal fats. And some experimental vehicles run on hydrogen, natural gas, or even synthetic fuels made from captured CO_2.

Alternative fuels reduce dependence on petroleum and can lower emissions, but they come with trade-offs (lower energy density, infrastructure challenges, cost). We dive deeper into alternative fuels in Chapter 10.

LOOKING AHEAD: THE FUTURE OF ENGINES

The internal combustion engine has been the dominant technology for over a century, but its days may be numbered. Electric vehicles are growing fast, and many countries have announced plans to phase out gas-powered cars entirely by 2030 or 2040. But combustion isn't dead yet — and it's evolving in fascinating ways.

Hydrogen fuel cells generate electricity by combining hydrogen and oxygen, with water as the only byproduct. *Hydrogen vehicles* are essentially electric vehicles, but instead of charging a battery, you refuel with hydrogen in minutes (just like gas). The technology is promising, but infrastructure is the big challenge — very few hydrogen stations exist, and building them is expensive.

Synthetic fuels (also called e-fuels) are made by capturing CO_2 from the air and combining it with hydrogen to create liquid fuel that's chemically identical to gasoline or diesel. The idea? You can run a traditional combustion engine on a fuel that's carbon-neutral (because the CO_2 released when you burn it was captured from the atmosphere in the first place). It's expensive and energy-intensive to produce, but it could extend the life of combustion engines in a zero-emission future.

Next-Gen EV Tech: Solid-State Batteries and Beyond

Electric vehicles are improving fast — like, really fast. If you think today's EVs are impressive, just wait.

Solid-state batteries are the next big thing. Current EVs use lithium-ion batteries (the same basic tech as your phone, just way bigger). *Solid-state batteries* replace the liquid electrolyte inside with a solid material, which sounds boring but is actually a game-changer. They promise:

- Higher energy density for more range in a smaller, lighter battery
- Faster charging means less time waiting at charging stations
- Longer life so that the battery lasts longer before it degrades

Think of a solid-state battery like going from a flip phone battery to a smartphone battery — same idea, but way better performance.

Wireless charging could eliminate the need to plug in entirely. Just park your car over a charging pad in your garage (or even in a parking spot), and it charges automatically. No cables, no fumbling in the rain, no forgetting to plug in. It's like wireless phone charging, but for your whole car.

Vehicle-to-grid (V2G) technology is even cooler. Your EV's battery could act as a backup power source for your home during outages, or even sell electricity back to the grid during peak demand times. Imagine your car paying you back by powering your house during a storm or earning you credits on your electric bill. It's like having a giant portable generator that also happens to drive you to work.

The future is electric, but it's also flexible, adaptive, and full of possibilities we're only beginning to explore. Cars won't just be transportation — they'll be mobile power sources, smart devices, and part of a bigger energy ecosystem.

REMEMBER

No matter what powers your car — gas, diesel, hybrid, or electric — the principles are the same: Convert stored energy into motion, do it efficiently, and minimize waste. The technology changes, but the goal doesn't.

2 Powering Up with Air, Fuel, and Fire

IN THIS PART . . .

See how your car's electrical system powers everything.

Diagnose battery, starter, and wiring problems the right way.

Follow fuel from the tank to the engine.

Maintain your fuel system and avoid costly mistakes.

Understand exhaust, emissions, and what they do.

Learn how hybrids and EVs really work.

Master diesel basics and maintenance.

IN THIS CHAPTER

» Seeing how electricity keeps everything from starters to screens alive

» Meeting batteries, starters, and ECUs as a starting team

» Understanding alternators and modern voltage regulation

» Meeting ECUs and other modules that control fuel, spark, and ignition systems

» Making sense of warning lights and basic OBD-II diagnostics

» Seeing how BCMs and hybrid/EV systems handle comfort features and high-voltage safety

Chapter 5
The Electrical System: Your Car's Digital Nerve Center

Think of this chapter as a roadmap showing how your car's electronics connect and work together. Electricity does more than start the engine; it powers the computers, sensors, screens, lights, comfort features, and safety systems that make a modern car work. You meet the big players (battery, starter, alternator, ECU, BCM), learn what warning lights are trying to tell you, and see how modern cars blend old-school 12-volt systems with high-voltage hybrid and EV tech.

The Car's Digital Nerve Center

Under the hood — and under the dashboards, seats, and carpet — your car is wired like a small building and a laptop had a baby. You still have mechanical parts like pistons, gears, and axles, but now they're surrounded by wiring and computers that tell them what to do and when to do it. Figure 5-1 shows the major pieces of a typical automotive electrical system.

You've got:

- **Power sources:** A 12-volt battery, an alternator, and (on hybrids/EVs) a high-voltage pack.
- **Brains:** The Engine Control Unit (ECU) and a growing crowd of other modules.
- **Nerves:** Wiring harnesses and data networks that link everything together.
- **Muscles:** Motors, solenoids, coils, and relays that move parts and make spark.

All of these items sit on top of the mechanical systems we describe in Chapter 4. The digital side doesn't replace those systems; it controls and coordinates them so that the car starts quickly, runs efficiently, stays comfortable, and warns you when something goes wrong.

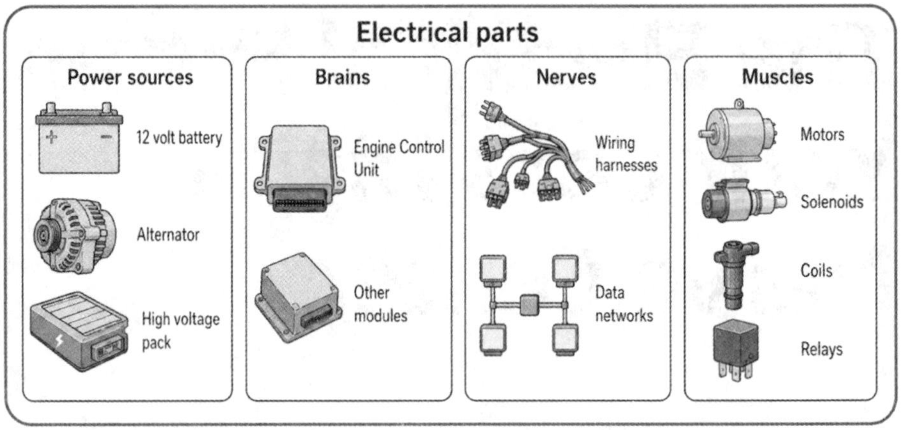

FIGURE 5-1: Electrical system overview.

Generated with AI using OpenAI

How electricity powers modern vehicles

If you've ever wondered what happens in the split second between pressing the Start button and hearing the engine roar to life, you're about to find out. Modern vehicles run on a carefully choreographed electrical dance that starts with a

12-volt battery, moves through a powerful starter motor, hands off to a belt-driven alternator, and then settles into a steady rhythm controlled by computers. It all happens so fast and so reliably that most drivers never think about it — until something goes wrong. We break down that dance step by step so that you understand not just what happens, but why each part matters.

Here's the big picture for a typical gas or diesel vehicle:

1. **The 12-volt battery wakes the car up and powers locks, computers, and the starter.**
2. **The starter motor cranks the engine, spinning it fast enough for combustion to begin.**
3. **Once the engine is running, the alternator takes over, powering the car and recharging the battery.**
4. **The ECU and other modules watch sensors and command coils, injectors, pumps, fans, and more to keep everything running smoothly.**

Hybrids and EVs add another layer: a high-voltage battery pack and one or more inverters and DC-DC converters. Those components move power between the drive motors, the big battery, and the familiar 12-volt system that still runs lights, locks, and control modules.

REMEMBER

Even in a hybrid or EV, a weak or dead 12-volt battery can strand you just as effectively as a dead battery in an older gas car. That tiny box still wakes up the computers and closes the high-voltage contactors before anything else can happen.

The rise of ECUs and BCMs

If you could travel back to the 1970s and pop the hood of a typical car, you'd find a fairly simple electrical system: a battery, an alternator, a distributor for spark, and enough wiring to run the lights, horn, and radio. Fast-forward to today, and that same engine bay is packed with computers, sensors, and enough wiring to make an electrician nervous. What changed? The answer is *control modules* — small but powerful computers that turned your car from a mechanical machine into a rolling network of interconnected brains.

Today's electrical system isn't just about spark and lights anymore. It's the central nervous system that coordinates, monitors, and controls nearly everything your car does. Here's who's running the show:

- The *Engine Control Unit* (ECU) runs fuel delivery, spark timing, and many emissions devices, making constant adjustments based on sensor data.

- The *Body Control Module* (BCM) orchestrates comfort and convenience features: windows, locks, interior lights, wipers, and more.
- Additional modules may handle ABS and stability control, airbags, electric power steering, infotainment, telematics, ADAS (advanced driver-assistance systems), and hybrid/EV systems.

You don't need to memorize every three-letter acronym or know exactly which module does what on your specific car. What matters is understanding that multiple computers share power and information over data networks, talking to each other dozens of times per second. That's why a weird symptom — like flickering interior lights combined with random warning chimes — might be electrical (a loose ground or failing alternator), electronic (a confused module), or both. Modern diagnostics often mean following the conversation between modules, not just testing individual wires.

The Starting System: Battery, Starter, and ECU

When you hit the Start button or twist the key, a whole mini-drama happens in one or two seconds. The battery, starter, and ECU all have starring roles.

Battery basics: More than a box of lead

The 12-volt battery does more than sit under the hood waiting to be blamed when the car won't start. It stores the low-voltage power your vehicle needs to wake up computers, run accessories, and crank the engine. Clean, tight terminals matter, and early clues such as slow cranking, dim interior lights, disappearing radio presets, or a resetting dash clock can point to 12-volt trouble before the battery leaves you stranded. During starting, the battery:

- Supplies high current (hundreds of amps) to the starter motor.
- Powers ECUs, fuel pumps, ignition coils, and injectors while the engine is cranking.
- Acts as a voltage buffer, smoothing out swings when big loads switch on and off.

Modern vehicles may use standard flooded-lead batteries, AGM (Absorbed Glass Mat), or even 12-volt lithium batteries. You can find out how to test them with multimeters and battery testers in Chapter 6.

TIP

If your radio presets vanish, the dash clock keeps resetting, or the car seems to forget settings, treat those as early hints of 12-volt trouble — not just annoyances.

Starter motors: The heavy lifters

If the battery is the alarm clock that wakes your car up, the starter motor is the personal trainer that gets it moving. Think of the starter as a very strong, short-duty power tool bolted directly to the engine — one that's built to deliver massive torque for just a few seconds at a time. Its entire job is to spin a cold, stationary engine fast enough to get combustion started, and then it immediately steps aside and lets the engine do the rest.

Here's what happens in those critical first seconds when you press Start:

1. **A small gear (pinion) on the starter slides forward and engages a large gear (ring gear) on the engine, creating the mechanical link between the starter motor and the crankshaft.**
2. **The starter spins the engine fast enough — usually a few hundred RPM — for the ECU to see crankshaft position and begin commanding fuel and spark.**
3. **Once the engine fires and runs on its own, the starter disengages and goes back to sleep until the next time you need it.**

The whole process takes one or two seconds when everything is healthy. But when something goes wrong, starter problems announce themselves pretty clearly. You might hear a single loud click with no cranking (often a bad starter solenoid or very weak battery), a very slow, labored rrrr-rrrr-rrrr drag (weak battery, bad connections, or a failing starter motor), or complete silence when you turn the key (electrical issue, failed relay, or anti-theft lockout).

Chapter 6 shows you how to test the battery, charging system, and starter circuit with a multimeter, battery tester, and scan tool. If the car won't start at all, Chapter 22 walks you through no-start triage so you can separate a weak battery, failing starter, bad connection, key/immobilizer issue, or something else entirely.

The ECU's role in starting

On older vehicles, turning the key sent power more or less directly to the starter circuit — it was a straightforward mechanical and electrical handshake. On modern cars, that handshake goes through a gatekeeper first. The ECU acts as the bouncer at the door, checking credentials before allowing the starter to run. This added layer of control improves safety, prevents accidental starts, and helps protect against theft, but it also means that "the car won't start" can have more causes than just a dead battery or bad starter.

Before the ECU gives the green light to crank the engine, it runs through a quick checklist of conditions. Figure 5-2 shows the basic starting system flow. Here's what it's looking for and why each one matters:

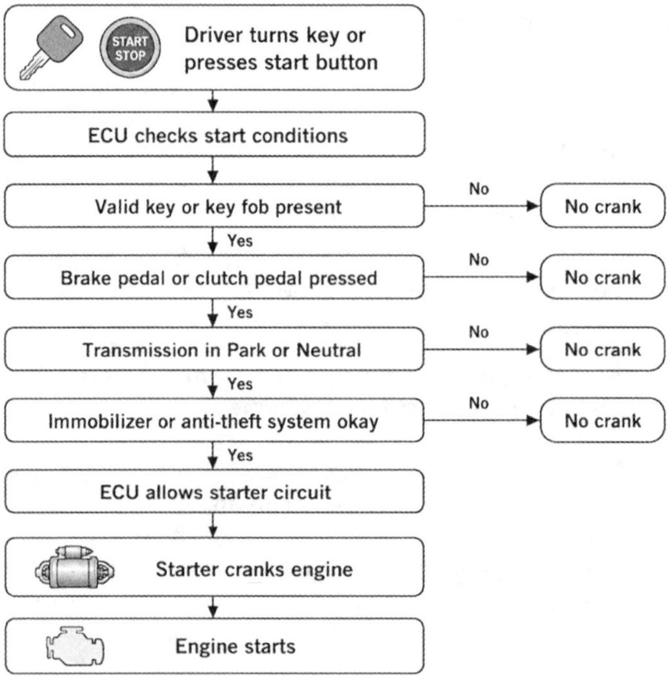

FIGURE 5-2: Starting system flow diagram.

Generated with AI using OpenAI

» **Is a valid key or key fob present?** Modern cars use transponder chips or proximity sensors to verify that the key trying to start the car is actually programmed for that vehicle. If the immobilizer system doesn't recognize the key, the ECU won't allow cranking — even if the battery is perfect and the starter is brand new. This check is your car's first line of defense against theft.

- **Is the brake pedal (or clutch pedal on a manual) pressed?** The brake-pedal or clutch-pedal requirement is a safety interlock. If the car started without you pressing the brake, it may lurch forward unexpectedly if it's in gear (or if the transmission has an internal fault). Requiring a pressed brake pedal ensures that you're in the driver's seat, paying attention, and ready to control the car the moment it starts. On manual transmissions, the same logic applies to the clutch pedal — pressing it disengages the transmission so that the engine can spin freely without trying to move the car.
- **Is the transmission in Park or Neutral?** The *neutral safety switch* (also called the park/neutral position switch) tells the ECU whether the transmission is in a safe position to start. If the transmission is in Drive or Reverse, the ECU refuses to crank — otherwise, the car could jump forward or backward the instant the engine fires. This safeguard is especially important on automatic transmissions, where the torque converter is always trying to transfer power when the engine is running.
- **Is the immobilizer/anti-theft system happy?** Beyond just recognizing the key, the immobilizer system may check for tamper signals, recent alarm triggers, or other security faults. If the system detects something suspicious — or if a glitch occurs in the security module — it can lock out the starter entirely. Sometimes a simple issue like a weak key fob battery or a recent battery disconnect can confuse the immobilizer and prevent starting until the system is reset or relearned.

If everything checks out — valid key, brake pressed, transmission in Park or Neutral, no security faults — the ECU grounds a relay or sends a command to a starter control module, which actually powers the starter motor and gets the engine cranking. Some hybrids and vehicles with automatic stop/start systems may not even have a traditional starter motor. Instead, an integrated starter-generator (ISG) or the main drive motor spins the engine directly, making starts nearly silent and almost instantaneous.

REMEMBER

"Nothing happens when I hit Start" can be many things: a dead battery, a bad starter, a failed sensor, loose or corroded connections, or the ECU refusing to crank for safety or anti-theft reasons. Don't just assume new starter is the answer — let the tests and scan data guide you. Modern no-start diagnosis often means checking inputs (brake switch, neutral safety switch, and key signal) just as much as testing outputs (battery voltage and starter current draw).

The Charging System: Alternator and Voltage Regulation

If the battery is your car's starting bank account, the alternator is its paycheck. Without a working charging system, even a brand-new battery will run down quickly.

The *alternator* is a belt-driven generator that turns mechanical energy from the engine into electrical energy. Figure 5-3 shows the basic charging system flow:

1. **Engine rotation spins a pulley on the alternator.**
2. **The alternator's rotor spins inside a stator, creating alternating current (AC).**
3. **Internal diodes convert that AC into direct current (DC) for the 12-volt system.**

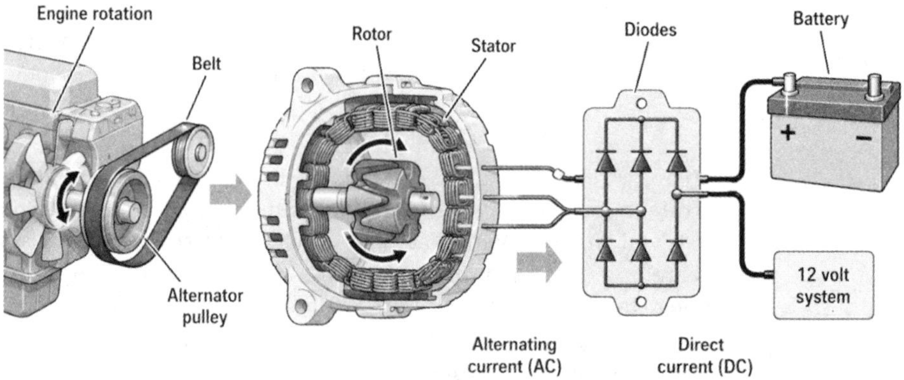

FIGURE 5-3: Alternator and charging system.

Older cars used separate, sometimes mechanical voltage regulators. Modern alternators use solid-state regulation, often built into the alternator housing and controlled by the ECU.

Solid-state and smart alternators

Many newer vehicles use smart alternators or computer-controlled charging. Instead of holding a fixed voltage, the charging system can adjust output based on:

- Battery type and temperature
- Electrical load (lights, heated seats, defrosters, and so on)
- Engine load, to reduce drag during acceleration and increase charging during deceleration

These strategies improve fuel economy and extend battery life, but they also mean that simple "looks like 14 volts, so it's fine" checks may not tell the whole story. In the next chapter, you can find out how to use a multimeter and scan tool together to see how the system behaves under different loads.

TIP

Some vehicles require specific alternator designs and programming. Dropping in the cheapest remanufactured unit you can find may cause charging problems and new warning lights. Always confirm the correct part number and any required relearn or programming steps.

Charging systems on hybrids and EVs

Charging systems on hybrids and EVs are where things get a little weird — in a cool, futuristic kind of way. Hybrids and EVs still have a 12-volt system (yes, even the fanciest electric car on the block), but they've ditched the belt-driven alternator for something that sounds like it belongs in a sci-fi movie: a DC-DC converter.

Think of the *DC-DC converter* as a very polite electrical transformer that takes the high-voltage power from the big battery pack — we're talking hundreds of volts — and steps it down to a friendly, familiar 12 to 14 volts to run your headlights, power windows, radio, and all the computers that keep the car from having an identity crisis. It also keeps the little 12-volt battery topped off, because even in a car that can silently glide down the highway on pure electricity, that humble 12-volt battery is still the one waking everything up in the morning.

On some hybrids, you may find both a traditional belt-driven alternator and a DC-DC converter working side by side, like a tag team. One covers for the other depending on whether the gas engine is running or the car is in electric mode. But the mission is always the same: Keep the 12-volt side alive and happy without overcharging it — because a fried 12-volt battery in a $60,000 EV is just as annoying (and just as expensive to tow) as one in a 20-year-old sedan.

Electronic Ignition Systems: Distributorless and COP

If you've ever watched an old car movie where the mechanic pops the hood, pulls off a round plastic cap, and pokes around at wires and a spinning rotor, you've seen a distributor in action. Classic distributor ignition systems used a spinning shaft and mechanical points to time and distribute spark to each cylinder in the correct firing order. They worked — your grandparents' cars ran on them for decades — but they had a lot of downsides that made mechanics and drivers equally frustrated:

- Points and rubbing blocks wore out and needed frequent adjustment. Miss a tune-up, and your engine would start running rough or refuse to start at all.
- Timing drifted as parts wore or as the distributor loosened in its mount, stealing power and fuel economy without you even realizing it.
- Moisture, carbon tracks, and worn caps or rotors caused misfires and hard starts, especially on damp mornings or after the car sat for a while.

As emissions rules tightened in the 1980s and fuel injection took over, automakers realized they needed more precision and less maintenance. Distributors gave way to electronic ignition and, eventually, distributorless and coil-on-plug systems that are smarter, more reliable, and a whole lot less fussy.

Distributorless ignition: Coil packs and waste spark

The first step beyond distributors was the *distributorless ignition system* (DIS), which uses coil packs instead of a single coil and spinning distributor. Instead of one coil feeding all the cylinders through a mechanical distributor, you get multiple coils grouped together in a pack or bank, with each coil responsible for one or two cylinders.

Here's how DIS works and why it's better:

- Each coil may fire two spark plugs at once — one cylinder on its power stroke (where combustion happens) and one on its exhaust stroke (where the spark does nothing useful, earning the nickname waste spark). It sounds inefficient, but it's simple, reliable, and eliminates all those spinning distributor parts.

- The ECU uses crankshaft and camshaft position sensors to know exactly where each piston is and when to fire each coil — no mechanical timing adjustments needed.
- No moving distributor parts means better reliability, more precise control, and fewer things to wear out or go out of adjustment.

Distributorless ignition was a huge leap forward, but engineers didn't stop there.

Coil-on-plug (COP): The modern standard

Many gasoline engines built from the early 2000s onward use coil-on-plug ignition, and once you understand it, you'll see why it's become the gold standard. In this setup, each spark plug gets its own dedicated coil, mounted directly on top of the plug under a small plastic cover. No shared coils, no waste spark, no compromises — just one coil per cylinder, doing exactly what that cylinder needs, exactly when it needs it.

The benefits are impressive:

- Shorter high-voltage paths mean less chance of energy loss, arcing, or crossfire between cylinders. The spark goes straight from coil to plug with almost no wiring in between.
- Individual control of each cylinder's spark timing and dwell lets the ECU fine-tune ignition for maximum power, efficiency, and emissions control — even adjusting for differences between cylinders.
- Longer intervals between tune-ups, especially when paired with long-life iridium or platinum spark plugs, means that many COP systems can go 100,000 miles or more before needing new plugs.

Coil-on-plug ignition is one of those quiet engineering victories that makes modern cars so much easier to live with. You don't think about it until something goes wrong — and when it does, the ECU usually knows exactly which cylinder is misbehaving and lights up the Check Engine light to let you know.

REMEMBER

If the Check Engine light is flashing (not just steady) while the engine is running, that usually means a severe misfire that can overheat and damage the catalytic converter in minutes. Ease off the throttle, avoid heavy acceleration, and treat it as a "get this checked now" situation, not a "maybe next month" chore. A flashing light is your car's way of screaming for help.

Engine Control Units: Brains behind the Sparks

The ECU is the conductor of the mechanical orchestra — the brain that coordinates air, fuel, and spark to make combustion happen. Think of the ECU as a tireless air traffic controller, constantly reading dozens of sensors, making thousands of decisions per second, and sending commands to actuators all over the engine. It never sleeps, never takes a coffee break, and never guesses — it just reads, calculates, and acts, over and over, as long as the engine is running. (For more on the ECU, see Chapter 4.)

Inputs: What the ECU listens to

Chapter 4 introduces the sensors that feed data to the ECU — the mass airflow sensor measuring incoming air, oxygen sensors sniffing exhaust, the throttle position sensor tracking your right foot, and all the others working together to give the ECU a real-time picture of what the engine is doing. You may be wondering what the ECU actually does with all that information.

The ECU's job starts with listening — constantly, relentlessly, thousands of times per second. It's reading sensor voltages, comparing them to expected values, watching for trends, and building a complete picture of engine conditions. But while Chapter 4 talks about what those sensors measure, in this chapter, we talk about how the ECU interprets that data and uses it to make decisions.

Here's what's happening behind the scenes:

- **Crankshaft and camshaft position sensors** don't just tell the ECU where the pistons are — they give it the timing reference it needs to fire injectors and coils with millisecond precision. Miss that timing by even a few degrees, and you get misfires, lost power, or engine damage.
- **MAF or MAP sensors** help the ECU figure out how much air the engine is taking in. A MAF sensor measures incoming air directly; a MAP sensor measures pressure in the intake manifold so the ECU can estimate engine load and airflow. The ECU uses that information to decide how long to open the fuel injectors, aiming for the right air-fuel mixture — about 14.7 parts air to 1 part fuel during normal gasoline operation — and then adjusting as conditions change.
- **Throttle position or electronic throttle** data tells the ECU not just how much power you're asking for, but how fast you're asking for it. Stomp the pedal, and the ECU knows you want maximum acceleration — it enriches the

fuel mixture, advances timing, and (on turbocharged engines) commands the wastegate to build boost.

- **Coolant and intake air temperature sensors** provide the context the ECU needs to adjust for real-world conditions. Cold engine? Add more fuel and raise idle speed. Hot intake air on a summer day? Pull back timing to avoid knock.
- **Oxygen sensors** are the ECU's feedback loop, constantly checking whether the last combustion cycle was rich, lean, or just right. The ECU uses this data to make tiny corrections (called *fuel trims*) hundreds of times per second, keeping emissions low and efficiency high.
- **Knock sensors** are the ECU's early warning system. If they detect the sound signature of *detonation* — abnormal combustion that can punch holes in pistons — the ECU immediately retards ignition timing to protect the engine, even if it means sacrificing a little power.

But the ECU doesn't work in isolation. It's also listening to messages from other modules over the *CAN bus* (Controller Area Network) — the vehicle's internal data highway. The transmission module tells the ECU when a shift is about to happen so that it can momentarily cut power for a smoother transition. The ABS module reports wheel slip so that the ECU can cut engine power and help traction control do its job. On hybrids, the hybrid control module coordinates when the gas engine should run, when the electric motor should take over, and when to recharge the battery.

It's a constant conversation between dozens of computers, all sharing data and making decisions together. That's why modern cars feel so refined and responsive — it's not just one brain running the show, it's a whole network of brains working in perfect harmony.

Outputs: What the ECU controls

Reading sensors is only half the job. The ECU also has to do something with all that information — and fast. Based on sensor data and its internal programming, the ECU commands a small army of actuators and devices scattered throughout the engine. Think of actuators as the muscles that carry out the brain's orders: Open this valve, spray that fuel, and fire this coil. Here's what the ECU is controlling, and why it matters:

- **Fuel injectors:** These tiny, electrically controlled spray nozzles sit in (or near) each cylinder. The ECU controls how long each injector stays open (measured in milliseconds), which determines exactly how much fuel gets sprayed in. Open it longer, you get more fuel (more power, but worse fuel economy).

Open it for less time, you get less fuel (better economy, but less power). The ECU is constantly adjusting injector timing to match what you're asking the engine to do.

- **Ignition coils:** These are the devices that build up electrical energy and release it as a high-voltage spark to ignite the air-fuel mixture. The ECU decides when to fire each coil (timing is everything; fire too early or too late, and you lose power or damage the engine) and how long to charge the coil before releasing the spark. More charge time means bigger, hotter spark. The ECU adjusts spark timing and coil charge time on the fly based on engine speed, load, and fuel quality.
- **Idle speed control or electronic throttle opening:** On older cars, idle speed was controlled by a mechanical valve or motor. On modern cars with drive-by-wire throttles, the ECU controls the throttle plate directly, opening it just enough to keep the engine running smoothly at stoplights and responding instantly when you press the gas pedal. You're not directly connected to the throttle anymore — you're sending a request to the ECU, and it decides how much throttle to give you based on conditions.
- **Turbo wastegates or electronic boost controllers:** If your engine is turbocharged, the ECU manages *boost pressure* (the amount of compressed air being forced into the engine). Too little boost, and you're leaving power on the table. Too much boost, and you risk engine damage from detonation or overheating. The ECU constantly adjusts the *wastegate* (a valve that bleeds off excess exhaust pressure) to keep boost in the safe zone while maximizing performance.
- **Variable valve timing actuators:** These solenoids or motors adjust camshaft position to change when the intake and exhaust valves open and close. The ECU commands these actuators to optimize valve timing for the current driving situation: low-end torque for city driving, high-end power for highway passing, or maximum fuel economy for cruising. It's like having multiple camshafts in one engine, all controlled by software.
- **EGR valves, purge solenoids, and other emissions devices:** The ECU also manages a bunch of emissions-control hardware that most drivers never think about. The *EGR (Exhaust Gas Recirculation) valve* routes a small amount of exhaust back into the intake to lower combustion temperatures and reduce nitrogen oxide emissions. The *purge solenoid* controls when fuel vapors from the gas tank get burned in the engine instead of escaping into the atmosphere. These systems work quietly in the background, keeping emissions low and preventing that dreaded Check Engine light from ruining your day.

Because the ECU is software-driven, automakers can tweak its behavior with updates and reflashes when they discover issues, improve fuel economy, or refine performance. It's like getting a software update on your phone that makes the camera better or fixes a bug — except in this case, the update may give you better gas mileage, smoother shifts, or more power. When it works, it's pretty cool. When it doesn't . . . well, that's what recalls are for.

Diagnostics: Codes, freeze frames, and monitors

When something falls outside of expected ranges — a sensor reading that doesn't make sense, a misfire, or a system that's not responding — the ECU doesn't just shrug and keep going. It takes notes and tries to help you figure out what's wrong. The ECU:

- Stores a Diagnostic Trouble Code (DTC) that you can read with an OBD-II scanner, giving you a starting point for diagnosis
- Saves a freeze-frame snapshot of sensor values at the exact moment the fault occurred — like a black box recording of the crime scene
- Turns on a warning light (usually the Check Engine light) to let you know something needs attention
- Tracks readiness monitors that show whether the ECU's self-tests have completed after codes were cleared — important for emissions testing and verifying that repairs actually worked

The ECU is trying to help you, but it's not handing you the answer on a silver platter. It's giving you clues, and it's up to you (or your mechanic) to follow those clues to the root cause.

REMEMBER

A trouble code is a clue, not a verdict. A code like "System Too Lean (Bank 1)" doesn't automatically mean "replace the oxygen sensor." It means the ECU is seeing a lean condition — too much air or not enough fuel — and wants you to investigate vacuum leaks, fuel pressure, clogged injectors, intake gasket leaks, MAF sensor issues, and yes, maybe the O_2 sensor. Don't just throw parts at the problem. Let the data guide you.

Warning Lights and Diagnostic Systems

Every time you turn the key to ON (before starting), the dash lights up like a holiday tree. That's a bulb test. Once the engine is running, most of those lights should go out. What stays lit, or starts flashing, is your car's way of saying, "Hey, something's up."

Check Engine light (MIL) basics

The Check Engine light — also called the Malfunction Indicator Lamp (MIL) — is at the heart of OBD-II diagnostics:

A steady Check Engine light indicates a problem, but the ECU doesn't think damage is imminent. The vehicle is usually safe to drive a short distance, but schedule a scan soon.

On the other hand, a flashing Check Engine light signals a severe misfire or another condition that can damage the catalytic converter. You need to reduce load or stop and get help.

Common Check Engine light triggers include misfires, emissions faults, fuel system lean/rich conditions, and sensor range/performance issues. You'll see these code families in Chapter 6 for ignition and misfire checks, Chapters 7 and 8 for fuel-system lean/rich and fuel-trim problems, and Chapter 9 for emissions, oxygen-sensor, EVAP, EGR, and catalyst codes.

Other warning lights

Your dash carries more messages than just Check Engine. A few important ones include:

- **Battery/charging system icon:** Alternator or charging fault. See Chapter 6.
- **Oil pressure light:** Low oil pressure (different from an oil-change reminder). See Chapter 14.
- **Brake warning:** Low fluid, parking brake set, or system fault. See Chapters 15 and 16.
- **ABS and stability control lights:** Anti-lock and stability aids possibly limited or disabled. See Chapter 15.
- **Airbag/SRS light:** Airbag system fault; bags may not deploy in a crash. See Chapter 20.
- **TPMS light:** Low tire pressure or a fault in the tire pressure monitoring system. See Chapter 18.

TIP

As a simple rule: Red or flashing lights deserve immediate attention; amber, steady lights call for a scan and a plan.

OBD-II basics (without the jargon headache)

Every modern car sold in the United States since 1996 has a standardized OBD-II port hiding somewhere within reach of the driver's seat, usually under the dashboard, near your left knee. It's a 16-pin trapezoid-shaped connector that looks vaguely important, and it is. This port is your car's confessional booth, diagnostic hotline, and tattletale all rolled into one little plastic socket.

When you plug in a scan tool or Bluetooth dongle (see Chapter 3), you get access to a treasure trove of information that the ECU has been quietly collecting. Here's what you can read:

- **Generic codes (P0xxx):** These codes are standardized trouble codes that mean the same thing across all brands. A P0171 on a Honda means the same thing as a P0171 on a Ford, a Toyota, or a Tesla. It's like a universal language for car problems, which is refreshingly rare in the automotive world where every manufacturer loves to do things their own way.
- **Manufacturer-specific codes (P1xxx and beyond):** These brand-specific codes are for systems that aren't covered by the generic standard. Think of them as the manufacturer's secret menu — codes for things like "Ford's variable intake runner control stuck open" or "GM's active fuel management system performance issue." You'll need a more advanced scan tool or online code database to decode them, but these codes are incredibly useful when diagnosing weird, brand-specific gremlins.
- **Freeze-frame data:** This data offers a snapshot of sensor readings at the exact moment the ECU detected a fault and turned on the Check Engine light. It's like a black box recording of the crime scene: engine speed, coolant temperature, throttle position, fuel trims, and more, all frozen in time. This data is gold for diagnosis because it tells you what the engine was doing when the problem happened — idling at a stoplight? Wide-open throttle on the highway? Cold start on a winter morning?
- **Readiness monitor status:** The ECU runs a series of self-tests (called *monitors*) to verify that emissions systems are working properly. If you've recently cleared codes or disconnected the battery, these monitors reset and need to run to completion before your car will pass an emissions test. *Readiness status* tells you which monitors have completed and which are still pending. It's like a checklist the ECU keeps to make sure everything is healthy before giving you a clean bill of health.

TIP

Here's the most important thing to understand about OBD-II codes: The code is a clue, not a verdict. Think of it like a headline in a newspaper. It tells you what the problem is, but not why it's happening or how to fix it.

For example, a P0171 "System Too Lean (Bank 1)" code means the ECU is detecting too much air or not enough fuel in the exhaust. But that code could be caused by any of the following:

- A vacuum leak sucking in extra air
- A weak or dying fuel pump not delivering enough fuel
- A dirty or failing MAF sensor giving bad readings
- An exhaust leak upstream of the oxygen sensor
- Clogged fuel injectors
- A bad oxygen sensor (though it's less common than people think)

See the problem? One code, six possible causes — and that's not even the full list. The code tells you what the ECU is seeing (a lean condition), but it's up to you to figure out why. That's where live data, freeze-frame analysis, and good old-fashioned detective work come in. Chapter 6 shows you how to use scan data, simple tests, and wiring checks to move from code to root cause without just throwing parts at the problem and hoping something sticks.

WARNING

Don't clear codes "just to see if they come back" before you write them down, snap a photo, or save the freeze-frame data. Here's why: Clearing codes also clears freeze-frame snapshots and resets readiness monitors — in other words, you're erasing all the clues the ECU collected before you even had a chance to read them. It's like burning the evidence before the detective arrives. Write down the codes, save the freeze-frame data, and then decide whether to clear them. Your future self (and your mechanic) will thank you.

The Body Control Module: Comfort, Convenience, and Quirks

If the ECU handles "go and stop," the Body Control Module (BCM) handles a lot of the "live with" stuff. Different manufacturers spread tasks among modules in different ways, but BCMs typically manage:

- Power windows and sometimes mirrors
- Power door locks and keyless entry

- Interior lights and their fade-out behavior
- Wiper and washer logic (speeds, intervals, rain sensing)
- Horns, alarms, and sometimes remote start
- Turn signals, hazards, and some exterior lighting

Power windows and locks

Modern window and lock systems look simple on the surface: Push a switch, and the window moves or the doors lock. Behind the scenes:

- The BCM monitors switches and door-ajar sensors.
- It drives window motors and lock actuators via relays or internal solid-state drivers.
- It may watch current draw for pinch protection and reverse a window if it hits an obstruction.

Common complaints like "this one window won't go up" or "this door never locks with the rest" usually start with simple checks, not an automatic BCM replacement. If only one door or window acts up, try both the local switch and the master switch, listen for the motor or lock actuator, and inspect the rubber wiring boot between the door and body for broken or frayed wires. The fix may be as simple as repairing a broken wire, cleaning a connector, replacing a faulty switch, or replacing a tired window motor or lock actuator. If several windows or locks stop working at once, check the related fuse, relay, power feed, and ground before blaming the module.

Chapter 6 walks you through those fuse, relay, power, ground, and basic wiring tests. If testing points to the BCM itself or the repair requires module programming, that's usually shop territory.

Lighting control and infotainment

If your car can fade interior lights, keep headlights on after you shut the car off, or turn lights on automatically in the dark, you're seeing lighting logic controlled by the BCM or a related module.

In many cars, the BCM (or a gateway module) also acts as a traffic cop for communication between infotainment, telematics, and driver-assist systems. That's why simple stereo swaps on newer vehicles can go badly unless they're done with the right interfaces and wiring diagrams.

REMEMBER

When diagnosing lighting or convenience features, don't assume bad bulb or bad radio is the only option. Fuses, relays, modules, grounds, and data networks all play a role.

Other Electrical Gadgets: Beyond the Big Stuff

Once you understand the heavy hitters — battery, alternator, ECU, and BCM — the rest of your car's electrical accessories start to make a lot more sense. Strip away the fancy features and complicated names, and you'll find that almost every electrical device in your car follows the same basic pattern. It's like realizing that every recipe is just some combination of heat, ingredients, and time. Once you see the pattern, the mystery disappears.

Here's the formula for nearly every electrical accessory in your car. Figure 5-4 shows the power-control-load pattern:

- **A power feed:** Electricity has to come from somewhere, usually the battery or a fused circuit that's always hot or switched on with the ignition. This feed is almost always protected by a fuse or circuit breaker so that if something goes wrong, the fuse blows instead of the whole car catching fire.
- **A control path:** Something has to tell the device when to turn on and off. Sometimes it's a simple switch you press (like a window button). Sometimes it's a module command from the BCM or another computer (like automatic headlights that turn on when it gets dark). Often, it's both — you press a button, which sends a signal to a module, which then powers the device.
- **A load:** The load is the thing that actually does the work: a motor (window, sunroof, seat), a heater element (seat warmer, rear defroster), an actuator (door lock, trunk latch), or a lamp (interior lights, headlights). The load is what consumes the electricity and converts it into motion, heat, or light.

That's it. Power in, control signal, load does the work. Once you see this pattern, diagnosing electrical problems becomes way less intimidating.

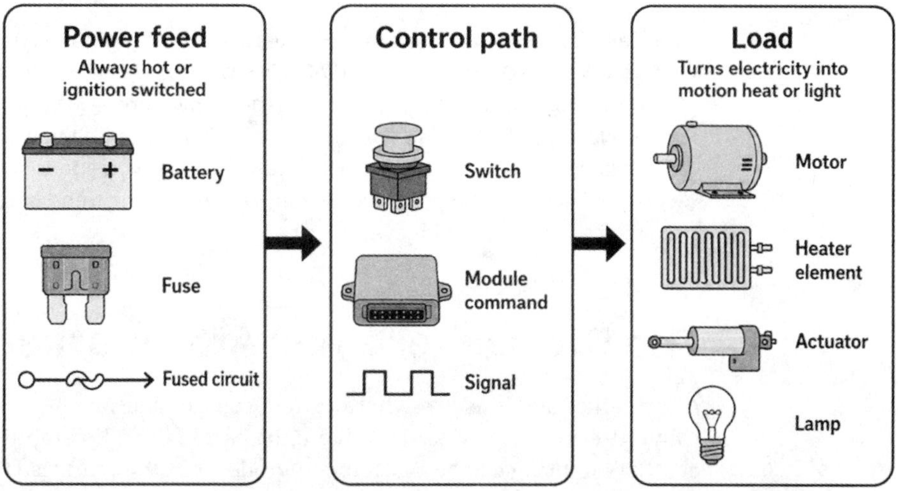

FIGURE 5-4: Power-control-load pattern.

Generated with AI using OpenAI

Everyday electrical accessories

Look at a few everyday electrical accessories and see how they fit the pattern of power in, control signal, load does the work:

- **Seat and steering-wheel heaters:** The power feed is from a fused circuit, controlled by a switch on the dash or center console, and the load is a resistive heating element woven into the seat or steering wheel. Press the button, the BCM closes a relay, current flows through the heating element, and your backside (or hands) get toasty. It's simple, effective, and one of the best inventions in modern cars.
- **USB ports and 12-volt accessory sockets:** These items are just power feeds with built-in fuses or circuit breakers. Plug something in, and it draws power directly from the 12-volt system. No fancy control logic, no modules — just straight-up power delivery. That said, some newer cars have smart USB ports that can communicate with your phone and adjust charging speed, but the basic idea is the same.
- **Sunroofs, power liftgates, and sliding doors:** These motor-driven systems are controlled by switches and (usually) a module that monitors position, detects obstructions, and prevents pinching. Press the button, the module checks that it's safe to move and then powers the motor in the correct direction. Release the button or hit an obstacle, and the motor stops (or reverses). It's more complex than a seat heater, but it still follows the same power-control-load pattern.

- **Cameras and parking sensors:** These sensors feed video and sensor data to your infotainment system and ADAS (Advanced Driver Assistance Systems) modules. The cameras and sensors themselves are loads (they consume power), but they're also data sources, sending information over the vehicle's data network so the car can help you park, warn you about obstacles, or even steer itself in tight spots. They're part of the growing trend of cars becoming rolling computers with eyes.

The DIY danger zone: Aftermarket add-ons

Aftermarket add-ons are where things can go sideways — literally and electrically. Aftermarket accessories like light bars, big audio amplifiers, winches, and auxiliary lighting can be awesome upgrades, but they can also turn your car into a rolling fire hazard if they're installed poorly.

The problem? Many of these devices draw way more current than the factory wiring was designed to handle. Tap into an existing circuit to power your 200-watt light bar, and you can overload that circuit, melt the wiring, blow fuses repeatedly, or — in the worst case — start an electrical fire.

Here's how to install aftermarket electrical add-ons safely:

- **Use proper fusing.** Every aftermarket device should have its own fuse, sized correctly for the load. If the device draws 10 amps, use a 15-amp fuse (not a 30-amp "just to be safe"). The fuse is there to protect the wiring, not the device.
- **Install a relay.** High-current devices (anything over 10 to 5 amps) should be controlled by a relay, not directly by a switch. The switch sends a low-current signal to the relay, and the relay handles the heavy lifting. This setup keeps high current out of your dash switches and prevents melted buttons and fried wiring.
- **Run dedicated power feeds from the battery.** Don't tap into existing circuits. Run a new, properly sized wire directly from the battery (with an inline fuse near the battery) to your accessory, which keeps the load off factory circuits and ensures you have clean, reliable power.
- **Avoid random taps into existing wiring.** Scotch-locking into a random wire under the dash may seem easy, but it's a recipe for problems: voltage drops, blown fuses, weird electrical gremlins, and potential fires. Do the wiring right the first time or pay a pro to do it for you.

WARNING

Aftermarket electrical work gone wrong is one of the top causes of vehicle fires. If you're not confident in your wiring skills, don't guess — ask for help or hire a professional installer. A few hundred bucks for proper installation beats a few thousand (or more) for fire damage, a totaled car, or worse. That's how you prevent DIY projects from turning into DIY smoke shows — and trust me, nobody wants to be that person explaining to their insurance company how their light bar mod turned their truck into a bonfire.

Future Electrical Systems: BMS, High Voltage, and Beyond

Modern cars are already rolling computers, and the trend is accelerating. Hybrids and EVs add larger batteries, powerful inverters, and more complex cooling systems. Even gas-only vehicles now rely on smart battery management, advanced charging, and software updates.

Battery Management Systems (BMS)

If the ECU is the brain that runs the engine, the Battery Management System (BMS) is the overprotective parent watching over the high-voltage battery pack in hybrids and EVs. And trust me, it needs to be overprotective because these battery packs are expensive, temperamental, and absolutely critical to keeping the car running. A single mistake — overcharging a cell, letting the pack get too hot, draining it too low — can cost thousands of dollars in repairs or even total the battery pack entirely.

Here's what the BMS does, 24/7, without ever taking a break:

- **Monitors individual cell voltages, temperatures, and currents.** A hybrid or EV battery pack isn't just one big battery. It's made up of hundreds (sometimes thousands) of individual cells wired together. The BMS watches every single one, checking voltage, temperature, and current flow to make sure no cell is being overworked, overheated, or left behind. It's like being a teacher in a classroom of 400 students and somehow knowing exactly what each one is doing at all times.
- **Balances cells so no single one is over- or under-charged.** Over time, individual cells can drift out of sync — some charge faster, some discharge faster. If left unchecked, this imbalance shortens battery life and can even cause safety issues. The BMS actively balances the cells, redistributing charge

so that they all stay in harmony. Think of it like making sure every kid gets the same amount of cake at a birthday party — nobody gets too much, nobody gets left out.

- **Controls charge and discharge limits to protect battery life.** The BMS decides how much power can flow in (during charging) and out (during driving) based on temperature, state of charge, and battery health. Push too hard, and you risk damaging the cells. The BMS is the referee that keeps everything within safe limits, even if it means limiting your acceleration or charging speed temporarily to protect the pack.
- **Talks to cooling systems to keep the pack in its happy temperature range.** Batteries hate extreme temperatures. Too hot, and they degrade fast (or catch fire). Too cold, and they lose capacity and can't deliver full power. The BMS constantly communicates with the cooling system (liquid cooling on most EVs, air cooling on some hybrids) to keep the pack in its sweet spot — usually between 60°F and 80°F. It's like having a thermostat that's obsessed with keeping the battery comfortable.

But here's the thing: BMS technology isn't just for hybrids and EVs anymore. Many newer gas vehicles also use a 12-volt BMS to manage the traditional 12-volt battery. This system tracks battery state of charge, adjusts smart-alternator behavior (charging more during deceleration, less during acceleration), and helps decide when the auto stop-start system should operate. If the 12-volt battery is weak or cold, the BMS tells the car "don't shut off the engine at this stoplight — we might not have enough juice to restart." It's a small but smart addition that extends battery life and prevents annoying no-start situations.

High-voltage safety in hybrids and EVs

WARNING

We'll be blunt: High-voltage systems in hybrids and EVs operate at hundreds of volts — typically 200 to 400 volts, and sometimes even higher in performance EVs. For context, your household outlet is 120 volts, and that's already enough to give you a nasty shock (or worse). The voltage in an EV battery pack is high enough to be dangerous or fatal, if mishandled. This isn't a "maybe don't touch that" situation — it's a "touch that and you could die" situation.

The good news? Automakers know this risk, and they've built multiple layers of safety into these systems to protect you, first responders, and technicians. Here's what's keeping everyone safe:

- **Bright orange sheathing on high-voltage cables:** If you see thick cables wrapped in bright orange insulation, that's the universal warning sign for high voltage. It's like the automotive equivalent of a DANGER: HIGH VOLTAGE sign on an electrical substation. Orange means don't touch, don't cut, and don't mess with it unless you're trained and have the right tools. This color-coding is standardized across all hybrids and EVs, so there's no confusion.

- **Automatic disconnects and contactors that open in a crash or fault:** High-voltage battery packs have built-in contactors (heavy-duty relays) that physically disconnect the pack from the rest of the car if the system detects a crash, a short circuit, or another fault. Think of them like circuit breakers in your house; if something goes wrong, they cut power instantly to prevent fires, shocks, or further damage. In a serious crash, these contactors open automatically, isolating the battery and making the car safer for first responders to approach.
- **Interlock circuits that shut the system down if covers or service plugs are opened:** Many hybrid and EV battery packs have service disconnect plugs or covers with built-in interlock switches. Open the cover or pull the plug, and the system immediately shuts down and discharges any residual high voltage. It's a fail-safe that prevents accidental contact with live high-voltage components. Some systems even have a mandatory waiting period (5 to 10 minutes) after pulling the service plug to let capacitors discharge fully before it's safe to work on the car.
- **Dedicated cooling loops for batteries and power electronics:** High-voltage batteries and inverters generate a lot of heat, so they have their own cooling systems separate from the engine cooling system. These separate systems are usually liquid-cooled loops with pumps, radiators, and temperature sensors. The cooling system keeps the battery pack and electronics in their safe operating range, and the BMS monitors it constantly. If the cooling system fails, the BMS will limit power or shut the car down entirely to prevent thermal damage.

Here's the bottom line: This book is all about empowering you to work on your own car, but high-voltage hybrid and EV systems are the exception. Visual inspections from a safe distance are fine — checking for damaged orange cables, looking for warning lights, making sure the 12-volt battery is healthy. But anything beyond a visual check — opening high-voltage covers, probing circuits, or working on the battery pack or inverters — belongs strictly in the hands of trained professionals with specialized tools, insulated gloves, and proper safety procedures.

WARNING

Never probe, open, disconnect, or "just tighten" anything marked with orange sheathing or high-voltage warning labels. Even if the car is off, capacitors can hold lethal voltage for minutes (or longer) after shutdown. If you're curious about how these systems work, great — read about them, watch videos, or ask questions. But leave the hands-on work to certified EV technicians. Your life is worth way more than the cost of a service call.

IN THIS CHAPTER

» Keeping your 12-volt battery health

» Understanding alternators and smart charging

» Solving starter and stop/start problems

» Caring for modern plugs and coils

» Tracking down fuse, relay, and wiring faults

» Staying safe around hybrid and EV high-voltage systems

Chapter 6 Tuning Your Electrical System

Think of this chapter as the difference between reading a recipe and actually cooking dinner. You're going to test batteries, check charging systems, diagnose why your car clicks instead of starts, and figure out which fuse just killed your radio.

Battery Basics in the Digital Age

If the electrical system is the body's nervous system, the 12-volt battery is the heart that gets it all beating. Every time you hit the Start button or turn the key, that small box under the hood (or in the trunk) wakes up dozens of modules, powers the starter or high-voltage contactors, and brings the car to life.

Even in hybrids and EVs, the humble 12-volt battery still controls the computers, locks, lights, and more. If it's weak or failing, your car can act possessed: random warning lights, "no key detected" messages, glitchy infotainment, or a dead-as-a-doornail no-start.

Meeting your modern battery types

Old-school cars mostly used flooded lead-acid batteries — the kind with caps you could pry off to peek at the electrolyte. Modern cars still use lead-acid chemistry, but the packaging and behavior have changed a lot.

Here are the main types you'll see today:

- **Flooded maintenance-free:** Still lead-acid, but sealed. You can't top off water or peek inside, and you shouldn't try. They're designed to live and die as one unit.
- **AGM (Absorbed Glass Mat):** The electrolyte is soaked into fiberglass mats, which makes the battery more vibration-resistant and spill-proof. AGMs handle deep discharges better and are common in cars with stop/start systems, heavy electrical loads, or advanced audio.
- **Lithium 12-volt batteries:** These batteries are still rare in mainstream cars but show up in some EVs, performance models, and custom builds. They're lighter and can deliver strong cranking power, but they need specific charging and care. You don't treat them like a lead-acid.

REMEMBER

Always replace a battery with the same type unless the manufacturer has approved an upgrade. Swapping a standard flooded battery into a car designed for AGM (especially stop/start vehicles) can cause charging problems, short battery life, and weird electrical behavior.

Reading the label

Pop the hood and take a look at your battery. See that label covered in numbers, codes, and fine print? It looks like someone tried to cram an entire technical manual onto a sticker the size of a credit card. But don't let it intimidate you — only three things really matter when you're buying a replacement battery, and once you know what to look for, the rest is just noise.

Here's what you actually need to pay attention to:

- **Group size** is the physical dimensions and terminal layout of the battery, usually listed as a number like Group 24, 35, 48, or 51R. Think of it like shoe sizes for batteries — your car was designed for a specific group size, and if you stray too far, you'll end up with cables that don't reach, hold-down brackets that won't clamp, or a battery that rattles around like a bowling ball in the trunk.

- **Cold Cranking Amps (CCA)** tells you how much current the battery can deliver at 0°F (–18°C) for 30 seconds while still maintaining enough voltage to crank the engine. In plain English? It's the battery's ability to start your car on a freezing winter morning when the oil is thick, the engine is cold, and everything is working against you. Higher CCA is better, especially if you live somewhere cold, drive a truck with a big engine, or have a lot of electrical accessories.
- **Reserve Capacity (RC)** is how long (in minutes) the battery can run a moderate electrical load, such as your headlights, wipers, and radio, if the alternator dies and stops charging. Think of it as your "get home safely" buffer.

Figure 6-1 shows the three battery-label details that matter most when choosing a replacement battery: group size, cold cranking amps, and reserve capacity.

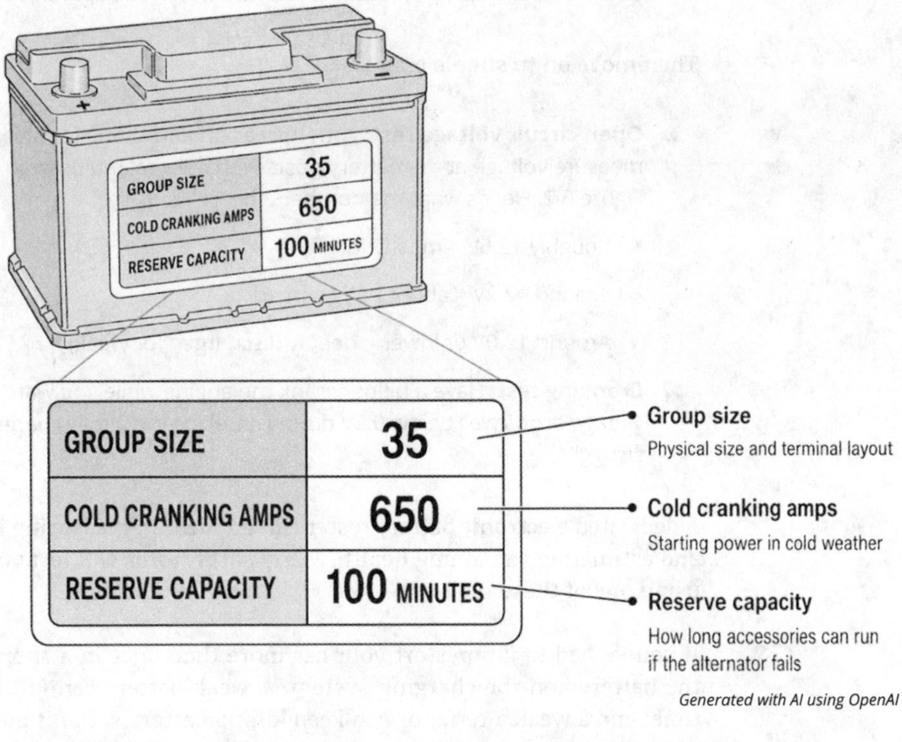

FIGURE 6-1: Reading a battery label.

Testing the battery without drama

Chapter 2 covers the quick monthly battery check: looking for corrosion, making sure the terminals and cables are clean and snug, and noticing slow-start or weak-accessory warning signs. Here, you go a bit deeper with simple voltage checks and a cranking test.

Start with a quick visual check:

- **Look for swelling or bulging cases.** That's a sign of overheating or overcharging.
- **Check for cracked cases or obvious leaks.** That's a scrap-pile battery.
- **Inspect terminals for heavy white/green corrosion.** Clean gently with a proper battery brush or baking soda solution, then rinse and dry.
- **Check for loose battery cables.** The cable ends should sit snugly on the battery posts and shouldn't twist by hand. A loose connection can act just like a dead battery: click-click-click, flickering lights, or no start at all. Tighten the cable clamp if it's loose, but don't crank down so hard that you damage the terminal. If the clamp is cracked, stretched, or won't tighten, replace it.

Then move on to simple tests:

- **Open-circuit voltage test:** With the car off and sitting for at least a few hours, measure voltage at the battery posts with a digital multimeter, as shown in Figure 6-2. Here's what the numbers mean:
  - Roughly 12.6V = mostly full
  - Around 12.2V = about half charged
  - Around 12.0V or lower = deeply discharged (or weak)
- **Cranking test:** Have a helper crank the engine while you watch the meter. If voltage drops well below 9.6V during cranking (on a fully charged battery), it's struggling.

A dedicated electronic battery tester can go further, measuring internal resistance and estimating remaining health. Many parts stores will test your battery for free using one of these tools.

TIP

If you've had to jump-start your car more than once in a short period, test both the battery and the charging system. A weak battery can kill an alternator over time, and a weak alternator can keep killing batteries. Don't guess — test.

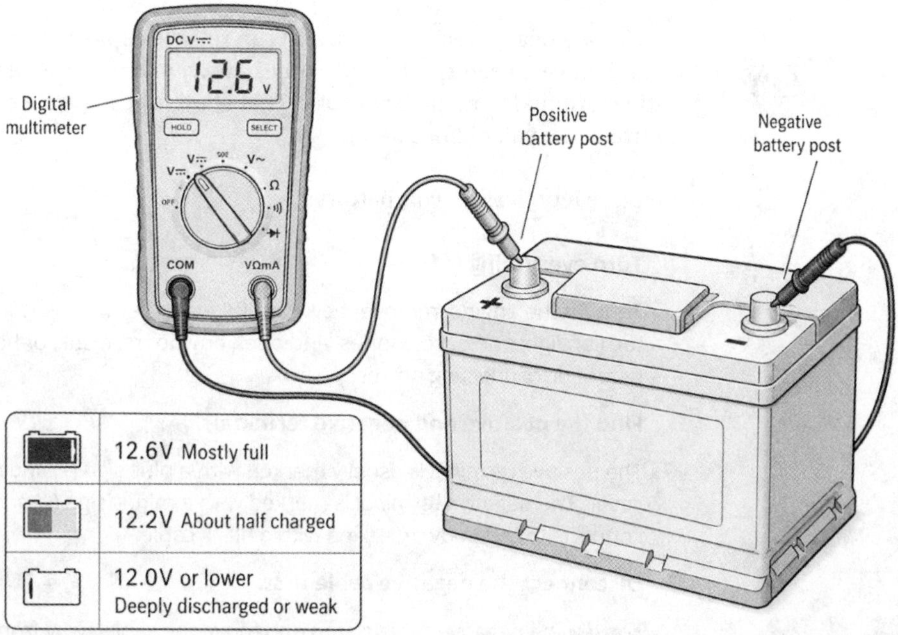

FIGURE 6-2: Multimeter testing battery voltage.

Generated with AI using OpenAI

Replacing a 12-volt battery safely

If your battery fails the voltage or cranking tests described in the preceding section or if a battery tester says it's reached the end of the road, replacement may be the right move. The job is usually straightforward, but modern cars are picky. The wrong battery type, a loose connection, or a skipped relearn can create the same weird electrical problems you were trying to fix.

Before you grab a wrench, confirm three things:

- **The replacement battery matches your vehicle.** Use the correct group size, battery type, cold cranking amps, and reserve capacity. For help decoding those numbers, see the section "Reading the label," earlier in this chapter.
- **Your vehicle doesn't require a special reset or registration.** Some vehicles need the new battery registered with a scan tool so that the charging system knows a fresh battery has been installed.
- **You can access the battery safely.** Some batteries live under the hood. Others hide in the trunk, under a seat, or beneath plastic covers. If getting to the battery requires disturbing orange high-voltage cables or high-voltage covers on a hybrid or EV, stop and call an EV-qualified technician.

WARNING

Batteries are heavy, can leak acid, and can release explosive gas. Wear eye protection and gloves, keep sparks and flames away, and never let a wrench bridge the positive terminal to metal bodywork. That shortcut can turn a simple battery swap into fireworks you did not order.

To replace a typical 12-volt battery:

1. **Turn everything off.**

   Shut off the engine, remove the key or keep the key fob away from the vehicle, turn off lights and accessories, and open any doors, trunk, or hood you need before disconnecting power.

2. **Find the positive and negative terminals.**

   The positive terminal is usually marked with a plus sign (+) and may have a red cover. The negative terminal is marked with a minus sign (–) and usually connects to the body or engine with a black cable.

3. **Disconnect the negative cable first.**

   Loosen the negative cable clamp and move the cable away from the battery so that it can't spring back and touch the post. Removing the negative cable first helps prevent accidental shorts.

4. **Disconnect the positive cable second.**

   Lift the red cover if there is one, loosen the positive cable clamp, and move the cable away from the battery.

5. **Remove the hold-down bracket.**

   Most batteries are secured by a clamp, strap, or bracket. Remove it and set the hardware somewhere safe. Don't skip reinstalling it later — the hold-down keeps the battery from sliding, tipping, or bouncing around.

6. **Lift the battery straight out.**

   Use the handle if the battery has one and keep the battery upright. A car battery is heavier than it looks, so use both hands and don't set it on paint, carpet, or anything you care about.

7. **Clean the tray and cable ends.**

   Wipe dirt from the battery tray and clean corrosion from the cable ends with a battery brush or baking soda solution. Rinse and dry the area before installing the new battery.

8. **Set the new battery in place.**

   Make sure the positive and negative posts are on the correct sides. A battery that physically fits but has reversed terminals can leave you with cables that don't reach — or worse, cables that get connected backward.

9. **Reinstall the hold-down bracket.**

   The battery should sit firmly in the tray and should not slide or rock. Tighten the hold-down enough to secure the battery, but don't crush the case.

10. **Connect the positive cable first.**

    Install the positive cable on the positive post and tighten the clamp until it is snug. Replace the red protective cover if your vehicle has one.

11. **Connect the negative cable last.**

    Install the negative cable on the negative post and tighten the clamp. The clamp should not twist by hand, but don't crank down so hard that you damage the terminal.

12. **Reconnect any vent tube or battery sensor.**

    Some batteries, especially those in trunks or under seats, use a small vent tube to route gases outside the vehicle. Some modern cars also have a battery sensor on or near the negative cable. Make sure anything you unplugged goes back exactly where it belongs.

13. **Start the vehicle and check for warning lights.**

    The engine should crank normally, and the battery warning light should go out after startup. Some vehicles may need idle relearn, window reset, clock reset, radio reset, or battery registration after replacement.

14. **Recycle the old battery.**

    Don't throw it in the trash. Auto parts stores, repair shops, and recycling centers usually accept old car batteries, and many stores charge a core fee that you get back when you return the old one.

TIP

Take a photo of the old battery before you disconnect anything. That picture gives you a quick reference for cable routing, terminal position, vent tubes, sensors, and hold-down hardware.

REMEMBER

Battery replacement isn't just "does it fit in the tray?" Match the battery type and rating, tighten the cables, secure the hold-down, and handle any required registration or relearn. A sloppy battery swap can cause no-starts, warning lights, charging problems, or a battery that dies young.

Charging and maintaining the battery

So your battery is low — not dead-dead, just sad and tired. Maybe you left the dome light on overnight. Whatever the reason, the battery is sulking, and you need to perk it back up.

Enter the smart battery charger (also called a battery maintainer or tender). This gadget isn't your grandpa's trickle charger that you had to babysit for hours and hope it didn't boil the battery dry. Modern smart chargers are like having a tiny, patient robot that knows exactly how much charge your battery needs, delivers it gently, and then stops before anything bad happens. They're cheap, they're foolproof, and they're one of the best investments you can make if you own a car that doesn't get driven every day.

Here's what makes a smart charger actually smart, and what to look for when you're shopping:

- **Automatic multi-stage charging:** A good smart charger doesn't just blast electricity at the battery and call it a day. It goes through stages: *bulk charge* (the fast initial boost), *absorption* (topping it off carefully), and *float mode* (maintaining the charge without overcharging).
- **Compatibility with your battery type:** Not all batteries are created equal. If you've got a standard flooded lead-acid battery, almost any charger will work. But if you've got an AGM (Absorbed Glass Mat) or a fancy lithium 12-volt battery, you need a charger that knows how to talk to it. AGM batteries are more sensitive to overcharging, and lithium batteries have their own quirks.
- **Safety features that save you from yourself:** Look for chargers with short-circuit protection (so that you don't start a fire if the clamps touch each other) and reverse-polarity protection (so that the charger yells at you — usually with a loud beep or flashing light — if you hook positive to negative and negative to positive).
- **Quick-connect pigtails (the lazy person's dream):** Many smart chargers come with a little harness you can permanently attach to your battery terminals and tuck under the hood. The harness has a weatherproof quick-connect plug that hangs out somewhere accessible. When you want to charge the battery, you just pop the hood, plug in the charger, and walk away.

TIP

For cars that sit a lot — weekend toys, project cars, RVs, seasonal vehicles, or that Miata you only drive when the sun is shining and your hair looks good — a smart maintainer is cheap insurance.

Using portable jump packs

We'll paint a picture. It's 6:30 a.m., you're running late for work, you turn the key (or press the Start button), and . . . nothing. Just a sad little click, or maybe a slow, labored rrrr-rrrr-rrrr that tells you the battery is toast. Your phone is at 12 percent, your neighbor's car is already gone, and the idea of waiting around for roadside assistance makes you want to crawl back into bed and call in sick.

Now imagine this scenario instead: You pop the trunk, grab a compact battery pack about the size of a hardcover book, clamp it onto your battery terminals, press a button, and start your car. Thirty seconds later, you're on your way. No strangers. No jumper cables. No drama. That's the magic of a portable jump pack, and it's one of the best $50 to $100 you'll ever spend on car stuff.

Portable jump packs (also called jump starters or booster packs) are essentially rechargeable lithium-ion batteries with heavy-duty clamps attached. They're small enough to live in your glove box or under a seat, powerful enough to crank over most engines, and smart enough to protect you from doing something dumb — like hooking them up backward and turning your battery into a science experiment.

Here's what to look for when you're shopping for one:

- **Enough peak amps for your vehicle:** Jump packs are rated by how much current they can deliver in a short burst, usually measured in peak amps. A small four-cylinder car may need only 400 to 600 peak amps. A V8 truck or SUV may need 1,000-plus amps, especially in cold weather when the engine oil is thick and the battery is already struggling.
- **Clearly labeled clamps with idiot-proof design:** The clamps should be big, beefy, and clearly marked: red for positive (+), black for negative (–). Some jump packs have clamps with built-in LED indicators that light up green when you've connected them correctly and flash red (or refuse to work) if you've got them backward.
- **Reverse polarity protection (because we all make mistakes):** This is the jump pack's way of saying, "Hey, buddy, you've got this backward. Fix it before you fry something." If you accidentally clamp positive to negative and negative to positive, a good jump pack will refuse to deliver power and will beep, flash, or otherwise alert you to the problem.
- **Built-in extras that make life easier:** Many jump packs come with bonus features like a built-in flashlight (so that you can actually see what you're doing at night), USB charging ports (so that you can top off your phone while you're waiting for roadside help), and even an air compressor (for topping off a low tire).

TIP

Keep your jump pack charged. We know, we know — this advice sounds obvious. But jump packs lose charge over time, even when they're just sitting in your trunk.

WARNING

Always follow the jump-start instructions in your owner's manual. Seriously. Some modern cars have dedicated jump posts under the hood (often marked with a little red plastic cover and a + symbol), and connecting directly to the battery terminals can damage sensitive electronics or confuse the car's computer.

Alternators and Charging Systems

Chapter 5 introduces the alternator as the part that keeps the 12-volt system charged after the engine starts. Here, you're not taking the alternator apart or memorizing rotor-and-stator theory. You're looking for signs that the charging system isn't keeping up.

In a gas or diesel vehicle, the alternator charges the battery and powers the electrical system while the engine is running. In most hybrids and EVs, a DC-DC converter does the same basic job for the 12-volt system, using power from the high-voltage battery pack. Either way, the mission is the same: Keep the 12-volt side of the car alive so the computers, lights, locks, infotainment, and safety systems can do their jobs.

Common charging-system warning signs include:

- **A battery warning light while driving.** That little battery-shaped icon usually means the charging system isn't charging properly. If it comes on while you're driving, you're running on whatever charge is left in the battery.
- **Dim or flickering lights.** Headlights, interior lights, or dash lights that brighten and dim with engine speed can point to charging trouble.
- **Repeated dead batteries.** A new battery that keeps going dead may not be getting recharged.
- **Slow cranking after a normal drive.** If the battery tests okay but acts weak after driving, the charging system may not be replacing the power used during starting.
- **Electrical weirdness.** Random warning lights, resets, or modules acting flaky can happen when system voltage is too low or unstable.

Checking charging voltage

A basic multimeter can tell you a lot. Before blaming the alternator, run the battery voltage and cranking checks we describe in the earlier "Testing the battery without drama" section. Then start the engine and check charging voltage at the battery posts following these steps:

1. **Set your digital multimeter to DC volts.**
2. **Touch the red lead to the positive battery post and the black lead to the negative battery post.**

   TIP With the engine off, a healthy, fully charged battery should be around 12.6 volts.
3. **Start the engine and check the reading again.**

On many traditional charging systems, you'll usually see about 13.5 to 14.8 volts with the engine running. That higher voltage is what pushes charge back into the battery.

But don't panic if a newer car doesn't sit at one perfect number. Many modern vehicles use smart charging, so voltage may rise, fall, or hover lower than you expect depending on battery temperature, electrical load, and driving conditions. That's why you're looking for patterns, symptoms, and warning lights — not one random reading.

Smart alternators and weird voltages

Older cars often charged at a fairly steady voltage whenever the engine was running. Modern charging systems can be much more flexible. The computer may reduce alternator output to save fuel, increase charging during deceleration, or change voltage based on battery temperature and state of charge.

That flexibility means a reading in the low 13-volt range isn't automatically bad if the car starts normally, the lights are bright, and no warning lights are on. But these readings deserve more attention:

- **Around 12.6 volts or lower with the engine running:** The charging system may not be charging.
- **Consistently above about 15 volts:** The system may be overcharging, which can damage the battery and electronics.
- **Voltage that drops when lights, blower motor, or rear defroster are turned on:** The alternator may be weak, the belt may be slipping, or a connection may be poor.

» **Voltage that looks okay but the battery keeps dying:** The problem may be intermittent, computer-controlled, or caused by a parasitic draw when the car is off.

TIP

If your charging voltage looks strange on a newer vehicle, don't condemn the alternator based on one meter reading. Check the battery condition first, look for warning lights, scan for charging-system codes, and check your owner's manual or service information for how that vehicle manages charging.

Doing quick visual checks

Before you assume the alternator is bad, look for the simple stuff:

» **Check the serpentine belt.** If the belt is cracked, glazed, loose, missing ribs, or squealing, the alternator may not spin properly.

» **Look at the battery terminals.** Loose or corroded connections can make a good alternator look bad.

» **Inspect the alternator connector.** A loose plug, damaged wire, or oil-soaked connector can interrupt charging-system control.

» **Listen for bearing noise.** A grinding, whining, or growling sound from the alternator area can point to a failing pulley or alternator bearing.

REMEMBER

A weak battery can make the alternator work overtime, and a weak charging system can keep killing batteries. Test both before replacing either one.

Charging systems in hybrids and EVs

In hybrids and EVs, the 12-volt battery still matters, but the charging source is usually a DC-DC converter, not a belt-driven alternator. Chapter 5 explains how that system works. For DIY purposes, keep your checks on the 12-volt side:

» Test the 12-volt battery with a multimeter or battery tester.

» Check for loose or corroded 12-volt battery connections.

» Watch for warning messages about the charging system, 12-volt battery, or electrical system.

» Leave orange high-voltage cables, inverter wiring, and high-voltage battery components alone.

WARNING

Do not probe, disconnect, tighten, or test orange high-voltage cables or high-voltage components. If a hybrid or EV has a DC-DC converter fault, high-voltage warning, or charging-system message that involves the inverter or battery pack, that's a job for an EV-qualified technician.

Starters and Stop/Start Systems

When you turn the key or press the Start button, the starter system has one basic job: Spin the engine fast enough for it to catch and run on its own. Chapter 5 explains how the battery, starter, and ECU work together to start the engine. Here, you're not rebuilding a starter or memorizing the pinion-and-ring-gear dance. You're using symptoms, simple checks, and scan-tool clues to narrow down why the car won't crank normally.

When a starting problem shows up, pay attention to what the car actually does:

- **Rapid clicking:** Start with the battery and cable connections. A weak battery or a loose or corroded cable is more likely than a bad starter.
- **One solid click but no crank:** The battery may be weak, the starter solenoid may not be engaging, or the starter circuit may have a poor connection.
- **Slow, dragging crank:** Check battery charge, cable condition, and engine grounds before blaming the starter.
- **Grinding during start:** Stop cranking. The starter gear may not be engaging properly, or the flywheel/flexplate teeth may be damaged.
- **Complete silence:** Look for dash messages first. "Press brake to start," "Key not detected," or "Shift to P to start" points you toward the brake switch, key fob, park/neutral switch, immobilizer, or control logic — not necessarily the starter.

Before you condemn the starter, check the basics:

- Run the battery voltage and cranking checks in the section "Testing the battery without drama," earlier in this chapter.
- Make sure the battery cables are clean and snug.
- Look for corrosion at the terminals and major ground connections.
- Check the starter fuse or relay if your vehicle uses one.
- Scan for codes, even if the Check Engine light isn't on, because some starting-system, body-module, and immobilizer codes are stored quietly.

TIP

A loose battery cable can act exactly like a bad starter: clicks, flickers, or total silence. Always check the cheap, easy stuff before pricing a starter.

Many newer vehicles also use stop/start systems, which shut the engine off at stoplights and restart it when you lift off the brake. Because these systems restart the engine many times during a single drive, they use tougher parts than older starting systems.

Depending on the vehicle, a stop/start system may use:

- A heavy-duty starter designed for frequent restarts
- An AGM or EFB battery built for repeated cycling
- An integrated starter-generator, also called an ISG, that can help start the engine and assist with charging

An ISG may be belt-driven, mounted where an alternator might normally live, or built into the transmission or flywheel area.

For DIYers, stop/start hardware means two important things:

- **Battery and starter replacement aren't "pick anything that fits" jobs.** Use the exact battery type, size, and rating the vehicle requires. For help reading battery labels and choosing the right replacement, see the "Reading the label" section, earlier in this chapter. For safe battery replacement steps, see the earlier "Replacing a 12-volt battery safely" section.
- **Some vehicles need a reset or relearn after battery or starter work.** The ECU may need to be told that a fresh battery or related component has been installed. Chapter 3 covers scan-tool basics, and Chapter 22 walks through no-start triage when the car still won't cooperate.

Modern starting problems aren't always old-school starter problems. The ECU may refuse to crank the engine if it doesn't see the right inputs from the brake switch, clutch switch, park/neutral switch, key fob, immobilizer, or other modules.

When a starting problem is intermittent, do three things before replacing parts:

- Write down exactly what happens: rapid clicks, one click, slow crank, grinding, or silence.
- Save any dash messages or warning lights.
- Scan for codes in the engine, body, immobilizer, and starting-system modules if your scan tool can access them.

Between the battery test, cable check, fuse/relay checks, and scan data, you can usually narrow the problem to the battery, wiring, starter, relay, or control logic. For the full step-by-step no-start path, see Chapter 22.

REMEMBER

A starter complaint isn't always a starter problem. Low voltage, loose cables, bad grounds, failed relays, security lockouts, and missing brake/park/clutch signals can all stop the starter from doing its job.

Ignition in the Modern Era

Modern cars have turned ignition maintenance from a regular chore into something you do maybe once or twice in the life of the vehicle. The ECU handles all the timing, there are no points to fiddle with, and spark plugs can cruise along for 60,000 to 100,000 miles or more before they need replacing.

But — and this point is important — that doesn't mean you can ignore the ignition system forever. When it finally does need attention, you'd better do it right, because modern ignition systems are less forgiving than the old stuff.

Long-life spark plugs (platinum/iridium)

Most modern engines use spark plugs tipped with platinum or iridium — precious metals that sound fancy because they are. These tips resist erosion way better than old-school copper plugs, maintaining a sharp edge and consistent spark energy for tens of thousands of miles. It's like the difference between a cheap kitchen knife that goes dull after a week and a high-end chef's knife that stays sharp for years.

What this means for you:

- **Longer replacement intervals:** Check your owner's manual, but many cars can go 60,000, 80,000, even 100,000 miles on a set of plugs. That's a lot of commutes.
- **Less frequent maintenance, but way more critical when the time comes:** When those plugs finally do wear out, you can't just ignore it and hope for the best. Worn plugs cause misfires, waste fuel, and can even damage your catalytic converter if you let it go too long.
- **Higher plug prices:** Yeah, iridium plugs cost more than the old copper ones. But when you divide that cost over 80,000 miles instead of 12,000, it's actually a bargain.

Symptoms of worn spark plugs

As plugs age, the electrode gap slowly widens (thanks to thousands of tiny electrical arcs eating away at the metal), and eventually the spark gets weak and inconsistent. That's when you start noticing problems, especially under heavy load — like when you're passing on the highway, climbing a steep hill, or if you've got a turbocharged engine that demands strong, reliable spark every single time.

Symptoms of worn spark plugs include:

- **Rough idle:** The engine feels like it's missing a beat.
- **Poor fuel economy:** A weak spark = incomplete combustion = wasted gas.
- **Hesitation or stumbling under acceleration:** You press the gas, and the engine stutters instead of pulling smoothly.
- **A flashing Check Engine light under load:** This light is the ECU's way of screaming "ACTIVE MISFIRE! PULL OVER!" (See Chapter 22 for what to do when that happens.)

Coil-on-plug systems

Modern engines use coil-on-plug (COP) ignition, where each spark plug gets its own dedicated coil mounted directly on top of it. No wires. No distributor. No mess.

This setup is better because it:

- **Eliminates long plug wires,** which were a common failure point (cracked insulation, carbon tracking, and crossfire between cylinders). Fewer parts means fewer problems.
- **Lets the ECU control timing and spark energy per cylinder** so that the computer can fine-tune ignition for maximum power, efficiency, and emissions control.
- **Improves spark accuracy and strength** because the electrical path from coil to plug is only a few inches long instead of several feet.

When a coil-on-plug fails (and eventually, they all do), the engine will usually throw a misfire code for that specific cylinder — something like P0302, which means "misfire detected, cylinder 2." That's your starting point.

A quick way to confirm a bad coil is to swap it with a coil from another cylinder and see whether the misfire follows. Here's the basic idea:

1. **Read the misfire code with your scan tool.**

   A code such as P0302 means the ECU detected a misfire on cylinder 2.

2. **Turn the engine off.**

   Let it cool and keep the key or fob away from the vehicle.

3. **Locate the coil on the misfiring cylinder.**

   If needed, use the engine diagram, service information, or a reliable parts-location guide for your vehicle.

4. **Unplug the coil connector carefully.**

   Don't yank on the wires.

5. **Remove the coil hold-down bolt, if your vehicle uses one, and lift the coil straight up off the spark plug.**

6. **Swap that coil with a coil from another easy-to-reach cylinder.**

7. **Reconnect both coils, reinstall the hold-down bolts, and start the engine.**

8. **Scan again after the engine runs.**

   If the misfire moves with the coil — for example, from cylinder 2 to cylinder 4 — the coil is the likely problem. If the misfire stays on the same cylinder, look at the spark plug, injector, compression, wiring, or connector instead.

Figure 6-3 shows how a coil-on-plug setup places one ignition coil directly over each spark plug.

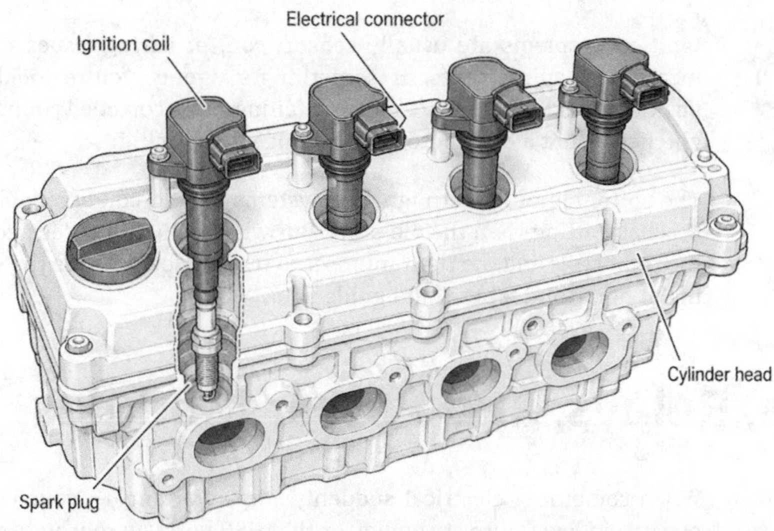

FIGURE 6-3: Coil-on-plug ignition system.

Generated with AI using OpenAI

TIP

A quick way to confirm a bad coil is to swap it with a coil from another cylinder and see whether the misfire follows. If cylinder 2 stops misfiring and cylinder 4 starts, congratulations — you just diagnosed a bad coil without spending a dime on a mechanic.

ECU-controlled ignition timing

Chapter 4 explains how ignition timing moved from old-school distributor adjustments to computer control. For this chapter, the important point is simpler: On most modern vehicles, you no longer set the timing with a wrench and a timing light. The ECU handles spark timing automatically based on sensor data.

If the engine is misfiring, hesitating, pinging, or running poorly, don't start looking for a distributor to twist. Start with the things the ECU depends on:

- **Trouble codes and freeze-frame data:** Scan first and save the codes before clearing anything.
- **Spark plugs and coils:** Worn plugs or weak coil-on-plug units can cause misfires under load.
- **Crankshaft and camshaft position sensors:** If the ECU loses timing reference, the engine may misfire, stall, or refuse to start.
- **Knock-sensor clues:** If the ECU detects knock, it may pull timing back to protect the engine, which can make the car feel weak or sluggish.
- **Wiring and connectors:** Loose, corroded, oil-soaked, or heat-damaged connectors can imitate a bad sensor or coil.

TIP

Ignition problems are usually sensor, coil, or wiring issues rather than simple mechanical adjustments. If something's wrong, you're looking at crankshaft position sensors, camshaft sensors, failing coils, corroded connectors, or software glitches — not a distributor cap that needs replacing.

The bottom line? Modern ignition systems are incredibly reliable and require way less babysitting than the old stuff. But when something does go wrong, you need the right tools and the right mindset to track it down. Leave the shade-tree guessing at home and let the data guide you.

Fuses, Relays, and Power Modules

When something electrical suddenly stops working — your radio goes silent, a power window refuses to budge, or that USB port you rely on to charge your phone decides to take a permanent vacation — your first instinct is probably to blame the device itself. Bad radio. Broken window motor. Cheap phone charger. But nine times out of ten, the real culprit is hiding in a little plastic box under your hood or dashboard: a blown fuse.

Fuses are the unsung heroes of your car's electrical system. They're designed to be the weakest link in the chain, sacrificing themselves to protect expensive components when something goes wrong. Think of them as the electrical equivalent of a stunt double — they take the hit so the star (your $500 radio or $1,200 power window motor) doesn't have to.

But here's the thing: On modern cars, fuses are only part of the story. Many circuits are now controlled by smart power modules and solid-state drivers that make decisions about when to send power, how much to send, and when to shut things down to protect themselves. It's like your car hired a team of tiny, paranoid bodyguards for every electrical circuit.

We break down how to find fuses, test them properly, and know when the problem is something more complicated than a $2 piece of plastic. Figure 6-4 shows the two common fuse-panel locations, a typical fuse-panel cover map, and the main fuse and relay types you're likely to find.

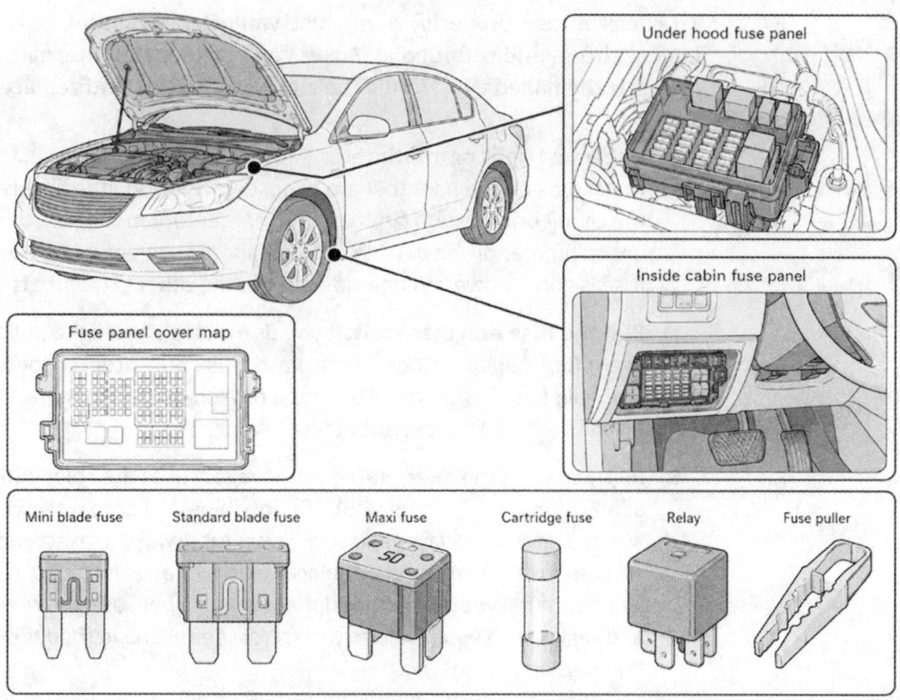

FIGURE 6-4: Fuse panel map and fuse types.

Traditional fuse replacement

Most cars have at least two fuse panels, and they're usually hiding in places that seem designed to test your flexibility and patience:

- **Under the hood:** This panel handles high-current circuits like the engine management system, cooling fans, fuel pump, charging system, and headlights. It's usually a black plastic box near the battery or along the firewall. Pop the lid, and you'll find rows of colorful blade fuses and maybe some larger cartridge fuses or fusible links for really heavy-duty circuits.
- **Inside the cabin:** This one covers lighting, accessories, infotainment, power outlets, and all the creature-comfort stuff. It's often tucked under the dashboard on the driver's side (good luck reaching it without a yoga background), behind a panel on the side of the dash, or sometimes in the glove box.

TIP

Your owner's manual will have a map of each fuse panel showing which fuse does what and the correct amperage rating for each slot. If you've lost your manual (no judgment — we've all been there), most manufacturers have PDFs available online, or you can usually find a diagram printed on the inside of the fuse panel cover itself.

To check a fuse properly, don't just yank it out, squint at the tiny metal strip inside, shrug, and call it good. Fuses can crack or fail internally in ways you can't see with the naked eye. Here's the right way to test and replace them:

- **Use a test light or multimeter.** Most modern blade fuses have two small metal tabs on the back that are exposed even when the fuse is installed. With the circuit powered on (ignition on, or accessory mode), touch your test light or multimeter probe to each tab. You should see power on both sides if the fuse is good. Power on one side but not the other? The fuse is blown.
- **Pull the fuse and inspect it.** If you don't have a test light, pull the fuse out (most fuse panels include a little plastic fuse puller tool clipped inside the lid) and hold it up to the light. Look for a broken or melted metal strip inside the plastic body. If it's broken, it's toast.
- **Replace with the exact same amperage.** Fuses are color-coded by amperage: 5-amp (tan), 10-amp (red), 15-amp (blue), 20-amp (yellow), 25-amp (clear), 30-amp (green). Always replace a blown fuse with the exact same rating. A 10-amp fuse gets a 10-amp replacement. Not a 15. Not a 20. Not a piece of aluminum foil wrapped around the terminals because you're out of fuses and really need your radio to work. (Yes, people have tried this — don't be that person.)

REMEMBER

Fuses blow for a reason: There's a short circuit, a failing component, or damaged wiring somewhere downstream. The fuse is trying to protect your car from turning into a rolling barbecue. Find the problem. Fix the problem. Then replace the fuse with the correct rating.

WARNING

Never "upgrade" a blown fuse to a higher-amp rating. A higher-amp fuse can let the circuit overheat before the fuse blows, which can melt insulation, damage modules, or start a fire. The fuse protects the wiring, not just the accessory that stopped working.

Smart power distribution modules

Welcome to the future, where not every electrical circuit gets its own individual fuse and relay anymore. Instead, many modern vehicles use *smart power distribution modules* (also called intelligent junction boxes or integrated power modules) to control and protect electrical loads. These modules are like the bouncers at an exclusive nightclub — they decide who gets in, how long they can stay, and when it's time to kick them out.

Here's what these modules do that old-school fuses and relays can't:

- **Contain solid-state drivers:** Instead of mechanical relays that click on and off, these modules use electronic switches (think tiny, fast-acting transistors) to control power delivery. They're quieter, more reliable, and can switch on and off thousands of times without wearing out.
- **Monitor current draw for each circuit:** The module constantly watches how much current each circuit is pulling. If it sees something weird — like a power window motor drawing way more current than it should because it's jammed or failing — it can shut that circuit down to protect itself and prevent damage.
- **Can shut down or pulse outputs if they detect faults:** Some modules will completely cut power to a circuit if they sense a problem. Others will pulse the power on and off rapidly (called PWM, or *pulse-width modulation*) to reduce load or manage heat. PWM is why you might see a power outlet that works fine for a few minutes and then mysteriously shuts off — it's not a blown fuse, it's the module saying, "Nope, something's not right here" and protecting itself.

For DIYers, here's the reality check: If a circuit is acting weird (working intermittently, shutting off under load, or just refusing to cooperate) and you've already checked the basics (fuses are good, no obvious wiring damage, connectors are tight), you're probably dealing with a module issue. And that's where things get tricky, because diagnosing smart modules usually requires:

- » A scan tool that can communicate with the body control module or power distribution module
- » Access to the module's fault codes and live data
- » Wiring diagrams and technical service bulletins
- » Sometimes, software updates or module reprogramming

The safe DIY play: Check the basics first (fuses, obvious wiring damage, and loose or corroded connectors). If those are all good and the circuit is controlled by a smart module, consider handing it off to a shop with the right scan tools, wiring diagrams, and factory software access.

REMEMBER

There's no shame in knowing when you've hit the limit of what you can reasonably diagnose in your driveway. These systems are complex, and sometimes the answer is buried three menus deep in a module's diagnostic data or requires a software flash that only the dealer can perform.

When relays still apply

Even in the age of smart modules, traditional electromechanical relays are still alive and well in many modern cars. They're used for high-current circuits like cooling fans, fuel pumps, starter motors, headlights, horns, and A/C compressors — basically anything that draws enough current to make a simple switch cry for mercy.

What is a *relay?* It's an electrically controlled switch. A small control current (usually from a switch or the ECU) energizes an electromagnet inside the relay, which pulls a set of heavy-duty contacts closed, allowing a much larger current to flow to the load. It's like using a light switch to control a floodlight — the switch handles only a tiny amount of current, but the floodlight can pull as much as it needs.

To test a relay when something stops working, you have several options:

- » **Swap it with an identical relay.** Many cars use the same relay part number for multiple circuits (horn, fuel pump, cooling fan, and so on). If you suspect a bad relay, find another relay in the same fuse box with the same part number, swap them, and see whether the problem moves. If the horn suddenly works but the fuel pump doesn't, congratulations — you just diagnosed a bad relay without spending a dime.

- **Listen or feel for a click.** When a relay is commanded on (turn the key, press the horn button, and so on), you should hear or feel a distinct click as the contacts close. No click? The relay might be bad, or it's not getting the signal to turn on (which could be a wiring issue, a bad switch, or a module problem).
- **Use a multimeter or relay tester.** If you're comfortable with electrical work and have a wiring diagram, you can test the relay's control circuit (pins 85 and 86 on a standard automotive relay) and the load circuit (pins 30 and 87). Inexpensive relay testers that make this process foolproof are also available.

REMEMBER

Relays are cheap, easy to replace, and one of the last truly DIY-friendly electrical components left in modern cars. If you've got a dead fuel pump, a cooling fan that won't run, or a horn that won't honk, swapping the relay is always worth a shot before you start throwing expensive parts at the problem.

Wiring and Modules

Modern car wiring isn't just a bunch of colored spaghetti stuffed behind the dashboard anymore. It's a carefully engineered nervous system carrying power, sensor signals, and high-speed data — all bundled together and routed through the car like a digital highway. When it works, it's invisible. When it doesn't, it can turn your car into a haunted house on wheels. We talk about what's under all that tape and loom, and why you should think twice before grabbing the wire cutters.

Wiring harness basics

A *wiring harness* is basically a pre-assembled bundle of wires, connectors, and terminals that's been carefully designed, routed, and secured with clips, grommets, and protective loom. Think of it as the circulatory system of your car — except instead of blood, it's carrying electricity, sensor data, and the occasional angry message from the ECU telling the transmission to stop being dramatic.

Modern harnesses carry three main types of signals, often running side-by-side in the same bundle:

- **Power and ground:** The heavy hitters, these are the wires feeding current to motors, lights, pumps, and anything else that needs serious juice to do its job.

- **Sensor signals:** These low-voltage wires carry information from sensors (throttle position, coolant temp, wheel speed, and so on) back to the control modules. They're sensitive and don't appreciate being messed with.
- **High-speed data networks:** CAN bus, LIN bus, and other communication protocols let modules talk to each other without needing a dedicated wire for every single message. This area is where things get complicated fast.

Unlike the simple two-wire circuits of older cars (power in, ground out, done), today's harnesses are like a crowded subway car at rush hour — everything's packed in tight, and one problem can cause a chain reaction. Sloppy repairs, poor splices, or tapping into the wrong wire can cause bizarre electrical gremlins that'll have you questioning your sanity.

Follow good wiring practices to keep your car from becoming a science experiment:

- **Support the harness properly.** Don't let wires hang by their connectors like they're bungee jumping. Use the factory clips and routing paths. Gravity and vibration are not your friends.
- **Keep wires away from heat and sharp edges.** Exhaust pipes melt insulation. Sharp metal edges cut through it. Neither of these outcomes is good. Route carefully.
- **Use proper loom or tape when opening a harness.** If you have to unwrap a section to inspect or repair it, rewrap it properly with split loom, cloth tape, or adhesive-backed wrap. Don't leave bare wires flapping in the breeze.
- **Never drill or screw into mystery sheet metal.** Before you mount that new accessory bracket or run a self-tapping screw through the firewall, check what's on the other side. You don't want to discover a wiring harness the hard way.

Body Control Module (BCM)

Chapter 5 introduces the Body Control Module — the BCM — which is basically the middle manager of your car's electrical system. It doesn't do the glamorous work like making the engine run or shifting gears, but it handles all the comfort and convenience stuff: power windows, door locks, interior lights, wipers, and sometimes even the horn and alarm. It's also constantly chatting with the engine computer, transmission, and other modules over the car's data networks, coordinating everything like an overly organized wedding planner.

From your DIY perspective, the BCM is:

- **The "boss" for many interior and lighting circuits:** If something electrical inside the cabin stops working and it's not a blown fuse, there's a decent chance the BCM is involved.
- **The gatekeeper for diagnostics:** Some BCMs control whether other modules wake up and respond to scan tools. If your scanner can't talk to a module, the BCM may be blocking the conversation (or it might be asleep itself).
- **A common source of weird, intermittent problems:** Loose connections, corroded grounds, or water leaks near the BCM can cause all kinds of strange behavior: windows that work sometimes but not others, lights that flicker for no reason, or doors that lock and unlock like they're possessed.

Before you blame the BCM and start shopping for a replacement, check these basics first:

- **Grounds:** The BCM needs a solid connection to ground (the car's metal body/frame). If the ground bolt is rusty, loose, or corroded, the module can't function properly. Find the ground point (usually a bolt on the body or frame near the module), remove it, clean the metal surfaces until they're shiny, and reinstall it tight.
- **Connectors:** Pull the BCM's wiring connectors and inspect them closely. Look for bent or pushed-back pins, moisture, or that telltale green/white crusty corrosion that means water has been sneaking in. A little contact cleaner and a careful pin adjustment can sometimes bring a "dead" module back to life.
- **Power feeds:** Use a multimeter to confirm the BCM is actually getting proper voltage on its power and wake-up lines. If the module isn't getting fed, it's not going to do anything — and that's not the module's fault.

CAN bus communication

CAN stands for Controller Area Network, and it's the most common data network in modern cars. Instead of running individual wires from every sensor and switch back to a central computer (which would require hundreds of wires and turn your car into a rolling wire factory), CAN lets multiple modules share a pair of twisted data wires and take turns talking. It's like a party line from the old telephone days, except way faster and with better manners.

Other networks — LIN (Local Interconnect Network), FlexRay, and even automotive Ethernet on newer high-end cars — may also be layered on top, but CAN is the workhorse that runs most of the show.

You don't need to become a network engineer, but here's what you should know:

- **Many modules share the same data lines.** The engine computer, transmission, ABS, airbag system, BCM, and infotainment might all be on the same CAN bus. That setup means one short, one bad termination resistor, or one module throwing a tantrum can take down multiple systems at once. It's the automotive equivalent of one person at the party ruining it for everyone.
- **Do NOT test CAN lines with a test light.** CAN wires carry sensitive, low-voltage, high-speed signals. (We're talking millions of messages per second.) Stabbing them with a test light or poking them with a regular multimeter probe can disrupt communication, corrupt data, or even damage a module. If you need to test CAN, use a proper scan tool or oscilloscope and know what you're doing.
- **Cutting, splicing, or probing CAN wires incorrectly is a recipe for disaster.** You can cause no-start conditions, widespread fault codes, intermittent electrical problems, and the kind of diagnostic nightmares that make mechanics weep.

Why DIY splicing is discouraged

Yes, there are correct ways to repair automotive wiring: soldered joints with proper strain relief, high-quality crimp connectors with adhesive-lined heat-shrink tubing, OEM-style terminals and connectors that match the factory stuff. Done right, a wiring repair can be as reliable as the original harness.

But we'll be honest — most DIY wiring repairs are not done right. They're done with whatever's in the junk drawer: wire nuts stolen from a light fixture, household electrical tape that turns into goo after six months, and twist-and-tape joints that look like they were assembled by someone wearing oven mitts in the dark.

Here's what goes wrong with poor splices:

- **Increased resistance and voltage drop:** A sloppy connection creates resistance, which means less voltage reaches the component at the other end. The extra resistance and voltage drop can cause dim lights, weak fuel pumps, sluggish motors, and fault codes for low voltage.

- **Corrosion wicking into the copper:** If the splice isn't sealed properly, moisture sneaks in and starts corroding the copper strands from the inside out. Eventually, the wire fails completely — usually at the worst possible time.
- **Wires breaking at the splice:** A rigid splice (like a wire nut or a blob of solder with no strain relief) creates a stress point. Every time the car hits a bump or the harness flexes, the wire bends right at that spot. Eventually, it fatigues and breaks. It's like bending a paperclip back and forth until it snaps.
- **Interference on sensitive signal and data lines:** Poor splices can act like little antennas, picking up electrical noise and injecting it into sensor signals or data networks. Electrical noise from poor splices can cause erratic sensor readings, communication errors, and fault codes that make no sense.

If you absolutely must repair wiring yourself, here's how to do it right:

- **Match the wire to the job.** Use the correct gauge and insulation type for the circuit you're fixing. A fuel pump circuit pulling 10 amps doesn't care about your leftover lamp cord from Home Depot. Use automotive-grade wire that matches (or exceeds) the original spec.
- **Invest in proper connectors.** Skip the cheap crimp connectors and household heat-shrink. Get quality crimp connectors with adhesive-lined heat-shrink tubing. When you heat it, the adhesive melts and seals out moisture like a waterproof cocoon. It costs an extra two bucks and will save you from redoing the job six months later when corrosion eats through your bargain splice.
- **Use OEM repair pigtails whenever possible.** Many manufacturers sell pre-made connector repair sections with the correct terminals, wire gauge, and insulation already attached. You just cut out the damaged section, splice in the pigtail, and you're done. It's faster, cleaner, and way more reliable than trying to rebuild a connector from scratch with a bag of random pins you found on Amazon.
- **Provide proper strain relief.** Don't leave your repair hanging in mid-air like a tightrope walker. Secure the harness on both sides of the splice with clips, zip ties, or loom so there's zero tension on the joint. Wires that dangle and flex will eventually break at the splice — it's not a matter of if, it's when.
- **Know when to walk away.** If the damaged wiring is part of a high-speed data network (CAN, LIN, FlexRay) or a safety-critical system (airbags, ABS, stability control, lane-keeping assist), stop. Put down the wire strippers. This is not the place to learn on the job. Replace the entire harness section with an OEM part or hand the repair to a professional with the right tools, connectors, and training.

High-Voltage Safety (Hybrids and EVs)

Hybrids and EVs are amazing pieces of technology — quiet, efficient, and packed with more computing power than the Apollo moon lander. But they also come with something traditional gas cars don't have: high-voltage electrical systems that can range from about 100 volts to over 400 volts (and even higher on some performance models). That's enough energy to cause serious injury or death if you touch the wrong thing.

The good news? Automakers design these systems with multiple layers of safety, and they're clearly marked with bright orange cables and warning labels. The best practice for most DIYers is beautifully simple: Respect the orange and don't touch it.

We talk about what's under the hood (and under the car), what you need to stay away from, and what you can still safely work on without risking a trip to the emergency room.

Battery management systems (BMS)

Chapter 5 introduces the Battery Management System, or BMS, as the system that watches over a hybrid or EV's high-voltage battery pack. Here, the important takeaway is simple: If the BMS sees something unsafe, the vehicle may limit power, slow charging, disable electric drive, or turn on a warning message to protect the battery and the people around it. The BMS keeps track of several high-voltage battery conditions:

- **Cell voltages and temperatures:** The BMS monitors individual battery cells to make sure none are overcharging, undercharging, or getting too hot.
- **State of charge:** The BMS tracks how much usable energy is left in the battery pack.
- **Charge and discharge limits:** The BMS controls how quickly the pack can charge and how much power the motors can safely draw.
- **Cooling:** The BMS communicates with the battery cooling system to help keep the pack in a safe temperature range.

For DIYers, the message isn't "grab a meter and investigate." It's the opposite. BMS diagnosis requires specialized scan tools, training, service information, and high-voltage safety procedures. If your hybrid or EV shows a high-voltage battery fault, BMS error, reduced-power warning, or "service high-voltage system" message, stop at the 12-volt checks and call a shop with EV-qualified technicians.

WARNING

Do not probe, unplug, tighten, or test high-voltage battery wiring or orange-cabled components while chasing a BMS warning. The BMS may be reporting a battery, cooling, isolation, or safety-interlock problem, and those checks belong in professional hands.

Orange high-voltage cables

If you see bright orange cables or components anywhere on your hybrid or EV, that's the universal automotive warning sign for HIGH VOLTAGE DO NOT TOUCH. It's like the electrical equivalent of a rattlesnake's rattle: nature's way of saying "back off, buddy."

WARNING

Here's the rule: If it's orange, leave it alone.

Specifically, do not:

- Probe, cut, splice, or disconnect anything orange.
- Run accessory wiring or tie-wraps alongside high-voltage cables.
- Use test lights, multimeters, or any tools on high-voltage circuits unless you're a trained EV technician with the right personal protective equipment and procedures.

You'll see orange cables:

- **Under the car:** Running from the battery pack (usually under the floor) to the motor and inverter
- **In the engine bay:** On hybrids, connecting the engine, generator, and high-voltage battery
- **To the charging port:** On plug-in hybrids and EVs
- **To heat pumps or high-voltage accessories:** On some EVs, power cabin heating and A/C compressors

WARNING

Never cut into, drill near, or even lean tools against orange-sheathed cables. And never assume a high-voltage system is off just because the car is shut down or the key is out. High-voltage service requires special insulated tools, high-voltage gloves rated for the system voltage, face shields, and step-by-step shutdown procedures. High-voltage systems are not DIY territory. Period.

Shutdown systems

Hybrids and EVs use *contactors* (heavy-duty electrical relays) and *interlocks* (safety switches) to keep high voltage isolated and safe when the car isn't running — or when something goes wrong.

Here's how they work:

- **Interlocks:** Opening certain doors, removing service covers, or disconnecting specific plugs sends a signal to the BMS, which immediately opens the contactors inside the battery pack. This action physically disconnects the high-voltage system, isolating it from the rest of the car. Think of it like pulling the main breaker in your house: Power stops flowing.
- **Crash shutdown:** If the car detects a collision (via airbag sensors and accelerometers), it automatically opens the high-voltage contactors and shuts down the system to protect first responders and passengers. Some cars even have a manual service disconnect (a brightly colored pull handle or plug) that emergency crews can use to kill the high-voltage system at the scene of an accident.
- **Official shutdown procedures:** Service manuals describe exact power-down procedures for technicians working on high-voltage systems.

Official shutdown procedures usually involve:

1. **Turning off the car and removing the key (or fob).**
2. **Disconnecting the 12-volt battery (to prevent the BMS from waking up).**
3. **Removing a service plug or opening a specific panel to trigger the interlock.**
4. **Waiting a specified time (often 5 to 10 minutes) for capacitors to discharge.**
5. **Using a high-voltage meter to verify zero voltage before touching anything.**

High-voltage shutdown isn't something to guess at, improvise, or figure out as you go. If you're not following the manufacturer's exact procedure with the right tools and training, you're gambling with your life.

When to call a professional

If your hybrid or EV has any of the following issues, do not attempt a DIY fix. Call a shop with EV-certified technicians:

- High-voltage battery fault codes or warnings
- "Service high-voltage system" or "Propulsion system malfunction" messages
- Loss of electric drive or reduced power with a turtle icon (common on some EVs)
- Coolant leaks near orange components (high-voltage battery or inverter cooling systems)
- Any damage to orange cables or high-voltage components
- Charging issues that involve the onboard charger, inverter, or battery pack (not just the charging cable or port door)

IN THIS CHAPTER

» Following fuel from tank to injector

» Tracing the jump from carburetors to computer-controlled injection

» Meeting modern fuel hardware

» Watching the ECU fine-tune the mix with fuel trims

» Exploring alternative fuels

» Using OBD-II clues to spot fuel-system trouble

Chapter 7 Re-imagining Fuel Systems

Modern fuel systems? They're not fuel delivery so much as fuel choreography. Instead of slurping gas like a kid with a juice box, today's engines measure fuel in milliseconds, adjust on the fly using sensor feedback, and follow a computer strategy designed to squeeze out more power, better mileage, and cleaner emissions — often all at once. It's less watering hose and more medical IV drip, with the ECU playing the role of the nurse who never sleeps and absolutely refuses to guess.

The good news: You don't need a lab coat or a programming degree to understand what's going on. You just need a clear map of the system and a sense of what each part is trying to do.

Fuel: The Lifeblood of Combustion

Fuel is stored energy. Your engine's job is to turn that stored energy into motion — smoothly, efficiently, and without setting off the Check Engine light just to keep life interesting. In Chapter 4, you can find out how combustion works — how your engine turns fuel into motion through the four-stroke cycle. In this chapter, we follow the fuel itself: how it gets from the tank to the combustion chamber, and what happens when that delivery system isn't quite right.

Efficient combustion works only when fuel is delivered in one of four "just right" ways:

- **In the right amount (not too rich, not too lean):** Think recipe. Too much fuel, and the engine runs *rich* (wastes gas, can smell fuel-ish, may feel boggy). Too little, and it runs *lean* (can feel weak, run hotter than it should, and complain with warning lights).
- **At the right time (when the engine can actually use it):** Modern engines don't just send fuel. They schedule fuel — tiny bursts timed to engine speed and load. If timing is off, you'll feel hesitation, stumbling, or that annoying "I pressed the pedal . . . hello??" delay.
- **At the right pressure (enough push to do the job):** Fuel has to arrive with consistent pressure so that the system can deliver the same amount of fuel again and again. Low or unstable pressure is like trying to water your lawn with a kinked hose — sometimes it works, sometimes it dribbles, and nothing is happy.
- **In the right form (a fine mist, not sloppy droplets):** Engines don't want fuel poured in like a drink. They want fuel atomized — fine mist that mixes with air easily and burns evenly. Big droplets burn poorly, waste fuel, and can make the engine run rough.

When fuel delivery is even a little off, you'll usually notice it in real life (not just on a scan tool):

- **Hesitation:** When you press the gas, and the car "thinks about it"
- **Rough idle:** Shaky at stoplights
- **Loss of power:** Especially on hills or merging
- **Poor mileage:** Same driving, more money
- **Warning lights:** Dashboard tattling at the worst possible time

From tank to injector

Picture the fuel system like a delivery service. The tank is the warehouse, the pump is the delivery truck, the lines are the roads, and the injectors are the doorbells that drop the package at the exact right house.

Here's the route, step by step:

- **Fuel tank (where it all starts):** The tank doesn't just hold gas. It's designed to keep fuel from sloshing like a washing machine during turns and braking. It also has plumbing that helps manage vapors and pressure changes.
- **Fuel pump (the muscle of the system):** Most modern vehicles use an electric in-tank pump. When you turn the key or press Start, you may hear a faint hum for a second or two — that's the pump priming the system so that the engine can start quickly.
- **Pickup screen/strainer (the first bouncer at the door):** Before fuel even leaves the tank area, a small screen helps catch bigger debris. It's not a fine filter — it's more like a doorman stopping the obvious troublemakers.
- **Fuel filter (the cleanup crew):** Some cars have an easy-to-replace inline filter. Many newer cars tuck the filter into the tank module or design it as lifetime. Translation: It may not be a regular DIY service item anymore, but clean fuel still matters. (We get practical about that in Chapter 8.)
- **Fuel lines (the delivery route):** Fuel travels forward through lines designed to handle pressure and heat. Modern setups are sealed and precise — less rubber hose everywhere, more purpose-built plumbing.
- **Pressure control (keeping delivery consistent):** Controlling pressure is the part most drivers never see, but it's a big deal. Modern systems often control pressure by:
  - Varying fuel pump speed (instead of running full blast all the time)
  - Using sensors to monitor pressure in real time
  - Avoiding a traditional return line on many vehicles (less heat, fewer vapors, and cleaner efficiency)
- **Fuel rail (the staging area):** Think of the fuel rail as the loading dock that feeds each injector. It holds fuel at the proper pressure so that each injector can draw from a steady supply.
- **Injectors (the precision sprayers):** Injectors are basically high-speed spray nozzles controlled by the computer. They open and close in milliseconds, delivering fuel in a fine mist, and may be either:
  - **Port injection:** Sprays fuel into the intake path before the cylinder

- **Direct injection:** Sprays fuel directly into the cylinder (more precise, often higher pressure, and different hardware)

» **Computer control (the conductor):** The engine computer (ECU) decides how much, when, and sometimes how fuel is delivered based on sensor feedback. This sensor-based control allows your car to adjust fuel delivery instantly for cold starts, hard acceleration, altitude, and even changing fuel quality. Figure 7-1 shows the path fuel follows from the tank to the combustion chamber.

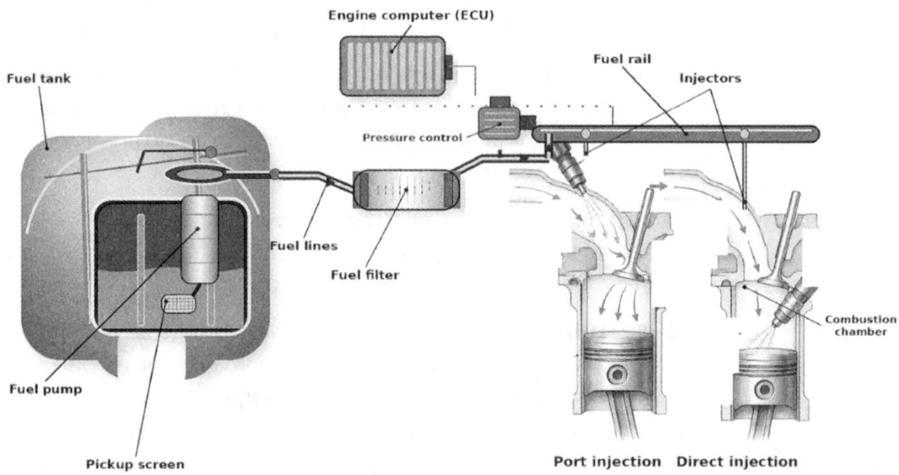

Generated with AI using OpenAI

FIGURE 7-1: How fuel travels from the tank to the combustion chamber.

WARNING

Fuel systems can stay pressurized even after the engine is off. Modern systems (especially direct injection) can run at very high pressures. The risk of pressurized fuel spraying out is why "just crack a line and see what happens" is a hard no.

Gasoline, diesel, ethanol, and blends

Not all fuel is the same, and your fuel system is designed around what you put in the tank. Use the right fuel, and everything runs smoothly. Use the wrong one, and your car will have a very expensive tantrum.

Here's the everyday-driver guide to common fuel types and blends:

» **Gasoline (most common — spark-ignition engines):** Gasoline engines rely on a spark to ignite the air/fuel mixture. What matters most at the pump:

- *Octane rating:* Octane is about knock resistance, not power juice. If your car calls for regular, premium won't magically turn it into a sports car — it'll just make your wallet lighter.

- *What the manual recommends:* The engine and computer are tuned for that fuel.
- *Contamination or age:* Bad gas happens. Contamination or very old fuel can cause rough running and hard starts.

» **Diesel (compression-ignition engines):** Diesel engines don't use spark plugs to ignite fuel the same way gas engines do. They rely on heat from compression and very precise fuel delivery. Diesel fuel systems often run higher pressures and can be more sensitive to contamination.

» **Ethanol blends (E10, E15, E85):** Ethanol is commonly blended into gasoline. The blend affects how the engine runs and how far you go on a tank:

- *E10:* Very common (10 percent ethanol). Most modern gas cars are designed for it.
- *E15:* A gasoline blend containing 15 percent ethanol. Some vehicles can use it, but others shouldn't. Check the owner's manual.
- *E85 (flex-fuel):* High ethanol content. Only use if your vehicle is specifically flex-fuel capable. Also, note that ethanol has less energy per gallon, so mileage usually drops on E85 (even if it's cheaper at the pump).

From Carburetors to Computers

Carburetors were clever little mechanical problem-solvers. They didn't need sensors, software updates, or a computer with opinions. They used engine vacuum and tiny fuel jets to pull gasoline into the incoming air stream — basically a carefully controlled sip-and-swirl system.

And when everything lined up just right? A carb could run great.

The issue is that everything rarely lined up just right. Cars got faster, cleaner, and more efficient, and emissions rules got tighter. Carburetors didn't get worse — they just got outgrown.

Carburetors

A *carburetor* mixes air and fuel using airflow and vacuum. As air rushes through a narrowed passage (a *venturi*), it creates suction that pulls fuel through small passages called *jets*. The carburetor works like a mechanical perfume atomizer — no electricity required.

But carbs came with a list of personality traits (and not the fun kind):

- **Sensitive to temperature and altitude:** Carbs don't know the weather changed. Cold air, hot air, thin mountain air, humid air — each one changes how fuel and air mix. Drive up a mountain? The mixture can go off. Cold morning? Fuel doesn't vaporize as well, so the engine needs extra help to start and run.
- **Required manual tuning:** In other words, become your car's part-time therapist. Carbs often needed fiddling — idle screws, mixture screws, choke adjustments, or jet changes. If you like tinkering, it was kind of satisfying. If you just wanted your car to start and go to work, it was like having a pet that behaves only when you feed it the exact right brand of kibble.
- **Not precise enough for modern emissions rules:** Emissions standards don't care that your carb is pretty close. They demand consistent, exact control of the air and fuel mixture.
- **Often struggled during cold starts:** Cold engines need a richer mix to run smoothly at first. That's why carbs used chokes — extra fuel (and often higher idle) until the engine warmed up. When things weren't perfect, cold starts could turn into long cranking and stalling.

Fuel injection basics

Fuel injection replaced carbs for one big reason: control. Fuel delivery becomes a calculation instead of a guess. Instead of relying on vacuum and tiny jets to pull fuel, fuel injection uses:

- **A fuel pump** to deliver fuel under pressure
- **Injectors** (electrically controlled valves) to spray fuel
- **The ECU** (engine computer) to decide exactly how much fuel to deliver and exactly when to do it

Here's what computer-controlled fuel injection looks like in everyday-driver language:

- **Injectors are precision sprayers.** Each injector opens for a tiny amount of time — often milliseconds — to deliver fuel. Longer open time means more fuel. Shorter open time means less fuel. It's like the computer controlling a spray bottle with a stopwatch.

- **Sensors tell the computer what's happening right now.** The ECU looks at things like airflow, engine temperature, throttle position, and oxygen levels in the exhaust. Then it adjusts fuel delivery constantly so that the engine runs smoothly whether you're driving up a mountain or in traffic with the A/C on blast.
- **The ECU self-corrects while you drive.** Instead of you tuning screws, the ECU makes tiny adjustments automatically. Modern cars can run cleanly and consistently for years without you ever touching a mixture screw (because you don't have one — welcome to the future).

Most classic fuel injection is port fuel injection, where fuel is sprayed into the intake path just before it enters the cylinder. It's reliable, smooth, and plenty precise. But then engineers said, "Cool. Now let's get even pickier."

Direct injection revolution

Direct injection (DI) takes fuel delivery to the next level by spraying fuel directly into the combustion chamber, not into the intake path. To spray fuel directly into the combustion chamber, DI systems use much higher fuel pressure and more precise injection timing.

Here's why automakers love direct injection:

- **More efficiency and power from smaller engines:** DI can control fuel delivery extremely precisely, which helps engines squeeze more usable energy out of each combustion event.
- **Plays really well with turbocharging:** Many modern turbo engines use DI because it helps manage combustion more precisely under boost (when engines are working harder).
- **Better atomization means cleaner burn:** Spraying fuel directly at high pressure can create a very fine mist, which burns more efficiently — when everything is working as designed.

But DI also comes with trade-offs (because, of course, it does):

- **More complexity and higher pressures:** DI systems add parts like high-pressure pumps and DI injectors that operate under serious pressure. Translation: Great performance, but not as simple as the old days.
- **Possible intake valve carbon buildup:** Because fuel isn't washing over the intake valves in many DI-only designs, deposits can build up over time on certain engines. (Don't panic; intake valve carbon buildup is one of those good-to-know items, and we talk maintenance realities in Chapter 8.)

» **Possible use both systems (dual injection).** To get the best of both worlds, some manufacturers combine port injection and direct injection. The computer chooses what to use depending on conditions.

Figure 7-2 shows the different types of fuel injection systems.

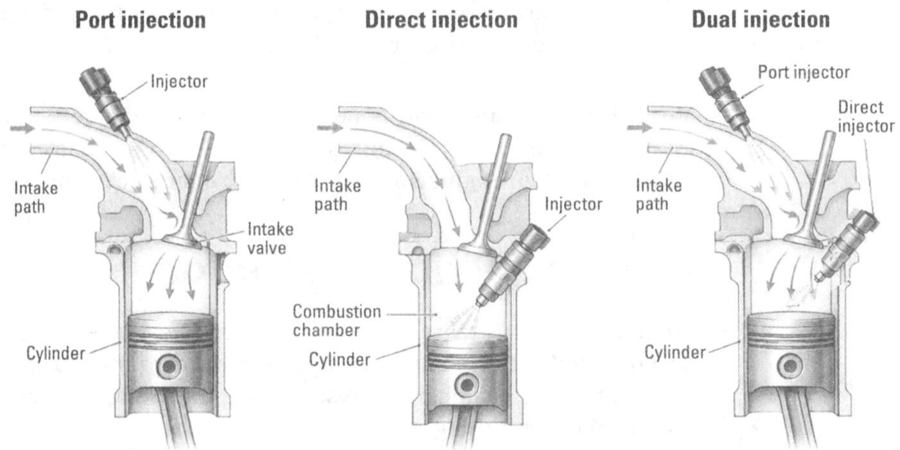

FIGURE 7-2: Types of fuel injection systems.

REMEMBER

Carbs mixed fuel mechanically. Fuel injection mixes fuel electronically. Direct injection takes it further by delivering fuel right where combustion happens — with higher pressure and tighter control.

Fuel Delivery in Today's Engines

Because fuel injection has turned fuel delivery into a computer-controlled math problem, you need to meet the hardware that makes that math real. Think of the fuel system like a two-stage delivery service:

1. **Move fuel forward (from the tank to the engine reliably).**
2. **Spray it precisely (at the right pressure and in the right mist for clean combustion).**

Depending on the engine, your car may use one pressure stage (most port-injected gasoline engines) or two pressure stages (direct injection and modern diesels).

Electric in-tank fuel pumps

Most modern cars use an electric fuel pump inside the tank, usually as part of a pump module assembly. This workhorse pushes fuel forward so that the engine always has a steady supply ready to go.

Here's the everyday-driver breakdown:

- **What it does:** The pump pulls fuel through a small pickup screen and pressurizes the fuel line so that the fuel can travel to the engine without relying on gravity, vibes, or wishful thinking.
- **Why it lives inside the tank:** Being submerged in fuel helps the pump stay cool and lubricated. Electric pumps can get hot — fuel is basically their built-in cooling jacket.
- **Why your car can't just sip fuel anymore:** Older systems could tolerate a little inconsistency. Modern systems can't. The engine computer expects stable fuel pressure so that it can accurately calculate fuel delivery. If pressure is bouncing around, the ECU is basically trying to measure ingredients during an earthquake.
- **How modern pumps are controlled (it's not always full blast):** Many vehicles use variable-speed pumps controlled by the ECU (or a fuel pump control module). Instead of pumping max pressure constantly, the system adjusts pump output to match demand, which means less heat, less noise, and often better efficiency.
- **What you might notice as a driver when the low-pressure side is unhappy:** Without getting too deep into troubleshooting (Chapter 8 is where we go hands-on), common big-picture symptoms can include:
  - Longer cranking before the engine starts
  - Hesitation when you accelerate
  - Power loss under load (like merging or climbing a hill)

TIP

Running your tank very low occasionally won't instantly destroy anything, but living on the fuel light 24/7 can make the pump run hotter over time.

High-pressure pumps for direct injection

If your engine uses direct injection (DI), it usually runs a two-pump setup, because the fuel has a tougher job to do than it did in the old "spray it in the intake and hope for the best" days.

First, an electric low-pressure pump in the tank sends fuel up to the engine — think of it like the delivery truck getting everything to the right neighborhood. Then a high-pressure pump mounted on the engine takes over and cranks that pressure way up, because DI injectors aren't gently misting fuel into open airflow . . . they're firing it straight into a hot, pressurized combustion chamber. Injecting fuel directly into a hot, pressurized combustion chamber is a whole different sport. Direct injection requires high fuel pressure to turn fuel into a fine, clean mist at exactly the right moment — more medical IV drip, less garden sprayer with attitude.

Why direct injection matters for performance and efficiency

Direct injection earns its keep by spraying fuel directly into the cylinder. Because the fuel goes directly into the cylinder, the ECU can control when and how fuel shows up with ridiculously tight precision. Precise control of injection timing and fuel quantity helps the engine make strong power without wasting fuel, reduces emissions, and works especially well with turbocharging.

In plain English: DI helps your engine squeeze more useful work out of the same gallon of fuel — like getting more miles out of a pair of shoes before they fall apart.

Why DI systems feel more high-tech

DI systems feel fancy because they're constantly watching and adjusting, like a helicopter parent with a stopwatch. The system keeps an eye on fuel rail pressure (so the computer knows what pressure is actually happening in real time) and then it tweaks the pump output and injector timing on the fly to match what you're doing — idling at a light, cruising, or punching it to merge like your lane just disappeared.

And because the pressures are so high, the system also has built-in "protect the engine" logic: If pressure goes out of range, it may cut power, throw a warning light, or put you in a reduced-performance mode to prevent damage. Basically, DI gives you better performance and efficiency, but it also means the fuel system has a lot less tolerance for "close enough."

WARNING

Direct injection fuel systems operate at very high pressure. Loosening a direct-injection fuel line to "see what happens" is dangerous because high-pressure fuel can spray out and cause injury. If you ever smell fuel in the engine bay or suspect a leak, that's a stop-and-address problem.

Common rail diesel systems

Diesel fuel systems are a different animal. A gasoline engine is like cooking on a kitchen stove: Mix fuel and air, add spark, and done. A diesel engine is more like a pressure cooker: It squeezes air until it's hot enough to mean it and then it injects fuel at just the right moment and lets physics handle the fireworks.

That's why most modern diesels use common rail injection. Picture a shared, super high-pressure fuel reservoir (the *rail*) that stays pressurized and ready, feeding all the injectors whenever the engine calls for it. Instead of each injector having its own little pressure supply, they all drink from the same firehose — more like a pressurized water main feeding multiple sprinkler heads than a bunch of separate garden hoses.

Here's why diesels need that setup: Diesel combustion is incredibly picky about how the fuel gets injected. It's not just "get fuel in there." It's "get it in there as a fine mist, at the perfect time, in the perfect amount." Common rail systems make that possible, because they can atomize fuel extremely well (cleaner burn), and they can do multiple tiny injections during a single combustion cycle. That's a fancy way of saying the engine can tap fuel in smoothly instead of dumping it in all at once — so diesels run quieter, pull smoother, and get better efficiency with lower emissions than the old-school diesel setups.

If a diesel fuel system starts getting stressed, you'll usually feel it before you fully understand it: hard starts, rough running, reduced power, and warning lights that show up right when you're trying to be somewhere important. We break down the "what it means" side in Chapter 8, but for now, just remember that diesels love precision and they demand clean fuel.

REMEMBER

Gas systems want fuel delivered precisely. Diesel systems want fuel delivered precisely and cleanly. Diesels are amazing, but they don't tolerate "close enough."

Turbocharged fuel delivery

Turbocharging is basically your engine saying, "I'd like more air, please." And the fuel system has to respond with, "Cool — then you're getting more fuel, too."

A turbo forces extra air into the engine, which means the ECU must add fuel to match that air. If fuel can't keep up, performance drops, and the engine may protect itself.

Here's what changes when a turbo enters the chat:

- **More air in means that more fuel is required.** Turbo engines can go from gentle cruising to high demand very fast. The fuel system must respond quickly — no delays, no drama.
- **Fuel pressure has to stay stable under boost.** The ECU is constantly managing fuel delivery so that the injector spray stays consistent, even when the intake air is pressurized.
- **The computer watches everything more closely.** Turbo engines typically rely heavily on sensor feedback (airflow/boost readings, fuel pressure readings, oxygen sensor feedback) to keep combustion safe and efficient.
- **Fuel quality matters more on many turbo engines.** Many turbo gasoline engines are designed around specific fuel recommendations (often related to knock control). Using the correct fuel helps the ECU deliver the power the engine was designed for — without constantly pulling timing or protecting itself.

Filters and Flow

All the high-pressure pumps and fancy injectors in the world can't help you if fuel can't get there cleanly and consistently. Think of fuel flow like your morning coffee routine: It doesn't matter how premium the beans are if the straw is clogged.

Modern inline and in-tank filters

Fuel filters have one job: Keep junk out of the parts that cost real money. Modern systems usually filter out debris in one of two ways with diesels being in their own ball game:

- **Inline fuel filter (along the fuel line):** Sits somewhere between the tank and the engine like a little security checkpoint. It's often easier to service, but where it's located (and whether it's even serviceable) depends on the car.
- **In-tank fuel filter (part of the pump module):** Lives inside the fuel tank, usually built into the fuel pump assembly. Translation: It's protected and nicely packaged, and it's usually not a quick "grab-a-wrench-in-the-driveway" swap.
- **Diesel filtration (extra serious mode):** Diesels usually run more filtering (often with water separation) because diesel pumps and injectors are precision parts. Dirt and water don't just cause issues; they can cause expensive issues. Diesel components don't enjoy "hydrating."

Signs of clogged fuel systems

A clogged filter (or any restriction in the fuel system) often shows up like the engine starts "running out of breath" when it needs fuel the most. Think of trying to drink a milkshake through a coffee stirrer.

Common signs you may notice as a driver:

- **Hesitation when you accelerate** (especially merging or passing)
- **Loss of power under load** (hills, towing, hot days with the A/C blasting)
- **Hard starts or longer cranking** (especially after it sits)
- **Surging or stumbling** like the engine can't decide what it wants
- **Rough running** when pressing the gas pedal
- **A Check Engine light** that may pop up with lean/rich or misfire-related codes

REMEMBER

One important reality check: These symptoms can also come from a weak fuel pump, dirty injectors, vacuum leaks, or sensor issues, so don't let "it feels sluggish" automatically turn into "must be the fuel filter."

When to replace filters

Fuel filter replacement is where the old versus modern difference really matters. If your vehicle has a serviceable external filter (more common on older cars and many diesels), then replacement is a normal maintenance item. If you're not sure when it was last changed and the car has a lot of miles, it's reasonable to put it on the catch-up maintenance list — because it's cheap protection for pumps and injectors.

If your vehicle has an in-tank filter that's part of the pump module (a setup used on many gasoline vehicles), then it's usually not treated like a routine service item. In that world, filters are often replaced only when there's a reason, such as:

- **Confirmed contamination,** such as bad fuel, water in fuel, or debris in the tank
- **A fuel pressure problem** that testing points toward a restriction or weak pump
- **A pump/module replacement,** where the filter gets replaced because it's part of the assembly

In plain English: Don't go hunting a modern in-tank filter on a hunch, because it may not be a standalone part, and it may not be accessible without dropping a tank (which is not most people's idea of a relaxing Saturday).

REMEMBER

If your car has an easy, serviceable filter, great — treat it like a normal maintenance item. If it's a modern in-tank setup, treat it like a diagnose-first item. Filters are cheap. Guessing is expensive.

Smart Fuel Management

Old systems basically delivered fuel and hoped for the best. Modern systems deliver fuel, watch what happens, adjust, and then do it again thousands of times. Your engine computer is basically running a nonstop cooking show: "A little more fuel . . . a little less . . . perfect . . . oops, someone opened a vacuum leak."

Role of ECUs in fuel trim

The ECU (engine computer) is constantly trying to hit the sweet spot — enough fuel for smooth power and efficiency, but not so much that you're wasting gas or dirtying emissions.

The ECU fine-tunes the air/fuel mixture with fuel trims, adjusting fuel delivery on the fly. If conditions change — cold start, hot day, altitude, traffic crawling, you flooring it — the ECU adapts.

TIP

Think of fuel trims like adjusting the shower temperature: You don't set it once for the rest of your life. You tweak it every time someone else in the house touches the handle.

Oxygen sensors and feedback

Oxygen sensors are basically your car's taste testers. They sit in the exhaust and report back to the ECU: "Yep, that burn was good" or "Nope, we're running lean/rich — fix it."

The ECU uses that feedback to correct fuel delivery in real time. Correcting fuel delivery in real time is a big reason modern engines can be powerful, efficient, and clean all at once — because they're not guessing. They're measuring.

Evap systems: Canisters and purge valves

This one surprises people: Your fuel system isn't just about liquid fuel — it's also about fuel vapors.

Gasoline evaporates easily, so modern cars capture those vapors in a charcoal canister (think of it like a sponge for fumes). Then, at the right time, the purge valve opens, and the engine drinks those stored vapors and burns them — cleanly and legally. (We explore how the exhaust system handles emissions in Chapter 9.)

If something in the EVAP system acts up, you may see a:

- Fuel smell
- Rough idle (sometimes especially after filling up)
- Check Engine light that feels personal

WARNING

Don't top off the tank after the pump clicks off. That habit is a great way to annoy your EVAP system, and it will absolutely retaliate with a warning light.

Alternative Fuels

Alternative fuels are basically the automotive world saying, "Okay . . . what else can we run on without burning the planet and our wallets?" Some are common, some are niche, and some are still in the "cool idea, call us in ten years" phase.

Flex-fuel (E85)

E85 is a high-ethanol blend (up to about 85 percent ethanol, depending on season and region). Flex-fuel vehicles can handle it because the ECU is programmed to adjust fuel delivery for ethanol's different behavior.

The simple takeaway:

- If your vehicle is flex-fuel, it can run E85 (and blends).
- If it's not, don't experiment — your fuel system didn't sign up for that science project.

Also, ethanol contains less energy per gallon than gasoline, so many drivers notice lower MPG on E85. Sometimes, it's cheaper at the pump, but you may visit the pump more often. Pick your poison.

Biodiesel basics

Biodiesel is a diesel fuel made from renewable sources, often blended into regular diesel. (You'll see labels like B5 or B20.) Many diesel vehicles can handle certain biodiesel blends, but not all, and not always in every condition.

The everyday-driver version:

- Check what your vehicle allows, because some systems are picky.
- In cold weather, some blends can be more prone to gelling issues.
- Cleanliness still matters a lot — diesel components are precision parts.

Hydrogen and synthetic fuels

Hydrogen is the no tailpipe emissions dream, especially in fuel cell vehicles where the only exhaust is water. The big challenge is infrastructure: You need fueling stations, storage, and distribution.

Synthetic fuels (often called e-fuels) are basically engine-friendly fuels made in a lab, sometimes using captured CO_2 and hydrogen. The idea is to keep combustion engines alive with a smaller carbon footprint, but cost and production scale are the hurdles.

REMEMBER

Alternative fuels aren't automatically better — they're just different. The best fuel is the one your vehicle is designed to use, consistently and cleanly.

Fuel System Diagnostics

Modern vehicles come equipped with sophisticated onboard computers that constantly monitor your fuel system's performance. When something goes wrong, your car's computer will detect the problem and alert you — usually with that dreaded check engine light. While this technology is incredibly helpful for identifying fuel system issues, the computer communicates through diagnostic trouble codes that look like cryptic alphabet soup (think P0171 or P0300).

The good news is that once you understand how to read these codes and what they're telling you, diagnosing fuel system problems becomes much more manageable. In this section, you discover how to retrieve these codes, interpret what they mean, and use them as your roadmap for troubleshooting common fuel system problems.

OBD-II codes for lean and rich conditions

Your car's computer is constantly checking whether the fuel-to-air mixture is just right — kind of like Goldilocks testing porridge. When the mixture is off, you'll get codes telling you it's either *lean* (not enough fuel) or *rich* (too much fuel).

Lean conditions happen when there's too much air or not enough fuel. Common culprits include:

- Vacuum leaks (unmetered air sneaking in where it shouldn't)
- Low fuel pressure (the fuel pump isn't keeping up)
- Dirty or clogged injectors (fuel can't spray properly)
- Faulty sensors (giving the computer bad information)

Rich conditions occur when too much fuel is in the mix, and it can be caused by:

- The fuel system delivering more fuel than commanded
- Leaking injectors dripping fuel when they should be closed
- Sensor malfunctions telling the computer to add more fuel
- Restricted airflow, where not enough air is getting in

Here's the important part: These codes don't tell you to replace the fuel pump or buy new injectors. They're more like your car saying, "Hey, something's off with the mixture — time to start detective work."

Injector misfire and fuel pressure codes

When your fuel system can't deliver fuel properly, your car will complain in two main ways: misfire codes and fuel pressure codes.

Misfire codes mean the engine isn't firing smoothly in one or more cylinders — it's like trying to ride a bike with a wobbly wheel, and you'll definitely feel it. Fuel pressure codes, on the other hand, indicate the fuel system can't reach or maintain the pressure it needs, kind of like trying to water your garden with a kinked hose. The water's there, but it just can't flow the way it should.

In plain English, what these codes are really telling you is that your engine either isn't getting enough fuel, isn't getting it at the right pressure, or the injectors aren't spraying it cleanly into the cylinders. Once you understand what your car is trying to say, you can start narrowing down where the problem actually is.

Using a Scan Tool for Diagnostics

A scan tool is your personal translator between you and your car's computer. If you don't have one, Chapter 3 covers what to look for in an OBD-II scanner. You don't need an expensive professional-grade tool — even a basic model (around $20 to $50) can help you:

- Read trouble codes so that you're not playing guessing games
- Check fuel trims to see whether the computer is constantly trying to correct the mixture
- Monitor sensor data in real-time to spot problems as they happen
- View freeze-frame data that shows exactly what was going on when the check engine light came on

TIP

Don't clear those codes right away! Read them first, write them down, and use them as clues to solve the mystery.

Hybrids and Beyond

Here's the plot twist: Hybrids still have all the usual fuel system parts — tank, pump, injectors, the works. The difference? The engine is basically on a part-time schedule. It shuts off at red lights, takes breaks when the electric motor can handle things, and clocks in only when absolutely necessary. It's the lazy coworker of engines, but in a good way.

The fuel system still needs to stay healthy, but here's the catch: If your hybrid sits around a lot, that gas gets old and stale. When the engine finally wakes up from its nap, it may sputter and complain like you would after sleeping weird on the couch.

REMEMBER

Hybrids still have all the usual fuel system parts — they just use them part-time.

Electric vehicles, on the other hand, said "no thanks" to the entire fuel system: no tank, no pump, no injectors, no gas cap to forget to tighten. No fuel means no fuel problems — it's beautifully simple in that department.

Of course, EVs have their own drama (batteries, cooling systems, and charging quirks), but the whole fuel delivery headache? Gone. It's like trading in your high-maintenance gas grill for a plug-in induction cooktop — completely different beast, completely different problems.

IN THIS CHAPTER

» Seeing why clean fuel matters

» Understanding high-pressure safety basics

» Handling filters, injectors, and pumps

» Sorting helpful additives from hype

» Using scan tools for clues

» Planning for hybrid/EV fuel realities

Chapter 8
Maintaining Your Fuel System

Fuel systems used to be fairly forgiving. If an older car ran rough, you blamed the weather, turned a screw, and pretended smelling like gasoline was part of your personality. Today's computer-controlled fuel systems are precision equipment, with exact pressures, tiny passages, and injectors that spray fuel more like medical equipment than a squirt gun. The payoff is better power, mileage, and emissions. The trade-off is less patience for dirty fuel, water, stale gas, and the timeless repair strategy known as "eh, it's probably fine."

Chapter 7 explains how fuel travels from the tank to the engine and how the computer controls delivery. This chapter focuses on keeping that system healthy. You discover how cleanliness, filters, fuel flow, injectors, and pumps affect everyday driving; which warning signs deserve attention; and where sensible DIY work ends before high-pressure fuel turns curiosity into an urgent-care visit. We also sort through ethanol blends, biodiesel, additives, and miracle-in-a-bottle promises that mostly perform magic on your wallet.

Basic scan-tool codes and fuel-trim trends can also provide early clues, although they point you toward a problem rather than handing you a confession.

Hybrids still need clean fuel even when the engine works part-time, while electric vehicles skip tanks, pumps, injectors, and the entire gasoline soap opera. Whatever you drive, the goal is fewer surprises, fewer check-engine-light ambushes, and a fuel system that quietly does its job without demanding its own reality show.

Why Fuel Cleanliness Still Matters

Fuel quality is one of those boring adult topics — right up until your car starts hesitating, idling like it had too much caffeine, or lighting the Check Engine light like it's trying to get your attention at a party. The tricky part is that modern fuel systems are incredible at delivering smooth power and great mileage, but they're also pickier than older systems. In other words, today's engines are less "I'll eat anything" and more "I have dietary restrictions, and I will complain."

Fuel as a precision fluid in modern engines

Modern fuel systems aren't just moving liquid from Point A to Point B. They're doing something more like a high-speed, high-precision spray job, thousands of times per minute. Delivering fuel in precise, rapid sprays means the fuel itself has to behave like a "good ingredient," not a mystery liquid.

Think of your fuel system like a fancy espresso machine: It can make amazing coffee, but only if the water is clean and the beans aren't stale. Dirty water or old beans don't just make it taste bad — they clog things and shorten the machine's life.

In a modern vehicle, fuel has to:

- Slip through tiny passages without clogging them
- Spray through injector tips with microscopic openings
- Stay consistent so that the computer can meter the right amount every time

That's true for gasoline engines — and it matters even more for direct injection and diesels, where fuel pressure and precision are turned up to "no room for nonsense." (For more on these types of engines, see Chapter 7.)

REMEMBER

Fuel system repairs can get expensive fast because the parts doing the precision work (pumps and injectors) don't tolerate contamination. Clean fuel is cheaper than replacing hardware that doesn't like dirt, water, or sludge.

Contaminants causing loss of power and efficiency

When fuel isn't clean, your engine usually doesn't fail dramatically in one big cinematic moment. It gets annoying first — the kind of annoying that makes you question whether you're imagining it. You're not.

Fuel problems usually come from a few repeat offenders:

- **Dirt/debris:** The tiny clog problem. It can restrict flow, wear components, and mess with spray patterns.
- **Water:** More common than people think (bad station fuel, condensation, diesel sensitivity). Water and precision parts are not friends.
- **Stale fuel/varnish:** The "car sat too long" problem. Old fuel can gum things up and make starting or running rough.
- **Wrong fuel:** The "one mistake, big bill" problem. Misfueling can damage pumps and injectors fast.

TIP

If symptoms start right after a fill-up, don't ignore that timing. Note the station and pump, keep the receipt, and consider switching fuel sources before you assume the car suddenly developed random issues.

WARNING

If you smell raw fuel, see wet lines, or spot dripping, stop and address it now. Fuel leaks aren't a "monitor it" situation — they're a fire risk.

From Carbs to Direct Injection

Fuel delivery has gone from turn a screw and hope to keep it clean and let the computer be picky. This section isn't a history lesson — it's the maintenance translation. You see what the jump from carburetors to fuel injection (and then to direct injection) changes for day-to-day care, what habits prevent the most problems, and where the DIY line is when fuel pressure and precision start getting serious.

Carburetors as history only

If you drive something modern, you're probably never going to maintain a carburetor — and honestly, that's a gift. Carbs are great museum pieces (and they're still alive and well in classic cars), but modern fuel-system maintenance isn't about tweaking screws and hoping the weather cooperates. It's about keeping a precision system clean, consistent, and unbothered.

The maintenance difference in one line:

Carbs tolerated close enough. Modern injection expects exactly right.

That's why this chapter leans hard into habits and prevention — because precision systems run beautifully . . . right up until they don't.

Basics of fuel injection

If you don't know what fuel injection is, check out Chapter 7. What matters here is how to live with it without turning every hiccup into a shopping spree.

Fuel injection maintenance is mostly about protecting the precision sprayers (injectors) and the system feeding them (pumps, filters, pressure control), which means:

- **Keeping fuel clean and fresh** (especially if the car sits a lot).
- **Keeping pressure stable** (by not ignoring early symptoms).
- **Not guessing when the car acts up** (because "fuel-ish" symptoms can also be air, ignition, or sensor issues).

Where people get into trouble is usually one of these four moves:

- **Skipping filter intervals** (diesel owners, this is your villain origin story).
- **Topping off after the pump clicks** (hello, EVAP problems).
- **Throwing additives at symptoms** instead of confirming what's wrong.
- **Replacing expensive parts** based on vibes instead of evidence.

REMEMBER

A bottle of cleaner can't fix a weak fuel pump, a vacuum leak, a bad sensor, or an ignition problem. It's a helper for mild deposit issues — not a mechanic in a container.

Direct injection and high-pressure systems

Direct injection is where modern fuel systems stop being DIY curious and start being respect the hardware. DI systems can run at very high pressure, and that changes your maintenance mindset in three big ways:

- **Treat the high-pressure side as pro territory.** Unless you have the right tools and the correct depressurizing procedure, don't open high-pressure components just to check. DI is not the place for improvisation.
- **Expect different long-term quirks.** Some DI engines are more prone to intake valve deposits over time. That's not a reason to panic — it's a reason to maintain smartly (good oil, correct intervals, and occasional longer drives) and to choose proven cleaning methods when needed.
- **Oil maintenance matters even more.** DI engines can be pickier about oil specs and change intervals because oil vapor and deposits are part of the real-world equation. Follow the manufacturer's oil spec and interval. (Chapter 14 goes deeper.)

WARNING

High-pressure fuel systems aren't "crack a line and see" systems. High-pressure fuel can be dangerous. If you suspect a DI leak or pressure issue, this is a stop-and-handle-correctly situation — not an experiment.

Fuel Filters and Flow

Fuel filters don't get any glory. They just quietly keep expensive parts from eating dirt for breakfast. In maintenance terms, this section is about two things: knowing what filter setup your vehicle actually has, and not turning a small suspicion into a big project.

Inline versus in-tank filters

Here's the quick reality: "Fuel filter" doesn't mean the same thing on every vehicle anymore. Before you plan any service, figure out which setup you have.

The fastest way to tell what you're working with is to check your owner's manual maintenance schedule or the service info for your exact vehicle. If it lists a fuel filter interval, it's usually a serviceable design. If it never mentions a fuel filter, it may be an in-tank lifetime setup.

Fuel filters fall into three common buckets: external inline filter, in-tank filter, and diesel filter, as shown in Figure 8-1.

TIP

If replacing the filter means dropping the fuel tank, don't do it "just because it might help." Treat that as scheduled-by-the-manufacturer or diagnose-first work.

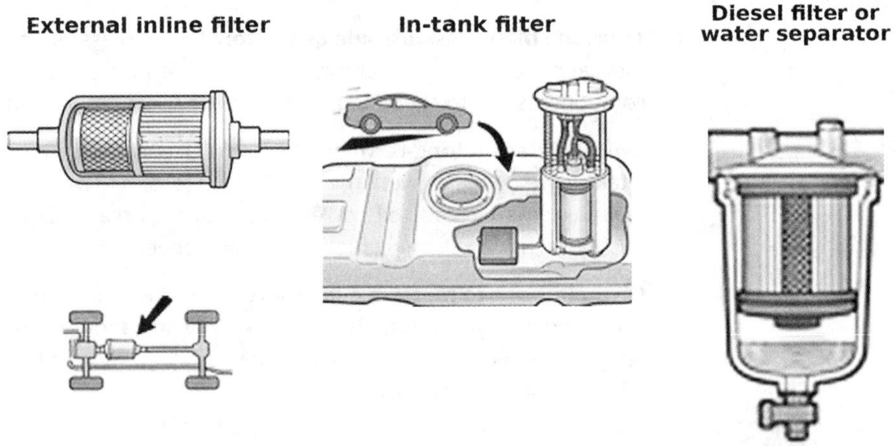

FIGURE 8-1: Types of fuel filters.

Generated with AI using OpenAI

External inline filter

The external inline filter is serviceable and is the classic maintenance-friendly situation. An external inline filter is:

- Common on many older gasoline vehicles and lots of diesels
- Often a scheduled service item
- Usually accessible without dropping the fuel tank
- Often DIY-possible if you follow safety steps and the correct depressurizing procedure

In-tank filter

An in-tank filter is often built into the pump module and is the "modern packaging" situation. An in-tank filter is:

- Common on newer gasoline vehicles
- Often not a routine service item
- May require tank access or tank removal to replace

TIP

Translation: It's not a casual "I've got time this weekend" job — and it's rarely the first move without evidence.

Diesel filter or water separator

A diesel filter or water separator is serviceable and serious. Diesels treat contaminated fuel like a personal attack. This type of filter usually requires:

- » Usually scheduled maintenance — don't skip it
- » Often includes water separation/draining
- » Possibly priming/bleeding steps afterward
- » A specific procedure (sometimes scan-tool-assisted) to prime correctly on some vehicles

Signs of a clogged filter

A fuel filter usually doesn't fail in a dramatic way. It fails like a clogged straw: Everything's fine, until you try to take a big sip.

So instead of listing a bunch of repeat symptoms (Chapter 7 covers general restriction behavior), here are the everyday moments that can point to a restriction:

- » **On-ramp disappointment:** You press the gas to merge and the car responds with "best I can do is . . . meh."
- » **Hill amnesia:** It climbs like it forgot how, especially with passengers/cargo/towing.
- » **Passing power disappears:** It cruises okay, but asking for more feels weak or inconsistent.
- » **Start-up stubbornness:** It starts, but it takes longer than it used to especially after sitting.
- » **Hot-day drama:** Problems show up more when it's hot out, and you're running A/C (higher load means higher fuel demand).

Before you blame the filter, ask three quick questions:

- » **Is the filter a scheduled service item on your vehicle?** If it's a modern in-tank setup, it's usually not the first target without testing.
- » **Did the problem start right after a fill-up?** That sign leans more toward fuel quality/contamination than a slowly clogging filter.
- » **Does it mainly happen under load?** Restrictions tend to show up when the engine is asking for more.

REMEMBER

This section helps you decide whether a restricted fuel filter is a likely cause of the symptoms before you buy any parts. The goal is to check the evidence first instead of replacing fuel-system components on a hunch.

Lifetime filters in modern vehicles

Lifetime fuel filter sounds like the filter is immortal. What it usually means is that it's not a scheduled replacement item under normal conditions. That's it. It doesn't mean it can never clog or fuel can never be contaminated.

A modern in-tank filter/pump module may still need attention if:

- You had a bad fuel event (water/contamination).
- Testing supports a delivery restriction or weak fuel pressure.
- The pump module is being replaced anyway (the filter is often part of the assembly).

Here's what you should do before you assume you need an expensive in-tank service:

- **Check your maintenance schedule** (don't fight the manual).
- **Look for patterns** (right after fueling vs gradual change).
- **Start with the low-risk wins** (good fuel habits, storage stabilizer when needed, and stop topping off).
- **Test or confirm before any tank-drop decision** (verify low fuel pressure or a delivery restriction before removing the tank).

TIP

If your vehicle has no scheduled fuel filter replacement and it runs well, don't go hunting for a tank-drop project. Your best lifetime filter strategy is clean fuel habits and catching changes early — not preemptive surgery.

Injectors: Precision Sprayers

Fuel injectors are tiny, hardworking overachievers — and like most overachievers, they don't complain until they're really unhappy. When they're doing their job correctly, you never think about them. The engine starts easily, idles smoothly, pulls cleanly, and gets decent mileage. Life is good. But injectors don't just send fuel. They deliver it with surgical precision, opening and closing thousands of times per minute and spraying fuel in a very specific way. When that precision slips, the engine notices — even if you don't at first.

The problem is that injectors are picky eaters. They don't like dirty fuel, water, or old gas that's been sitting around thinking about its life choices. Even small deposits can mess with how fuel leaves the injector, and when that happens, combustion gets a little sloppy. The computer will do its best to cover it up, but it can only fake it for so long. That's why injector issues usually don't show up as dramatic failures — they show up as subtle annoyances, like rough idle, hesitation, or slowly worsening MPG that makes you wonder if you suddenly forgot how to drive.

How injectors atomize fuel

Injectors don't just deliver fuel — they deliver it as a very specific mist. That mist is what lets the fuel mix with air evenly and burn smoothly.

When deposits build up (even small ones), the spray pattern can get sloppy. Instead of a nice "fog", you can end up with more of a "garden-hose-with-a-thumb-over-it" situation — uneven fuel delivery that makes combustion less consistent. The computer will try to compensate, but it can cover up only so much before you feel it as roughness, hesitation, or lost efficiency. Figure 8-2 compares a clean injector spray pattern with a deposit-affected pattern, showing how buildup can turn an even mist into an uneven spray.

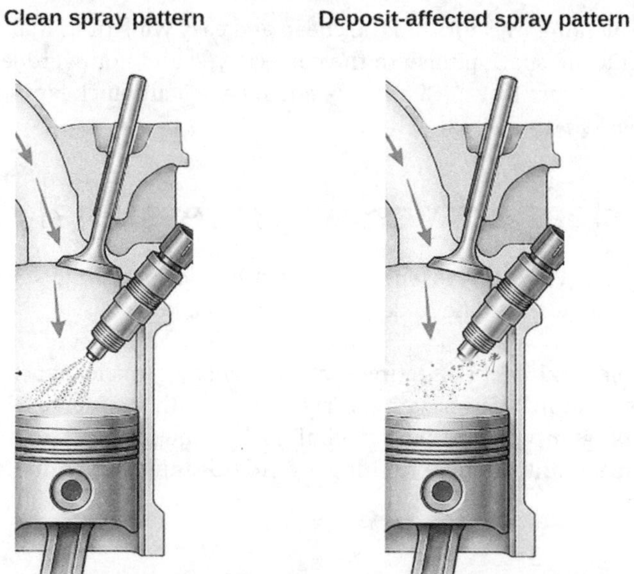

FIGURE 8-2: Injector spray patterns: Clean versus deposit affected.

Generated with AI using OpenAI

REMEMBER

If spray quality drops, combustion quality drops. And when combustion quality drops, your car starts compensating, which usually means worse MPG and worse manners.

Symptoms of dirty injectors

Dirty injectors rarely announce themselves with one obvious symptom. They show up as little behavior changes — the kind you notice because the car suddenly feels less smooth than it used to be.

Common "this might be injector-related" moments include:

- **The stoplight shuffle:** It idles rougher than normal once it's warmed up.
- **The gentle-throttle stumble:** Light acceleration feels hesitant, like the engine has to think about it first.
- **The MPG creep:** Your fuel economy slowly gets worse, even though your driving hasn't changed.
- **The random misfire vibe:** It occasionally feels like a cylinder missed a beat, especially on cold starts or after the car sits.

Here's the money-saving reality check: Those same symptoms can also come from spark plugs/coils, vacuum leaks, airflow sensors, or low fuel pressure, so don't skip straight to "injectors are bad" because the internet said so.

TIP

Before blaming injectors, do the cheap and easy wins first: Make sure the air filter is decent, the spark plugs are the correct type and not overdue, and there are no obvious vacuum leaks. (Chapters 5 and 6 have your quick ignition and basic scan-tool checks.)

DIY cleaners versus professional cleaning

Cleaning fuel injectors is where people either do something smart or start pouring random liquids into the tank like it's a science fair.

A *fuel injector cleaner* (sometimes labeled fuel system cleaner) is a detergent additive you pour into the gas tank. It rides along with the fuel and helps dissolve light deposits (gum/varnish) that can build up in the fuel system and on injector tips over time. Think of it like running a gentle cleaning cycle through the system, not rebuilding it.

Doing it yourself

You can buy injector cleaner at:

- **Auto parts stores** (in the fuel-additive aisle)
- **Big-box stores** (automotive section)
- **Online retailers**
- **Some gas stations** (usually small bottles near the counter)

TIP

Buy a product clearly labeled for your fuel type (gasoline versus diesel) and follow the directions exactly. More is not better here.

DIY cleaner can make sense when:

- The issue is mild (a little roughness, slight hesitation, small MPG drop).
- You do lots of short trips (engine rarely gets a long, hot run).
- The vehicle sits often.
- You're trying to prevent deposits — not revive a failing system.

WARNING

Be cautious with miracle additives and aggressive DIY intake-spraying shortcuts. If the method isn't known-safe for your specific engine, you can damage sensors or emissions components — and turn a small problem into a big bill.

A smart DIY approach looks like the following steps:

1. **Start with one tank of good-quality fuel from a busy station.**

   You want to buy from a busy place because it'll have high turnover.

2. **Add one reputable injector cleaner as directed.**

   You'll usually pour it into a low tank and then fill up.

3. **Drive normally and evaluate after one to two tanks.**
4. **If nothing changes, stop adding hope and move on to real diagnosis.**

REMEMBER

An injector cleaner is a maintenance tool, not a miracle fix. If the problem is severe, a bottle won't outsmart physics.

DIY cleaner will not fix:

- A leaking injector
- Heavy contamination or a serious clog
- Weak fuel pump or low fuel pressure
- Air leaks or sensor issues
- Mechanical engine problems

WARNING

If the car is shaking badly, power is dropping hard, or the Check Engine light is flashing, skip the additive experiment and diagnose the issue by jumping to Part 5.

Opting for a profession

So when does it make sense to skip the bottle and go pro? Professional injector service is worth it when:

- The problem is persistent, not occasional.
- You have repeat drivability complaints or repeat codes.
- Basic ignition or air checks didn't solve it.
- A shop can confirm a fuel-delivery issue with proper testing.

A professional may do:

- On-car pressurized cleaning, where a cleaner is through the fuel rail under controlled conditions
- Injector removal plus bench/ultrasonic cleaning, which is more thorough and depends on engine
- Replacement if an injector is leaking, electrically failing, or damaged

Diesel injector sensitivity to contamination

If gas engines are picky, diesels are picky and petty. Diesel fuel systems run super tight tolerances, and the injectors/pumps are basically precision instruments that don't enjoy a little water or a little grit. Not even as a treat.

If you drive a diesel, your injector survival plan is simple:

- Follow the fuel filter and water separator schedule like it's law.
- Buy fuel from reputable, high-turnover stations (fresh diesel, fewer surprises).
- Take Water in Fuel warnings seriously (don't clear and ignore).
- Don't delay when symptoms start — diesel fuel problems can snowball fast.

REMEMBER

For diesels, fuel cleanliness isn't a nice to have. It's survival.

Smart Fuel Pumps

If injectors are the spray nozzles, the fuel pump is the heart of the system. When it's healthy, you never notice it. When it's struggling, the car starts acting like it's running a marathon while breathing through a coffee stirrer.

Figure 8-3 compares an electric in-tank pump, variable-speed pump control, and the high-pressure pump used by direct-injection systems.

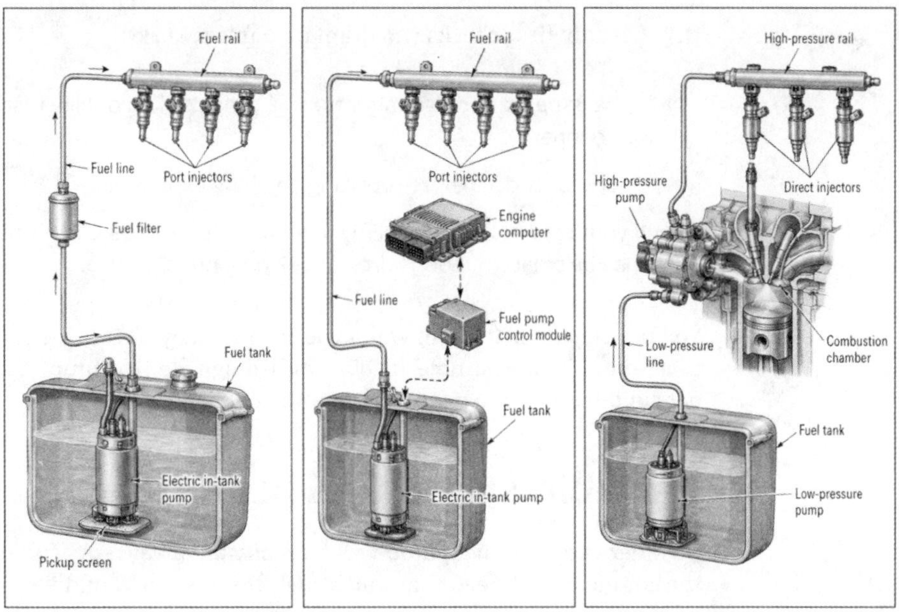

FIGURE 8-3: Smart fuel pumps.

Generated with AI using OpenAI

Electric in-tank pumps

Most modern vehicles use an electric fuel pump inside the tank. This in-tank setup sounds fancy, but the maintenance idea is simple: The pump likes cool fuel, clean fuel, and not being abused.

Certain habits help pump life:

- **Don't live on the fuel light.** Running low occasionally is fine. Running low all the time makes the pump run hotter.
- **Avoid repeat bad-fuel episodes by choosing good stations.** Choose a station that is busy, reputable, and clean-looking.
- **Address symptoms early.** Pumps often fade before they die. Don't wait for the full no-start finale.

When a pump is getting tired, you may notice:

- Longer crank time before it starts
- Power loss under load (hills, merging, and towing)
- Intermittent hesitation, often worse when the tank is low

DIY-friendly first checks (no drama, no guesswork):

- If the issue started right after fueling, consider fuel quality first (bad gas happens).
- Check for codes before replacing anything expensive.
- If your car has an external fuel filter and it's overdue, catch-up maintenance may be smart (but don't drop a tank on a hunch).

TIP

You may hear a brief hum when you turn the key to ON; it's the pump priming. If that sound changes, note it, but don't diagnose by pump vibes alone. Use scan data and testing or a shop if symptoms persist.

Variable-speed fuel pumps

On older cars, the fuel pump was basically an always-on, full-blast device. When the engine didn't need that much fuel, the system would just send the extra fuel back to the tank (kind of like running a garden hose wide open and letting the extra water spill back into the bucket). It worked, but it wasted energy and heated the fuel.

On many modern cars, the pump is smarter. Instead of running at 100 percent all the time, the car changes the pump's speed depending on what the engine needs right now. Think of the system as a dimmer switch or a variable-speed ceiling fan: low setting when you're cruising gently, higher setting when you stomp the gas, climb a hill, or tow something.

What controls fuel-pump speed?

Usually the ECU (engine computer) or a fuel pump control module tells the pump when to turn it down or turn it up. By varying the pump's speed, the controller maintains the required fuel pressure where it needs to be without making the pump work harder than necessary.

Cars use variable-speed fuel pumps to provide several benefits:

- **Less heat in the fuel system:** Hot fuel means an unhappy fuel system.
- **Less noise:** The pump doesn't have to scream all the time.
- **Better efficiency:** Less electrical load means a tiny bit less work for the engine and charging system.
- **Often fewer vapor/emissions headaches:** The system stays cooler and more controlled.

REMEMBER

A pump that isn't always loud (or a voltage reading that changes) is often normal on these systems.

In addition, if you're troubleshooting, you can't always use the old-school logic of "it should be steady all the time." Some cars need a scan tool to see what the pump is being told to do versus what it's actually doing.

TIP

Simple rule: If the car runs smoothly and starts normally, don't worry that the pump isn't full blast all the time — that's the point of variable-speed control.

High-pressure pumps for DI systems

Direct injection adds a second, engine-mounted pump that boosts fuel pressure from strong squirt to industrial pressure washer. That's where you shift from DIY curiosity to DIY caution.

The DI maintenance takeaways are to:

- **Follow the correct oil spec and interval** to help control deposits and protect expensive hardware.

- **Watch for fuel smells or dampness in the engine bay** (stop-and-check, not wait and see).
- **Get a pro diagnosis for pressure-related faults before buying parts** because DI parts aren't cheap.

WARNING

Don't loosen, crack, or "just check" DI high-pressure lines. The system can stay pressurized even after shutdown, and high-pressure fuel can spray, penetrate skin, and create a fire risk. If the fix involves opening the high-pressure side, it's generally a pro-level job.

Maintaining Fuel Quality

Chapter 7 explains gasoline, diesel, ethanol blends (including E10, E15, and E85), and biodiesel, along with the vehicles that can use each type.

For maintenance, follow the fuel specifications in your owner's manual. If the vehicle is driven infrequently, also follow the manufacturer's fuel-storage recommendations. On diesel vehicles, service the fuel filter and water separator according to the recommended maintenance schedule.

REMEMBER

Diesels are amazing, but they're not forgiving. Keep fuel clean, follow filter intervals, and buy from stations with high turnover.

Fuel System Diagnostics

This chapter isn't turning you into a diagnostic technician — that's not the goal. But you can use basic scan info as an early-warning system so that you don't wait until a small issue becomes expensive.

OBD-II codes for lean/rich conditions

Chapter 7 explains what these codes mean. Here's how to treat them in a maintenance chapter:

- **Lean/rich codes:** The computer is working hard to keep the mixture happy.
- **Misfire codes:** Combustion isn't consistent.

- **Fuel pressure-related codes:** You have delivery problems you shouldn't ignore.

Your job isn't replacing whatever Google says. Your job is to capture the clues.

TIP

Don't clear codes immediately. Write them down (or screenshot them) and note when they appear: cold start, highway cruise, heavy acceleration, or right after fueling. Timing is a huge clue.

Fuel trim interpretation

Fuel trims are percentage adjustments the engine computer makes to the amount of fuel delivered by the injectors. A positive fuel-trim number means the computer is adding fuel; a negative number means it's subtracting fuel. Scan tools usually display short-term fuel trim, which changes quickly, and long-term fuel trim, which reflects corrections learned over time.

You don't need to become a fuel-trim scientist. Think of trims as your car's effort meter. If the computer is constantly making big corrections, something is changing.

Here's a simple maintenance routine (quick trend check):

1. **Warm the engine fully.**
2. **Check trims at idle.**
3. **Check trims again around 2,500 rpm.**

If trims seem extreme or are trending worse over time, plan diagnosis or a professional evaluation.

REMEMBER

Trims point to a condition, not a guaranteed bad part.

When to consult a professional mechanic

Get professional help when you have:

- Any fuel leak or strong fuel smell
- A flashing Check Engine light
- Persistent drivability problems that don't improve with basic maintenance
- Suspected DI high-pressure issues

» Repeated lean, rich, or misfire codes after completing checks, including reading the codes, considering fuel quality, and checking whether a serviceable fuel filter is overdue

» Diesel water/contamination concerns you can't resolve safely

WARNING

If you misfuel (gas in diesel or diesel in gas), don't start the engine. Tow it and have it handled correctly.

Hybrids and EVs

Fuel maintenance now depends on how often your engine actually runs — and for hybrids, that's the sneaky part. A hybrid can go long stretches barely sipping gas, which is great for your wallet, but it also means the fuel in the tank can sit around long enough to get stale. And stale fuel is like old milk: You don't notice it until you really notice it. Hybrids still have the same basic fuel-system players (pump, injectors, and lines), so they still need clean, fresh fuel to behave.

The maintenance fix isn't complicated — it's just a little more intentional. Try not to let a tank of fuel sit for months, especially if you mostly drive short electric-heavy trips. Every so often, take the car on a longer drive that fully warms up the engine and burns through some of that older fuel. And if your vehicle has a fuel maintenance mode or prompts that encourage the engine to run for fuel freshness, don't ignore it — that's the car doing you a favor. Put simply: If your hybrid mostly runs electric, don't make half a tank of old gas your long-term lifestyle choice.

EVs, on the other hand, skip the entire fuel-system world — no tank, no pump, no injectors, no EVAP system, and no mystery Check Engine light after a fill-up because there is no fill-up. No fuel system removes a whole category of maintenance headaches, but it doesn't mean EVs are maintenance-free. They still need tires, brakes (often less wear thanks to regenerative braking), cooling-system care, and 12-volt battery attention. The key idea is simple: No fuel system doesn't mean no maintenance — it just means different maintenance.

IN THIS CHAPTER

» Following exhaust from the manifold to the tailpipe

» Understanding catalytic converters, DPFs, and other cleanup hardware

» Meeting oxygen sensors and how they keep the mixture honest

» Making sense of EGR and EVAP systems without the jargon headache

» Separating legal sound and performance upgrades from expensive mistakes

» Using OBD-II codes and common symptoms to spot emissions trouble fast

Chapter 9

Exhaust and Emissions: Cleaning Up after the Combustion Party

Every time your engine runs, it produces a hot stream of exhaust gases. Some of that stream is harmless (mostly nitrogen and water vapor). Some of it is not (carbon monoxide, unburned hydrocarbons, and nitrogen oxides). And all of it is loud enough to make your neighbors rethink their life choices if you let it out unchecked.

This chapter is your map of that whole cleanup operation — from the exhaust manifold to the tailpipe, from oxygen sensors to diesel particulate filters, and from "this sounds cool" mods to "this will fail inspection and light up the dash." The next time you smell something weird, hear a new rattle, or see a P0420 code, you'll know what your car is trying to tell you.

Exhaust 101: The Journey Out

If the intake system is the engine's front door, the exhaust system is the back door — and it's handling hot, fast-moving gases under pressure. How well the exhaust system does its job affects power, fuel economy, cabin comfort, and how clean (and legal) your car is.

Your exhaust system has three big jobs:

- Move exhaust gases out of the engine efficiently (without leaking into the cabin).
- Quiet things down so that the car doesn't sound like a lawn mower in a metal trash can.
- Clean up emissions using catalysts, filters, and sensors that keep the ECU honest.

Exhaust manifold and header design

The *exhaust manifold* bolts to the engine and collects exhaust gases from each cylinder. Its job sounds simple — gather exhaust and send it downstream — but the details matter because the exhaust manifold is where exhaust heat and pressure are at their peak.

You'll usually see one of these setups:

- **Cast-iron or cast-steel manifold:** A cast-iron or cast-steel manifold is durable, compact, and common on everyday cars because it handles high exhaust heat well and fits neatly in tight engine bays.
- **Tubular headers:** This performance-style manifold is made of individual tubes. Headers can improve exhaust flow and scavenging (helping cylinders empty more efficiently), but they can also be noisier and more prone to leaks if installed poorly.

» **Turbocharger integrated into the manifold:** On turbo engines, the exhaust stream spins a turbine before heading downstream. This turbocharger setup means exhaust plumbing is doing double duty: It's both waste flow and a power source.

TIP

A ticking sound on cold start that fades as the engine warms up is a classic exhaust manifold or manifold-gasket leak symptom. Heat makes parts expand and can temporarily seal small leaks — which is why they're easiest to hear when the engine is cold.

Handling manifold leaks safely

So, you've got that ticking sound, huh? It may be your manifold saying, "Hey, I'm leaking!" First, you need to figure out if it's just a gasket or something bigger:

1. **Inspect the area.**

   Look for dark soot marks around the manifold or gasket.

2. **Feel for leaks.**

   When the engine is cold, feel carefully for escaping air.

3. **Loosen with care.**

   If bolts are stuck, apply penetrating oil and let it sit.

4. **Check the gasket.**

   If it's worn or damaged, replace it.

5. **Tighten to spec.**

   Check Chapter 3 for how to use a torque wrench properly and reference Chapter 1 to find your vehicle's torque specs.

6. **Recheck.**

   After tightening, start the engine cold and listen for leaks. If you still hear a sound, the manifold may be cracked — and it's time to get a shop involved for a closer look!

REMEMBER

If the bolts start acting like they own the place, you've got options.

From manifold to tailpipe

Once exhaust leaves the manifold (and the turbo, if you have one), it travels through a series of pipes and components designed to control heat, noise, and emissions.

Figure 9-1 shows the full exhaust system layout, from the exhaust manifold at the engine all the way back to the tailpipe.

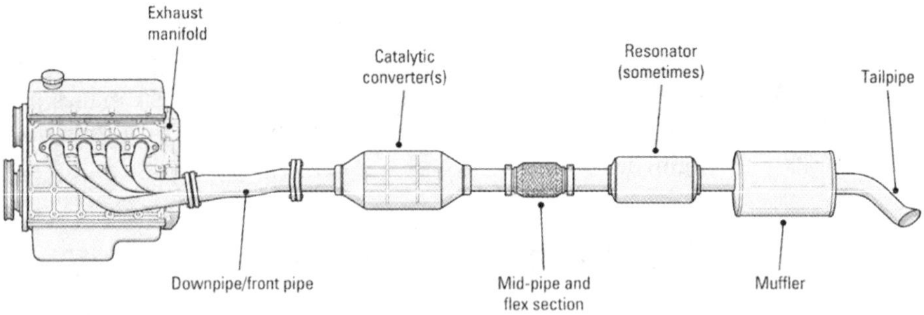

Generated with AI using OpenAI

FIGURE 9-1: Exhaust system overview.

Here's the typical route on a gasoline vehicle:

- **Downpipe/front pipe:** The first section after the manifold or turbo.
- **Catalytic converter(s):** The emissions-cleanup unit or units that help turn carbon monoxide, unburned hydrocarbons, and nitrogen oxides into less harmful gases. For the full breakdown, see the section "Catalytic Converters," later in this chapter.
- **Mid-pipe and flex section:** A flex joint that lets the exhaust move with the engine without cracking hard pipes.
- **Resonator (sometimes):** The part that tunes out specific frequencies (think "drone control").
- **Muffler:** The main sound reducer.
- **Tailpipe:** The final exit.

A few small parts do a lot of work along the way:

- **Heat shields:** Thin metal shields that protect nearby parts (and you) from exhaust heat.
- **Hangers and rubber isolators:** Flexible supports that hold the exhaust in place while letting it move and flex without rattling the whole car.
- **Clamps, flanges, and gaskets:** The seams in the system — and the most common leak points.

WARNING

Exhaust leaks are more than annoying noise. Leaks upstream of the cabin can let carbon monoxide (CO) into the vehicle. If you ever smell exhaust inside, feel dizzy, or get headaches while driving, treat it as an urgent safety issue — fix the leak before you keep driving.

Mufflers and resonators for sound control

People often say "my muffler is bad" when they really mean "my exhaust is loud." But mufflers aren't the only sound-control parts in the system.

Here's the quick translation:

- **Resonator:** Targets specific tones and frequencies. It's like a noise-canceling headset for your exhaust note — it doesn't always make the car quiet, but it can make it less droney or boomy.
- **Muffler:** Reduces overall volume. Mufflers use chambers, baffles, and acoustic packing to calm the exhaust before it exits the tailpipe.
- **Active or variable exhaust valves:** Change exhaust flow and sound. Many modern cars have a valve that opens or closes to make the exhaust quieter in normal driving and louder in sport or performance modes. See the section "Performance and Sound," later in this chapter.

Catalytic Converters

Catalytic converters (cats) are the reason modern cars can make power and still run clean enough to pass emissions standards. They're also one of the most misunderstood (and most stolen) parts on the vehicle.

How catalytic converters reduce emissions

A gasoline engine produces three major problem pollutants:

- **Carbon monoxide (CO):** A poisonous gas from incomplete combustion.
- **Unburned hydrocarbons (HC):** Fuel that didn't fully burn (also contributes to smog).
- **Nitrogen oxides (NOx):** Formed when combustion temperatures get very high.

A three-way catalytic converter tackles all three using precious-metal catalysts (typically platinum, palladium, and rhodium). In plain English, the converter helps turn those bad molecules into less harmful ones (mostly carbon dioxide, nitrogen, and water).

Two practical realities matter for DIYers:

- **Cats need to get hot before they clean well.** That's why many cars have a close-coupled converter located near the engine — it warms up quickly after a cold start.
- **Cats don't like misfires or raw fuel.** A flashing Check Engine light (misfire) can overheat a converter fast. Fix misfires promptly. It's cheaper than replacing a cat.

Dual converters and high-flow systems

Many vehicles have more than one catalytic converter. V-engines may have a converter for each bank. Some vehicles use a small pre-cat near the engine plus a larger under-floor converter downstream. (If you're shopping for exhaust parts (axle-back, cat-back, downpipes), go to the "Performance and Sound" section, later in this chapter.)

WARNING

Removing, disabling, or bypassing emissions equipment (catalysts, DPFs, EGR, SCR/DEF systems) is illegal in many places and can also damage the vehicle or trigger constant warning lights. This book focuses on keeping your car reliable and compliant — not on deleting the parts that keep the air breathable.

TIP

Catalytic converter theft is common because converters contain valuable metals. If your car suddenly sounds like a race car and the Check Engine light turns on at the same time, look under the car — a missing converter is unfortunately a real possibility.

Diesel particulate filters (DPFs)

Diesel exhaust cleaning is its own world. Most modern diesels use a chain of components, often including:

- **Diesel Oxidation Catalyst (DOC):** Helps reduce HC and CO and supports later stages.

- **Diesel Particulate Filter (DPF):** Traps soot (particulate matter) so that it doesn't go out the tailpipe.
- **Selective Catalytic Reduction (SCR):** Uses DEF (diesel exhaust fluid) to reduce NOx.
- **Sensors everywhere:** NOx sensors, temperature sensors, differential pressure sensors, and more.

Figure 9-2 shows how these diesel aftertreatment components are arranged in sequence, from the oxidation catalyst through the DPF and into the SCR/DEF system.

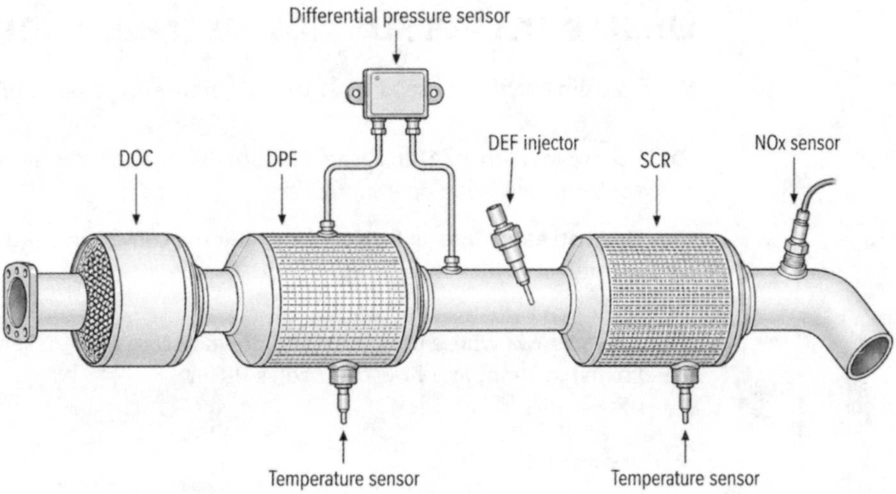

FIGURE 9-2: Diesel aftertreatment chain.

Generated with AI using OpenAI

The DPF deserves special attention because it's basically a soot filter that has to clean itself.

Here's the everyday-driver translation of regeneration (regen): The vehicle periodically raises exhaust temperature so that the soot trapped in the filter burns off and turns into ash.

During a regen, you may notice:

- A higher idle speed, hotter smell, or cooling fans running after you park
- Slightly worse MPG during the event (extra fuel/strategy to raise temps)
- A dashboard message or warning light on some vehicles

REMEMBER

Short trips are rough on DPF systems because the exhaust may never stay hot long enough for passive cleaning. If you drive a diesel, pay attention to regen messages and don't ignore them. (Chapter 11 goes deeper on diesel life.)

Oxygen Sensors: The Exhaust Watchdogs

Chapter 7 introduces O_2 sensors as the ECU's taste testers. Here's what matters on the exhaust side: where they sit, what upstream versus downstream means, and why they trigger catalyst codes.

Upstream versus downstream sensors

Most gasoline vehicles use at least two oxygen sensors per bank:

- **Upstream (Sensor 1/2):** Located before the catalytic converter. Used for fuel control (closed-loop operation).
- **Downstream (Sensor 1/2):** Located after the converter. Used mainly to monitor catalytic converter efficiency.

Figure 9-3 shows where upstream and downstream oxygen sensors are located in the exhaust system, and how their roles differ.

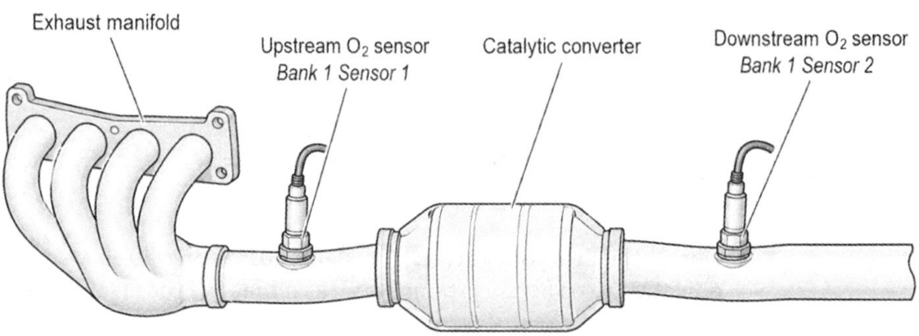

FIGURE 9-3: O_2 sensor locations.

Generated with AI using OpenAI

Some vehicles use wideband air-fuel ratio sensors upstream instead of the older narrowband style. The idea is the same: feedback that helps the ECU adjust fuel trims.

QUICK DECODER FOR O_2 SENSOR NAMES

Bank is the engine side, and *Sensor* is the position.

Bank 1 is the side of the engine that contains cylinder #1. (Bank 2 is the other side; inline engines usually have only Bank 1).

Sensor 1 is upstream (before the catalytic converter). Sensor 2 is downstream (after the converter).

So "Bank 1 Sensor 2" refers to the O_2 sensor after the catalytic converter on the Bank 1 side.

Role in closed-loop fuel management

When the engine is warmed up, it usually runs in a closed loop: The ECU commands fuel, reads the oxygen sensor feedback, and then corrects fuel delivery in real time. That's how modern cars stay smooth, efficient, and clean across huge changes in temperature, altitude, and driving style.

REMEMBER

An oxygen-sensor code doesn't automatically mean replace the oxygen sensor. Exhaust leaks, wiring issues, vacuum leaks, fuel pressure problems, and misfires can all confuse the sensor and trigger codes. Treat codes as clues, not verdicts.

Common failure symptoms

Oxygen sensors don't usually fail dramatically. They age. The sensor slows down, readings get lazy, and the ECU has to work harder to keep the mixture in check.

Common signs include:

- **Check Engine light** with O_2 sensor or heater codes.
- **Worse fuel economy** without a clear driving change.
- **Rough idle or hesitation** (sometimes), especially if fuel trims are swinging.
- **A catalyst efficiency code** (P0420/P0430) that turns out to be an exhaust leak or sensor problem — not a bad converter.

TIP

If you're chasing a catalyst efficiency code, check for exhaust leaks ahead of the downstream sensor first. A small leak can let fresh air into the exhaust stream and make the converter look inefficient on scan data.

Smog Control and Emissions Systems

Modern emissions control isn't just a catalytic converter in a pipe. It's a whole ecosystem of systems designed to reduce NOx, capture fuel vapors, and keep the engine operating in a clean window.

EGR valves

EGR stands for Exhaust Gas Recirculation. It routes a small amount of exhaust back into the intake under certain conditions. That sounds counterintuitive, but it lowers combustion temperatures — and lower temperatures reduce NOx.

Common real-world EGR issues look like the following:

- **EGR stuck open:** Rough idle, stalling, or a "running like it has a vacuum leak" feel.
- **EGR stuck closed or restricted:** Higher NOx emissions and possible pinging or knock on some engines, plus EGR flow codes.

REMEMBER

On many engines, EGR problems can masquerade as intake or idle problems. Don't let the name fool you — EGR affects how the engine runs, not just what comes out of the tailpipe.

EVAP systems and how they connect to emissions monitoring

Your fuel system makes vapors even when the engine is off. The EVAP system captures those vapors in a charcoal canister and then purges them into the engine to be burned at the right time.

The EVAP system is also a major source of mystery Check Engine lights because it's monitored by leak tests and valves. Common culprits include loose gas caps, cracked hoses, stuck purge valves, and vent valve issues.

If you find yourself with an EVAP issue, refer to Chapter 7 for more help.

DEF systems for diesels (SCR)

Many modern diesels use Selective Catalytic Reduction (SCR) to reduce NOx. SCR injects diesel exhaust fluid, or DEF (basically urea in water) into the exhaust stream upstream of a catalyst. The chemistry turns NOx into nitrogen and water.

Here is what matters for drivers:

- **DEF is a consumable.** You have to refill it periodically.
- **Quality matters.** Contaminated or incorrect fluid can trigger warnings and reduced-power modes.
- **The vehicle monitors SCR efficiency.** Ignoring DEF warnings can eventually lead to no-start countdowns on some systems.

WARNING

If you drive a diesel, don't ignore DEF or DPF warnings. These systems protect both emissions compliance and engine operation — and "just driving it until it fixes itself" often ends in limp mode or expensive repairs.

Performance and Sound

Wanting your car to sound better isn't a crime. (Well, not automatically.) The trick is understanding what you're changing and what the car — and the law — expects.

Variable exhaust valves in modern performance cars

Active exhaust systems use valves to change flow paths. In quiet mode, exhaust is routed through more muffling. In sport mode, valves open and the exhaust takes a louder, freer path.

These systems can fail, too. A stuck valve can cause:

- A car that's "too quiet" in sport mode (valve stuck closed)
- Rattles or buzzing noises (loose valve hardware or broken actuator gears)
- A warning light on some vehicles if the actuator is monitored

Performance mufflers and aftermarket systems

Aftermarket exhaust parts range from harmless to headache-inducing. These systems usually fall into a few buckets:

- **Axle-back:** Replaces the muffler section only. Mostly sound.
- **Cat-back:** Replaces everything after the catalytic converter. Often the easiest way to change sound without touching emissions hardware (but noise laws still apply).
- **Downpipe/header changes:** Can affect catalysts and sensor locations. More likely to trigger codes, fail inspections, or require tuning.

One more real-world note: Drone is real. A louder exhaust can sound great at full throttle and miserable at 2,100 rpm on the highway. Resonators exist for a reason — your commute doesn't need to sound like it is trapped inside a tuba.

TECHNICAL STUFF

The old "backpressure makes torque" myth is oversimplified. Engines want efficient scavenging and properly sized piping — not random restriction. Bigger isn't always better, and removing key components can create tuning problems, not free horsepower.

REMEMBER

A louder exhaust isn't automatically more power. On many modern engines, the ECU and turbocharging strategy matter far more than raw pipe volume. Sound and performance are related, but they're not the same thing.

Legal versus illegal modifications

The line between legal and illegal modifications is simple:

- **Legal mods** typically keep emissions hardware intact (cats/DPF/SCR) and change sound after the cleanup parts.
- **Illegal mods** usually remove or disable emissions controls or require cheating the ECU to hide it.

REMEMBER

Even if your area doesn't do emissions testing, the vehicle is still designed to run with its emissions systems in place. Keeping them working is usually the most reliable (and least headache) choice.

Diagnostics and Troubleshooting: When the Dash Starts Judging You

Emissions systems have a gift: They often warn you before something becomes a complete failure. The downside is that the warning usually comes as a cryptic code and a glowing light.

OBD-II codes in the emissions world

Here are some common code families and what they usually point to:

- **P0420/P0430:** Catalyst efficiency below threshold (Bank 1/Bank 2). Often triggered by a tired converter, but also by exhaust leaks, misfires, or sensor issues.
- **P013x/P015x series:** O_2 sensor signal or heater faults (upstream/downstream).
- **P0440–P0456 family:** EVAP leaks, purge/vent problems, loose gas cap behavior.
- **P0401/P0402:** EGR flow issues (too little/too much).
- **Diesel examples:** P2002 (DPF efficiency), DPF pressure/regen codes, and SCR/DEF efficiency codes on newer systems.

TIP

Before clearing codes, save them. Screenshot your scan tool, write down the code list, and note when it happens (cold start, highway cruise, right after fueling, heavy acceleration). That context is half the diagnosis.

How to recognize emissions-system failures

Some emissions issues are silent until the light comes on. Others announce themselves with classic symptoms:

- **New exhaust noise:** Roaring, ticking, or hissing — often a leak or broken hanger
- **Rattling under the car:** Sometimes a loose heat shield; sometimes a converter substrate breaking apart
- **Sulfur (rotten egg) smell:** Can be converter-related or a sign of rich running/misfires overheating the catalyst
- **Soot streaks at joints:** A visual clue of an exhaust leak
- **Diesel messages about regen/DPF/DEF:** Not optional reading

DIY-friendly checks that won't get you in trouble

You can do a lot with your eyes, ears, and a scan tool without turning into an exhaust surgeon.

- Look for obvious leaks, broken hangers, and missing heat shields (with the engine cool).
- Check the gas cap seal and tighten it properly if you see EVAP codes.
- Inspect oxygen-sensor wiring and connectors for melting or chafing near hot pipes.
- If you have a misfire code and a flashing Check Engine light, address the misfire first. Don't keep driving and hope the catalyst survives.
- Use live data to look at fuel trims and O_2 sensor activity (Chapter 6 covers scan-tool basics).

WARNING

Don't run a car in an enclosed garage "just to listen for leaks." Exhaust fumes can build up quickly. If you're diagnosing sounds, do it outside or with proper ventilation.

TECHNICAL STUFF

Clearing codes resets readiness monitors. You can have no codes but still fail inspection for Readiness due to a diagnostic system or OBD reader clearing DTC codes. The vehicle must be driven 50 to 100 miles after clearing any code before getting emissions testing completed.

When to call a professional

Hand the job off when you're dealing with:

- Welding repairs, manifold replacement, or leaks near the firewall/turbo where access is tight and heat is extreme
- Catalytic converter replacement (especially on vehicles where the converter is integrated into the manifold)
- Diesel DPF/SCR faults that require forced regen procedures, specialized diagnostics, or emissions-system testing
- Any situation where exhaust fumes are getting into the cabin

Hybrid and EV Context

Not everyone's exhaust system lives the same life anymore. Hybrids and stop/start vehicles cycle the engine on and off so often that the exhaust system is constantly warming up, cooling down, and collecting moisture. Those duty-cycle differences affect everything from catalyst efficiency to how quickly pipes can rust in certain climates.

Hybrid exhaust systems and reduced emissions

Hybrids still have exhaust systems, catalytic converters, and oxygen sensors, but the engine doesn't run continuously. That difference changes a few things:

- **More cold starts per mile:** Stop/start and engine-off coasting can mean the catalyst cools down more often, so the system relies on smart warm-up strategies.
- **More condensation:** Short engine run times can mean more water vapor in the exhaust that doesn't fully steam out, which can accelerate rust in some climates.
- **Fewer total engine hours:** Many hybrids simply run the engine less, which can reduce total emissions — one reason they do so well in city driving.

TIP

If your hybrid does mostly short trips, a longer drive now and then helps fully warm the engine and exhaust system — which is good for both fuel freshness (see Chapter 8) and emissions-system health.

Why EVs don't need exhaust systems

EVs don't burn fuel, so there's no exhaust stream to clean. No manifold, no catalytic converter, no muffler, no oxygen sensors — and no Check Engine light because of a loose gas cap because there isn't one.

No exhaust system doesn't mean EVs are maintenance-free (tires, brakes, cooling systems, and 12-volt batteries still matter), but the entire exhaust-and-emissions category disappears.

IN THIS CHAPTER

» Comparing what's in a hybrid to what's in an EV

» Understanding regenerative braking without needing a physics minor

» Making sense of charging levels, charging speed, and real-world range

» Seeing why battery temperature matters

» Meeting the other future fuels

Chapter 10
Driving into the Future: A Deep Dive into EVs and Hybrids

The future of cars isn't one shiny spaceship parked in your driveway. Depending on where you live and what you drive, the future may look like a hybrid that takes naps at stoplights, a plug-in hybrid that behaves like an EV during the week, or a full battery-electric vehicle that skips gas stations entirely.

And it's not just electricity. Ethanol blends are already everywhere, some fleets run on natural gas, and hydrogen fuel-cell vehicles exist — yes, they're real — even if you don't see many of them at your local supermarket.

This chapter is your simple map of the modern powertrain landscape: what changed, what stayed the same, and what actually matters for ownership and maintenance. You don't need to memorize acronyms or become a charging-station detective. You just need the basics so that you can make good decisions — and avoid the expensive misunderstandings.

Hybrid Vehicles: The Best of Both Worlds

Hybrids are the best of both worlds when your driving includes lots of stop-and-go traffic, short trips, and low-speed cruising. Instead of making the gasoline engine do all the work all the time, a hybrid lets electric power handle the parts where gas engines are at their least efficient.

The usual payoff is better city fuel economy, smoother stoplight takeoffs, and less time idling like a bored teenager in a driveway. But hybrid isn't one design — it's a whole family, and the differences matter.

What's under the hood (and under the floor) in a hybrid

Think of a hybrid as a gasoline car with an electric teammate and extra hardware to manage high-voltage power. The exact layout varies, but most hybrids share the same core ingredients:

- **A gasoline engine** (often tuned for efficiency rather than max power)
- **One or more electric motor/generators** (to drive the wheels, start the engine, and recharge the battery)
- **A high-voltage (HV) battery pack** (the energy buffer for electric driving and regeneration)
- **An inverter** (converts HV battery DC power into AC power for the motor, and back again during regen)
- **A DC-DC converter to keep the 12-volt system charged** (no alternator in many hybrids)
- **Control modules** (the computers that coordinate the whole "who does what, when" strategy)

Figure 10-1 shows the main pieces of a hybrid powertrain and how the gasoline engine, electric motor, inverter, and battery work together. Many hybrids also have extra cooling hardware. Some have separate coolant loops for the inverter, motor, or battery pack, because power electronics hate overheating the way cats hate baths.

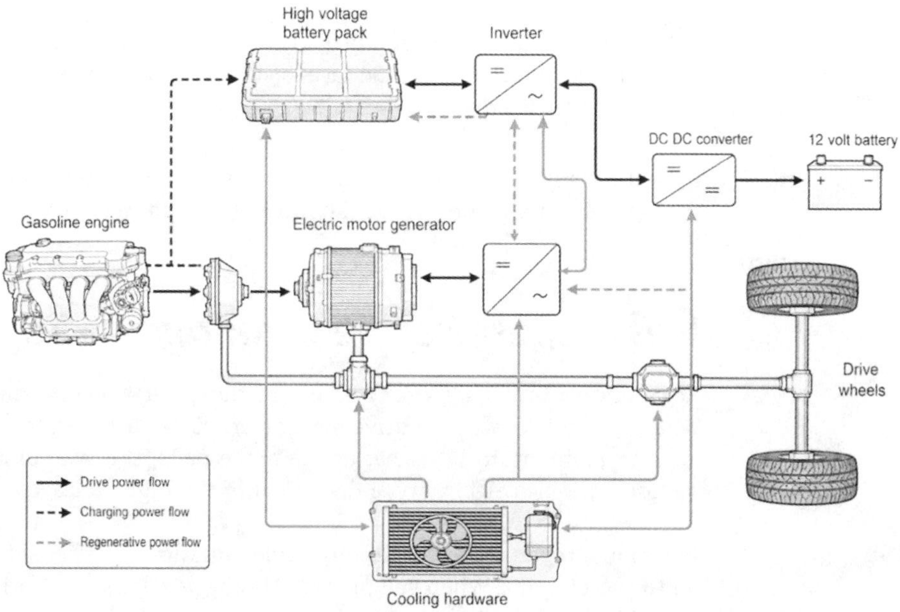

FIGURE 10-1: Hybrid powertrain essentials.

Generated with AI using OpenAI

Sorting hybrid types without going cross-eyed

Hybrid terminology can feel like a marketing maze with extra dead ends because it's describing two different things at once. Some labels tell you how much electric driving the car can do (mild, full, and plug-in). Others describe how the drivetrain is arranged (series, parallel, and multi-mode). Brochures love to mix those labels together, but you don't need to untangle every engineering detail. Here's a practical way to think about the main hybrid types you'll actually encounter:

- **Mild hybrid (often 48-volt):** The electric system assists the engine and smooths stop/start, but usually can't drive the car on electricity alone. This type is great for efficiency gains without major complexity for the driver.
- **Full hybrid (parallel hybrid):** The engine and electric motor can both drive the wheels. The car can creep or cruise short distances on electric power, especially at low speed.
- **Series hybrid:** The gasoline engine mainly acts as a generator. Electric motors do the driving. This design can feel EV-like, especially around town.
- **Plug-in hybrid (PHEV):** This design features a hybrid with a larger battery that you can charge from the grid. Many PHEVs can cover daily errands on electricity and then operate like a regular hybrid on longer trips.

- **Two-mode and multi-mode hybrids:** More complex drivetrains that can operate in multiple mechanical and electric modes. You don't need to memorize the details — just know the hardware can be more complicated.

REMEMBER

Hybrid doesn't automatically mean plug-in. If your trunk doesn't have a charge port or cord, it's a conventional hybrid — it recharges itself through the engine and regenerative braking.

How regenerative braking works

Regenerative braking (regen) is one of the biggest hybrid and EV party tricks. When you slow down, the drive motor can act like a generator. Instead of turning all your momentum into heat at the brake pads, the system turns some of that motion back into electricity and stores it in the high-voltage battery.

In real life, regen feels like gentle engine braking — the car slows down as you lift off the accelerator. When you press the brake pedal, many hybrids blend two kinds of braking together:

- **Regenerative braking:** The motor or generator creates electrical drag and charges the battery.
- **Friction braking:** Traditional brake pads and rotors provide stopping power, especially at low speed or in hard stops.

You don't get 100 percent regen all the time, though (sadly, physics won't sign off on free energy):

- A full battery can't accept much more charge, so regen is reduced.
- A very cold battery may limit regen until it warms up.
- Hard braking still requires friction brakes (physics doesn't negotiate).

TIP

If a hybrid feels grabby or inconsistent in the last few feet of a stop, that's often the system handing off from regen to friction braking at low speed. It's usually normal. But if it's severe or comes with warning lights, get it checked.

REMEMBER

Regen reduces brake wear, but it doesn't delete your brakes from existence. You still need friction brakes for hard stops, and you still need periodic brake service to prevent sticking calipers and rusty rotors.

Hybrid performance and efficiency benefits

Hybrids shine in the exact situations that make gasoline engines inefficient: creeping, idling, short hops, and stop-and-go traffic. Electric motors deliver instant torque at low RPM, so takeoffs can feel smooth — and sometimes surprisingly peppy.

On the efficiency side, hybrids win by cutting idle time, capturing energy during deceleration, and letting the engine operate in its happy zone more often instead of lugging around at inefficient loads.

TECHNICAL STUFF

Don't be surprised if a hybrid's engine sounds a little different from a traditional automatic. Many hybrids use eCVT-style drivetrains that let engine speed change independently of road speed. It can sound like the engine holds RPM — that's usually normal behavior, not slipping.

Hybrid maintenance: What's the same, what's different

A hybrid still has plenty of normal car maintenance, because it still has an engine, coolant, brakes, tires, and suspension. But some tasks happen less often, while a few new ones show up.

Here's the practical checklist — no secret handshake required — and what's basically the same as a nonhybrid:

- Oil changes still matter, so follow the oil-life monitor or the manual — don't make up intervals.
- Air filters, cabin filters, wiper blades, tires, and brake fluid service still apply.
- Engine cooling system service still matters on engine-based hybrids.

And here's what's different or extra on many hybrids:

- The 12-volt battery is still critical (and sometimes smaller than you expect). A weak 12-volt can cause bizarre "computer says no" behavior.
- Some hybrids have dedicated inverter or motor coolant loops. Use the correct coolant type — mixing whatever's on the shelf is a great way to create expensive problems.
- Battery cooling systems may have filters or ducting that need to stay clean (especially if a cabin-air intake vent is near a rear seat).

- Brakes can rust from underuse. Occasional firm stops (when safe) help keep rotors clean and calipers moving.

WARNING

High-voltage hybrid components and orange cables aren't DIY-friendly. Looking is fine. Probing, disconnecting, or opening high-voltage components is not. Treat orange like a Do Not Touch sign.

Electric Vehicles (EVs): Going Fully Electric

An EV skips the entire combustion side of the story: no fuel tank, no exhaust, and no engine that needs sparks, air-fuel mixing, and emissions cleanup. Skipping the combustion hardware removes a huge list of parts — and a huge list of classic failure modes.

But EVs aren't maintenance-free. They just shift your attention to different systems: tires, brakes, cooling loops, software updates, and that still-important 12-volt electrical system.

EV basics: Batteries, motors, and inverters

Strip an EV down to essentials, and it's a big battery feeding one or more electric motors. The complicated-sounding parts are mostly the grown-ups in the room that manage and protect that energy flow.

Here are the building blocks you'll hear about most often (with the plain-English job description):

- **Battery pack (high-voltage DC):** Stores energy, usually in a large pack under the floor for safety and space efficiency.
- **Battery Management System (BMS):** Monitors cell voltages and temperature, controls charging/discharging, and protects the pack.
- **Inverter:** Turns battery DC into AC for the drive motor(s) and converts AC back into DC during regenerative braking.
- **Electric motor(s):** Provide torque to move the vehicle. Some EVs use one motor, others use two or more for AWD and performance.
- **Reduction gear (single-speed):** Reduces the electric motor's high-speed rotation into usable wheel speed, usually without the multi-speed transmission found in gasoline vehicles.

» **Onboard charger:** Converts AC power from Level 1/Level 2 charging into DC power for the battery.

» **DC-DC converter plus 12-volt battery:** Runs the regular car electronics and wakes up the computers, just like a gas car.

Figure 10-2 shows the basic EV powertrain layout, tracing energy flow from the high-voltage battery through the inverter and motor to the wheels. Unlike a gasoline vehicle, an EV usually has no exhaust system and no multi-speed transmission shifting through gears. Power moves through a much simpler path — battery to inverter to motor to reduction gear to wheels — which is one reason EVs feel so smooth and quiet.

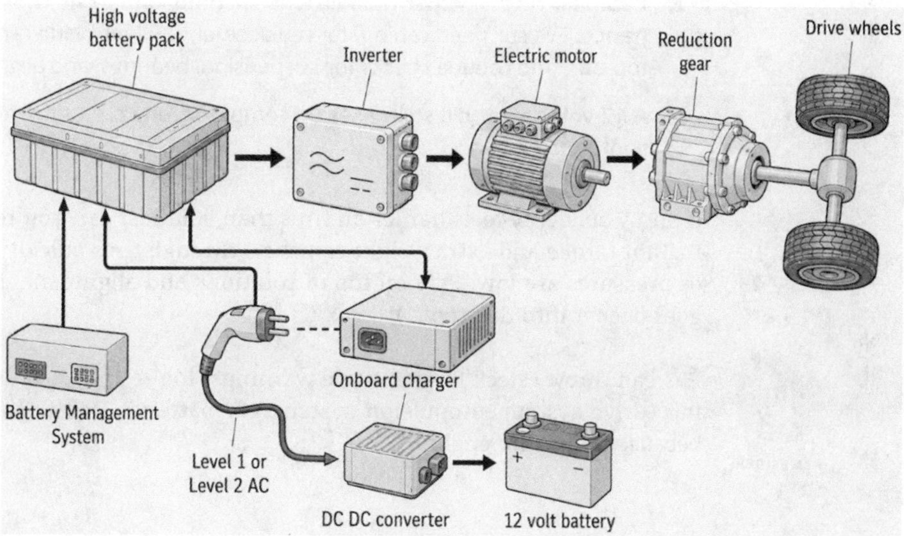

FIGURE 10-2: EV powertrain basics.

Generated with AI using OpenAI

Maintenance differences from combustion vehicles

EV maintenance is mostly about what disappears — and what stubbornly remains. Here's the quick, real-world comparison on the things EVs usually don't have (and therefore don't service):

» Oil changes, spark plugs, timing belts/chains related to an engine, and most engine-air/fuel hardware

» Exhaust systems and emissions components, including catalysts, O_2 sensors, and mufflers

» Traditional automatic transmission service (many EVs use a simple reduction gear instead)

Things EVs still have (and still need attention) include

» **Tires:** EV torque and vehicle weight can accelerate tire wear. Rotation and correct inflation matter more than ever.

» **Brakes:** Regen reduces wear, but brakes still need periodic use and inspection to prevent rust and sticking hardware.

» **Cooling systems:** Many EVs have coolant loops for the battery, inverter, and motor. Coolant type and service intervals still matter.

» **Cabin air filters, wiper blades, washer fluid, and basic chassis maintenance:** EVs still need cabin-filter replacements, wiper-blade care, washer-fluid top-offs, and routine checks for suspension, bearings, and alignment.

» **A 12-volt battery:** It still wakes up computers and closes the high-voltage contactors.

TIP

If an EV suddenly feels harder on tires than your last car, you're not imagining it. Instant torque and extra weight can chew through tires quickly if alignment is off or pressures are low. Stay on top of rotations and alignment checks. (Chapter 18 goes deeper into this topic.)

REMEMBER

EVs can throw Check Engine-style warnings, too — they just use different wording (drive system, propulsion system, HV battery). Don't ignore warnings just because there's no engine.

Charging 101: Levels, charging times, and range considerations

Charging is the EV version of fueling — but instead of one pump speed, you have several charging levels with very different power rates. The good news is that daily charging is usually easy: Plug in at home or work, wake up with a full enough battery, and repeat.

The confusing part is the vocabulary: Level 1, Level 2, DC fast charging, kW, kWh, and why charging slows down as the battery fills. Let's translate it into human.

AC charging versus DC fast charging

Level 1 and Level 2 charging are AC charging. That means the car's onboard charger does the work of converting AC wall power into the DC power the battery can store.

DC fast charging is different: The charging station does the conversion, and the car accepts high-power DC directly into the battery — under strict temperature and safety control.

Charging levels in plain English

Charging speed depends on the charger, the car, battery temperature, and state of charge. But you can still think in useful ballparks:

- **Level 1 (120V household outlet):** Slow, but convenient. Best for low daily mileage or overnight top-offs.
- **Level 2 (240V home charger or public AC):** The daily sweet spot for most EV owners. Much faster than Level 1 and gentle on the battery.
- **DC fast charging (public highway chargers):** Best for road trips and quick boosts. Fast at low state of charge, slower as the battery fills.

Figure 10-3 compares the three main charging levels — Level 1, Level 2, and DC fast charging — so that you can see how dramatically charging speed changes.

It also explains why most EV owners rely on Level 2 for daily driving and save DC fast charging for road trips.

TECHNICAL STUFF

kW is charging speed (power). kWh is battery size/energy (how much fuel you have). Think of kW as the flow rate and kWh as the bucket size.

Quick math you can actually use: Charging time (hours) ≈ kWh you need to add ÷ kW you're charging at.

Range considerations (why the estimate moves around)

An EV's range estimate is like a weather forecast (or your phone's battery percentage): useful, but not a sworn oath. Drive faster, climb hills, blast heat, or fight a headwind, and the estimate drops — because physics is doing its thing. Unlike gas cars, many EVs can be more efficient in city driving (regen helps) and less efficient on the highway (wind resistance wins).

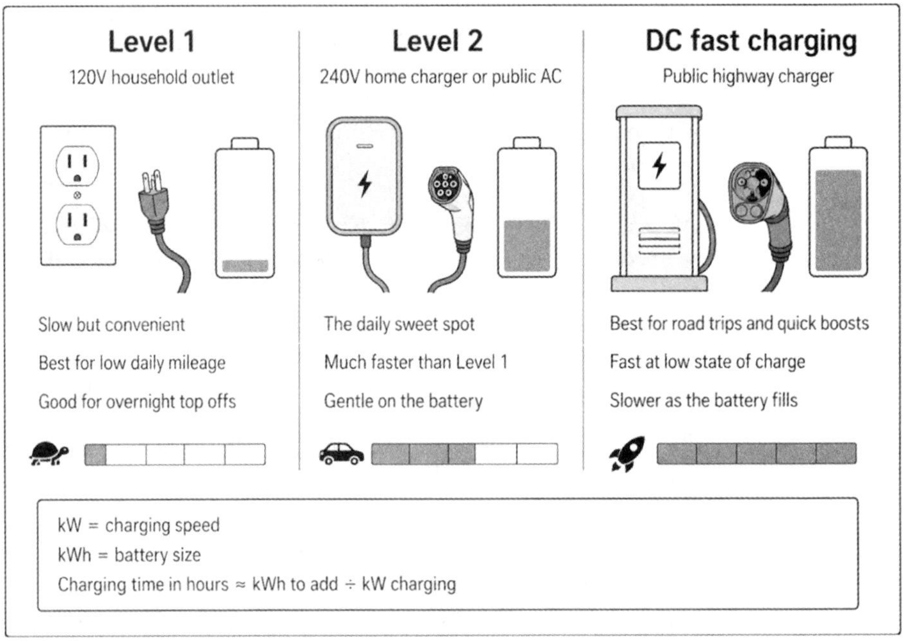

FIGURE 10-3: Charging levels at a glance.

Generated with AI using OpenAI

The biggest real-world range influencers are usually:

- **Speed:** Highway speeds burn energy faster than city driving (air resistance rises sharply as speed increases).
- **Temperature:** Cold weather reduces battery performance and increases heating demand; extreme heat increases cooling demand.
- **Tires and pressure:** Underinflation and aggressive tread can reduce range.
- **Cargo, roof racks, and towing:** Extra weight and drag cut range — sometimes dramatically.
- **Elevation and wind:** Long climbs and headwinds are energy-hungry; long descents can recover some energy with regen.

TIP

For road trips, arrive at fast chargers with some battery left — not nearly empty — and plan more frequent, shorter charging stops instead of one giant charge-to-100-percent session. Most EVs charge fastest in the lower part of the battery and slow down above roughly 70 to 80 percent.

Battery Thermal Management

Batteries are picky about temperature. Too cold, and they deliver less power and accept charge slowly. Too hot, and they age faster — and the car will protect itself by limiting power or charging speed.

Thermal management is the system that keeps the battery in its comfort zone. It's a big reason modern EVs and hybrids can be quick, safe, and reliable without cooking their own batteries.

What thermal management actually does

Depending on the vehicle, thermal management can include liquid cooling, electric heaters, heat pumps, valves, pumps, radiators, and a whole lot of sensors. The goal is simple: Keep the battery (and power electronics) near the temperature range where they perform best and last longest.

You see thermal management in action when:

- Fast charging slows down because the battery is heating up and the car is protecting it.
- Cold weather reduces regenerative braking until the pack warms.
- The car preconditions the battery before a fast-charge stop when you navigate to a charger.

Practical habits that protect battery health

Battery life isn't magic — it's the result of good design plus decent habits. You don't need to baby your EV, but a few simple behaviors can reduce long-term stress on the pack.

Here are smart habits most manufacturers agree with:

- Use a daily charge limit (often 70 to 90 percent) if your car offers it and only charge to 100 percent when you need the range soon.
- Avoid leaving the car sitting at 100 percent for days in hot weather (high state of charge plus heat is a stress combo).
- Don't make arrive at 0 percent your personality. Low state of charge is fine occasionally, but living there adds stress.
- If possible, park in shade or a garage in extreme temperatures.

- » Let the car precondition before fast charging (using the built-in navigation when available).

REMEMBER

Charging slowing down at higher state of charge is normal. It's the car protecting the battery. If you need 100 percent for a trip, charge to 100 percent as close to departure time as practical.

WARNING

Never open, drill into, or "just inspect" a high-voltage battery pack. Even when the car is off, high-voltage components can be dangerous. Cooling-system service on EV battery loops can also require special procedures — when in doubt, use a qualified shop.

Ethanol and Flex-Fuel Vehicles

In addition to hybrids and EVs, other future fuels are already in the mix — starting with ethanol. In many places, E10 (10 percent ethanol) is the everyday default, and higher blends are popping up at more stations every year.

WARNING

Most modern gasoline vehicles are perfectly fine with the blends approved by the manufacturer — but only if you know what your car is designed to tolerate. The big mistake is assuming every gasoline engine is flex-fuel. (It isn't).

What are flex-fuel vehicles?

A *flex-fuel vehicle* (often labeled FFV) is designed to run on gasoline, ethanol blends, and — on many models — E85 (up to 85 percent ethanol, depending on season and region). "Designed to" is the key. FFVs use fuel-system materials that can handle higher ethanol content, and their computers are calibrated to adjust fueling when the blend changes.

Your engine computer doesn't guess the blend by vibes. Flex-fuel systems either use a sensor to measure ethanol content or infer it from how the engine responds and then automatically tweak fuel delivery and ignition timing.

You can tell whether your vehicle is flex-fuel (without playing "hope this is the right fuel") by:

- » Checking the owner's manual or the fuel-door label (best source).
- » Looking for Flex-Fuel, FFV, or E85 labeling on the fuel door, window sticker, or under-hood emissions label.

- Using a VIN/parts lookup or the manufacturer's app/site if you're unsure (some trims have it, others don't).

REMEMBER

If your vehicle isn't explicitly rated for E85, don't use it just to see. E85 in a non-FFV can cause drivability problems and, in some cases, damage fuel-system components.

Pros and cons of ethanol use in modern engines

Ethanol has real benefits — and real tradeoffs. Knowing both keeps you from buying fuel based on pump-label chaos or your neighbor's confident-but-wrong advice.

Here's the upside list (why ethanol exists in the first place):

- Ethanol has a high octane rating, which can support knock resistance in some engines.
- It can be produced from renewable feedstocks, which reduces petroleum dependence.
- Many modern engines and fuel systems are designed around E10 as the normal baseline.

And here are the trade-offs (or what you notice first at the next fill-up):

- **Lower energy content:** Ethanol contains less energy per gallon than gasoline, so MPG often drops as ethanol percentage rises.
- **Cold-start behavior:** High-ethanol blends can be fussier in cold weather (your car compensates, but it may not love it).
- **Storage sensitivity:** Ethanol blends can attract moisture and can go stale faster if the vehicle sits for long stretches.

TIP

If your car sits a lot (seasonal vehicle, short-trip lifestyle, or "I work from home now" reality), don't let half a tank of high-ethanol fuel age in place for months. Use a fuel stabilizer for long storage and take an occasional longer drive to fully warm the engine and burn older fuel. (Chapter 8 has the fuel-freshness habits.)

Hydrogen and Fuel Cell Technology

Hydrogen fuel-cell vehicles are the quiet cousin in the alternative-power family. They drive like EVs (electric motors, instant torque, and regenerative braking), but they store energy as hydrogen gas instead of in a giant battery pack.

If you've ever wished for EV driving with gas-station-fast refueling, fuel cells are the idea behind that wish.

How fuel cells generate electricity

A fuel cell stack makes electricity through a chemical reaction between hydrogen (from the tank) and oxygen (from the air). The byproducts are heat and water — which is why fuel-cell vehicles can have water dripping from the tailpipe area.

A simplified fuel-cell powertrain includes these main components:

- High-pressure hydrogen tank stores the fuel.
- Fuel cell stack generates electricity on demand.
- A small battery buffers power for acceleration and regenerative braking.
- An electric motor drives the wheels through a reduction gear.

Figure 10-4 shows how a fuel-cell vehicle generates electricity onboard, using hydrogen to feed a fuel-cell stack that powers an electric motor. The small battery in the system acts as a buffer, smoothing power delivery and capturing energy during regenerative braking.

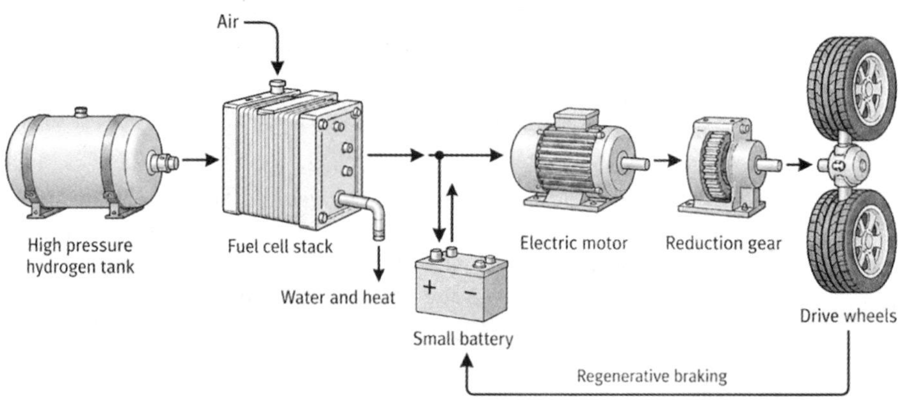

Generated with AI using OpenAI

FIGURE 10-4: Fuel-cell overview.

Advantages of hydrogen vehicles

Fuel-cell vehicles offer a few compelling upsides in the right context:

- **Fast refueling:** Minutes, similar to gasoline
- **Electric driving experience:** Smooth, quiet, instant torque
- **No tailpipe CO_2:** Water and heat at the tailpipe, useful in dense urban areas

Current challenges: Infrastructure, cost, and storage

Fuel cells aren't better EVs so much as EVs with different tradeoffs. The big hurdles today are less about the vehicle and more about the ecosystem around it.

Common real-world challenges include

- Limited fueling infrastructure, especially outside certain regions
- Variable hydrogen cost and supply, depending on location and availability
- High-pressure storage requirements, including expensive tanks and strict safety systems
- Limited low-carbon hydrogen production, especially at large scale

REMEMBER

Fuel-cell vehicles are still electric vehicles at the wheels. They just carry energy differently — in a tank of hydrogen instead of a huge battery.

Natural Gas and Other Alternative Fuels

Not every alternative-fuel story is about passenger cars. A lot of adoption happens in fleets first, where vehicles return to the same depot every night and fuel supply can be managed centrally.

That's why you'll hear about natural gas, renewable fuels, and synthetic fuels even if your personal next car is a hybrid or an EV.

Natural gas vehicles in fleets and commercial use

Natural gas vehicles (NGVs) typically run on compressed natural gas (CNG) or liquefied natural gas (LNG). They've been popular in some commercial fleets (buses, delivery trucks, utility fleets) because fuel cost can be competitive and tailpipe emissions can be lower than older gasoline or diesel designs.

The trade-offs are mostly practical:

- Fuel tanks are large, heavy, and high-pressure, which can reduce cargo space.
- Public fueling stations can be limited compared with gasoline/diesel.
- Conversions and modifications must be done correctly and legally (improper conversions can be dangerous and can fail inspections).

TIP

If you're considering an NGV conversion, treat it like emissions equipment: Use certified kits and professional installation and verify local inspection/legal requirements. Cheap, sketchy conversions are how you end up with a vehicle that's hard to service and hard to insure.

Other future fuels: Synthetic fuels, renewable options

Beyond electricity, hydrogen, and natural gas, you'll hear about synthetic fuels (sometimes called e-fuels) and renewable liquid fuels. The goal is to provide liquid fuel that can work in existing engines — ideally with lower net carbon impact — without rebuilding the entire fueling infrastructure overnight.

A few examples you might run into include:

- **Renewable diesel (different from biodiesel):** A diesel-like fuel made from renewable feedstocks, often used in fleets
- **Biodiesel blends (common in some regions):** See Chapters 8 and 11 for the details
- **Synthetic gasoline/diesel (e-fuels):** Made using captured carbon and renewable electricity, still expensive and not widely available

The big takeaway: These fuels may help in niches (aviation, heavy equipment, and legacy fleets), but for most drivers today, the practical future is hybrids, plug-in hybrids, and battery EVs — because those are already here and improving fast.

IN THIS CHAPTER

» Understanding diesel basics

» Following fuel delivery from old-school pumps to common rail systems

» Seeing how turbocharging and intercoolers create low-RPM torque and efficiency

» Starting strong in cold weather

» Living with clean-air tech

» Maintaining and diagnosing modern diesels

Chapter 11
Delving into Diesels

Diesel engines have a reputation: They're tough, they're torquey, and they'll run for what feels like three geological eras — as long as you treat them like a diesel and not like a gas engine that drank the wrong juice.

Here's the twist: A modern diesel isn't just an engine. It's an entire team sport — high-pressure fuel injection, turbocharged air management, and a cast of emissions characters (DPF, EGR, SCR/DEF) that all want the right driving habits and maintenance, or they'll throw a tantrum with a dashboard light show.

In this chapter, you get the owner-friendly roadmap: what's different, what's picky, what's pricey, and what you can do to keep your diesel out of limp mode and your savings account out of therapy.

Diesel Basics: What Makes Them Different

Before we dive into turbos and emissions hardware, we lock down the two fundamentals that explain most diesel behavior: how diesel combustion works and what diesel fuel is like. Get these right, and the rest of the chapter will feel a lot less like mysterious tractor magic.

Compression ignition versus spark ignition

A gasoline engine is like a kitchen stove: It mixes fuel and air, and then a spark plug provides the click that starts the burn right on schedule.

A diesel engine is more like a high-powered bicycle pump with attitude. It compresses only air so hard that the air gets hot enough to start a fight — and then the engine sprays fuel into that heat. The fuel lights off from temperature and pressure, so no spark is needed. In Figure 11-1, you can see how gas engines use a spark to start combustion; diesels use heat from compression.

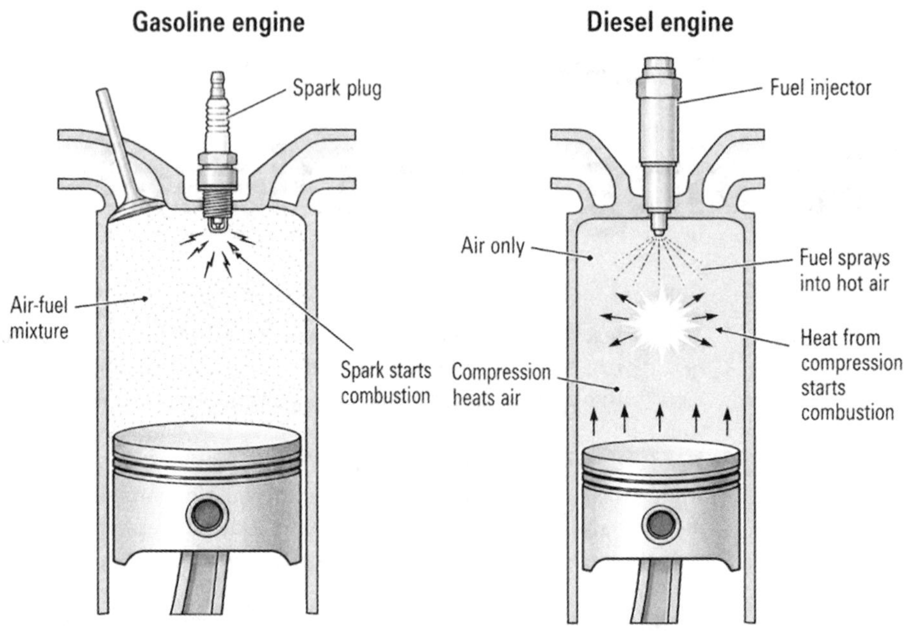

FIGURE 11-1: Diesel versus gasoline combustion.

Generated with AI using OpenAI

That one change rewrites the rulebook. Diesels run higher compression, create higher cylinder pressures, and depend on super-precise fuel delivery to control timing and power. It also explains the classic diesel clatter, especially at idle — you're hearing serious pressure changes happening fast, not a calm little candle flame.

REMEMBER

Diesels don't use spark plugs, but they often need help when it's cold. That's what glow plugs or intake heaters are for. See the section "Cold Starting and Glow Plugs," later in this chapter.

Diesel fuel properties and energy density

Diesel fuel is different from gasoline in ways that matter at the pump, in the tank, and inside the engine. It's less volatile (it doesn't evaporate as easily), and it packs more energy per gallon. That extra energy is a big reason diesels can deliver strong fuel economy — especially when you're hauling, towing, or climbing hills without begging the engine to downshift into next week.

Diesel is also rated by cetane, not octane. Think of it this way: Cetane is about how readily and consistently the fuel ignites under compression. Octane is about how stubbornly a fuel resists igniting too soon. Gas engines love that resistance. Diesels don't — in a diesel, reliable lights-on-time combustion is the whole point.

TIP

If you're coming from the gasoline world, ditch the higher-octane-is-better reflex. Diesels don't want premium-grade stubbornness — they want the correct diesel fuel for your region and season, plus whatever your owner's manual allows for biodiesel blends.

Fuel Delivery in Modern Diesels

A diesel lights fuel using compression and heat, so the next question is how does the fuel get delivered at exactly the right moment?

Spoiler: Diesel fuel delivery has evolved from rugged farm equipment to surgical robot with a PhD in timing, and that's a big reason modern diesels make great power and throw expensive tantrums when fuel quality is sloppy.

Mechanical pumps as history

Older diesels used mechanical injection pumps — basically a super-strong fuel metering device driven by the engine itself. No fancy computer decisions — just cams, springs, and precision machining doing the job.

These systems were tough and straightforward, like a cast-iron skillet: not delicate, not picky, and usually happy as long as you didn't feed them mud. The pump pushed fuel to the injectors at the right time, and the injectors popped open when pressure got high enough.

The downside? Mechanical systems weren't nearly as flexible or precise. Timing and fuel amount couldn't be adjusted on the fly the way modern engines do, so older diesels were often louder, smokier, and not as clean or efficient — especially during cold starts or sudden acceleration. Emissions and efficiency demands pushed diesel injection from purely mechanical timing to computer-controlled precision.

REMEMBER

Older mechanical diesels can be more forgiving, but forgiving doesn't mean they're invincible. Dirty fuel still causes wear — it just may take longer to show up (like cavities when you only sometimes floss).

Common rail systems

Modern diesels mostly use *common rail injection:* A high-pressure pump feeds a shared fuel rail, and the ECU tells each injector exactly when and how much fuel to spray. For the full fuel-system tour, see Chapter 7, especially the section "Fuel Delivery in Today's Engines."

Here's the diesel-specific takeaway: Common rail systems help modern diesels run quieter, cleaner, and more efficiently, but they're picky. The pump, rail, and injectors work with extremely tight tolerances, so clean fuel and proper filtration matter a lot. (For maintenance habits that protect those parts, see Chapter 8.)

Common rail systems are where the ECU really starts showing off: It can command multiple tiny injections during one combustion event — a small pre-injection, the main injection, and sometimes a post-injection. This multiple-injection strategy helps modern diesels run quieter, cleaner, and more efficiently because the fuel burn is smoother and better controlled.

Figure 11-2 shows the difference between an older mechanical pump design and a modern common rail system.

The trade-off is sensitivity: Common rail systems need clean fuel and proper filtration because the parts are built with ultra-tight tolerances. In diesel terms, close enough is another way of saying expensive.

WARNING

Common rail fuel pressure isn't high like a tire or a fuel pump on a gas engine — it's high like industrial equipment. Don't loosen fuel lines or crack fittings to see what happens. What happens can be injury . . . and a repair bill that makes your wallet leave the chat.

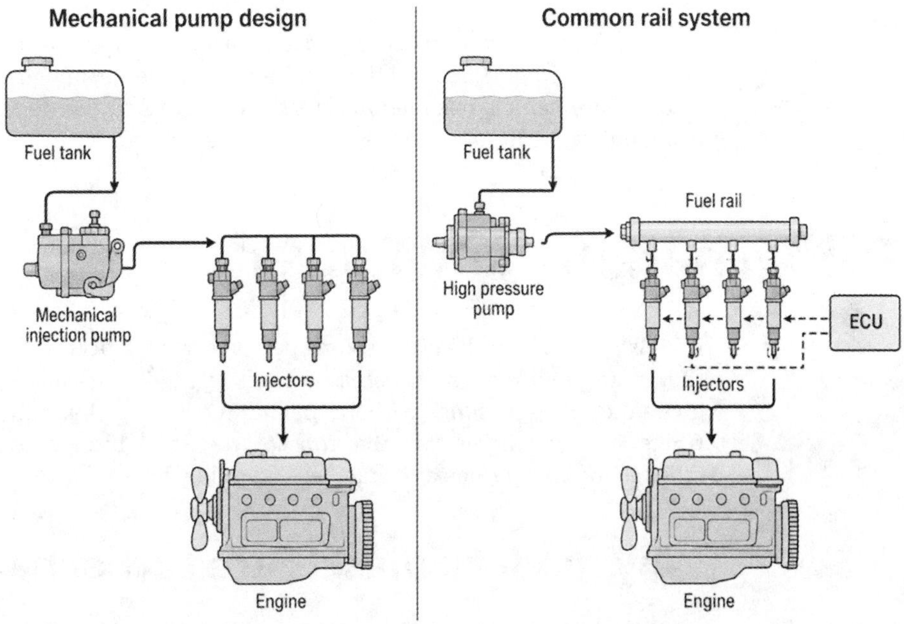

FIGURE 11-2: Older mechanical pump design versus modern common rail system.

Generated with AI using OpenAI

High-pressure injectors

Diesel injectors aren't just valves — they're precision spray devices that turn liquid fuel into an extremely fine mist. Instead of a squirt gun, think perfume atomizer. . . except the perfume is diesel, and the pressure can cut your confidence in half.

Because injector holes are tiny and tolerances are tight, injectors are sensitive to:

- **Dirt:** Acts like sandpaper
- **Water:** Causes corrosion and poor combustion
- **Poor fuel quality:** Can mess with spray pattern and timing

When injectors aren't happy, your diesel usually tells you with symptoms like:

- Hard starting
- Rough idle
- More smoke than usual
- Less power, worse mileage
- A knock or clatter under load

TIP

Want to be nice to your injectors? Do the boring stuff like a pro: Buy fuel from busy stations (fresh fuel), replace the fuel filter on schedule, and drain the water separator if your vehicle has one. Injectors love clean fuel the way humans love clean drinking water: It's not exciting, but it prevents drama.

Turbocharging and Power

Diesels make power the way a strong person carries groceries: They don't sprint — they grunt and move mountains. Turbocharging is basically how manufacturers give a diesel bigger lungs without making the engine physically the size of a mini fridge. Once you understand that concept, the turbo, intercooler, and boost control stop feeling mysterious and start feeling mildly bossy.

Why modern diesels are turbocharged

Most modern diesels are turbocharged because boost is the easiest way to give a diesel what it always wants: more air. More air lets the engine burn more fuel cleanly, which means more torque, less smoke, and better combustion — especially at the low RPM range where diesels like to live.

Turbocharging also lets manufacturers use a smaller engine that still pulls hard. So you get a vehicle that feels calm and confident when towing or climbing hills — without revving like it's trying to win a karaoke contest.

Role of intercoolers

Here's the turbo's little problem: When you compress air, you heat it up. And hot air is like a puffy winter coat — it takes up space but doesn't pack as much oxygen. Less oxygen means less efficient combustion and a harder time staying clean and happy.

That's why boosted engines use an intercooler to cool the compressed air before it goes into the intake. Cooler air is denser, which means the engine gets more oxygen in every gulp. Follow the air flow in Figure 11-3.

If a charge pipe splits, a clamp loosens, or the intercooler leaks, a diesel can suddenly feel weak or smoky — like the turbo showed up to work but forgot its badge.

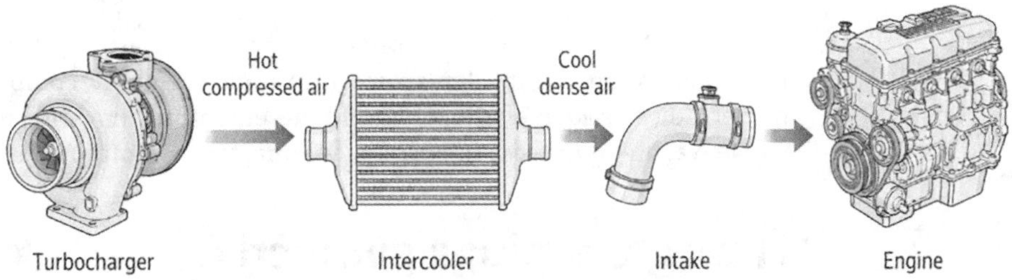

Generated with AI using OpenAI

FIGURE 11-3: Turbo plus intercooler air path.

Common clues include:

- A loud whoosh or hiss under acceleration
- A sudden loss of power (like the turbo stopped participating)
- More black smoke under load (fuel is there, but air isn't)
- A reduced power message or Check Engine light on many vehicles

TIP

Do a quick visual check for oily residue around boost hoses and intercooler connections. A light oil film can be normal in many turbo systems, but wet, messy oil plus a loose hose is a strong hint you've found a boost leak.

Boost and efficiency benefits

Many diesels use a *variable-geometry turbocharger* (VGT). Instead of a simple on/off approach with a wastegate, a VGT adjusts vane position to control how exhaust hits the turbine. In plain English: A VGT helps the turbo spool fast at low RPM (less lag) and helps prevent over-boost at higher RPM.

Because the ECU can control boost so precisely, it can balance power, fuel economy, and emissions more effectively. The same strategies that make a diesel feel strong and smooth can also help it hit soot and NOx targets — which is the automotive version of being powerful and well-behaved.

REMEMBER

A turbo code doesn't automatically mean the turbo is dead. Boost leaks, sensor problems, clogged air filters, and stuck actuators can all imitate turbo failure — so diagnose the easy stuff before you start shopping for expensive spinning metal.

Cold Starting and Glow Plugs

Cold weather is where a diesel's "I light fuel with heat" personality gets a little dramatic — because when the engine is freezing, it's harder to build enough heat for clean ignition. That issue is why *glow plugs* (and sometimes intake heaters) exist: They're basically the diesel's toaster oven, warming things up so the first few combustion events don't turn into a slow, smoky complaint. And because modern diesels love efficiency (and hate embarrassing cold-start behavior), the whole warm-up process is now faster, smarter, and often controlled by the ECU.

How glow plugs evolved

Early glow plugs took noticeable time to heat up, and cold starts could be a slow, smoky event. Modern glow plugs heat faster, last longer, and are often monitored by the ECU so that the system can detect a weak plug before it leaves you stranded.

Some diesels use intake air heaters (often a grid heater in the intake) instead of, or in addition to, glow plugs. The goal is the same: Get enough heat into the air and combustion chamber so that the first few injections burn cleanly.

ECU-managed preheating

On many vehicles, the Wait to Start or glow plug light is the ECU telling you it's preheating the engine. That little pause makes a big difference in cold weather: easier starting, less white smoke, and less strain on the starter and batteries.

WARNING

If your diesel has a Wait to Start light, actually wait. Starting early can mean rough running, white smoke, and longer crank times.

Modern cold-start strategies

Cold starts are not just about glow plugs. A diesel needs good cranking speed (because compression is high), the right fuel for the temperature, and enough heat in the right places. A few habits make winter much easier:

- **Keep the batteries healthy.** Weak batteries are one of the most common causes of hard starting on diesels.
- **Use winter-blend diesel** from a reputable, high-turnover station when temperatures drop.
- **Keep the tank above one-quarter** in very cold weather to reduce condensation and gelling risk.
- **If your manufacturer recommends** an anti-gel additive, use it correctly — and before the fuel gels.
- **If you have a block heater,** use it when temperatures are extreme (it reduces wear and improves starting).

WARNING

If your diesel suddenly won't start in extreme cold, avoid creative fixes like starting fluid unless the manufacturer explicitly allows it. Some engines and intake heaters can be damaged by it.

TIP

If your diesel cranks slowly, don't just blame diesel being diesel. Load-test the battery (or batteries) and check connections. Starting issues that look fuel-related can be electrical.

Diesel Emissions and Clean Air Tech

Modern diesel emissions gear is basically the engine's don't-be-a-chimney kit. It catches soot, cuts smog-forming gases, and tries to keep everything clean-ish — but it only works well when you drive and maintain the vehicle like it's a modern machine, not a 1993 tractor with unlimited free passes.

Figure 11-4 shows a typical diesel aftertreatment layout — from the turbo outlet through the DOC/DPF, DEF injector, SCR catalyst, and the sensors that keep the whole system honest.

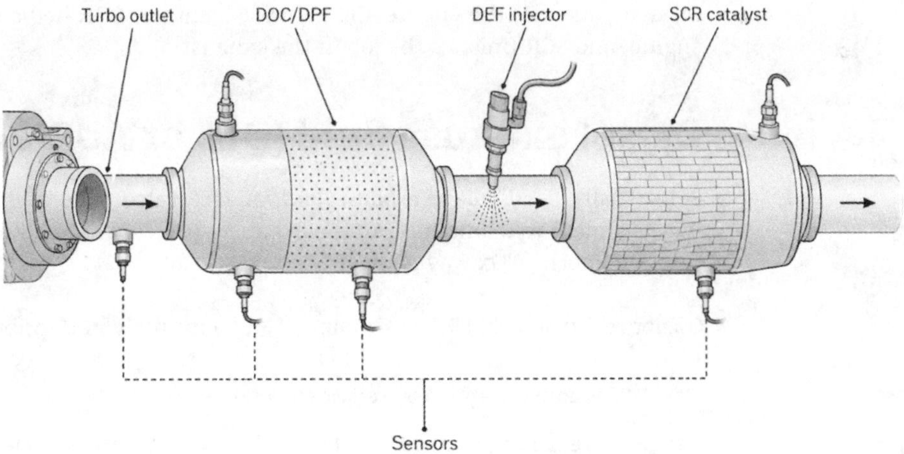

FIGURE 11-4: Diesel aftertreatment layout.

Generated with AI using OpenAI

Diesel particulate filters (DPF)

A *diesel particulate filter*, or DPF, is the exhaust system's lint trap. It catches soot so that it doesn't leave the tailpipe as that classic black "look at me" cloud. To keep from clogging, the DPF has to cook the soot into ash once in a while. That cooking process is called *regeneration* (regen).

Regen usually shows up in three styles:

- **Passive regen:** Happens naturally on longer, steady drives when exhaust temperatures are already high enough to burn off soot.
- **Active regen:** Happens when the computer turns up the heat on purpose, often by adding fuel or changing timing.
- **Parked/forced regen:** Happens when soot load gets too high, and the DPF needs a more controlled cleaning cycle, often started with a scan tool or performed at a shop.

REMEMBER

Regen burns soot into a tiny amount of ash. Soot is the part that can be burned off; ash is what slowly accumulates. Over time, that ash buildup can make the DPF need professional cleaning or replacement — especially if you use the wrong oil.

Selective catalytic reduction (SCR)

Selective catalytic reduction, or SCR, is the system that tackles NOx (smog-forming gases). Think of SCR as the exhaust's chemistry lab: When the exhaust is hot enough, the SCR catalyst helps convert NOx into less harmful stuff.

On many diesels, the engine and exhaust team up: EGR helps reduce NOx in the engine, and SCR finishes the job in the exhaust.

Diesel exhaust fluid (DEF or AdBlue)

SCR usually needs *diesel exhaust fluid*, or DEF (also called AdBlue). The vehicle injects a measured amount into the exhaust upstream of the SCR catalyst, and the reaction knocks NOx way down.

Owner reality check: DEF is simple . . . and absolutely not optional:

- **DEF is consumable.** You refill it sometimes.
- **DEF freezes around 12°F (−11°C).** That's normal; the vehicle is designed to thaw it.
- **DEF quality matters.** Contamination can trigger warnings and faults.
- **DEF warnings can escalate.** If DEF is low or a fault occurs, many systems can eventually reduce power or start a no-start countdown.

TIP

Keep the DEF filler area clean, use sealed containers, and don't experiment. DEF is not close enough to anything else.

Exhaust gas recirculation (EGR)

Exhaust gas recirculation, or EGR, reduces NOx by lowering combustion temperatures. EGR lowers the temperatures by feeding a measured amount of exhaust back into the intake — basically diluting the incoming air so that combustion runs cooler.

The downside is mess: EGR brings soot into the intake stream. Soot plus oil vapor equals sticky gunk, and over time, that gunk can clog EGR valves, coolers, and intake passages, which can lead to rough idle, reduced power, and flow-related trouble codes.

WARNING

Disabling or removing emissions equipment is illegal in many places and can create reliability and drivability problems. The goal is to keep these systems working, not delete them.

Maintenance Musts

Diesel maintenance isn't complicated; it's just less forgiving. Think of a modern diesel as a strong, hardworking machine with two rules: Keep its fuel and oil clean, and let the emissions system finish its self-cleaning routines once in a while.

TIP

Start with fuel filtration, because in diesel world, dirty fuel doesn't just cause a hiccup; it can write a very expensive love letter to your wallet.

Figure 11-5 shows the diesel maintenance priority pyramid: Start with clean fuel and good filtration, use the correct oil spec, let regens finish (and don't idle forever), and always scan codes and save freeze-frame data before you hit Clear like it's a magic erase button.

Fuel filters and water separation

If diesels care about one maintenance item more than most gasoline engines, it's fuel filtration. Diesel injectors and high-pressure pumps have tiny clearances, and dirt or water can cause expensive damage.

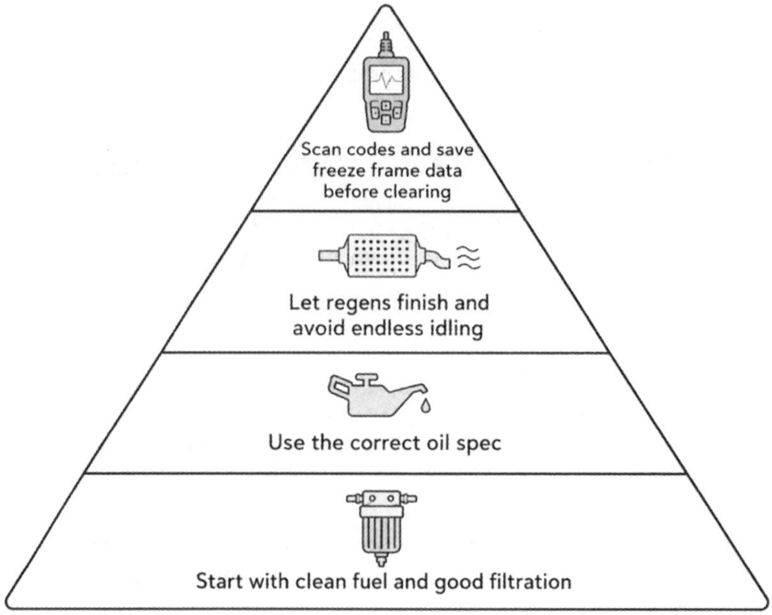

Generated with AI using OpenAI

FIGURE 11-5: Diesel maintenance priorities pyramid.

Many diesels include a water separator and a drain. Some have a water-in-fuel sensor. The goal is simple: Catch water before it reaches the high-pressure system.

Here are a few practical habits that can help:

- Replace fuel filters on schedule (or sooner if you suspect bad fuel).
- Buy diesel from high-turnover stations (fresh fuel, less chance of water).
- If your vehicle has a water separator drain, follow the owner's manual procedure and don't ignore a water-in-fuel warning.

REMEMBER

On many diesels, a clogged fuel filter doesn't just reduce performance; it can cause hard starting, stalling, and fuel-pressure codes.

Oil change intervals

Diesel engines often require oils with specific additive packages, and many modern diesels require low-ash (low-SAPS) oils to protect the DPF. Using the wrong oil can increase ash accumulation in the DPF over time — the slow, expensive kind of problem.

REMEMBER

Follow the exact oil spec in the owner's manual (not just the viscosity). On a modern diesel, the spec matters as much as the weight.

As for intervals, don't guess. Follow the manufacturer's schedule and pay attention to the oil life monitor if your vehicle has one. Short trips, heavy towing, and lots of idling can all shorten the normal interval because they increase soot loading and fuel dilution in the oil.

DPF regeneration cycles

The best practice is boring — and boring is good. If the vehicle tells you regen is in progress or asks you to keep driving, do it. A steady 15 to 30 minute drive (often at highway speeds) is a common way vehicles complete regen, but always follow the message and your owner's manual for your specific system.

WARNING

Ignoring repeated regen requests can lead to a clogged DPF, limp mode, and expensive repairs. Short-trip diesel life is hard on aftertreatment.

The following diesel-friendly driving habits help most emissions systems:

- **Give the vehicle regular fully warmed drives.** A longer trip every week or two helps.
- **Avoid excessive idling.** It creates soot without getting the exhaust hot enough to clean it.
- **Don't shut the engine off mid-regen, if you can help it.** Some vehicles resume later; others get grumpier.
- **Fix misfires, boost leaks, and fuel issues promptly.** They can overload the DPF quickly.

Special attention to injector cleanliness

Injector cleanliness is not just about a cleaner additive. It's mostly about prevention: clean fuel, good filtration, and no water in the system. Contamination that wouldn't bother an older diesel can damage common rail injectors.

REMEMBER

If your manual allows fuel additives, use only reputable diesel additives and follow directions. More is not better. The bigger win is consistent maintenance and avoiding questionable fuel sources.

Diagnostics in the Diesel Age

Modern diesels have more sensors than a spaceship, which means the engine computer usually tells you when it's unhappy — loudly. The goal here is to read the clues (codes, live data, and a few quick checks) so that you fix the real problem instead of guessing, panic-buying parts, or blaming the turbo for everything.

OBD-II diesel codes

Yes, diesels use OBD-II, and the Check Engine light is still the ECU asking for attention. The difference is what the ECU is watching: boost control, fuel pressure, emissions efficiency, soot load, and a lot of sensors that gasoline engines simply do not have.

When a warning light appears, start with a code scan. If your scan tool supports it, save freeze-frame data — it's basically a screenshot of what the engine was doing when it decided to complain.

TIP

If you get a reduced-power message, scan for codes before clearing anything. Clearing codes can erase clues and make an intermittent fault harder to find.

Regen cycle monitoring

Some vehicles show regen status on the dash. Others hint at it with higher idle speed, cooling fans running hard, or a hot smell near the tailpipe area. If your diesel offers a "DPF regen in progress" message, take it seriously and let the system finish.

Many scan tools can display useful diesel-specific data, such as soot load, exhaust temperature sensors, and regen counters. Those numbers can help you confirm whether a drivability problem is tied to aftertreatment or something else (like a boost leak).

NOx sensor faults

NOx sensors are part of the SCR system's feedback loop. They help the ECU determine whether the SCR catalyst is doing its job and whether DEF dosing is correct. When a NOx sensor fails or reads out of range, the vehicle may trigger warnings, set efficiency codes, and sometimes reduce power to protect emissions compliance.

Because NOx sensor problems can look like DEF problems (and vice versa), accurate diagnosis matters. A code scan is the starting point; a qualified shop may be needed for pinpoint testing.

DEF level and quality sensors

Modern DEF tanks often have level sensors, temperature sensors, and quality sensors. Those sensors are good for emissions control, but they also mean that the vehicle can complain loudly if the system thinks DEF is low, frozen, or contaminated.

If you see repeated DEF warnings, don't ignore them. Many vehicles use a countdown strategy that can eventually limit speed or prevent restarting until the fault is addressed.

WARNING

If you're losing coolant, overheating, and seeing persistent white smoke, don't keep driving and hope it disappears. That combination can indicate a serious engine problem.

Alternative Diesel Fuels

Diesel fuel isn't a single, boring one-size-fits-all liquid anymore — it's more like a menu with options, blends, and a few names that sound like sci-fi. The good news is you don't need a chemistry degree to navigate it; you just need to know what your engine is approved to drink (and what can cause cold-weather drama).

Biodiesel blends (B5, B20, B100)

The most common alternative you'll actually see at the pump are biodiesel blends. *Biodiesel* is a diesel-like fuel made from renewable oils or fats. It's often blended with petroleum diesel, such as B5 (5 percent biodiesel), B20 (20 percent), or higher blends in some regions.

Many modern vehicles are approved for lower blends, but don't assume every diesel is happy with every blend. Check the owner's manual for approved biodiesel percentages because high blends can affect cold-weather performance, fuel system materials, and warranty coverage.

TIP

If you use biodiesel in cold climates, pay extra attention to winter blend guidance. Some biodiesel blends can gel at higher temperatures than straight petroleum diesel.

Renewable diesel

Renewable diesel (often made by hydrotreating, sometimes called HVO) is different from biodiesel even though the names sound similar and is chemically closer to petroleum diesel. In many applications, renewable diesel can be used as a drop-in fuel with fewer cold-flow and stability issues than biodiesel blends.

Availability varies by region, but renewable diesel is growing because it can reduce lifecycle emissions while working within existing diesel infrastructure.

Synthetic diesel and future fuels

You'll also hear about synthetic diesel (sometimes called *e-fuels*) made using captured carbon and renewable electricity. The idea is to create a diesel-compatible fuel with lower net carbon impact without replacing every engine overnight.

Synthetic diesel and other e-fuels are still evolving. For most drivers today, the practical takeaway is simple: Use the fuel your engine is approved for, and treat any new diesel fuel claims with healthy skepticism until the manufacturer approves it.

Where Diesels Still Shine

Diesel isn't the best engine for everyone anymore — it's the right tool for the right job. Think of it like owning work boots: If you're climbing ladders and hauling lumber, they're perfect; if you're just walking to the mailbox, they're overkill and kind of annoying.

The following sections describe where diesels still earn their keep and feel like the smart choice, not the complicated one.

Heavy-duty towing and torque advantage

Diesels shine when they're used the way they were built to be used: towing, hauling, and long highway miles. Low-RPM torque makes heavy loads feel easier, and diesels often hold speed on grades without downshifting as aggressively as many gasoline engines.

If your life includes trailers, long climbs, or heavy payloads, a diesel can still be a smart tool — especially when matched to the right duty cycle.

Commercial fleet and long-haul trucking

In commercial service, diesel's strengths are hard to replace: long range, fast refueling, durability under steady load, and a mature support network for parts and service.

That is why diesel remains dominant in long-haul trucking and many fleet applications, even as electrification grows in local delivery and urban routes.

Declining role in passenger cars

In many markets, diesel passenger cars have become less common. The aftertreatment hardware adds cost and complexity, and emissions requirements are strict. For drivers with mostly short trips and stop-and-go commuting, hybrids and plug-in hybrids (see Chapter 10) often match the duty cycle better.

REMEMBER

A diesel that never gets fully warm is a diesel that will eventually get unhappy. If your driving is mostly short, cold trips, choose the powertrain that fits your routine.

Hybrid diesel applications in fleet use

Diesel-hybrid systems exist in some buses, work trucks, and specialized equipment. The idea is the same as any hybrid: Use electric assist and regenerative braking to reduce fuel use in stop-and-go duty cycles while keeping diesel for long-range and heavy-load capability.

For most everyday drivers, diesel-hybrid systems are more common in commercial fleets than in personal vehicles — but it's one more example of diesel evolving rather than disappearing.

3

Staying Cool and In Control

IN THIS PART . . .

Learn how your cooling system controls engine heat.

Troubleshoot overheating and cooling issues fast.

Understand engine oil and how to use it right.

See how brakes work and why they matter most.

Inspect brakes and bearings before problems grow.

IN THIS CHAPTER

» Discovering why engines need cooling — and why "it'll be fine" is not a cooling strategy

» Following the coolant loop from engine to radiator and back

» Understanding pressure caps, expansion tanks, pumps, thermostats, and fans

» Seeing how the heater core and sensors fit into the bigger picture

Chapter 12

Inside the Cooling System: How Heat Moves and Parts Work

Engines are basically metal boxes that make controlled explosions for a living. Explosions are great for moving a car. They're also great at making heat.

Unfortunately, overheating can turn a normal car into an expensive driveway ornament in a hurry. The good news is that the cooling system helps keep everything working properly. In this chapter, we explain how the cooling system works. Chapter 13 is the hands-on chapter for maintenance and troubleshooting.

For the quick monthly "Is my cooling system about to betray me?" check, refer to Chapter 2. If you already have an overheat, leak, or warning light, Chapter 13 is your next stop.

Why Engines Need Cooling

Combustion makes an enormous amount of heat. Only part of that heat becomes useful work pushing pistons down. The rest has to be managed so that the engine can stay strong, efficient, and predictable.

Heat from combustion

Every time fuel burns, heat tries to soak into the pistons, cylinder walls, head, valves, oil, and nearby hardware. The engine deals with that heat three main ways:

- Coolant carries heat away from the engine and releases it through the radiator.
- Oil helps cool and protect internal parts that coolant can't easily reach.
- Airflow removes heat from the radiator and hot engine components.

TIP

Modern engines are temperature-obsessed because efficiency and emissions rules are temperature-obsessed. The ECU wants the engine warm — not roasted.

Dangers of overheating

Overheating is not just "the needle went up." It means metal, plastic, oil, and coolant are being pushed outside the range they were designed to live in.

Here's what can happen, from bad to catastrophic:

- Coolant can boil and vent out, which leaves the system with even less cooling capacity.
- Cylinder heads can warp, and head gaskets can fail.
- Plastic tanks, fittings, and reservoirs can crack from heat and pressure.
- Misfires or poor running while hot can also stress emissions hardware, such as the catalytic converter.
- In severe cases, oil protection drops, and serious engine damage can follow.

WARNING

If the gauge spikes, an overheat message appears, or the vehicle tells you to pull over, treat it like a real safety issue — not a suggestion.

The Coolant System

The *cooling system* is the engine's heat-management team. It moves heat away from the engine, dumps it into outside air, and tries to keep everything in the temperature range where power, efficiency, and emissions all behave.

The cooling system, shown in Figure 12-1, consists of the following components:

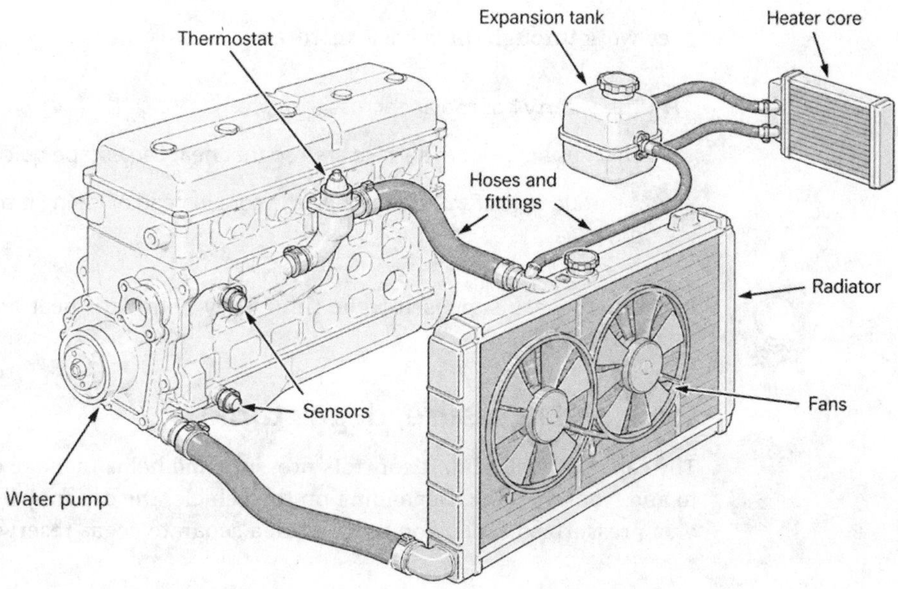

FIGURE 12-1: A simplified view of the cooling system.

- Thermostat
- Radiator and expansion tank
- Hoses and fittings
- Water pump
- Fans
- Heater core
- Sensors

The remainder of this chapter describe these components, and how they work, in more detail.

Radiator and expansion tank

The *radiator* is the heat exchanger. The *expansion tank is* where the system sends extra coolant when everything gets hot and crowded.

Aluminum/plastic design

Most modern radiators use an aluminum core with plastic end tanks because it balances heat transfer, packaging, cost, and weight.

They work through three basic features:

- Tubes carry hot coolant across the core.
- Thin fins add a lot of surface area so that heat can escape quickly.
- A shroud helps force air through the core instead of letting it sneak around the edges.

TIP

Radiator fins are supposed to be thin. They help with heat transfer, not structural strength.

Caps and pressure, degas tanks

The cap isn't just a lid. It controls pressure and helps manage coolant movement to and from the tank. Depending on the vehicle, the cap may live on the radiator, on a pressurized expansion tank, or on a separate degas reservoir.

A recovery or overflow tank catches expanding coolant and returns it later. A pressurized expansion or degas tank stays in the cooling loop and carries system pressure all the time.

WARNING

Never open a pressure cap on a hot engine. Hot coolant under pressure can spray out and burn you badly.

Hoses and fittings

Hoses and fittings live in a rough neighborhood: heat, vibration, chemicals, road grime, and years of temperature cycling. They usually give clues before they fail completely.

Modern systems often use molded hoses and quick-connect fittings, shown in Figure 12-2, so that everything routes tightly without kinks or awkward bends:

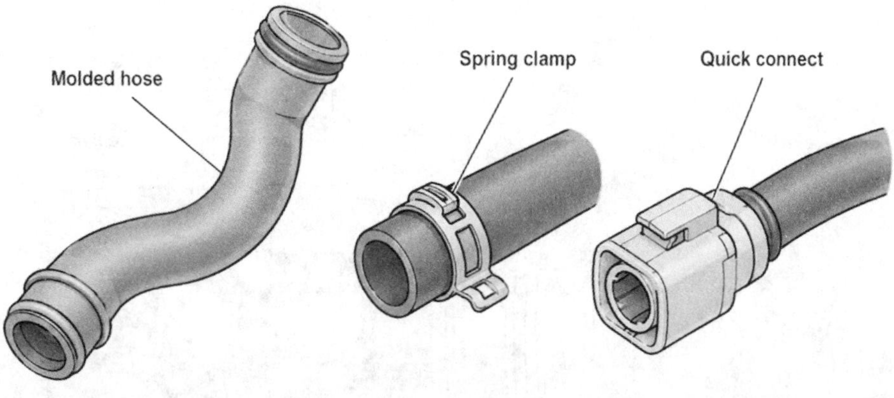

FIGURE 12-2: Common hose and fitting styles.

Generated with AI using OpenAI

- **Molded hoses** are shaped to fit around nearby parts without collapsing.
- **Spring clamps** keep tension as a hose expands and contracts with heat.
- **Quick-connects** save assembly time but depend on small seals and plastic locks that can age and crack.

REMEMBER

If a quick-connect feels brittle, believe it. Old plastic tabs snap easily and can turn a simple job into a parts hunt.

Common early-warning signs of wear include

- Bulges, swelling, or soft spots
- Cracks, splits, or a dry, chalky-looking surface
- Coolant crust or staining around a joint or clamp
- A sweet smell after driving
- A small puddle under the front of the car

Water pump

The *water pump* is what keeps coolant moving. If flow drops, the rest of the system can't do its job well, which is why pump problems can look like weak heat, overheating, or mystery coolant loss.

Mechanical impellers

Traditional pumps are belt-driven and use an impeller to push coolant through the block, head, and radiator (see Figure 12-3).

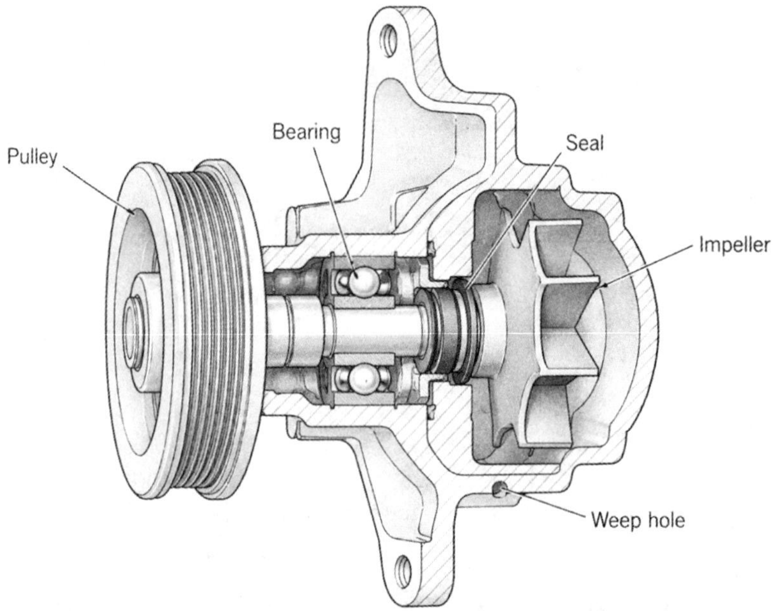

FIGURE 12-3: Mechanical water pump cutaway.

Generated with AI using OpenAI

A mechanical water pump depends on these basic parts working together:

- The *impeller* moves coolant.
- The *bearing* supports the shaft and pulley load.
- The *seal* keeps coolant inside the pump.
- The *weep hole* gives a failing seal somewhere to leak before the bearing gets contaminated.

TIP

A dried coolant trail near the pump is often an early clue that the seal is on its way out.

Electric pumps

Many newer vehicles use electric pumps as the main pump or as auxiliaries for turbos, hybrids, EV battery loops, and smart thermal-management systems.

Their advantage is control: They can run only as fast as needed and, on some designs, keep circulating coolant after shutdown to manage hot spots.

You'll often see electric pumps on turbocharged engines and electrified vehicles because those systems benefit from flexible, computer-controlled cooling.

Thermostats

The *thermostat* is the gatekeeper that helps the engine warm up quickly and then stay near its target temperature once everything is hot.

Mechanical wax-pellet thermostats

A traditional thermostat uses a wax pellet that expands with heat and opens a valve when coolant reaches its designed temperature. Figure 12-4 shows the thermostat in its two basic positions: mostly closed when the engine is cold and open when the engine is warm enough to send coolant through the radiator.

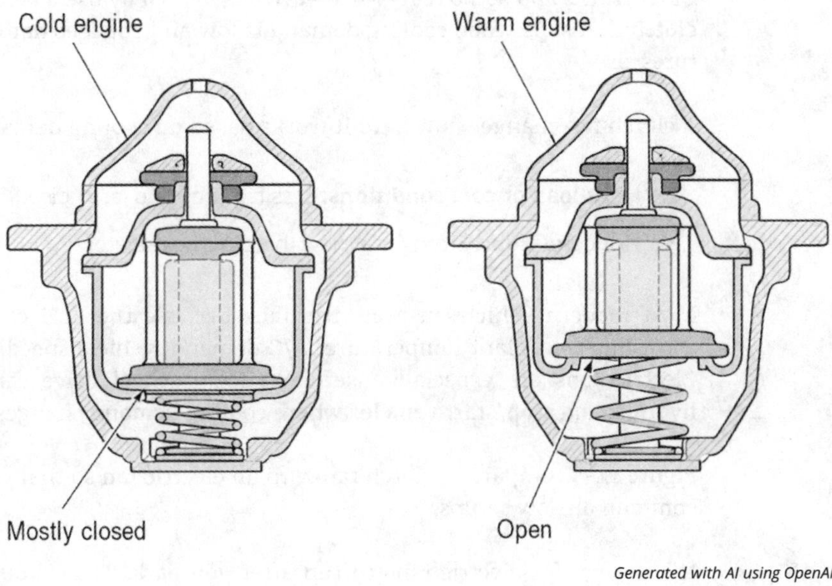

FIGURE 12-4: Wax-pellet thermostat operation.

The thermostat's position changes as coolant temperature rises:

- **Cold engine:** Mostly closed, so coolant stays in the engine and bypass circuit for faster warm-up.
- **Warm engine:** Open, so coolant can flow through the radiator for cooling.

REMEMBER

A thermostat doesn't "make the engine cool." It helps the engine reach and hold the correct operating temperature.

Some newer systems let the ECU influence thermostat behavior so the engine can run a bit hotter for efficiency or a bit cooler under heavier load.

TIP

If scan data shows coolant targets that move around, it can be normal on a smart thermal-management system.

Fans and airflow

Coolant can carry heat to the radiator, but airflow is what actually removes that heat from the vehicle.

Older trucks and some rear-wheel-drive layouts may use a belt-driven fan with a clutch that slips when cooling demand is low and engages harder when temperatures rise.

A clutch fan changes how hard it works based on cooling demand:

- **Light-load or cold conditions:** Less fan drag and less noise.
- **Hot conditions:** Stronger airflow through the radiator.

Most modern vehicles use electric fans because the ECU can switch them on according to coolant temperature, A/C demand, vehicle speed, and other inputs. Electric fans are especially useful on front-wheel-drive cars, turbo engines, hybrids, and stop/start vehicles where cooling demand changes quickly.

Figure 12-5 compares a clutch fan with an electric fan so that you can see the two common airflow setups.

REMEMBER

It's normal for electric fans to run after you park. That is often just heat-soak management, not the car forgetting to turn itself off.

Heater core

The *heater core* is a small radiator inside the dash. It gives you cabin heat and also provides useful clues about what the cooling system is doing.

Your cabin is heated when hot coolant flows through the heater core while the blower pushes air across it. Figure 12-6 shows the heater core inside the HVAC box, along with the coolant flow and blower airflow that create cabin heat.

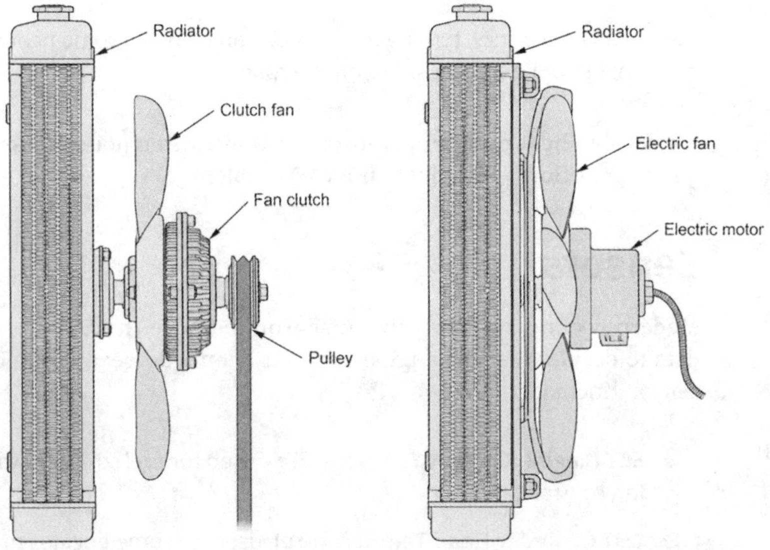

FIGURE 12-5: Clutch fan versus electric fan.

Generated with AI using OpenAI

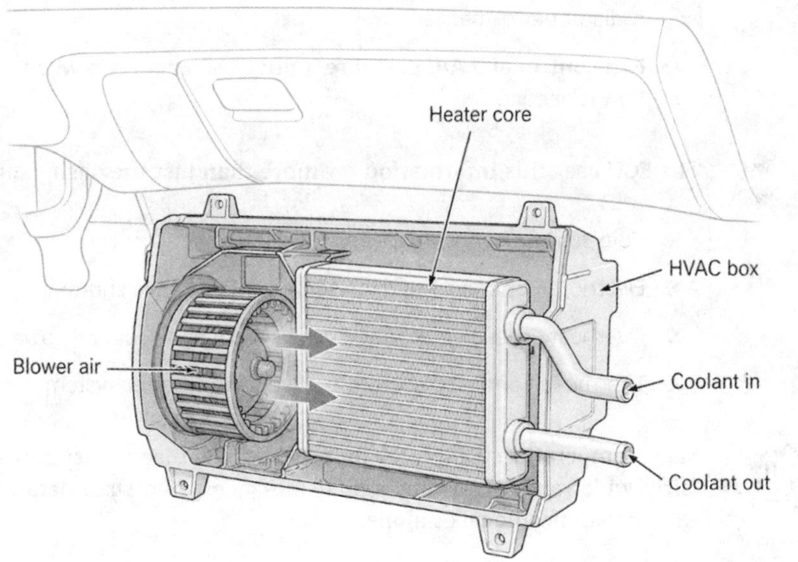

FIGURE 12-6: Heater core and HVAC box.

Generated with AI using OpenAI

The heater core serves several roles in the coolant loop:

- It adds a little extra cooling capacity and system volume.
- On many designs, it also acts as part of the bypass path when the thermostat is closed.

» In an emergency, turning the heat on can help pull some heat out of the engine while you get safely off the road.

TIP

Weak cabin heat plus temperature weirdness often points to low coolant, trapped air, or poor flow — not just an HVAC problem.

Sensors

Modern cooling systems rely on sensors because the ECU uses real temperature data to decide what the engine and fans should do next. Common cooling-related sensors include:

» **ECT (Engine Coolant Temperature)**, used for fuel strategy, warm-up, and fan control

» **CHT (Cylinder Head Temperature)**, used on some engines to monitor metal temperature directly

» **Radiator outlet temperature sensors**, used on some vehicles to judge radiator performance

» **Fan-control and A/C pressure inputs**, used to decide when more airflow is needed

The ECU uses this information for more than just the dash gauge:

» Cold-start fuel enrichment and idle strategy

» Electric fan operation and, on some vehicles, grille shutters

» Overheat protection actions, such as warnings, reduced power, or A/C shutoff

» Thermostat and electric-pump strategy on smarter systems

REMEMBER

Many temperature gauges are buffered, which means they can sit normal across a fairly wide range. Warning lights, messages, and scan data often tell the truth earlier than needle vibes alone.

How the Coolant System Works

Coolant is always doing laps: through the engine to grab heat, through the radiator to dump it, and back again. Once you understand that route, a lot of cooling-system problems stop feeling mysterious.

The coolant route

Here's the basic route in plain English:

1. **The water pump pushes coolant into the engine block.**
2. **Coolant circulates around the cylinders and moves into the cylinder head, picking up heat along the way.**
3. **From the cylinder head, the coolant heads toward the thermostat housing.**
4. **If the engine is cold, the thermostat stays closed, and coolant mostly circulates through a bypass so warm-up happens faster.**
5. **If the engine is warm, the thermostat opens and coolant flows through the radiator, where airflow removes heat.**
6. **Cooled coolant returns to the pump, and the cycle repeats.**

REMEMBER

The heater core is usually in parallel with the main loop, which is why you can often get cabin heat before the engine is fully warm.

Expansion and contraction cycle

Coolant expands when it gets hot and contracts when it cools down, so the system has to allow movement without letting the whole thing boil over or suck in air.

On a healthy system:

- Pressure rises as the engine warms.
- The cap holds that pressure up to its rating, which raises the coolant's boiling point.
- Excess coolant moves into a recovery or expansion tank instead of spilling onto the driveway.
- As the engine cools, coolant is drawn back into the system.

TECHNICAL STUFF

That pressure margin is the trick. It lets modern engines run hot enough for efficiency without turning coolant into a kettle.

IN THIS CHAPTER

» Checking coolant safely (no burns, no drama)

» Topping off correctly and avoiding "coolant soup"

» Finding leaks without guessing: visual checks, pressure tests, and dye

» Bleeding air after repairs so the heater works and the gauge stays sane

» Troubleshooting overheating by pattern (idle vs highway is a big clue)

Chapter 13
Cool under Pressure: Real-World Maintenance and Troubleshooting

Chapter 12 was the "how it works" tour. This chapter is the "okay, now my car is doing something weird" reality show.

Cooling-system problems have a special talent: They look dramatic, but the fix is often basic. Low coolant, a small leak, trapped air, or a lazy fan can make the temperature gauge act like it is auditioning for a horror movie.

Your mission here is simple: Check the easy stuff first, confirm problems before buying parts, and keep your skin unscalded in the process. (Hot coolant isn't a spa treatment.)

If you're unsure what each part does (radiator, cap, pump, thermostat, fans, heater core), flip to Chapter 12 before you start wrenching. Understanding the normal coolant loop saves you from replacing parts out of pure frustration.

Cooling-System Safety Rules

Cooling systems are pressurized on purpose. That pressure raises the boiling point and helps prevent boiling over. It also means that "just crack the cap real quick" is a terrible plan when the engine is hot.

Cooling-system checks fall into two temperature groups. This list isn't a step-by-step order; it tells you which checks belong on a cold engine and which checks require the engine to be running or warming up.

- **Cold checks:** Check coolant level, remove the pressure cap, pressure-test the system, top off coolant, and inspect hoses only when the engine is cool. A cold system is safer because it isn't holding hot pressure that can spray coolant.
- **Warm checks:** Fan operation, thermostat opening behavior, and cabin heat performance only when the procedure calls for the engine to run. Keep your hands, face, sleeves, and tools away from fans, belts, pulleys, and any place coolant could splash.

REMEMBER

When in doubt, start cold. Only run the engine when the check specifically requires it and have a plan before you do.

WARNING

Never open a pressure cap on a hot engine. If the system is hot and pressurized, coolant can flash-boil and spray out. Wait until the upper radiator hose feels cool and soft, or just wait longer. Patience is cheaper than urgent care.

A safe cap-check routine

WARNING

Even on a cool engine, open a pressure cap slowly and deliberately. Do not remove it in one twist. Use this routine only after the engine is cold:

1. **Confirm the engine is cold.**

   The upper radiator hose should feel cool and soft.

2. **Place a thick towel over the pressure cap.**

   The towel gives you a little protection if any surprise pressure is left.

3. **Loosen the cap slowly to the first stop.**

   Don't put your face over the cap while you do this step.

4. **Pause and listen for any hiss.**

   If you hear pressure escaping, wait until it stops.

5. **Remove the cap slowly.**

   Press down if your cap requires it, turn it the rest of the way, and lift it off carefully.

Figure 13-1 shows the same cold-engine cap-removal routine.

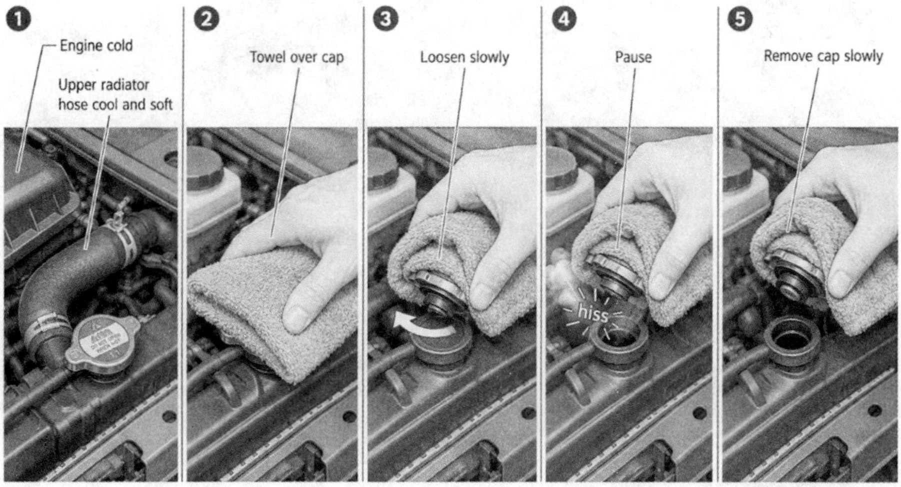

FIGURE 13-1: Safe pressure-cap check.

TIP

If you can't honestly say the engine is cold, don't open anything. Use the time to grab tools, find the flashlight, and pretend you meant to be this organized all along.

Quick Checks That Prevent Parts Roulette

Before you replace anything, do a quick reality check. The goal is to answer two questions:

- Is there enough coolant?
- Is it staying where it belongs?

Check the coolant level and the right reservoir

Many vehicles want you to check the coolant level at the expansion or degas tank, not at the radiator. Check the level only when the engine is cold. Look for marks such as MIN, MAX, FULL COLD, or COLD on the tank. On a cold engine, the coolant should sit at the COLD mark or safely between MIN and MAX. Do not fill the tank to the brim; coolant needs room to expand as it warms up.

Figure 13-2 shows typical expansion-tank level marks and where the coolant level should sit when the engine is cold.

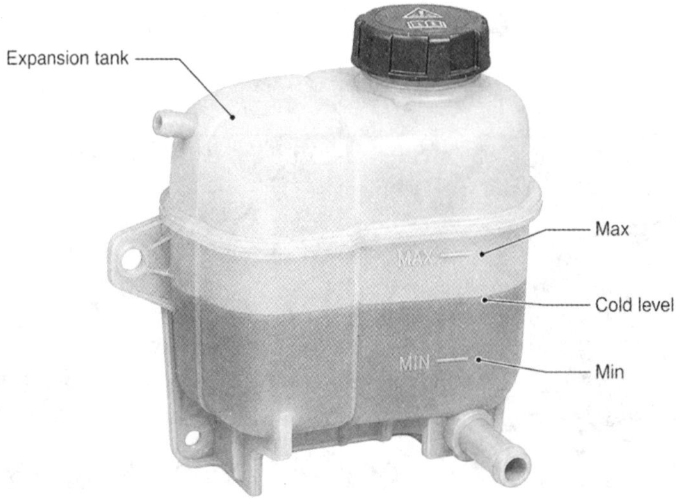

FIGURE 13-2: Expansion tank level marks (MIN/MAX) and what normal looks like cold.

Generated with AI using OpenAI

REMEMBER

A low coolant level can cause weak cabin heat, temperature spikes, and mystery overheating. Low coolant isn't a symptom; it's a clue. Something is leaking, boiling over, or being consumed.

Check coolant condition (quick and nonscientific)

You don't need a laboratory to check the condition of your coolant. You just need eyeballs. Coolant should look like coolant, not like rusty iced tea or a glitter smoothie.

Healthy-ish coolant has a clear, consistent color, with no chunks, no oily sheen, and no burnt smell. Coolant is suspect if it looks brown or rusty, contains sludge, has oil floating on top, or gives off a strong exhaust smell in the tank.

TIP

If you see oil in the coolant or coolant that looks like chocolate milk, skip the "maybe it's fine" phase. That discovery is a stop-and-diagnose moment, not a top-off moment. (See the section "Recognizing When to Stop and Get Help," later in this chapter.)

Look for leaks (dry first and then wet)

Start with a dry inspection of the coolant. Dried coolant leaves chalky trails and crusty deposits. Then look for fresh wet spots. A bright flashlight and a calm attitude do more here than panic does. Make sure you:

- **Check hose ends and clamps** (especially at the radiator and thermostat housing).
- **Look at radiator end tanks and seams** (plastic tanks love to crack where they crimp).
- **Look under the water pump for a dried trail or drip** (weep hole clues).
- **Check the inside** (sweet smell or damp passenger carpet can point to the heater core).

REMEMBER

For the full "what is this puddle?" decoder ring, see Chapter 21. Cooling leaks are often obvious once you know where to look and what dried coolant looks like.

Choosing Coolant (the Safe, Boring Way)

Use the coolant specification your vehicle calls for. Don't rely on color alone. Many coolants are dyed different colors for branding, not for accuracy.

If you have the owner's manual, follow it. If you don't have the manual, look up the OEM spec for your exact vehicle. You can find that information from the dealer or in a reliable parts catalog.

If you're stranded, you can use plain water as an emergency move, not a lifestyle. Fix the leak and restore the correct mix as soon as possible.

WARNING

Avoid mixing coolant types unless the product specifically says it's compatible with your vehicle's spec. Mixing can cause sludge, corrosion, and heater-core clogs. Your cooling system doesn't need to become a science fair project.

TECHNICAL STUFF

A 50/50 mix of coolant concentrate and distilled water is common because it balances freeze protection, boiling-point margin, and corrosion protection. Some vehicles use pre-mix, some use different ratios, and some use specialty formulas. The spec matters more than the ratio meme.

Topping Off Coolant without Creating a Chemistry Experiment

Adding coolant is easy. Adding the wrong coolant is easy, too. The difference is that one helps your engine, and the other quietly starts a long-term argument inside the cooling system.

Use the right fill point

Some vehicles are filled at the radiator, some at a pressurized degas tank, and some have both an overflow bottle and a separate pressurized tank. Figure 13-3 shows these three common setups.

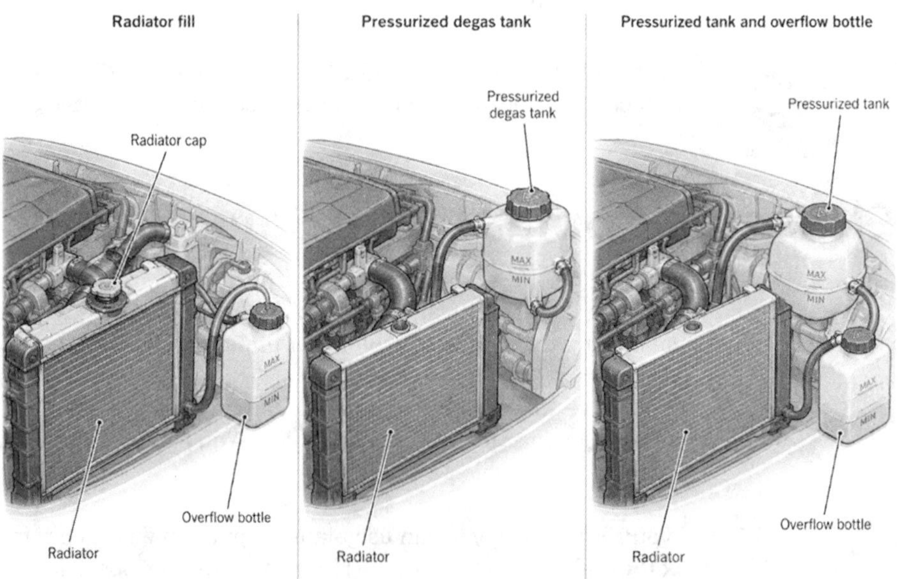

FIGURE 13-3: Where to add coolant.

Generated with AI using OpenAI

The simple top-off procedure

Use the following steps when the system is just a little low and you're not doing a full drain/refill:

1. **Start with a cold engine on level ground.**

   If it's hot, walk away and let it cool. Your skin will thank you.

2. **Identify the correct reservoir or fill point.**

   Use the radiator, pressurized expansion or degas tank, or overflow bottle your vehicle calls for. Look for a cap with a pressure rating, such as psi or kPa, or a "Do not open when hot" warning. If you see either one, treat that cap as pressurized.

TIP

3. **Open the pressurized cap slowly.**

   Follow the safe cap-check routine earlier in this chapter: Cover the cap with a thick towel, loosen it slowly to the first stop, pause for any hiss to finish, and then remove it carefully. Don't put your face over the cap while opening it.

4. **Check the correct level mark (FULL COLD, MIN, or MAX).**

   Some tanks have both hot and cold marks. If you are checking the level with a cold engine, use the COLD mark. Filling to the HOT line when cold is how you pre-order an overflow mess later.

5. **Add the correct coolant slowly until it reaches the proper mark.**

   Don't fill it to the brim; coolant needs room to expand as the engine warms up.

6. **Reinstall the cap fully.**

   Make sure the cap is seated and tightened securely. Tight is good; Hulk-tight is not necessary.

7. **Start the engine, set the heater to HOT, and idle a few minutes.**

   Watch for leaks and confirm warm cabin heat.

8. **Shut the engine off, let it cool completely, and recheck the level.**

   Add coolant only if the level drops below the correct cold mark.

9. **Top off once if needed, then watch the level.**

   If the level drops again after the next drive or two, stop topping off and go leak-hunting — coolant doesn't vanish, it escapes. For the full puddle decoder, see Chapter 21. For why the cooling system should work as a closed loop, see Chapter 12.

TIP

If the level drops again after one short drive, do not keep topping off forever like it's a subscription service. Find the leak. Chapter 12 explains why the system should be a loop, not a disappearing act.

Finding Leaks without Guessing

A cooling system can lose coolant in three ways: It leaks externally, it leaks internally, or it boils/vents out. The trick is confirming which one is happening before you buy parts.

Pressure testing (the "tell me the truth" tool)

A *cooling-system pressure test* is the closest thing to a lie detector for coolant leaks. You pressurize the system with the engine off and cold, which often makes leaks show themselves without heat, fan noise, or moving belts adding drama.

You can buy one at most auto parts stores (AutoZone, O'Reilly Auto Parts, Advance Auto Parts, NAPA Auto Parts), online (Amazon), or tool stores (Harbor Freight). Many parts stores also have loaner/rental tool programs, which is perfect if you plan to do this once and not start a pressure-tester collection.

TIP

If you've never done a pressure test, pull up a couple short videos online using search terms like "cooling system pressure test" plus your year/make/model. Watch how they attach the adapter and how they release pressure at the end — then follow these steps so you're not learning mid-spray.

WARNING

Only pressure-test on a cold engine. Hot systems can still be pressurized, and hot coolant is basically a boiling betrayal.

Use these steps to set up and run a pressure test:

1. **Start with the engine cold and remove the pressure cap safely.**

   Cold means sitting long enough that the upper radiator hose is cool to the touch. If the cap is on a radiator neck or a pressurized tank, use the safe cap-check routine earlier in "Cooling-System Safety Rules": Cover the cap with a thick towel, loosen it slowly to the first stop, pause for any hiss to finish, and then remove it carefully.

2. **Install the correct adapter and attach the hand pump.**

   Choose the adapter that matches your fill point. Use a radiator-neck adapter if your vehicle has a radiator cap. Use an expansion-tank adapter if the cap is on a pressurized tank. Make sure the adapter seal or O-ring is clean, seated flat, and not cracked. A crooked adapter can create a fake leak that is really just your tool complaining.

3. **Pump to the cap rating printed on the cap, but don't exceed it.**

   The cap usually lists a rating in psi or kPa, such as 16 psi/110 kPa. Pump up to that number — not "until it feels right." Over-pressurizing can create leaks that weren't there before. (Congrats, you invented a problem.)

4. **If the rating is missing or illegible.**

   Look up the spec for your vehicle or replace the cap first. After the system is pressurized, watch the gauge for a few minutes. A slow drop usually means a slow leak. A healthy system should hold fairly steady. A tiny initial dip can happen as hoses flex, but then it should settle. A fast drop usually indicates a big leak (or a bad adapter seal).

5. **While it's pressurized, inspect for fresh wetness from top to bottom.**

   Use a flashlight and start high, because coolant can run downward and make the leak look like it started somewhere else. Check hose ends and clamp areas, radiator seams and end tanks, thermostat housing and nearby fittings, the water pump area and weep hole, and heater hoses at the firewall.

6. **If the gauge is dropping but nothing is dripping, start looking in the usual hiding spots:**

   - Look under splash shields where coolant can pool and travel.
   - Inspect around the radiator cap or tank neck for hairline cracks or crusty staining.
   - Check the cabin for heater-core clues (foggy windows, a sweet smell, or damp carpet) because sometimes the leak is inside the car, not under it.

7. **If you can't find an external leak but pressure drops, suspect an internal leak.**

   Internal leaks don't always leave a puddle. Common clues include sweet-smelling exhaust, persistent white smoke after warm-up, bubbles in the reservoir, or oil that looks milky. This is where you stop guessing and follow the guidance in the upcoming section "Recognizing When to Stop and Get Help" before you start buying parts like it's a hobby.

8. **Release pressure, remove the tool, and reinstall the cap.**

   Use the tester's release valve (or bleed down slowly) before removing the adapter. Then reinstall the cap fully. Clean up any spilled coolant — pets think it smells tasty, and coolant is toxic.

Figure 13-4 shows the pressure-test setup used in the steps you just walked through: the correct adapter attached at the radiator neck or pressurized expansion tank, the hand pump connected, and the pressure gauge visible so you can watch whether the system holds pressure.

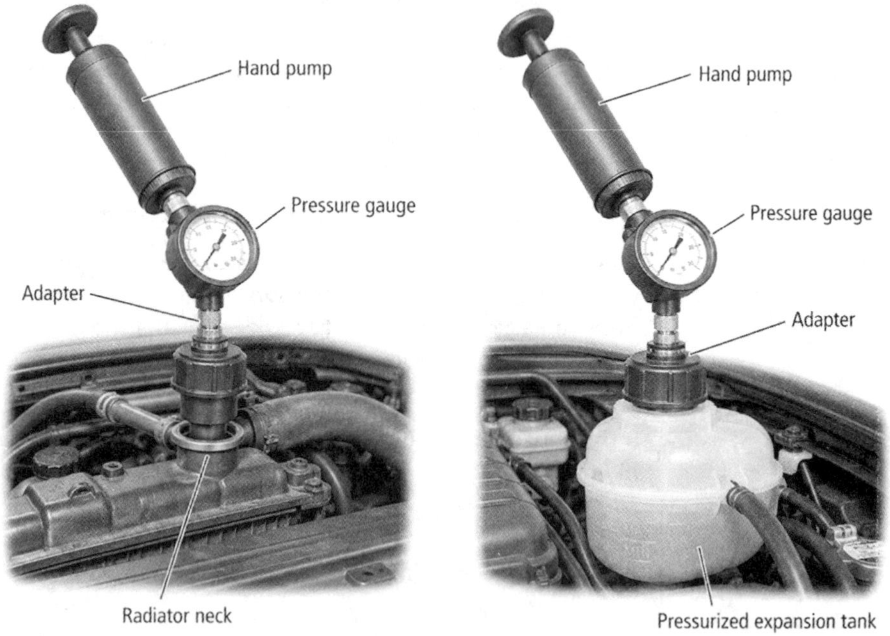

FIGURE 13-4: Cooling system pressure test setup.

Generated with AI using OpenAI

UV dye (the "why is it always leaking at night?" method)

If a leak only happens while driving or only when hot, UV dye can help. Add the dye, drive normally for a day or two, and then inspect with a UV light. Leaks glow like they're trying to get attention.

Follow these steps:

1. **Add dye to the coolant per the product instructions.**
2. **Drive until the system fully warms up.**

   The fans should cycle on at least once.
3. **Inspect with a UV light around joints, seams, and under the pump area.**

Common leak locations and the clues they leave

The following clues show what leaks in common cooling-system areas often look or smell like. Start with these spots before you start blaming the head gasket on the internet.

- **Hose ends and clamps:** A leak at a hose end or clamp may leave a wet ring at the joint or a crusty trail below the clamp.
- **Radiator seam and end tanks:** A leak at a radiator seam or end tank may leave wetness at the crimp seam or white, green, orange, or pink crust along the tank edge.
- **Water pump weep hole:** A leak at the water pump weep hole may leave a drip below the pump or a dried coolant trail.
- **Thermostat housing:** A leak at the thermostat housing may show up at the gasket surface, especially after a recent thermostat job.
- **Heater core:** A heater-core leak may cause a sweet smell inside the cabin, foggy windows, or damp carpet, often on the passenger side.

Figure 13-5 shows these common cooling-system leak points.

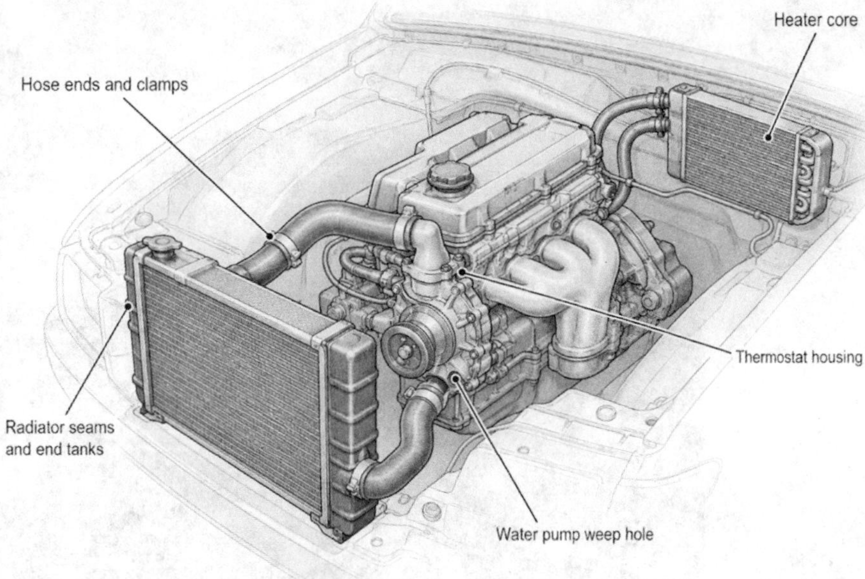

FIGURE 13-5: Common cooling-system leak points.

Generated with AI using OpenAI

Bleeding Air after Repairs

Air in the cooling system causes the greatest hits of confusion: no cabin heat, random temperature spikes, gurgling sounds, and "it overheats only sometimes" behavior. Air isn't evil. It's just in the wrong job.

Three common bleeding methods

Your vehicle may use one of these common methods to bleed air from the cooling system after coolant service or repairs:

- **Open a bleed screw.** Open a small screw at a high point while filling until coolant flows smoothly without bubbles.
- **Use a spill-free funnel.** Attach the sealed funnel at the radiator neck or pressurized fill tank and then run the engine so that trapped air can bubble out safely while the coolant stays contained.
- **Use a vacuum fill tool.** Connect the tool at the fill point, pull a vacuum on the system, and let the vacuum draw coolant in with fewer trapped air pockets.

Figure 13-6 shows the typical hardware you'll see.

FIGURE 13-6: Bleeding methods.

Generated with AI using OpenAI

A safe, general burp procedure

This general burp procedure works on many traditional systems. Always check your service info for special steps. (Some vehicles have bleed screws, specific fill ports, or electric pumps that require a scan-tool bleed routine.)

1. **With the engine cold, set the heater controls to HOT so that coolant can flow through the heater core.**
2. **Fill the system at the correct point.**

   If you're using a funnel, you need to install it now.
3. **Start the engine and let it idle while watching the coolant level and adding more as needed so that it doesn't suck air.**
4. **As the engine warms up, watch for bubbles escaping.**
5. **Squeeze the upper radiator hose gently to help move trapped air (gloves recommended).**

   When the thermostat opens, the upper hose usually gets hot and flow increases. You may see a bigger bubble "burp" out.
6. **Watch for bubbles to stop and the heater to blow consistently hot.**
7. **Install the cap (or remove the funnel and cap the system).**
8. **Let the engine cool completely.**
9. **Recheck the level the next morning and top off to the mark.**

REMEMBER

Weak heat is often the first sign of air or low coolant. The heater core is basically a built-in early warning system. Chapter 12 explains why it can act up before the gauge does.

Diagnosing Overheating by Pattern

When your engine overheats, the pattern of when it happens can reveal the culprit. Instead of guesswork, use Table 13-1 to match the scenario — whether it's overheating at idle, at speed, or randomly — with the likely causes and checks.

TABLE 13-1 Overheating Patterns

Overheating pattern	What it often means	Key checks and references	How to do these checks
Idle or traffic, cools at speed	Airflow problem — fans aren't cooling enough.	Check fans run (temp or A/C on). Inspect fuses, relays, connections. Radiator fins blocked?	Watch fans visually at idle or with A/C on. Feel upper radiator hose (hot) versus lower (cool).
Highway speed	Coolant flow issue — thermostat, pump, or radiator.	Confirm coolant level, bleed air. Check thermostat opens. Use an IR thermometer (see Chapter 16) or feel radiator hoses.	Confirm coolant in reservoir. Carefully feel for cold spots top-to-bottom on radiator.
Overheats randomly	Air, sticky thermostat, or sensor.	Compare scan tool temp to gauge. Watch fan command. If cabin heat goes cold, suspect air or low coolant.	Compare dash gauge reading to normal. Listen for fans engaging as temp rises.

Testing Fans, Thermostats, and Pumps Quickly

You can learn a lot about a problem without removing half the engine. These quick tests help you confirm a suspect before you commit to a Saturday-long repair.

Fan quick test (electric fans)

On many vehicles, turning the A/C on forces at least one radiator fan to run. It is a quick sanity check. Figure 13-7 shows the basic idea.

After you turn on the A/C, use what the fan does next to narrow the problem:

- **No fan with A/C on:** check fuses/relays, wiring, and the fan motor.
- **Fan runs but overheats at idle:** check radiator airflow and fan speed (some failures are "spins, but weak").

TIP

Be careful around fans. Electric fans can turn on with the key off. Treat the fan like a blender that is waiting for a reason.

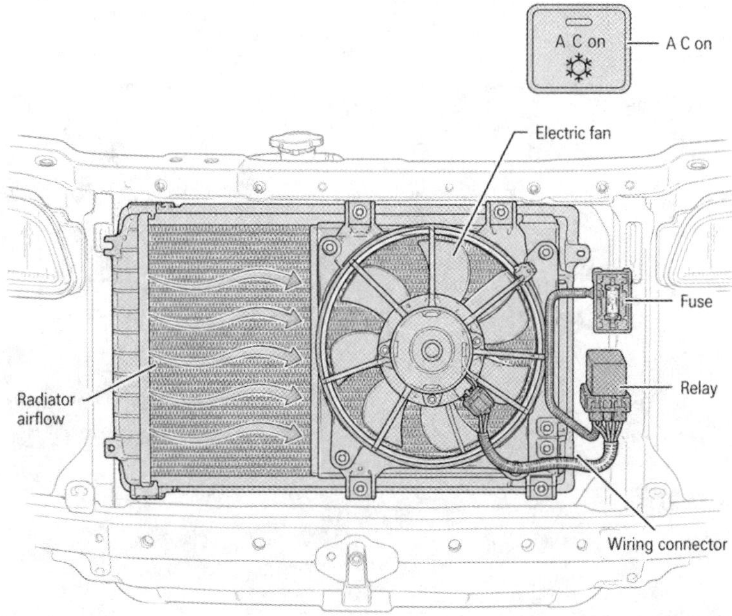

Generated with AI using OpenAI

FIGURE 13-7: Electric fan quick test and common check points.

Thermostat behavior test (no disassembly)

A thermostat stuck closed often causes overheating. A thermostat stuck open often causes slow warm-up and weak heat. You can check thermostat behavior by watching how the upper radiator hose warms up from a cold start. Keep the pressure cap installed during this test.

Start with a cold engine and confirm the coolant level is correct. Start the engine and let it idle while you watch the temperature gauge. Keep your hands, sleeves, and tools away from fans, belts, and pulleys. As the engine warms, check the upper radiator hose with an IR thermometer or use a gloved hand and touch carefully only from a safe position. The hose usually stays cooler at first. When the thermostat opens, hot coolant begins flowing to the radiator, and the upper hose should warm up quickly.

Figure 13-8 shows the basic clue: the upper radiator hose warming quickly when the thermostat opens.

Use the hose-temperature clue along with the warm-up behavior to narrow the problem:

- **If the engine is hot but the upper radiator hose stays cool,** suspect a stuck-closed thermostat or severe air pocket.

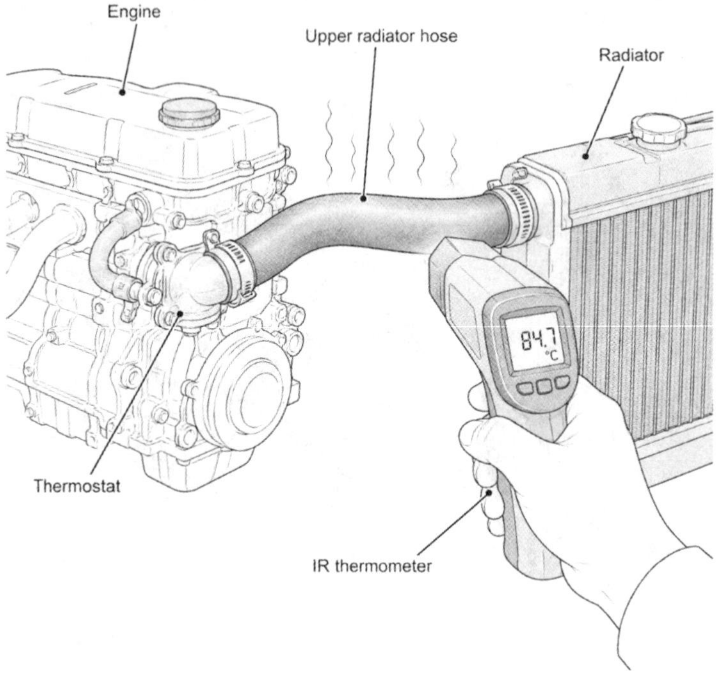

FIGURE 13-8: Thermostat opening clue (upper hose warms suddenly when thermostat opens; IR thermometer helps).

Generated with AI using OpenAI

» **If warm-up takes forever and the heater is weak at speed,** suspect a stuck-open thermostat.

Water pump clues (without removing it)

Water pumps usually give clues before they fail completely: leaks, bearing noise, or poor circulation. Use the following clues to help decide whether the water pump belongs higher on your suspect list:

» Look for dried coolant trails or a drip below the pump snout (see the section "Common leak locations and the clues they leave").

» Listen for squeaks/whines from the pump area and check for pulley wobble on belt-driven pumps.

» Suspect a flow problem from the water pump or trapped air if you have heat one minute and none the next, and the coolant level is okay.

The Overheat Emergency

If the temperature gauge spikes or you get an overheat warning, your goal is not to "make it home." Your goal is to reduce heat load, avoid engine damage and get to a safe stop. An overheated engine can go from warning light to expensive internal damage quickly, so treat the warning as a stop-and-reassess situation.

While you're still moving, do these three things right away:

- **Turn off A/C (it adds heat load).** The A/C adds heat load because the condenser sits in front of the radiator and dumps extra heat into the same airflow path.
- **Turn cabin heat to HOT and fan to HIGH.** This feels ridiculous in summer, but the heater core is a small radiator inside the dash. Running the heat can pull some heat out of the coolant while you look for a safe place to stop.
- **Ease off the throttle and look for a safe place to pull over.** Avoid hard acceleration, climbing harder than necessary, or trying to push through it. Less engine load means less heat.

Once you're stopped, the next step depends on what the vehicle is doing:

- **If steam is pouring out, shut the engine off and let it cool.** Steam means the cooling system is already hot, pressurized, and possibly venting coolant. Do not open the hood if steam is blasting out toward you. Give it time to calm down first.
- **If the temperature is high but not pegged and there is no steam, let the situation guide you.** Some vehicles may stabilize after a brief idle with the heater on high, especially if the overheat happened after a hard climb or stop-and-go traffic. Watch the gauge closely. If the temperature keeps climbing, shut the engine off.
- **If the gauge is pegged, a red warning appears, power drops, or the vehicle tells you to stop, shut it down.** At that point, the car is not asking for encouragement. It is asking for mercy.

After the engine is off, let it cool naturally. Do not open the pressure cap while the engine is hot. Do not add cold water to a hot radiator or hot engine. When the system is fully cool, you can check the coolant level using the safe cold-engine routine earlier in this chapter. If coolant is low, you see an obvious leak, the warning returns, or the engine overheats again, stop driving and get help.

WARNING

Never pour cold water into a hot engine or hot radiator. Rapid temperature changes can crack components. Let the system cool naturally. The only thing you should pour immediately is your respect for physics.

Recognizing When to Stop and Get Help

Most cooling issues are fixable at home. Some are big enough that you should stop, plan, and possibly tow. Towing isn't defeat; it's smart budgeting.

Following are some red flags that deserve a deeper diagnosis:

- Coolant disappears with no external leaks you can find (especially if the exhaust is white or sweet-smelling).
- Bubbles are constantly rising in the tank after warm-up (possible combustion gases in the coolant).
- Oil looks milky or overfull (coolant in the oil), or coolant has a thick oily film.
- Repeated overheating episodes occur, even after topping off and bleeding air.
- Heater core leak symptoms (wet carpet) plus electrical/airbag components under the dash (shop time for many people) occur.

WARNING

Overheating can damage head gaskets and warp cylinder heads. If you suspect an internal leak, avoid repeated "just drive it and see" tests. One more overheat is sometimes the one that turns a manageable repair into an engine rebuild story.

Deciding Where to Go from Here

If your cooling system passed the checks in this chapter, congratulations: you have a boring, functional cooling system. Boring is the dream.

If you found a leak, air problem, or weak fan, fix that first and then recheck coolant level cold to confirm stable temperature under the conditions that used to cause trouble. If you need to understand how the parts work together, Chapter 12 is your reference map. For leak-fluid identification and "what is that stain?" clues, Chapter 21 is your detective handbook.

IN THIS CHAPTER

» Discovering why oil matters more than ever in modern engines

» Finding out how oil moves through the engine and what it does when it gets there

» Choosing between conventional, synthetic, and extended-life/high-mileage oils

» Understanding oil-life monitors and modern service intervals

» Checking your oil correctly and doing a simple DIY oil change

Chapter 14
Liquid Gold: The Lifeblood of Your Engine

Chapters 12 and 13 are all about coolant and keeping your engine from turning into a sad, expensive fondue pot. In this chapter, you meet the other fluid your engine absolutely can't live without: oil — the lifeblood, bodyguard, and janitor all rolled into one amber package.

Oil doesn't just make things slippery. It keeps metal parts from grinding themselves into modern art, helps carry heat away from hot spots, suspends gunk so that the filter can catch it, and even helps seal the tiny explosion chambers where power is made. Basically, oil is the employee of the month . . . every month.

Why Oil Matters More than Ever

Your engine can't shrug off low, dirty, or wrong oil. Today's engines run with tighter clearances, higher temperatures, and more complicated hardware, so the right oil has to do several jobs at once: Lubricate moving parts, carry away heat, clean up tiny particles, and help protect internal surfaces. Your engine is a giant collection of metal parts moving at ridiculous speeds, under ridiculous heat, while tiny controlled explosions happen thousands of times a minute. Oil is the thin film that keeps those parts from high-fiving each other directly.

Here's the short list of oil's real jobs:

- **Lubrication:** Separates moving metal parts with a protective film (so friction stays a concept, not a lifestyle).
- **Cooling:** Carries heat away from places coolant can't easily reach, like bearings and turbocharger bearings.
- **Cleaning:** Holds soot and microscopic wear particles in suspension so that the filter can catch them.
- **Sealing:** Helps piston rings seal against the cylinder walls for better compression and less blow-by.

Older engines were more forgiving. Modern engines depend on precise oil specs. Modern engines use tight clearances, variable valve timing, direct injection, turbocharging, start/stop systems, and emissions hardware that all depend on oil behaving exactly as intended.

That's why manufacturers specify both a viscosity and a performance standard. Use the wrong oil, and you can trade a few dollars of savings for wear, deposits, or *low-speed pre-ignition,* known as *LSPI* — a harmful early combustion event that can happen in some direct-injection engines under load. For more on direct-injection engines and LSPI risk, see "Direct injection engines," later in this chapter.

WARNING

If you're low on oil, you're not just low on lubrication — you're low on cooling and cleaning capacity, too. That's why "just a little low" can turn into noise, wear, and overheating faster than your brain expects.

Oil Basics

Oil can seem like one of those "sure, whatever" car topics — until you realize it's doing multiple jobs at once while getting cooked, squeezed, and flung around at thousands of RPM.

TIP

To make sense of the bottle labels and specs, start with the basics: where oil goes, what it does when it gets there, and why modern oil is more than just slippery liquid.

How oil flows through the engine

Think of the oil system like a tiny city water system — except instead of pipes in your walls, it's passages inside an engine block, and instead of water, it's liquid "please don't explode."

Figure 14-1 shows the basic loop: Oil lives in the pan, gets pulled through a pickup tube, pressurized by the oil pump, cleaned by the filter, and then sent through internal passages (oil galleries) to bearings, camshafts, and other hard-working parts. After that, it drains back to the pan and does another lap. Engine cardio.

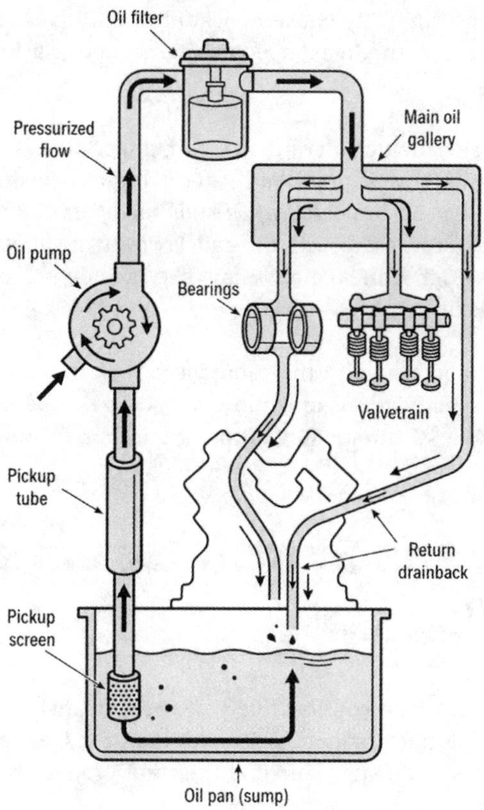

FIGURE 14-1: Basic engine oil flow.

Generated with AI using OpenAI

What oil actually does at a microscopic level

On a microscopic scale, engine parts look less like smooth metal and more like two mountain ranges trying to slide past each other. Oil's job is to keep those mountains from chewing each other up.

Sometimes oil forms a thick-enough film that parts ride on it *(hydrodynamic lubrication)*. Other times — like at cold start or on cam lobes — oil is more of a boundary layer where additives help prevent metal-to-metal contact. Either way, oil is basically the bouncer keeping trouble out of the club.

Oil chemistry: Detergents, additives, and viscosity modifiers

Oil is a base oil plus a carefully chosen cocktail of additives. The base oil is the liquid. The additives are the reason your engine doesn't turn into a smoky, sludgy regret.

Common additive jobs include detergents and *dispersants* (keep deposits from baking onto parts), *anti-wear protection* (guard high-pressure contact points), *antioxidants* (slow down oil breakdown), *friction modifiers* (help efficiency), *anti-foam agents* (bubbles aren't protective), and *viscosity modifiers* (help oil behave when cold and hot). High-mileage oils may also include *seal conditioners* to help older gaskets stay flexible.

REMEMBER

Oil isn't just oil. Two bottles with the same viscosity can behave very differently depending on their specifications and additive packages. Specs matter more than marketing slogans like "Ultimate Mega Protection Thunder Juice."

Conventional versus Synthetic versus Extended-Life Oils

If the oil aisle has ever made you feel like you need a translator and a mood ring, you're not alone. What matters most is simpler than the label poetry: Does the oil meet your engine's required spec, and is it the right type for the job?

OLD CONVENTIONAL VERSUS SYNTHETIC DEBATE

If the oil aisle has ever made you feel like you need a translator and a mood ring, you're not alone. What matters most is simpler than the label poetry: Does the oil meet your engine's required spec, and is it the right type for the job?

Conventional oil is refined from crude oil and can work well in engines that allow it. Synthetic oil starts with more heavily refined or engineered base oils and an additive package designed for better stability, cleaner performance, and stronger protection under heat, cold starts, and longer service intervals. Synthetic-blend oil lands in the middle, mixing conventional and synthetic base oils.

The choice isn't really about which bottle sounds fanciest. It's about what your engine calls for. If your owner's manual requires synthetic oil or a specific manufacturer approval, use that exact spec.

Now engines run hotter, are often turbocharged, and demand cleaner oil for longer. So the question isn't "Is synthetic worth it?" as much as "Does my engine call for it?" (Often, yes.)

Why synthetic is now standard

Synthetic oils generally handle heat better, flow better in the cold, resist sludge, and stay stable longer. That's why many manufacturers specify synthetic (or synthetic blends) — especially for modern turbo and direct-injection engines.

REMEMBER

Conventional oil isn't bad. It just has a smaller performance envelope. If your manual allows conventional and you change it on schedule, it can still do the job. The key is meeting the required spec.

Extended-life oils and high-mileage formulas

Extended-life oils are formulated to hold up for longer drain intervals — but only when your vehicle and your driving conditions support it. "I bought the long-life oil so I never have to change it again" is not a thing. Nice try, though.

High-mileage oils (usually for engines with 75,000 miles or more) may include seal conditioners and different additive balances to help reduce leaks and consumption. They're not magic potion, but they can be a helpful nudge for an older engine that's starting to . . . mark its territory.

TIP

If your engine is using or leaking oil, switching to high-mileage oil may help a little, but it won't fix a torn gasket or worn rings. Think supportive shoes, not new knees.

Viscosity Explained in Today's Terms

Viscosity sounds technical, but the numbers on the bottle are really just oil's "cold start versus fully hot" rating. You do not need a chart memorized — only what the numbers mean and why the manual is specific.

Viscosity is oil's resistance to flow — basically, how thick or thin it is. The numbers on the bottle look like a Wi-Fi password, but they're actually pretty simple once you decode them.

In a grade like 0W-20, the first number with the W (for winter) is cold-flow performance. Lower first numbers flow easier in the cold, which helps reduce wear at startup. The second number is how the oil behaves at operating temperature. Higher second numbers stay thicker when hot.

Your engine's manual isn't guessing here. If it says 0W-20, it means 0W-20 — not "whatever was on sale" and definitely not "my uncle says thicker is better."

Why thinner oils dominate today (efficiency and cold start)

Thinner oils (like 0W-20 and 0W-16) reduce internal drag, which helps fuel economy and emissions. They also move quickly on cold starts — and cold starts are where a lot of engine wear happens.

The trade-off is that thinner oils rely heavily on the correct additive package and the engine being designed for them. That's why specs matter so much now.

When thicker oils are still used (performance, heavy-duty)

Some engines still call for thicker oils like 5W-40, 0W-40, or 10W-30 — often for high-performance, heavy-duty use, or certain older designs. Towing, high heat, track days, and hard use can also push manufacturers to recommend a different grade (sometimes seasonally or by duty cycle).

TIP

Bottom line: Don't "upgrade" viscosity on a hunch. Follow the manual, and if you're doing severe-duty driving, look for the manufacturer's severe-service recommendation.

Oil-Life Monitoring Systems

Your *oil-life monitor* is basically your car's version of a smartwatch: not reading your mind, but doing math about how hard the oil has worked based on trip length, temperature, load, time, and engine speed.

Dashboard reminders and algorithms

That oil-life percentage on your dash isn't your car judging your moral character. It's an estimate based on driving conditions: temperature, trip length, engine load, RPM, time, and sometimes more. Your car is basically doing math so you don't have to (which is honestly very generous).

Some vehicles also use sensors that monitor things like temperature or conductivity, but most systems are algorithm-based. Either way, they're far smarter than the old "every 3,000 miles no matter what" rule.

Why 3,000-mile rule is outdated

Modern engines, oils, and filters are better than they used to be. Many vehicles have normal-service intervals in the 7,500 to 10,000 mile range (sometimes more), especially with the correct synthetic oil. The 3,000-mile rule stuck around because it's simple, memorable, and convenient for oil-change marketing.

That said, "outdated" doesn't mean "ignore maintenance forever." It means you should follow the manufacturer's schedule or oil-life monitor, not a superstition from 1996.

Condition-based oil changes (driving habits, climate, load)

Oil gets used up faster when you do lots of short trips (oil doesn't fully warm up), drive in extreme heat or cold, tow or haul, idle a lot, drive in dusty areas, or drive like every on-ramp is an audition for an action movie.

REMEMBER

Normal service and severe service are not judgments about your personality. They're about how hard your oil's life is. If your driving matches severe service, use the severe-service interval.

Filters: More than Just a Can

If oil is the engine's liquid gold, the filter is the unglamorous friend following behind with a trash bag. Its job is to catch the soot, metal dust, and microscopic junk the oil picks up before that grit keeps circulating.

Spin-on versus cartridge filters

Spin-on filters are the classic metal cans you twist on and off. A typical spin-on filter has a metal can, filter media that traps grit, a gasket that seals the filter to the engine, and, depending on the design, small internal valves that help manage oil flow.

Many spin-on filters include an *anti-drainback valve,* which helps keep oil from draining out of the filter when the engine is off. That can help oil pressure build faster at startup. Many also include a *bypass valve,* which allows oil to keep flowing if the filter media is restricted. Dirty oil is still better than no oil.

Cartridge filters use a replaceable paper element inside a reusable housing. On some cartridge setups, valve functions may be built into the housing or cap instead of the filter element itself, so the safest move is always to use the correct filter for your exact engine.

Figure 14-2 shows the common features you'll see on a typical spin-on filter.

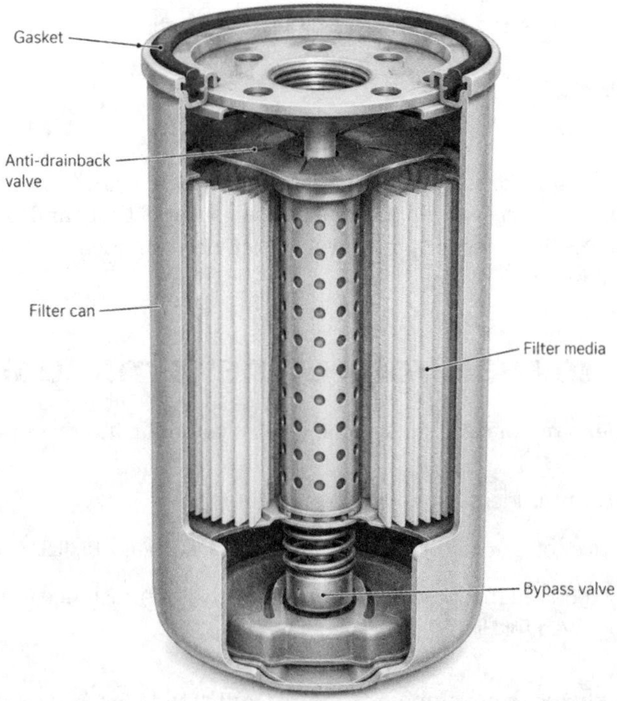

FIGURE 14-2: Typical oil filter features.

Generated with AI using OpenAI

REMEMBER

A bypass valve is an internal backup, not a warning light. You usually won't know exactly when it opens from the driver's seat. If the oil pressure light comes on, the engine rattles at startup, or the oil and filter have been neglected, change the oil and filter and diagnose the problem instead of assuming the bypass valve has everything handled.

Why using a quality filter matters as much as the oil itself

A quality filter isn't automatically the most expensive one on the shelf. Look for the correct part number for your exact year, make, model, and engine; a reputable brand; the right gasket or cartridge fit; and a filter that meets the manufacturer's requirements for your oil-change interval. If the filter includes an anti-drainback valve or bypass valve, those features also need to match the engine's design. For using your VIN to order the correct parts, see Chapter 1.

If your engine requires a specific filter type (especially cartridge housings and specialty filters), use the correct part number. Filters aren't the place for improvisation.

Modern Service Intervals and Manufacturer Specs

Modern oil service isn't "change it when it feels right" anymore. It's more like following a recipe where the oven costs several thousand dollars: The engine wants a specific viscosity plus the exact performance spec or approval it was designed around.

How to read your owner's manual oil spec

The owner's manual or under-hood label is your oil truth serum. It usually tells you:

- Viscosity grade, such as 0W-20 or 5W-30
- Service category or performance standard, such as API, ILSAC, or ACEA
- Any required manufacturer approval, such as a "must meet" or "approved for" line

Those alphabet-soup standards matter. API stands for American Petroleum Institute, ILSAC is a common gasoline-engine oil standard, and ACEA is a European oil-standard system. You don't need to memorize the organizations; you just need the letters on the bottle to match what your vehicle requires.

Figure 14-3 is your quick label cheat sheet. You're looking for three things: the viscosity grade, the service rating, and any required approval your vehicle demands.

OEM-specific oil requirements

Some manufacturers don't just say "use 5W-30." They also require a specific performance standard or approval. You'll see this as a line on the bottle that says something like "Meets . . ." or "Approved for . . .."

Examples include GM's dexos standards, VW/Audi approvals, and BMW Longlife (LL) approvals. The exact code depends on the engine and model year, so treat the manual as the boss, not the internet comment section.

TIP

If the manual requires an approval, find it printed on the bottle. "This is basically the same thing" is how you end up with basically the same problems.

FIGURE 14-3: Oil label cheat sheet.

Generated with AI using OpenAI

Why following spec is more important than brand loyalty

Oil brands are like pizza opinions: Everyone has one, and nobody is calm about it. The good news is your engine doesn't care about your brand loyalty — it cares about the correct viscosity and the correct spec/approval.

Choose any reputable oil that meets the required standards, change it on schedule, and your engine will usually live a long, boring (which is good) life.

Special Considerations

Not all engines live the same oil life. Turbos add heat, direct injection adds quirks, and hybrids can subject oil to lots of starts, stops, and short warm-up cycles, so the right oil and interval matter even more.

Turbocharged engines

Turbos are powered by exhaust heat, which means they live in an environment best described as "surface of the sun, but smaller." The turbo's bearings rely on a steady supply of clean oil.

If oil overheats in the turbo, it can bake into deposits *(coking)* that restrict oil flow and shorten turbo life. Using the correct synthetic oil, sticking to the right interval, and avoiding constant hot shutoffs after hard driving can help.

TIP

After a hard drive (towing, mountain climbs, spirited driving), give the engine a short cooldown idle before shutoff when practical. It's not a ritual — it's just letting temperatures settle so that oil doesn't get cooked in place.

Direct injection engines

Direct injection (DI) engines are efficient and powerful, but they can be prone to a nasty event called LSPI — low-speed pre-ignition. In plain English, the engine can "bang" before it's supposed to, under load at low RPM, and that can be hard on pistons and bearings.

One reason oil specs got stricter is to help reduce LSPI risk. Using the correct spec (and not randomly swapping viscosities) is part of keeping DI engines happy.

Hybrids

Hybrids love starting and stopping the gas engine. That can mean more cold starts and more moisture/fuel dilution in the oil if the engine doesn't get fully warm often.

Many hybrids also go longer between oil changes because the engine doesn't run constantly, but the oil still ages with time and contamination. Follow the oil-life monitor or the manual's time/mileage limits, whichever comes first.

How to Check Your Oil Correctly

Checking your oil is like checking your phone battery before you leave the house: It takes a minute, and it can save your day from going sideways. The goal is a quick, accurate reading — not a false alarm caused by checking on a slope or rushing the job.

Dipstick method

Checking oil is one of the highest-value maintenance habits you can develop. It takes a few minutes and can save you from the kind of repair bill that makes you consider bicycles as a personality change.

REMEMBER

For an accurate reading, park on level ground and give the oil a little time to drain back into the pan. Figure 14-4 shows a typical dipstick with MIN and MAX marks (or holes/lines). Your job is to stay safely between them — not to hit MAX like you're playing a carnival game.

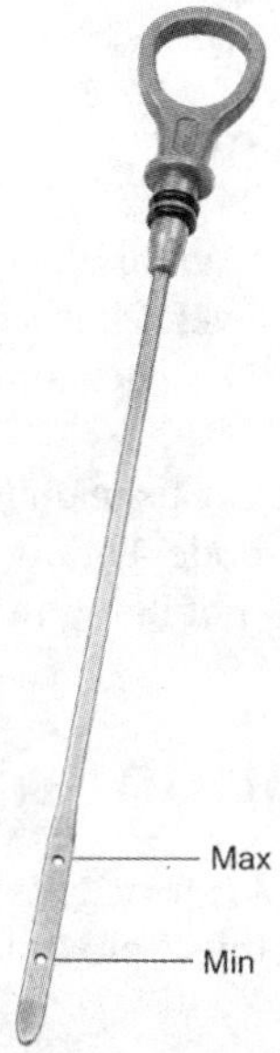

FIGURE 14-4: Dipstick level marks and what "between the lines" looks like.

Generated with AI using OpenAI

1. **Park on level ground and shut the engine off.**

   Wait 5 to 10 minutes so that oil can drain back into the pan. (Checking immediately after shutoff can read low because oil is still up in the engine.)

2. **Pull the dipstick, wipe it clean, and reinsert fully.**

   Make sure it seats all the way — a half-seated dipstick gives you a half-true reading.

3. **Pull it again and read the level.**

   Oil should be between MIN and MAX (or between the two holes/lines). If it's below MIN, you need to add oil.

4. **Take a quick look at the oil.**

   Dark oil can be normal. What you don't want is a burnt smell, metal glitter, or a milky chocolate shake look (possible coolant contamination).

5. **If needed, top off in small amounts and recheck.**

   Add a little, wait a minute, and recheck. Overfilling isn't extra protection. Too much oil can get whipped into foam by moving engine parts, and foamy oil does a lousy job lubricating and cooling. It can also get pushed into places it doesn't belong, causing smoke, leaks, or emissions-system trouble. If the level ends up above MAX, remove the extra oil until it's back in the safe range.

WARNING

If the dipstick shows no oil at all, don't start the engine "just to see." Add oil first and then reassess. No oil on the stick means you're already in the danger zone.

Digital oil level sensors

Some vehicles don't give you a traditional dipstick. Instead, they use a dashboard menu and a sensor to estimate oil level. That's convenient . . . until you're standing there wishing you could just pull a stick and know.

Digital systems usually require the car to be on level ground, at a certain temperature, and sometimes in a specific mode. Follow the on-screen instructions. If the car says "conditions not met," it's not being moody — it's trying to be accurate.

Oil color and condition

Oil color alone doesn't tell the whole story. Fresh oil darkens quickly, especially in engines that run hot or have direct injection. Dark doesn't automatically mean bad.

Things that should make you investigate further:

- **Milky or frothy oil:** Possible coolant contamination
- **Strong fuel smell:** Possible fuel dilution, especially with lots of short trips
- **Metal sparkles:** Wear debris — the opposite of a fun glitter craft
- **Oil level rising on its own:** Possible with fuel dilution — not normal

DIY Oil Changes: A Condensed Guide

Doing your own oil change is like cooking at home: cheaper, oddly satisfying, and somehow you still end up with a mystery smear on your elbow. The trick is having the right tools ready before you loosen the drain plug.

REMEMBER

An oil change is very DIY-friendly — as long as you take the safety part seriously. The goal isn't speed. The goal is no crushed fingers and no oil waterfall.

Gather the following tools and safety gear:

- Correct oil type and amount (check the manual/spec label)
- New oil filter (and a new drain plug washer, if your vehicle uses one)
- Drain pan (big enough for the full capacity)
- Socket/wrench for the drain plug and a filter wrench, if needed
- Funnel, gloves, shop towels, and safety glasses
- Ramps or jack stands and wheel chocks (never rely on a jack alone)
- A way to reset the oil-life monitor (usually a dash/menu procedure)

WARNING

Never get under a vehicle supported only by a jack. Use ramps or jack stands on solid ground and chock the wheels. This warning isn't being dramatic — it's staying alive.

Figure 14-5 shows the basic setup: safe vehicle support, a drain pan, the drain plug, and the filter location. Your vehicle may hide the filter behind a splash shield or tuck it sideways just to test your patience.

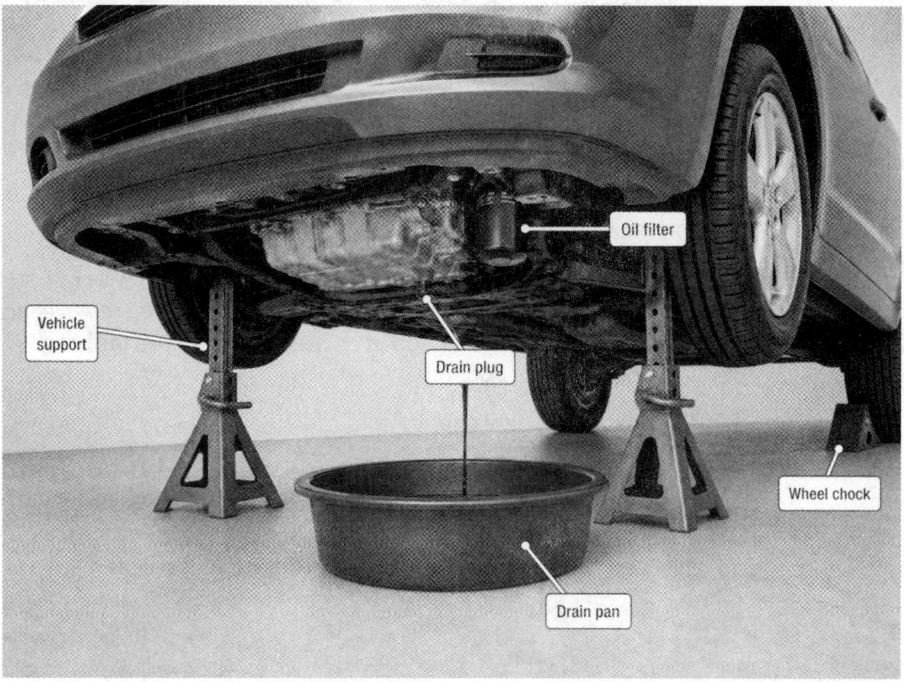

FIGURE 14-5: Basic oil change layout.

Generated with AI using OpenAI

Drain, filter, and refill basics

Once the vehicle is safely supported and your drain pan is in position, the basic oil-change rhythm is simple: Drain the old oil, replace the filter, refill with the correct oil, and verify the level before you call the job done.

1. **Warm the engine slightly and then shut it off.**

   A few minutes helps oil drain faster. Don't get it scorching hot if you're new to changing oil — hot oil burns.

2. **Safely raise and support the vehicle.**

   Set the parking brake, chock a wheel, and give the car a gentle shake test before you crawl under it. For safe lifting and support, see Chapter 1.

3. **Remove the drain plug and let the oil drain completely.**

   Place the drain pan under the plug, remembering that oil may shoot outward at first instead of dropping straight down. Use the correct-size socket or wrench to loosen the drain plug and then turn it counterclockwise by hand once it's loose enough. Keep light inward pressure on the plug until the last thread releases so that it doesn't fall into the drain pan like a tiny metal submarine. For socket and wrench basics, see Chapter 3.

4. **Reinstall the drain plug.**

   Wipe the plug, replace the drain plug washer if your vehicle uses one, and thread the plug in by hand first to avoid cross-threading. Then tighten it with the same socket or wrench. If you have the torque spec, use a torque wrench. "Snug" is good; "stripped oil pan" is not. For torque wrench basics, see Chapter 3.

5. **Remove the old filter.**

   If you have a spin-on filter, unscrew it counterclockwise by hand or with a filter wrench if it's stubborn. If you have a cartridge filter, remove the filter housing cap using the correct socket or wrench. Make sure the old gasket isn't stuck to the engine or housing.

6. **Install the new one.**

   Lightly oil the new gasket and then install the new filter. Tighten a spin-on filter by hand, usually about 3/4 turn after the gasket touches. Tighten cartridge housings to the vehicle's spec. For spin-on and cartridge filter differences, see "Spin-on versus cartridge filters," earlier in this chapter.

7. **Add fresh oil, start the engine briefly, and check for leaks.**

   Add the correct oil type and amount through the oil-fill opening using a funnel. Start the engine for 10 to 20 seconds and then shut it off and look around the plug and filter for leaks.

8. **Recheck the level and top off.**

   After a few minutes, check the dipstick (or sensor reading) and adjust the level to the proper range. Add oil in small amounts and recheck so that you don't overfill it.

9. **Reset the oil-life monitor.**

   If you skip this step, your car will keep reminding you forever. Cars don't forgive. If you don't know the reset steps, check the owner's manual or Google your year, make, and model plus "reset oil life" and follow the button/menu dance.

Proper disposal and recycling

REMEMBER

Used oil is recyclable, but it doesn't go in the trash, down a drain, into a storm sewer, onto the ground, or into a random "I'll deal with this later" container in the garage. Treat it like a fluid that needs a proper handoff.

After the oil cools, pour it into a clean, sealed jug, such as the empty oil bottles or another clean container with a tight cap. Keep the container upright, label it used motor oil if needed, and take it to a place that accepts used oil. Many auto parts stores, repair shops, recycling centers, and household hazardous waste, or HHW, drop-off sites accept used motor oil, often for free. Rules vary by location, so check before you go.

Do not mix used oil with coolant, brake fluid, transmission fluid, gasoline, water, or mystery garage liquids. Mixed fluids are harder to recycle and may be refused.

Used filters are often accepted, too, after they've drained for a few hours. Bag the filter, bring it with the used oil if your drop-off site accepts filters. Never dump oil in a storm drain, on soil, or anywhere you would prefer your drinking water not to come from.

Warning Signs of Oil Trouble

Oil problems rarely arrive like a movie explosion. They usually show up as a smell, a drip, a puff of smoke, or a warning light first — and catching those clues early can save an engine.

Dashboard low-oil pressure light

A dashboard low-oil pressure light is the big one. The oil-pressure light usually means the engine isn't getting the pressurized oil flow it needs right now. Not soon. Not later. Now.

Figure 14-6 shows a simple decision tree for what to do. It's short on purpose: When oil pressure is truly low, time is not your friend.

If the low-oil pressure light comes on while you're driving, treat it like an engine-protection emergency and follow these steps right away:

1. **Ease off the throttle and pull over safely.**

   Reduce load, find a safe spot, and don't keep driving to see whether it clears.

2. **Shut the engine off.**

   If pressure is low, every second of running is extra wear.

3. **Check the oil level after a few minutes.**

   If it's low, add oil until it's in the safe range.

4. **If the light stays on (or the engine is noisy), tow it.**

   Do not drive it. Not driving is how you save an engine.

WARNING

If you hear knocking, loud ticking, or grinding with an oil-pressure warning, do not restart the engine. Tow it. The engine is telling you it's out of protective film, and it's not being subtle.

Blue smoke

Bluish smoke from the exhaust often means the engine is burning oil. You may see it on startup, during hard acceleration, or on long downhill stretches. A little puff once in a while isn't always a crisis, but steady smoke is a sign to investigate.

Common causes include worn valve seals, worn piston rings, or turbocharger oil seal issues. Translation: Oil is sneaking into places it shouldn't and then getting turned into "perfume" you can smell at stoplights.

Oil leaks and stains

If your oil level drops and you're not seeing smoke, look for leaks. Fresh oil looks wet and shiny; older leaks collect dirt and turn into a greasy paste.

Figure 14-6 shows common leak areas: valve cover gaskets, oil pan gaskets, filter/housing seals, crank seals, and (on turbos) oil feed/return lines.

FIGURE 14-6: Common oil leak points.

Generated with AI using OpenAI

TIP

Trying to confirm a small leak? Park over a piece of cardboard overnight. It turns "maybe" into "yep" without you crawling around in the dark.

Engine knocking/tapping noises

Light ticking can be normal on some engines. Loud ticking, knocking, or a sudden new tap dance is not. If the ticking is paired with an oil warning light, low oil level, or a big leak, shut the engine down and investigate before you turn a small problem into a full engine rebuild.

REMEMBER

There is no shame in towing to prevent engine damage. Towing is expensive. Engines are more expensive. Math wins.

IN THIS CHAPTER

» Seeing how brakes turn motion into controlled stopping

» Comparing disc, drum, parking brake, and wear-sensor basics

» Understanding brake fluid, moisture, and service intervals

» Sorting out ABS, EBD, brake assist, ESC, and brake-by-wire

» Maintaining brakes on gas, hybrid, and EV vehicles responsibly

Chapter 15
Brake Check: How Stopping Power Has Evolved

Your car can do a lot of impressive things: Merge onto the highway, haul a week's worth of groceries, and somehow make your phone disappear into the seat crack like it entered a different dimension. But the most important thing it does? It stops. On purpose. Repeatedly. Without turning your commute into a low-budget action movie.

In this chapter, we show you how brakes turn pedal pressure into stopping power, why disc and drum brakes still share the road, how brake fluid and safety systems help keep stops controlled, and what changes when hybrids and EVs blend regenerative braking with friction brakes. You also get the maintenance clues that tell you when your brakes need attention before squeals, grinding, warning lights, or weird pedal feel turn into a bigger problem.

Why Brakes Are the Most Important Safety System

Going is optional. Stopping is mandatory. Brakes are the one system you use every single time you drive — sometimes gently, sometimes urgently, and sometimes with the emotional intensity of someone realizing a yellow light is shorter than it was in 2009.

Also, brakes don't just stop the car. They help you stop predictably, in a straight line, and with enough control to steer around trouble instead of starring in it. That's why the braking system has gotten smarter over the years — not because drivers got worse, but because traffic did.

Stopping = safety

Brakes are your car's most important safety system because they're the difference between a close call and a new bumper. A good braking system helps you:

- Keep a safe following distance (even when the driver ahead is emotionally attached to sudden stops)
- Stay in control when traction is limited (rain, snow, gravel, or panic)
- Reduce stopping distance when everything is working the way it should
- Maintain steering control so that you can avoid a hazard, not just meet it

Here's the big truth that surprises people (and occasionally offends them): Brakes don't create traction — tires do. Brakes only use the grip you already have. So if your tires are worn, underinflated, or basically smooth like a bowling ball, your brakes can be brand-new and still feel underwhelming. (For tire traction and stopping-distance reality checks, see Chapter 18.)

And one more thing that matters way more than most people realize: heat. Braking works by turning your car's motion into heat through friction. One hard stop is usually fine. Repeated hard stops — mountains, towing, stop-and-go, spirited driving — can heat things up until braking starts to feel weaker or less consistent — that's brake *fade,* which is a polite term for "my brakes are tired and would like a vacation."

REMEMBER

If your stopping distance feels longer than it should, don't just blame the brakes. Tires, road surface, load, and speed all matter — and speed matters a lot.

Redundancy in design

Engineers design brakes the way paranoid people pack for a weekend trip: with backups for the backups — plus snacks, plus a flashlight, plus a second flashlight "in case the first flashlight has feelings."

That's where a split hydraulic system comes in. In most modern cars, the master cylinder is basically a two-in-one setup (often called a tandem master cylinder). Instead of sending pressure through one single brake loop, it sends pressure through two separate hydraulic circuits. Your brake system isn't one long straw; it's two straws, each feeding part of the braking system.

What does a split hydraulic system get you? Insurance. If one circuit leaks (say, a brake line fails), you don't automatically lose all braking. You usually keep partial braking — enough to get safely stopped and get help.

Here's how that split is usually arranged:

- **Front/rear split:** One circuit handles the front brakes, while the other handles the rear brakes.
- **Diagonal split:** One circuit handles left-front and right-rear, and the other handles right-front and left-rear. (This split helps reduce hard pulling if one circuit fails, because you still have one front wheel braking.)

If one circuit fails, the pedal may suddenly feel like it has trust issues — it can go lower than normal, feel spongy, and require more effort to slow down. It's the automotive version of "I can still do the job, but I'd like you to notice I'm not happy."

Modern braking systems often include extra layers of help, such as:

- Split brake circuits so that one failure doesn't wipe out everything
- A brake booster to reduce pedal effort (vacuum, hydraulic, or electronic, depending on the vehicle)
- ABS and stability control to step in when the wheels start losing grip
- A parking brake system that can hold the car when parked — and can act as a limited backup in a true emergency

But here's the important part: Redundancy is for getting you safely stopped, not for "let's keep driving for a week and see what happens."

WARNING

If your brake warning light comes on, your pedal suddenly feels wrong (soft, sinking, or needing pumping), you hear grinding, or the car pulls when you brake, don't wait and see. That's how small issues become large invoices. For staying calm and handling emergencies, see Chapter 20. For tracking down odd sensations and noises, Chapter 21 is your decoder ring.

Basics of Hydraulic Braking

Hydraulic brakes are basically a legal way to turn your foot into super strength. You press the pedal with a human amount of force, and the system multiplies it into "clamp a spinning metal disc" force. It's one of the most satisfying cause-and-effect chains on the entire vehicle — when everything is working correctly, anyway.

Fluid pressure

Hydraulic braking works because brake fluid doesn't like being squished. When you press the pedal, you create pressure in the brake lines, and that pressure travels to the brakes at each wheel. The whole system depends on one key feature: It's sealed. (Air is the enemy — it compresses — which is why a spongy pedal often points to air in the lines. We talk bleeding in "Pads, rotors, and bleeding," later in this chapter.)

Figure 15-1 shows the basic path from your foot to the wheels — the simplest way to understand what's happening when you hit the brakes. When you press the brake pedal, the *brake booster* helps reduce the effort your leg has to provide. The *master cylinder* turns that pedal movement into hydraulic pressure. *Brake fluid* carries that pressure through the brake lines to the brakes at each wheel. On disc brakes, the *caliper* squeezes the brake pads against the rotor. On drum brakes, *brake shoes* press against the inside of the drum. The next sections break down those parts one at a time.

Master cylinder

The *master cylinder* is the brake system's headquarters. It converts pedal movement into hydraulic pressure and pulls brake fluid from a reservoir so that the system always has a supply. If you've ever popped the hood and seen a small plastic tank near the firewall labeled "brake fluid," that's the reservoir. It's not decorative. It's your stopping budget.

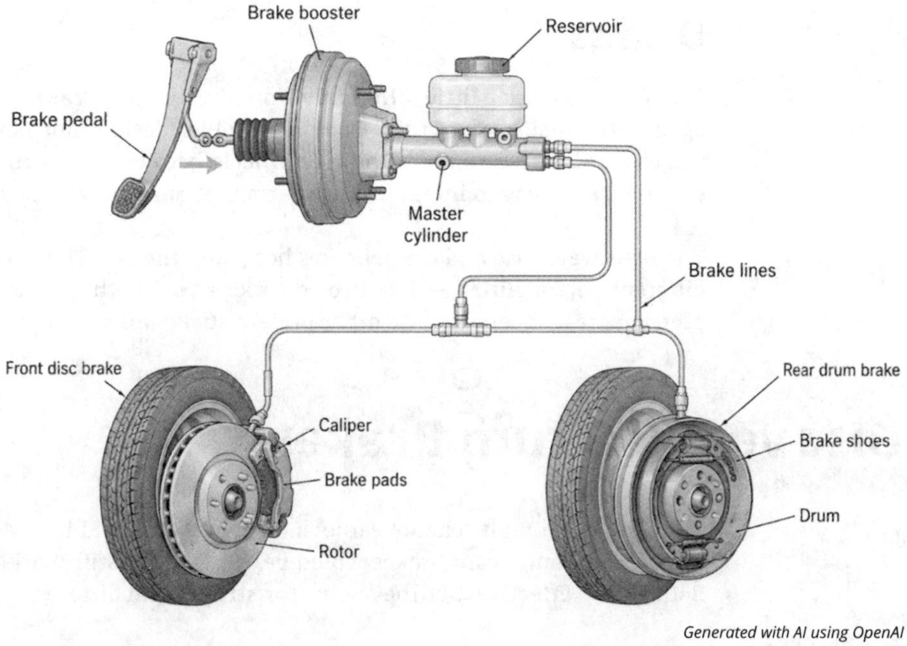

FIGURE 15-1: Basic hydraulic brake layout.

Most modern vehicles also use a brake booster (vacuum, hydraulic, or electric) to reduce how hard you need to press. Without it, your leg would get a workout every time you approached a stop sign — great for fitness, terrible for daily driving.

Disc brakes

On disc brakes, *calipers* squeeze brake pads against *rotors* (the metal discs attached to the wheels). That friction turns motion into heat (hello again, heat) — which is why braking hard down a mountain can make brakes smell like "hot metal plus regret."

A few normal-but-surprising brake realities:

- **Brakes are designed to get hot.** They just aren't designed to stay blazing hot forever.
- **A little brake dust on your wheels is normal.** Brake dust is annoying, but normal.
- **If you feel shaking while braking, it may be rotor issues** — or it may be something else up front. Chapter 21 helps you sort out those issues.

Drums

Drum brakes work a little differently from disc brakes: Brake shoes press outward against the inside of a drum. They're an older design, but not extinct — many vehicles still use drums on the rear wheels because they can be durable, cost-effective, and easy to integrate with certain parking brake designs.

The takeaway: Disc and drum brakes both stop the car. They just go about it with different personalities — like two coworkers who both get the job done, but one prefers spreadsheets and the other prefers sticky notes.

Disc versus Drum Brakes

If brakes had a high school yearbook, disc brakes would be "Most Likely to Keep Their Cool," and drum brakes would be "Still Here, Still Working, Stop Asking." Both can be effective, but they shine (or struggle) in different situations.

Disc brakes generally manage heat better, perform more consistently, and tend to shed water more easily in wet conditions. They're also often easier to inspect because the pads and rotors are more visible — which means fewer "surprise, you needed brakes last month" moments.

Disc brakes create friction when a caliper squeezes brake pads against a rotor. Drum brakes create friction when brake shoes press outward against the inside of a drum. In other words, disc brakes clamp from the outside, while drum brakes press from the inside. Disc brakes usually manage heat and repeated hard stops better, while drum brakes package the braking parts differently and can handle parking brake duty neatly. Figure 15-2 gives a quick visual of those two friction paths.

DRUMS THEN VERSUS NOW

Historically, drums were everywhere. They work fine for normal driving, but they can hold heat more than discs, which can lead to reduced performance during repeated hard stops. Today's drums are better than the old stereotypes, but the heat-management advantage still leans toward discs.

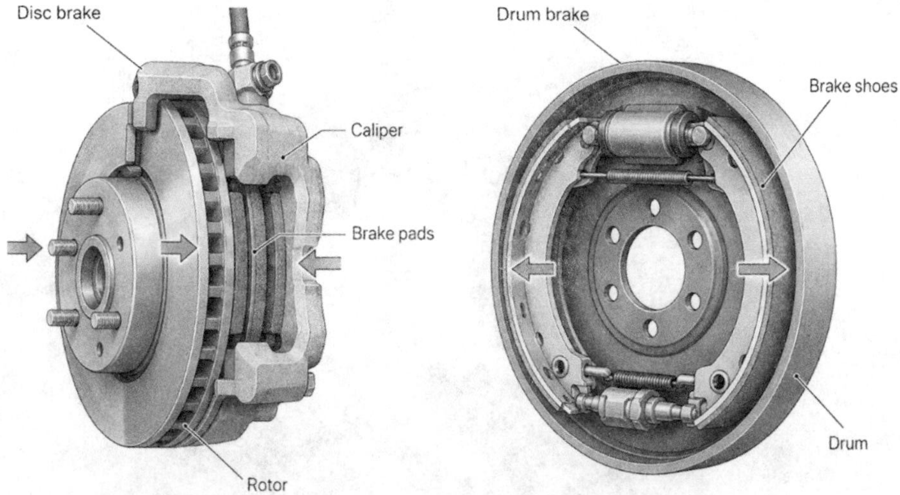

FIGURE 15-2: Disc versus drum brakes at a glance.

Generated with AI using OpenAI

Rear drum brakes still show up on some vehicles because rear brakes often do less of the stopping work in everyday driving. (Weight shifts forward when you brake.) Drums can also handle parking brake duties neatly. If your vehicle has rear drums, it doesn't mean it's outdated — it just means the manufacturer picked a design that fits the vehicle's needs and budget.

Brake Fluid

Brake fluid is the quiet hero that makes hydraulic brakes possible — and it gets almost no love until something goes wrong. It's also one of the few fluids in your car that can ruin paint faster than a bad DIY project. So yes: Respect the brake fluid.

DOT 3, 4, 5.1

Most cars use DOT 3, DOT 4, or DOT 5.1 brake fluid. The DOT number mainly reflects heat performance (boiling point) and, in some formulations, viscosity — which matters when ABS/ESC valves are working fast. The correct type is usually printed on the reservoir cap or listed in your owner's manual. The important rule is simple: Use exactly what your vehicle calls for. Choosing brake fluid is not a "close enough" situation.

Figure 15-3 shows where you'll usually find the brake fluid spec — on the reservoir cap that's usually near the firewall — and it's worth checking before you buy anything that comes in a bottle with lightning bolts on it.

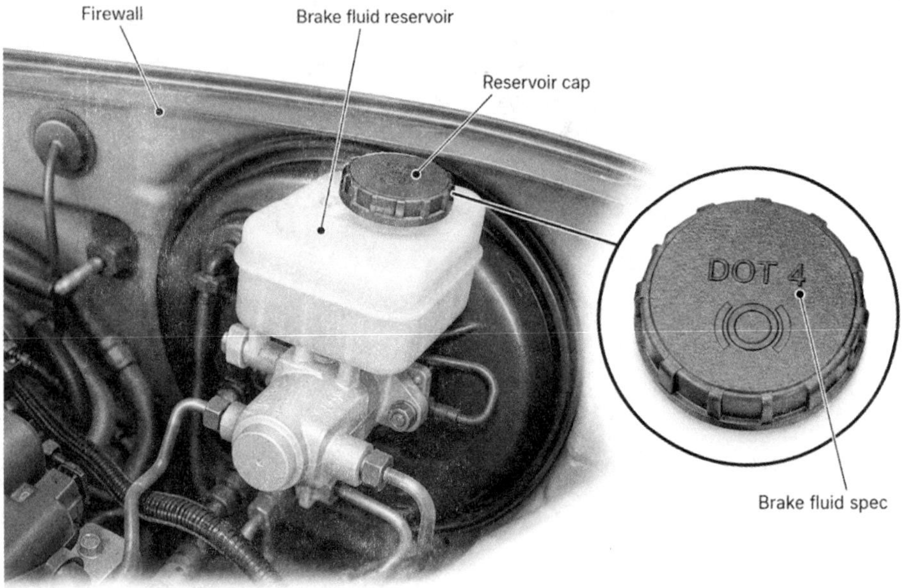

FIGURE 15-3: Brake fluid reservoir cap markings (DOT rating) and where to confirm specs.

Generated with AI using OpenAI

WARNING

DOT 5.1 isn't DOT 5. DOT 3/4/5.1 are glycol-based; DOT 5 is silicone-based and is generally not interchangeable. And whatever you do, don't spill brake fluid on painted surfaces — it can damage paint. If you spill it, wipe it up immediately and rinse with water.

Moisture absorption

Most brake fluid absorbs moisture from the air over time. That moisture lowers the fluid's boiling point and can encourage corrosion inside brake components. Translation: Old brake fluid can make hard braking less consistent — especially when the system gets hot — and it can help corrosion quietly rack up future repair bills.

A brake pedal that gets mushy after repeated hard stops can be a sign the system is overheated — sometimes from pad fade, sometimes from fluid getting too hot. Either way, it's your brakes asking for a cooldown. Don't ignore it — and don't keep pushing your luck downhill. (Mountain driving is a special kind of test for brakes.)

Service intervals

Brake fluid service intervals vary by vehicle and driving conditions, so your owner's manual gets the final vote. Many manufacturers recommend changing brake fluid periodically based on time — not just miles — because moisture buildup happens whether you drive a lot or a little.

For your monthly under-the-hood sanity check, Chapter 2 will keep you on track. You typically won't be changing brake fluid monthly — but you can absolutely keep an eye on the fluid level and look for leaks or sudden drops.

ABS and EBD

Anti-lock Braking System (ABS) is one of those systems you don't think about until it activates — and then you think about it a lot. The pedal pulses, the car makes noises, and your brain briefly wonders if the vehicle is doing interpretive dance. Relax. If ABS is working, it's trying to help you stay in control.

Skid prevention

ABS helps prevent wheel lock-up during hard braking. When wheels lock, steering control drops dramatically — you become a passenger, not a driver. ABS rapidly modulates brake pressure so the wheels keep turning enough for you to steer around trouble while still braking hard.

ABS often feels and sounds like:

- A vibrating or pulsing brake pedal, which is totally normal during ABS activation
- A grinding or buzzing sound from the ABS pump (normal, if brief)
- The car remains steerable — which is the whole point

One more dashboard translation: If the ABS warning light stays on (not just flashing when traction is sketchy), ABS and stability control may be disabled. You'll usually still have normal brakes — but without the anti-lock safety net — so get it checked.

REMEMBER

If ABS activates, keep firm pressure on the brake pedal and steer where you want to go. Don't pump the brakes like it's 1978 — ABS is already doing the pumping for you.

Figure 15-4 shows the basic ABS building blocks: wheel-speed sensors feeding an ABS module that can adjust brake pressure faster than any human foot.

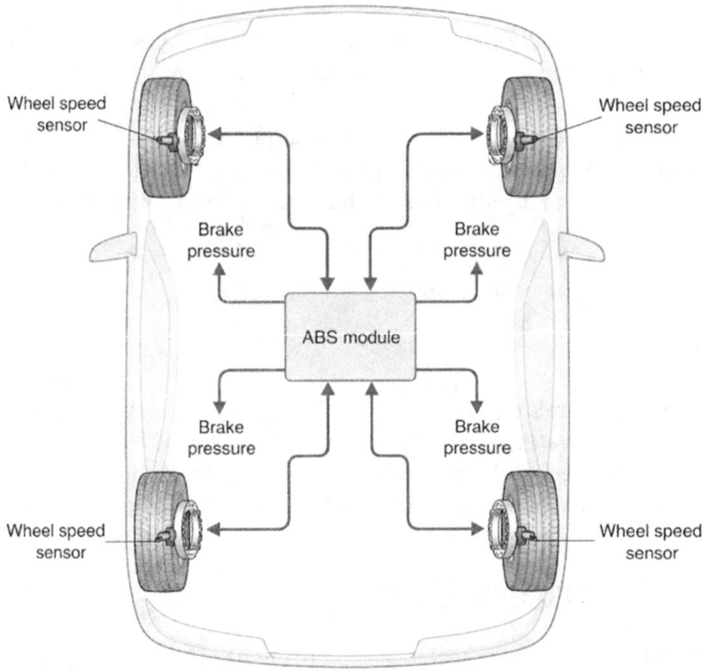

FIGURE 15-4: ABS basics.

Generated with AI using OpenAI

Electronic distribution

Electronic Brakeforce Distribution (EBD) is the quiet partner to ABS. It adjusts how much braking force goes to the front and rear based on load and traction, helping keep stops smooth and stable — especially when the vehicle is loaded down with passengers, cargo, or that one friend who packs like they're moving out.

Brake Assist and ESC

In a perfect world, everyone brakes smoothly, steadily, and with the calm precision of a driving instructor. In the real world, people panic-brake like they're trying to stomp a spider. Modern vehicles add extra systems to help you brake effectively when your brain is busy screaming.

Emergency boost

Brake assist looks for emergency-braking behavior (like a sudden slam of the pedal) and boosts hydraulic pressure if it thinks you're not pressing hard enough.

It's basically your car saying, "I understand you're scared — let me help you be more effective."

If you ever felt like you hit the brakes hard and the car somehow stopped even harder than expected, that may have been brake assist stepping in.

Stability control integration

Electronic Stability Control (ESC) is like a quiet referee for skids. If the vehicle starts to rotate more than you intended (oversteer/understeer), ESC can apply braking to individual wheels and sometimes reduce engine power to help you regain control. It's one of the most important modern safety technologies on the road.

ESC ties directly into the braking system, so when you see traction/stability lights flashing, it's often the brakes doing tiny, targeted corrections you may not even feel. For more on staying calm when things get sketchy, see Chapter 20.

Parking Brakes

The parking brake is your vehicle's "stay" command — like telling a dog not to chase a squirrel, except the dog weighs two tons and has questionable judgment on hills. Parking brakes don't get much attention until you need one that actually works.

Traditional parking brakes use a hand lever or foot pedal connected by cables to the rear brakes. They're simple, mechanical, and often very reliable — as long as they're used occasionally. A parking brake that never gets used can seize up or get weak, like a gym membership that only exists in theory.

Also, quick fun fact: Some cars with rear disc brakes still use a tiny drum-style parking brake inside the hat of the rotor. So, yes, you can have discs and a mini drum at the same time.

Electronic Parking Brake (EPB) replaces the lever with a button and uses electric motors to apply and release the brake. Many systems also include an auto-hold feature in traffic, which is basically a tiny luxury for your right foot.

Figure 15-5 compares the basic layouts of traditional cable parking brakes and electronic systems that clamp at the caliper.

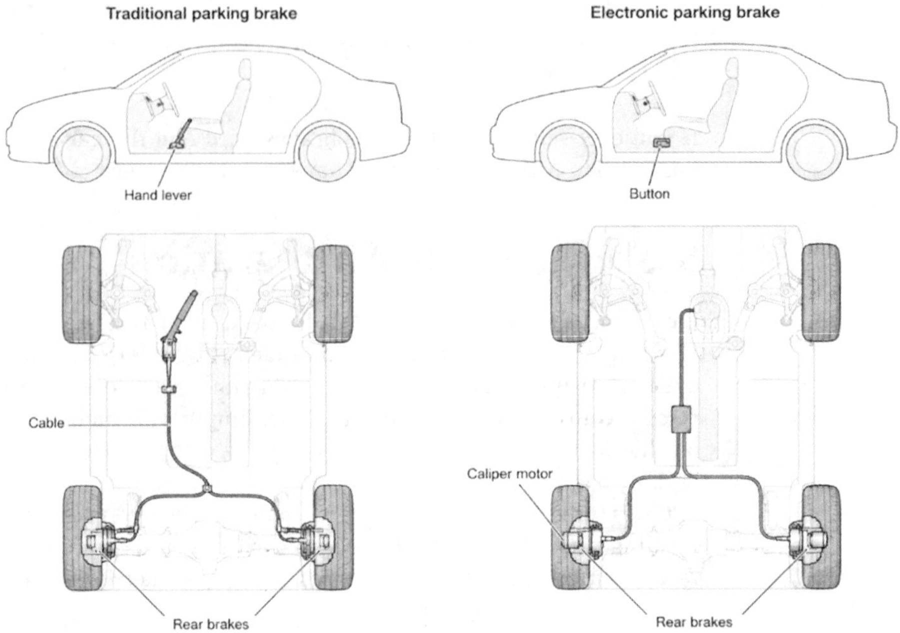

Generated with AI using OpenAI

FIGURE 15-5: Parking brakes (cable-operated) versus EPB (motor-on-caliper/button control).

TIP

On many automatics, using the parking brake before shifting into Park can reduce strain on the parking *pawl* — the small locking piece inside the transmission that helps hold the car in Park — especially on hills. It can also make it easier to shift out of Park later. Your transmission will quietly thank you.

Pads, Rotors, and Materials

Brake parts wear out. That's not a flaw — that's the plan. Pads are designed to sacrifice themselves so that your rotors, calipers, and wallet don't have to suffer unnecessarily. The trick is choosing parts that match your driving, not your favorite marketing slogan.

Ceramic versus semi-metallic pads

Most everyday vehicles use pads that fall into common families, such as ceramic or semi-metallic. Both can work well — they just have different tradeoffs.

Ceramic pads are often quieter, produce finer dust, and can feel smooth and consistent. Semi-metallic pads often have a strong bite and good heat handling, but they may be noisier and dustier.

TIP

The best pad is the one that matches your vehicle and driving (and meets any required specs).

Slotted, drilled, and coated

Rotors also come in different flavors: plain, coated, slotted, drilled, or any of these combinations. For most normal driving, quality plain or coated rotors are perfectly fine. Slotted or drilled rotors can have benefits in specific high-heat use, but they're not automatically better for daily commuting.

If you're choosing parts because you want a certain look behind the wheels, that's allowed — just don't sacrifice quality or correct fitment to achieve the aesthetic of "track day that never happens."

Brake Wear Sensors

Brakes don't usually fail in silence: They complain first. Sometimes they squeal. Sometimes they grind. Sometimes they light up your dashboard like a tiny, judgmental Christmas tree. Wear sensors exist to give you a heads-up before you go full metal-on-metal.

Some vehicles have brake pad wear sensors that trigger a dashboard warning when pads are low. Others rely on the classic squealer noise. Either way, the goal is the same: Replace pads before they chew into rotors and turn a routine job into a bigger repair.

Brake wear indicators usually come in two forms: a mechanical squealer (a small metal tab that squeaks when pads are thin) or an electronic sensor that triggers a warning light when wear reaches a limit.

Figure 15-6 shows both common designs — because once you know what they are, brake noises feel less mysterious and more like your car speaking in a very specific dialect.

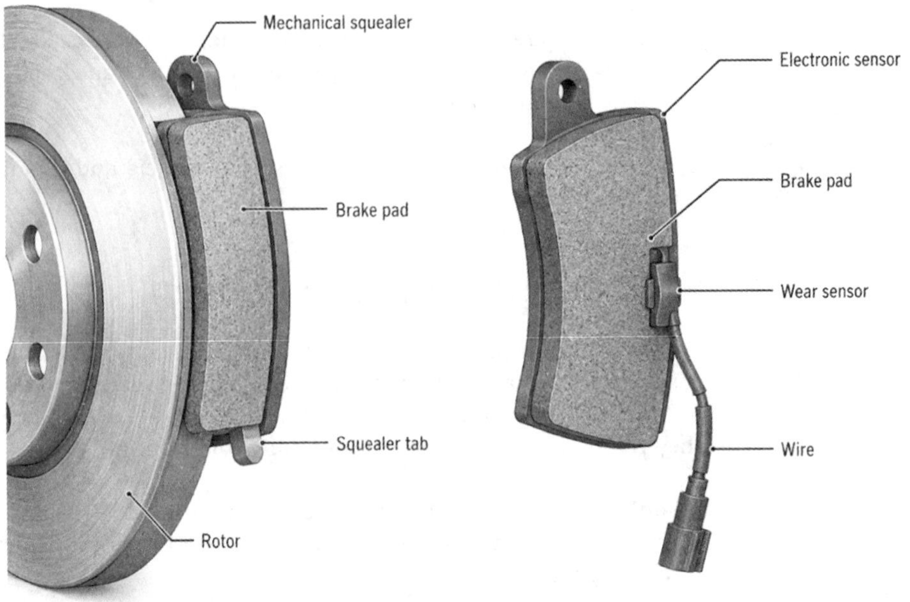

FIGURE 15-6: Brake pad wear indicators (mechanical squealer tab versus electronic wear sensor).

Generated with AI using OpenAI

Hybrid and EV Braking

Hybrids and EVs didn't just add batteries — they changed the whole slowing down vibe. In many cases, the car tries to slow you using the electric motor first and only calls on the friction brakes when it needs extra stopping power. It's like having two braking systems that share a group chat.

Regenerative braking

Regenerative braking uses the electric motor as a generator during deceleration, sending energy back into the battery instead of wasting it all as heat. The result can be improved efficiency and (often) less brake pad wear — especially in stop-and-go driving.

If you want the bigger picture on hybrids, EV components, and why regen feels different from car to car, Chapter 10 breaks it down.

Brake-by-wire

Some hybrids and EVs use brake-by-wire systems that blend regenerative braking with traditional friction braking. Your pedal input becomes a request, and the control system decides how much stopping comes from regen versus pads and rotors. When it's tuned well, you don't notice the handoff — you just stop smoothly.

Brake-by-wire also shows up on some gas-only cars, but it's most noticeable in hybrids and EVs because the system has to blend regen with friction braking smoothly.

Because brakes are a safety-critical system, brake-by-wire designs include redundancy and fail-safes. Still, if your hybrid or EV suddenly feels off when braking (or throws brake warnings), get it checked. A brake-by-wire problem is not a place to test your luck.

Maintenance and DIY

Brakes are one of the most commonly serviced systems — and one of the fastest ways to get in over your head if you rush or skip safety steps. The good news is you can do a lot as an owner: inspecting, listening, paying attention, and knowing when it's time to call a pro. (And if you want a more hands-on brake and bearing maintenance guide, Chapter 16 is where to go.)

Pads, rotors, and bleeding

At a basic level, brake maintenance is about three things: friction material (pads/shoes), smooth contact surfaces (rotors/drums), and healthy hydraulics (fluid and lines). If any one of those things is unhappy, the whole system feels it.

Here's a quick driveway inspection checklist:

- Look at pad thickness (if visible) and rotor condition through the wheel spokes.

  TIP

  Newer pads look thick and have plenty of friction material between the rotor and the metal backing plate. If the pad material looks thinner than about 1/4 inch, plan a closer inspection; if it's near 1/8 inch, uneven, or you can barely see material left, schedule brake service. For a more hands-on pad-and-rotor inspection, see Chapter 16.

- Check brake fluid level in the reservoir (sudden drops can mean leaks).
- Listen for new squeals, grinding, or scraping — especially when braking.
- Pay attention to pulling, vibrations, or a pedal that feels softer than usual.

Figure 15-7 highlights the common places to inspect and the "don't ignore this" trouble signs.

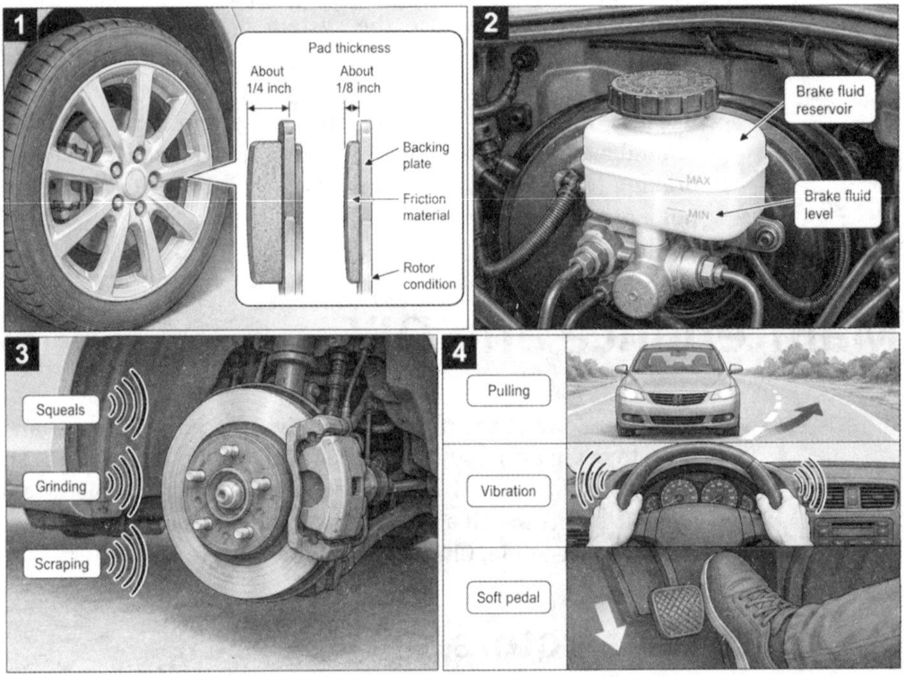

FIGURE 15-7: Quick brake inspection points.

Generated with AI using OpenAI

WARNING

If you're lifting the vehicle to inspect brakes, follow safe lifting practices (see Chapter 1) and use the right equipment (see Chapter 3). Never get under a car supported only by a jack. Brakes are important — but staying alive is even more important.

Bleeding brakes (removing air from the system) is a common DIY job, but it's also where many brake problems are accidentally created. If you're not confident in the process, it's completely reasonable to let a shop handle it. Air in the lines can reduce braking power, and reduced braking power isn't a fun learning experience.

ABS and EPB cautions

Modern brakes are tied into electronics in ways older cars never were. ABS modules may require specific bleeding procedures, and electronic parking brakes often need a service mode to retract properly during pad replacement.

TIP

If you're doing brake work and suddenly get warning lights, strange pedal feel, or an EPB that refuses to cooperate, don't keep forcing things. That's how connectors break, threads strip, and your simple weekend project becomes a multiweek saga. Chapter 23 can help you choose a shop, and Chapters 5 and 6 explain why modern electrical systems are so picky.

Environmental Responsibility

Brakes don't just stop your car — they create dust and waste, and brake fluid isn't something you want anywhere near your driveway drains. The good news: Being responsible here is easy, and you don't need to become an eco-monastic order of brake caretakers. Just handle the messy stuff correctly.

Copper-free pads

Brake pads have traditionally used copper in some formulations, and brake dust can wash into waterways. Many modern pads are trending toward low-copper or copper-free designs. If you have a choice and the parts meet your vehicle's needs, choosing lower copper pads is a simple "do better" move.

REMEMBER

And when you're cleaning or working around brakes, don't blow brake dust around like confetti. Use brake cleaner or wet methods, avoid inhaling dust, and wash up afterward.

Recycling fluid and pads

Brake fluid is hazardous waste — treat it like it. Keep it in a sealed container and take it to a shop or local hazardous-waste program that accepts automotive fluids. Many shops already have disposal systems in place, which is one reason brake fluid service is often worth paying for.

Used rotors and drums can often be recycled as scrap metal, and used pads should be disposed of according to local rules. If you want the fluid disposal mindset for everyday car ownership, Chapter 14's environmental section is a good companion — because nothing says adulthood like responsibly transporting a jug of questionable liquids.

Brakes have evolved from simple mechanical systems into smart, sensor-heavy safety networks, but the mission hasn't changed: Turn motion into controlled stopping. Keep your brakes healthy, keep your tires healthy, and your car will keep being boring in the best possible way.

IN THIS CHAPTER

» Seeing why brakes and wheel bearings are basically roommates

» Inspecting pads, rotors, and the "is this normal?" warning signs

» Spotting trouble early with noise clues, wheel play tests, and warning lights

Chapter 16

Stop and Roll: Keeping Brakes and Bearings in Check

Brake problems and bearing problems can sound and feel weirdly similar from the driver's seat. The goal isn't "guess and replace parts." The goal is "confirm and then fix." Your wallet will appreciate the difference.

In this chapter, we help you tell brake trouble from wheel-bearing trouble, spot early warning signs, inspect the parts you can see safely, and know when a wheel-end problem needs professional attention.

Why Brakes and Bearings Are a Team

Brakes and wheel bearings are like the two roommates who share a tiny apartment at the end of your axle: One's obsessed with stopping, the other's committed to spinning smoothly, and neither one appreciates surprise heat or random wobbling. When they're getting along, you never think about them. When they aren't, you get squeals, growls, and warning lights.

Bearings allow rolling, brakes stop safely

Your wheel-end is like a tiny neighborhood with a lot going on: The caliper squeezes the brake pads against the rotor to handle stopping, and the bleed screw sits on the caliper for brake bleeding, the hub and bearing handle smooth spinning, and the ABS sensor quietly judges everyone's behavior.

Figure 16-1 shows who lives in that neighborhood. You don't need to memorize it — just notice how close everything is.

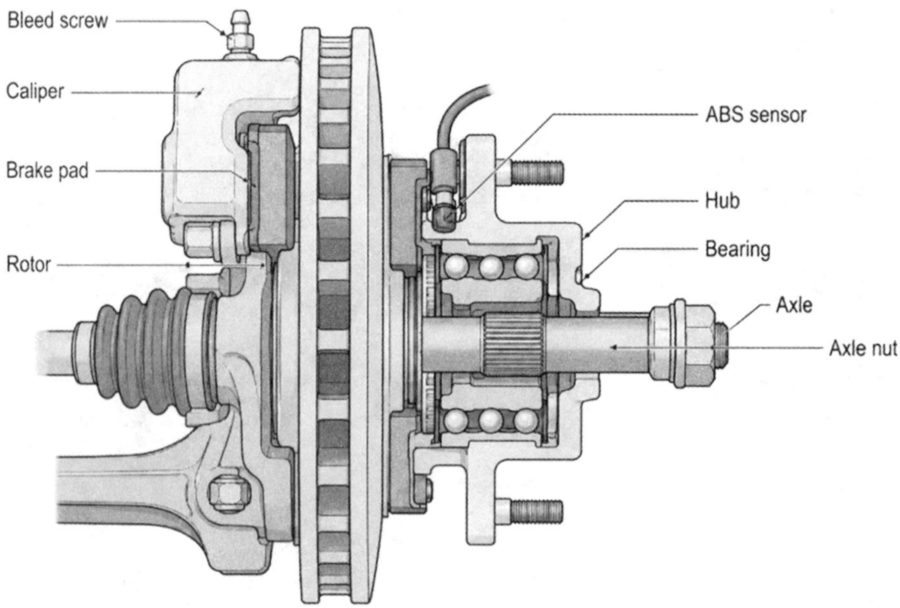

FIGURE 16-1: Wheel-end map.

Generated with AI using OpenAI

Failure in one affects the other

When the brakes or bearings fail, they affect each other.

When a brake problem bullies the bearing:

- A sticking caliper (or seized slide pins) can keep the pads lightly dragging, which creates heat. Heat is great for pizza. It's terrible for bearing grease.
- A warped or overheated rotor can transmit vibration that feels like a wheel issue, even when the bearing is fine.
- Brake fluid leaks or road grime can contaminate nearby components, including sensors and wiring.

When a bearing problem messes with the brakes:

- Bearing play can let the rotor wobble slightly, which can feel like a pulsation or vibration when you brake.
- A noisy bearing can sound like brake grinding (especially at low speeds), which leads people to replace perfectly good pads.
- Hub or bearing issues can upset wheel speed sensor signals, which can trigger ABS, traction, or stability lights.

TIP

If the noise happens only when you press the brake pedal, suspect brakes first. If the noise happens while cruising and changes with speed, suspect bearings (or tires) first. That one clue solves a shocking number of mysteries.

Brake Inspection 2.0

Brake inspection 1.0 is "I peek through the wheel spokes and hope." Brake inspection 2.0 is "I check the system in a way that actually answers questions."

Pads and rotors check

Start with the easy observations before you grab tools. The car will usually tell you what's wrong — it just speaks in squeaks, smells, and vibes.

On your next normal drive, note these clues:

- Pulling while braking (left or right)
- Steering wheel shake or pedal pulsation during braking
- Pedal feels spongy, sinking, or inconsistent
- New noises that show up specifically when you brake
- Brake, ABS, or traction lights that weren't there yesterday

WARNING

If the brake pedal suddenly sinks to the floor, the brake warning light comes on, or you hear grinding that gets louder with braking, stop driving and get help. (For emergency calm, see Chapter 20.)

After that normal-drive check, look at the brake fluid reservoir under the hood. You're looking for a sudden drop in level (possible leak or very worn pads) and for obviously nasty fluid.

Quick pad-and-rotor reality checks

When you look at pads and rotors, you're not trying to become a brake engineer. You're just answering three simple questions:

- **Are the pads wearing evenly?** Even wear means the caliper is moving like it should.
- **Is the rotor surface healthy?** The surface should be smooth-ish, not chewed up or heat-damaged.
- **Do I see any clues that something is dragging, overheating, or seizing?** These kind of clues are where the expensive drama begins.

Now here are the common "aha" clues:

- **Inner pad much thinner than the outer pad:** A thinner inner pad usually means the caliper isn't sliding freely — the slide pins are sticky or the caliper is partly seized. Translation: One pad is doing all the work while the other one is basically along for the ride.

  What to do: Check, clean, and lube the slide pins and hardware (with brake-safe lube) and make sure the caliper slide-pin boots aren't torn. For a refresher on how calipers, pads, and rotors work together, see Chapter 15.
- **A heavy rust ridge or deep grooves on the rotor:** A thin rust lip at the very edge of the rotor is common, but a big ridge or deep grooves means the pad and rotor have been in a bad relationship for a while. Either the pads wore down too far, debris got embedded, or the rotor surface is just past its good citizen stage.

  What to do: If the groove catches your fingernail or the ridge looks like a tiny cliff, plan on pads and rotors (or rotor replacement or resurfacing, if appropriate). For more on pads, rotors, and brake wear, see Chapter 15.
- **Blue/purple coloring on the rotor:** That coloring is a heat signature. It means the rotor got very hot — like "long downhill and riding the brakes" hot or "caliper dragging and nobody told you" hot. Heat can glaze pads, reduce stopping consistency, and shorten the life of nearby parts.

What to do: Don't just slap on new pads and call it a day. Look for the cause of the heat first: uneven pad wear, sticky slide pins, a dragging caliper, or a recent stretch of heavy braking. For the uneven-pad and slide-pin clues, see "Quick pad-and-rotor reality checks," earlier in this section. For brake-system basics, including how pads and rotors turn motion into heat, see Chapter 15.

- **Cracked rubber boots or torn slide-pin seals:** Those little rubber boots aren't decoration — they're the bodyguards. When they tear, water and road salt move in, corrosion starts, and the slide pins gradually turn into stuck pins. Then you get uneven pad wear and weird braking feel.

  What to do: Replace damaged boots and hardware and service the slide pins before the caliper starts acting like it's allergic to movement. For the uneven-pad clues that point to sticky slide pins, see "Inner pad much thinner than the outer pad" earlier in this section. For the brake-system basics behind calipers, pads, and rotors, see Chapter 15.

WARNING

If you see metal-on-metal scoring, hear grinding, or the rotor looks like it went through a cheese grater, stop driving it and fix it. That's not wear. That's "your rotor is being eaten in public."

Wheel bearings 101

Wheel bearings are the ultimate supporting actor part: They do their job flawlessly for years, get zero appreciation, and then — when they finally get tired — your car starts making a sound like a distant helicopter full of bees.

The good news is you don't need a lab coat to understand bearings. You just need to know what they do, what normal feels like, and how to spot the early warning signs before your wheel-end neighborhood turns into a reality show.

Role of bearings

Wheel bearings do two deceptively simple jobs:

- Let the wheel spin with minimal friction so that you don't waste power turning heat into sadness.
- Hold the wheel/hub in the correct position under load, such as cornering, braking, potholes, and your friend who packs like they're relocating.

When a bearing wears out, it can get noisy, develop play, and sometimes run hot. None of those are cute quirks. They're early warning signs.

Tapered roller versus sealed hubs

There are two main bearing worlds, and your vehicle lives in one of them:

- **Serviceable (older-school) bearings:** Often tapered roller bearings that can be cleaned, inspected, repacked, and adjusted
- **Sealed hub assemblies (modern reality):** A unitized hub/bearing assembly that you replace as a whole

Figure 16-2 shows the difference. Once you know which one you have, the maintenance decisions get a lot less mysterious.

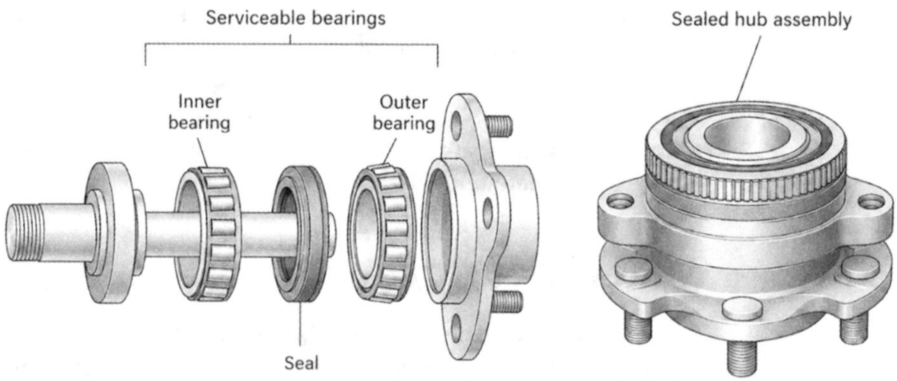

Generated with AI using OpenAI

FIGURE 16-2: Bearing types.

TIP

Not sure which setup you have? Look up the front wheel bearing part for your exact year, make, and model. If the listing says hub assembly, you're in sealed-hub land. If it lists separate inner and outer bearings and a seal, you're in serviceable-bearing land.

TECHNICAL STUFF

Many modern hubs rely on correct torque to set bearing preload. Translation: Torque specs aren't suggestions. Overtightening can shorten bearing life. Under-tightening can create play. Either way, the bearing loses, and your weekend gets weird.

Brake squeal versus bearing growl

Your car has two main complaint sounds in this chapter: brake squeal and a bearing growl.

Brake sounds tend to change with pedal pressure. Bearing sounds tend to change with vehicle speed and corner loading.

Table 16-1 is a quick translator so that you don't replace the wrong parts out of pure annoyance.

TABLE 16-1 Noise Translator

Noise	What it means
High-pitched squeal while braking	Pad wear indicator, pad material, light glazing, or hardware vibration
Grinding while braking	Pads may be worn to metal (sound of your rotors filing a complaint)
Clunk on first brake application after reverse	Pad shift or hardware play (often fixable with proper hardware/cleaning)
Low hum or growl that rises with speed	Classic bearing or tire noise
Noise changes when you gently swerve left or right at speed	Bearing becomes very suspicious
Rhythmic whup-whup	Possible tire issue, especially if tread is cupped or uneven

TIP

If you rotate tires and the noise moves with the tires, you just solved the mystery: it's probably tire-related. If the noise stays at the same corner, bearings or brakes move up the suspect list.

Packing Serviceable Wheel Bearings

Wheel bearings used to come with a bonus activity: a hands-on arts-and-crafts project starring you, a tub of grease, and a heroic amount of paper towels. If your vehicle (or trailer) has serviceable bearings, this messy little ritual actually matters because the difference between "smooth rolling" and "why is my wheel trying to pass me?" can be a thin film of lubrication.

We walk you through what the process of packing bearings really is, why modern cars mostly moved on, and how to do it without accidentally turning maintenance into premature failure with a side of grease perfume.

Grease packing

Packing bearings sounds like a moving day chore. It's actually the process of forcing fresh grease into a serviceable bearing so that the rollers have a healthy film of lubrication.

Done correctly, packing bearings can extend bearing life. Done incorrectly, it can shorten bearing life while also making your hands smell like grease until next Tuesday.

TIP

Before you start, make sure this job actually applies to your vehicle. Serviceable bearings can be cleaned, inspected, repacked, and adjusted. Sealed hub assemblies are replaced as a whole, not repacked. If you're not sure which setup you have, see "Tapered roller versus sealed hubs," earlier in this chapter. With that map in mind, here's the basic hand-packing process.

1. **Confirm the bearing setup.**

   Look up the wheel bearing part for your exact year, make, and model. If the parts listing shows separate inner and outer bearings and a seal, you're in serviceable-bearing land. If it says hub assembly, skip the grease and move to the next section.

2. **Lift and support the vehicle safely.**

   Work on level ground, set the parking brake, chock the wheels, lift at the correct jack point, and support the vehicle with jack stands. For the full safe-lifting routine, see Chapter 1. For jack stands, wheel chocks, sockets, wrenches, and torque wrenches, see Chapter 3.

3. **Remove the wheel and the parts in front of the hub.**

   Remove the wheel. Depending on the setup, you may need to remove the brake caliper, caliper bracket, and rotor to reach the hub. Hang the caliper so that it doesn't dangle by the brake hose. For calipers, pads, rotors, and brake inspection basics, see Chapter 15 and "Quick pad-and-rotor reality checks," earlier in this chapter.

4. **Take apart the serviceable bearing assembly.**

   Remove the dust cap, retainer or cotter pin if your setup uses one, spindle nut, washer, and outer bearing. Slide the hub or rotor assembly off carefully. The inner bearing and seal usually come out from the back side of the hub.

5. **Clean the bearings and races.**

   Wipe away old grease with shop towels and then clean the inner bearing, outer bearing, and races. The race is the smooth surface the rollers ride against. Do not use compressed air to spin a dry bearing; it can damage the bearing and send grime where you do not want it.

6. **Inspect before adding fresh grease.**

   Look for pitting, scoring, cracks, rough rollers, blue or purple heat marks, or a gritty feel. If the bearing or race is damaged, don't pack it and hope for the best. Replace the damaged parts or get help.

7. **Pack the bearing with fresh wheel-bearing grease.**

   Put a mound of the correct wheel-bearing grease in one gloved palm. Hold the bearing with the wide side facing the grease and then press the bearing edge into the grease until fresh grease pushes up through the rollers on the other side. Rotate the bearing and repeat until grease appears all the way around.

8. **Add a light coat of grease where it belongs.**

   Lightly coat the race and spindle surface with fresh grease. Don't fill the whole hub cavity like a frosting project unless the service information for that vehicle or trailer says to.

9. **Reinstall the inner bearing and seal.**

   Set the packed inner bearing back into the hub and then install a new seal squarely. A damaged or crooked seal can let grease escape and dirt enter, which is exactly how a freshly packed bearing gets betrayed.

10. **Reinstall the hub and outer bearing.**

    Slide the hub back onto the spindle carefully so that you don't damage the seal. Install the packed outer bearing, washer, and spindle nut.

11. **Adjust the bearing correctly.**

    Follow the service information for the exact spindle-nut adjustment or torque procedure. This is the part where "close enough" causes trouble: too tight can overheat the bearing, and too loose can create wheel play. Chapter 3 covers why torque wrenches matter, and earlier in this chapter, we explain why bearing preload isn't a guessing game.

12. **Finish and check your work.**

    Reinstall the retainer or cotter pin, dust cap, brake parts, and wheel. Torque the lug nuts to spec, pump the brake pedal if brake parts were removed, and test drive carefully. After the drive, listen for noise and check for looseness or unusual heat at that wheel.

Figure 16-3 shows the usual parts order for a serviceable bearing.

WARNING

If you can't confirm the bearing type, torque or preload procedure, or parts order for your exact vehicle or trailer, stop and get help. Wheel bearings are small parts doing a huge safety job. A bad adjustment can create heat, play, noise, or a wheel-end failure.

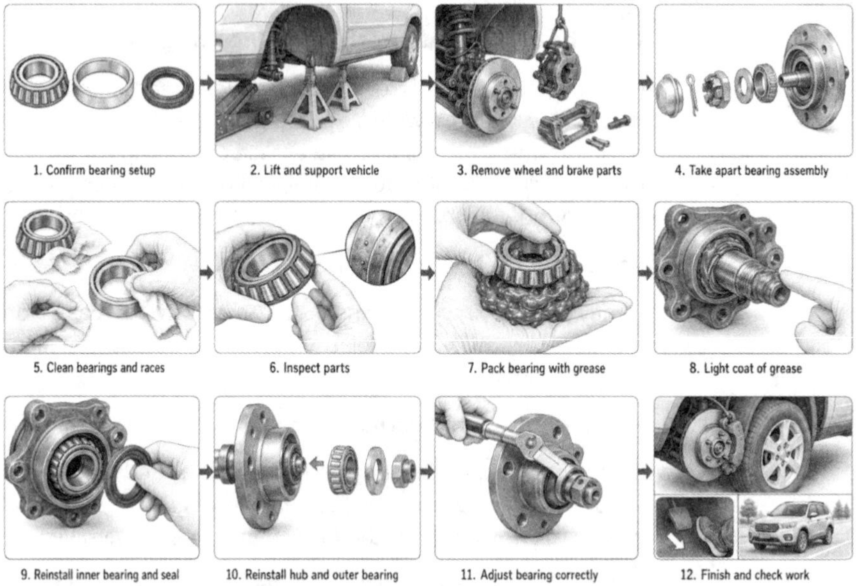

FIGURE 16-3: Serviceable bearing basics.

Generated with AI using OpenAI

Why sealed hubs replaced bearing packing

On most modern passenger vehicles, wheel bearings are sealed. In this section, newer means vehicles that use a sealed hub/bearing unit instead of separate serviceable inner and outer bearings. With a sealed hub assembly, you don't repack the bearing or just add grease. When the bearing gets noisy, develops play, or fails, you replace the hub/bearing assembly.

That doesn't automatically put the job off-limits for DIYers. Many sealed hub assemblies are bolt-in parts that a careful DIYer can replace with the right tools, safe lifting, and torque specs. For the basic replacement flow, see the next section. Sealed wheel bearings isn't manufacturers being cruel. It's the trade-off for compact design, integrated sensors, and predictable preload. It also means you don't have to do grease art in your driveway as often — the silver lining.

Replacing sealed hub assemblies

On many vehicles that use sealed hub assemblies, the wheel bearing arrives as part of a single hub/bearing unit. That means there's no repacking, no grease sculpture, and no guessing if you "got enough in there."

Instead, the job is more like a careful remove-and-replace project: Remove the parts in front, unplug what needs unplugging, unbolt the hub, and swap in the new one, with a quick side quest to defeat rust. The job is very doable for a beginner if you stay organized, handle the ABS wiring like it's made of feelings, and torque things to spec — not to "that feels about right."

Bolt-in hub assemblies

On many vehicles that use bolt-in sealed hub assemblies, the hub bolts to the *steering knuckle* — the sturdy steering-and-suspension part the wheel-end attaches to — from the back side. (For more on steering knuckles and related suspension parts, see Chapter 17.) The good news: You often don't need a shop press, the heavy tool used to push press-fit bearings in and out. The bad news: Rust can bond the hub to the knuckle like they're in a long-term relationship.

ABS tone rings and sensors

Wheel speed sensors and tone rings are how ABS and traction control know what each wheel is doing. A failing bearing can sometimes disturb that signal. Also, a damaged sensor harness can cause warning lights even when the bearing is fine, which is why a quick visual check is worth doing.

Replacement basics

Every vehicle is a little different, but the hub replacement rhythm often looks like this process:

1. **Loosen the lug nuts on the ground and then lift and support the vehicle safely.**

   Crack the lug nuts loose while the tire is still on the ground so that the wheel doesn't spin while you're fighting the wrench. Then lift the vehicle and support it securely — this is not a "trust the jack and hope" moment. See Chapter 1 if you're unsure how to lift and support the vehicle safely.

2. **Remove the wheel, caliper, and caliper bracket and hang the caliper so that it doesn't dangle by the hose.**

   Once the wheel is off, remove the caliper and bracket as needed. Support the caliper with a hook, bungee, or wire — because the brake hose isn't a suspension component.

3. **Remove the rotor and unplug the ABS sensor (if applicable).**

   Pull the rotor off (rust may make it act like it lives there now). If the hub has an ABS sensor harness, unplug it carefully and free the wiring clips so that you don't turn a simple job into a "why is the ABS light on now?" sequel.

4. **Remove the axle nut on driven wheels (often very tight).**

   On FWD/AWD/4WD hubs, the axle nut usually takes serious effort, which is normal. Use the right socket, solid leverage, and the correct procedure for your vehicle.

5. **Remove the hub mounting bolts and then remove the hub (rust may require persuasion).**

   Hub bolts usually come in from the back side of the steering knuckle. Once they're out, the hub should come free unless rust has bonded them like best friends. Penetrating oil, careful persuasion, and patience are your allies here.

6. **Clean the mating surface, install the new hub, and torque everything to spec.**

   Clean the knuckle's mounting surface so that the new hub sits flush (rust high spots can cause wobble and premature failure). Install the hub and torque the fasteners to spec — bearings love accuracy.

7. **Reinstall brakes and wheel; torque lug nuts correctly; test drive carefully.**

   Put everything back together in reverse order, torque lugs properly, and do a careful test drive. Before you roll, pump the brake pedal a few times to restore a firm pedal. Otherwise, your first stop will be more exciting than you wanted.

Figure 16-4 shows the overall replacement flow.

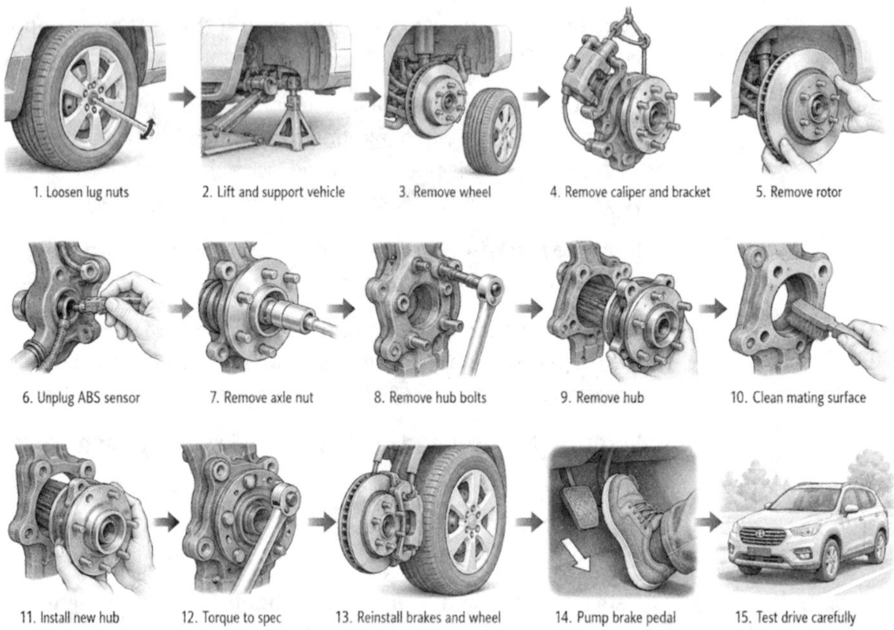

FIGURE 16-4: Bolt-in hub assembly replacement overview.

Generated with AI using OpenAI

WARNING

Some axle nuts are replaced after removal or torque-to-yield. If your service info says replace it, do it. Also, avoid using an impact to finish torque. Bearings and sensors prefer accuracy over enthusiasm.

Spotting Trouble Early

Wheel bearings usually don't fail out of nowhere — they hint first. The hints sound like a low hum that slowly turns into a growl, and they love to show up right when you're trying to enjoy a quiet drive. The good news is you can do a little car detective work with your ears (and a simple check or two) to narrow it down before it becomes a full-on roadside drama.

Noise diagnostics

For the basic sound-pattern clues, refer to Table 16-1 earlier in this chapter. That table helps you separate noises that change with brake pressure from noises that rise with vehicle speed or change during turns.

If the sound pattern points toward a possible wheel bearing, one safe next check is the gentle swerve test on an empty, straight road at steady speed:

- Gently drift left, then back to center, and then gently drift right (no sudden moves).
- If the noise gets louder when you load one side, the bearing on the opposite side often becomes the suspect. (Example: Louder on left drift can point to right-side bearing).
- If the noise doesn't change at all, it may be tires or something else.

Wheel play test

If you can safely lift the wheel, do the play check gently at two hand positions. For safe lifting and support, see Chapter 1. Grip the tire at 12 and 6 o'clock and rock the wheel in and out. Then grip it at 3 and 9 o'clock and rock it the same way. After that, spin the wheel by hand. Figure 16-5 shows the hand positions for the rock test and the spin check.

What you're looking for:

- Noticeable clunk or movement at the wheel
- Roughness or grinding sensation when spinning by hand
- A notchy feel that suggests internal damage

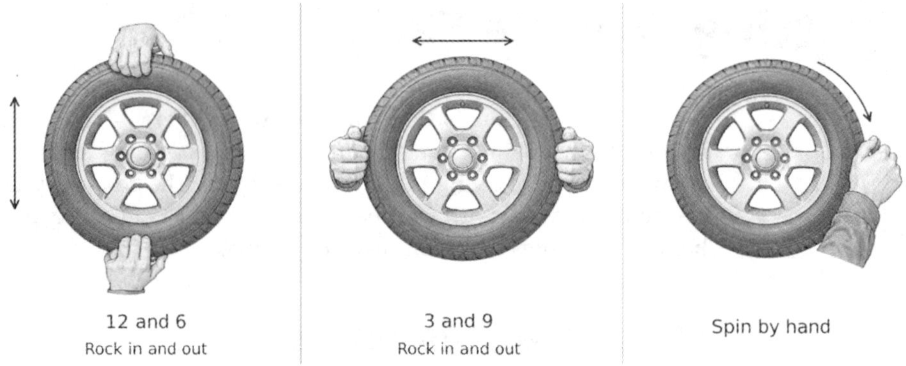

FIGURE 16-5: Wheel play test.

Generated with AI using OpenAI

ABS warning lights

If the ABS light (or traction or stability lights) shows up with a new hum or vibration, don't ignore it. It doesn't automatically mean the bearing is bad, but it does mean something at that wheel-end needs attention (sensor, wiring, tone ring, or hub).

TIP

A scan tool that reads ABS codes can point you toward the specific wheel speed sensor that's unhappy. It's like the car whispering, "It's the left rear. Please stop guessing."

A failing wheel bearing can also show up as heat. After a normal drive (no hard braking), a bad bearing will often run noticeably hotter than the others. If you've got an infrared (IR) thermometer, you can quickly compare hub temps side-to-side — the hot one is your clue.

You may be wondering what's a normal hub temp after driving? There's a range because temps change with outside weather, speed, vehicle weight, and braking. In normal cruising with light braking, you'll often see hubs somewhere around 100 to 160°F.

What matters most is the comparison:

- Left versus right on the same axle should be pretty close.
- If one hub is 20 to 30°F hotter than the other after the same drive, pay attention.
- If it's 50°F-plus hotter, that's a big red flag (bearing or brake drag are common suspects).

BUYING AN IR THERMOMETER

An IR thermometer is a handheld tool that reads surface temperature without touching the part. You point it at the hub/rotor area, pull the trigger, and it gives you a temp reading in seconds. It's basically a temperature gun for your car.

You can buy one at:

- Auto parts stores (AutoZone, O'Reilly, Advance)
- Hardware stores (Home Depot, Lowe's)
- Online (Amazon, for example)

You don't need anything fancy — just get one that reads at least up to ~500°F and has decent reviews.

WARNING

Don't touch the hub or rotor to see whether it's hot. Brakes aren't muffins. Use an IR thermometer or just keep your fingers as decoration.

Maintenance and DIY Tips

Wheel-end work is one of those simple, but not casual jobs: The steps aren't complicated, but the details matter. A hub that's installed cleanly and torqued correctly can run quietly for years; a hub that's installed close enough can come back with noise, vibration, or a brand-new attitude.

Torque specs for hubs and lugs

If there's one boring habit that prevents expensive problems, it's torquing fasteners correctly — especially wheels and axle nuts.

Lug nuts should be tightened in a crisscross star pattern instead of going around the wheel in a circle. The star pattern helps the wheel seat evenly against the hub, instead of pulling one side tight before the rest of the wheel is snug. Start the lug nuts by hand, snug them evenly, and use a torque wrench for the final tightening to the spec in your owner's manual or service information. For more on safe wheel work, see Chapter 1. For more on torque wrenches, see Chapter 3.

Axle nuts also need the correct torque spec. Do not tighten them by "feel," because too tight or too loose can shorten bearing life or create play. Some axle nuts are also replace-after-removal, so follow the service information for your exact vehicle.

Figure 16-6 shows the lug nut star pattern, the torque wrench on a lug nut, and the axle nut that also needs the correct spec.

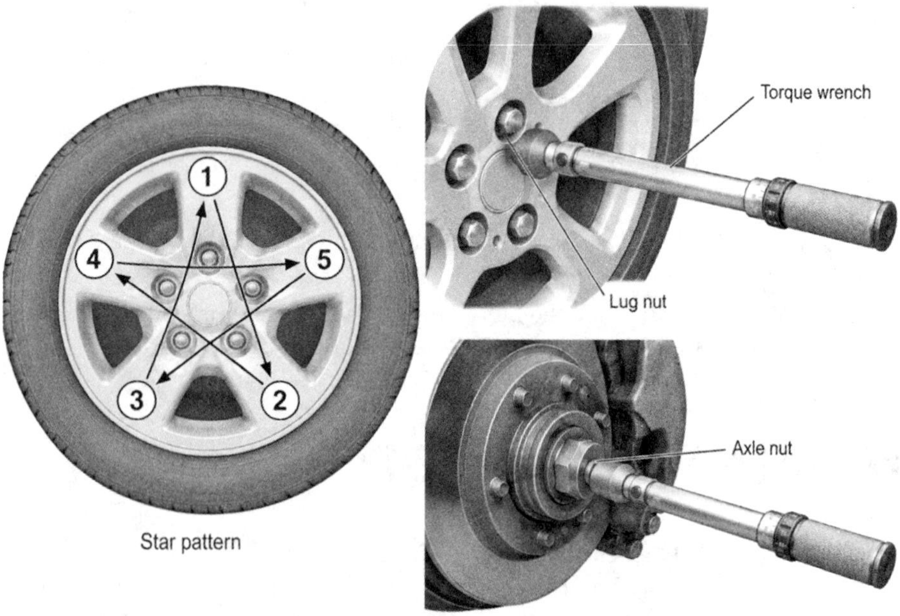

FIGURE 16-6: Lug nut star pattern and torque reminders.

Generated with AI using OpenAI

TIP

Use a torque wrench for final tightening. An impact gun is great for removal. For installation, it's like using a chainsaw to slice cake — possible, but not the vibe.

Pad and rotor versus hub replacement

When something feels off, the smartest move is to separate brake symptoms from bearing symptoms.

It's more likely a brake job (pads/rotors/hardware) when:

- Noise appears only when braking
- Pedal feel changes (soft, pulsing, or inconsistent)

- Pad thickness is low or uneven
- Rotors show heavy grooves, heat spots, or obvious damage

It's more likely a bearing/hub issue when:

- A hum or growl is present while cruising and rises with speed
- Noise changes when you gently swerve left or right
- The wheel has noticeable play when lifted
- The hub runs hotter than the opposite side after a normal drive

REMEMBER

If you're not sure, it's okay to bring your notes to a shop and ask for a diagnosis before authorizing parts. Chapter 23 helps you pick a mechanic who will explain what they found instead of just handing you a large invoice and a small shrug.

Hybrid and EV Bearings

Hybrids and EVs may feel smooth and futuristic, but their wheel bearings still do the same basic jobs: Support the vehicle's load and let the wheels spin with minimal friction. These vehicles often carry more weight because of the battery pack, and electric torque arrives instantly from a stop. That combination can be harder on wheel bearings, especially if you also run big wheels, low-profile tires, or hit potholes like they owe you money.

Regenerative braking can dramatically reduce brake pad wear because the electric motor helps slow the vehicle. That changes how much work the brake pads do, but it does not change the bearing's job. The wheel bearing still carries the load and supports every wheel rotation, whether the slowing comes mostly from regenerative braking or from the brake pads and rotors.

Figure 16-7 compares those two braking paths. In regenerative braking, the motor helps slow the vehicle. In friction braking, the brake pads squeeze the rotor. In both cases, the wheel still spins on the same bearing.

TIP

Because friction brakes get used less on some hybrids and EVs, rotors can rust more. An occasional firm stop (when safe) helps clean the rotor surfaces. For the bigger hybrid and EV systems tour, Chapter 10 is your friend.

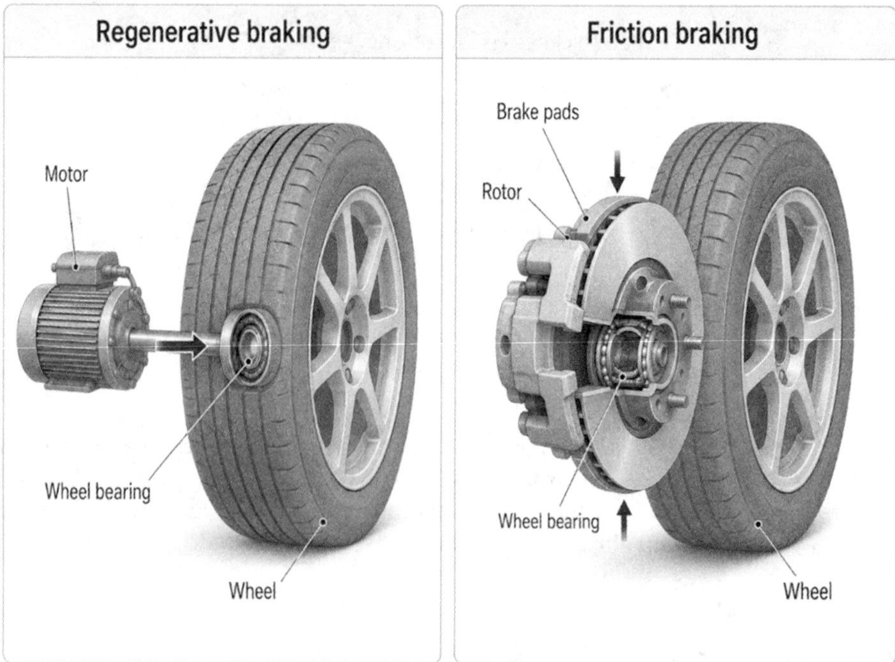

FIGURE 16-7: Regen versus friction braking.

Generated with AI using OpenAI

4

Smoothing the Ride: Steering, Tires, and Transmissions

IN THIS PART . . .

Understand the basics of steering and suspension.

Learn how tires, balance, and alignment affect your drive.

Follow how power moves through transmissions and drivetrains.

IN THIS CHAPTER

» Understanding what steering and suspension actually do

» Seeing how old-school linkages turned into rack-and-pinion and electric power steering

» Meeting springs, shocks, struts, control arms, and bushings

» Decoding modern steering tech like lane keep assist and self-parking

Chapter 17 Steering and Suspension Systems Smooth the Way

Steering and suspension are two of the least glamorous systems on the car — right up until one of them starts acting weird. Then suddenly every pothole has commentary, the steering wheel feels like it needs relationship counseling, and your peaceful commute turns into a rolling sound check.

You don't need a chassis-engineering degree for this tour. In this chapter, we translate steering and suspension into plain English: how your hand input reaches the wheels, how power assist changed over time, what the main parts do, and what common symptoms usually mean.

Steering Basics

A car that can go fast but not steer accurately is just a very organized mistake. *Steering* is the system that lets you choose a direction, hold that direction, and make small corrections when wind, road crown, bumps, or other drivers try to volunteer new plans.

Steering turns the front wheels so that the car changes direction. Good steering also feels predictable, responds without a big delay, and helps the car track straight without you making constant tiny corrections.

A healthy steering system helps you do three things well:

- Point the car where you want it to go, from gentle lane changes to sharp turns into a parking space.
- Make small corrections without drama when the road surface, crosswind, or vehicle load changes.
- Feel enough feedback through the wheel to know what the tires are doing — not every pebble, just the important gossip.

Figure 17-1 is the big-picture idea: Your hands create an input, the steering gear turns that input into wheel angle, and the tire contact patches do the actual work of changing the car's path.

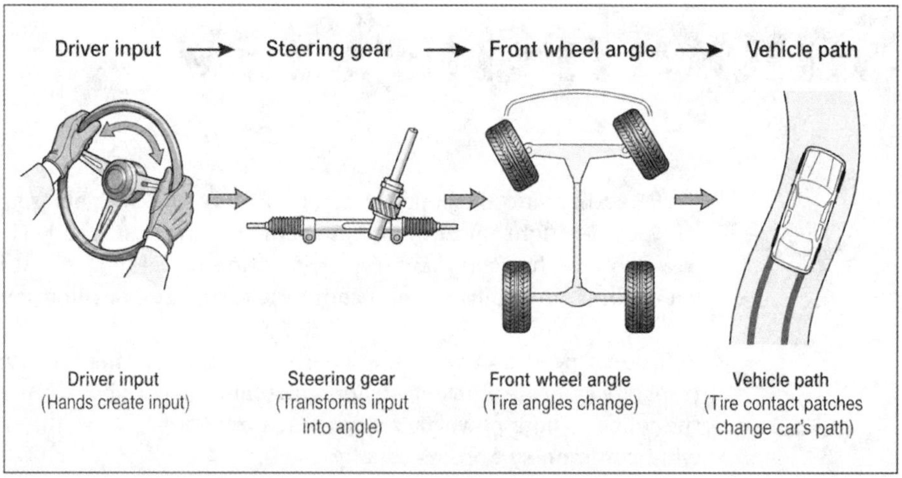

FIGURE 17-1: Steering at a glance.

Generated with AI using OpenAI

REMEMBER

The steering wheel doesn't directly drag the car around a corner. It changes tire angle. Tire grip does the rest. That is why steering, suspension, tire condition, and alignment are all basically coworkers, whether they like it or not.

Turning input to wheel movement

When you turn the steering wheel, that rotation travels down the steering column and into a steering gear. The gear then converts your hand movement into motion that can actually point the front wheels.

On most modern vehicles, the path looks like:

1. **The *steering wheel* is where the driver starts the conversation.**
2. **The *steering column* and *intermediate shaft* are the rotating connections between the wheel and the gear, often using small joints to snake past other components.**
3. **The *steering gear* or *rack* is the part that converts rotary input into the motion that can move the wheels.**
4. **The *tie rods* are the steering links that carry that motion out to the steering knuckles at each front wheel.**
5. **The *steering knuckle* and *hub area* are where the wheel assembly actually pivots left or right.**

Figure 17-2 follows that chain from top to bottom. The names may sound a little mechanical at first, but the logic is simple: Twist here, movement travels there, wheels turn over there. It's a relay race, not sorcery.

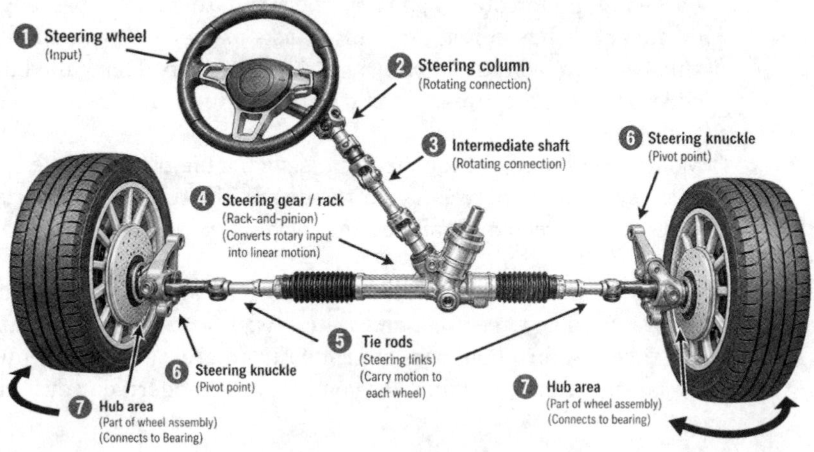

FIGURE 17-2: Steering input path.

Generated with AI using OpenAI

TIP

If the steering wheel is off-center after front-end work, don't treat it like a cosmetic issue. An off-center wheel often means the alignment or steering adjustment is off, and on newer cars, it can also confuse driver-assist systems that depend on steering-angle information. Chapter 18 goes deeper on alignment.

From linkages to rack-and-pinion

Older steering systems often looked like someone emptied a small hardware store under the front bumper. Modern systems are usually simpler, lighter, and more direct. That change is one reason newer cars tend to feel sharper and easier to package under the hood.

Old linkage systems

Many older rear-wheel-drive cars, body-on-frame SUVs, and trucks used a steering box with a maze of linkages. Instead of a compact rack moving left and right, these systems used a steering gear, a pitman arm, center link or drag link, an idler arm, and tie rods to pass motion across the front suspension.

The advantage was strength and durability, especially for heavier vehicles. The downside was that every extra joint was one more place for wear, looseness, and "why does this truck need two inches of steering wheel movement before anything happens?" to enter the chat.

Figure 17-3 shows the old linkage style system. You can compare this in the next section with the newer style systems.

Modern rack-and-pinion steering

Rack-and-pinion steering is now the standard on most passenger cars and crossovers, and it has spread to many trucks as well. In rack-and-pinion steering, a small gear called the *pinion* turns a straight toothed bar called the *rack*. As the rack slides left or right, it pushes and pulls the tie rods, which turn the wheels.

Modern rack-and-pinion steering is such a big deal because it's compact, direct, with fewer joints between your hands and the tires. Fewer parts often means less play, quicker response, and easier packaging.

Rack systems also use protective rubber boots at each end. Those boots aren't decorative. They keep dirt and water away from the moving inner joints and the rack itself. A torn boot can let grime in and grease out, and future repair bills get ideas. Figure 17-4 familiarizes you with this modern day system.

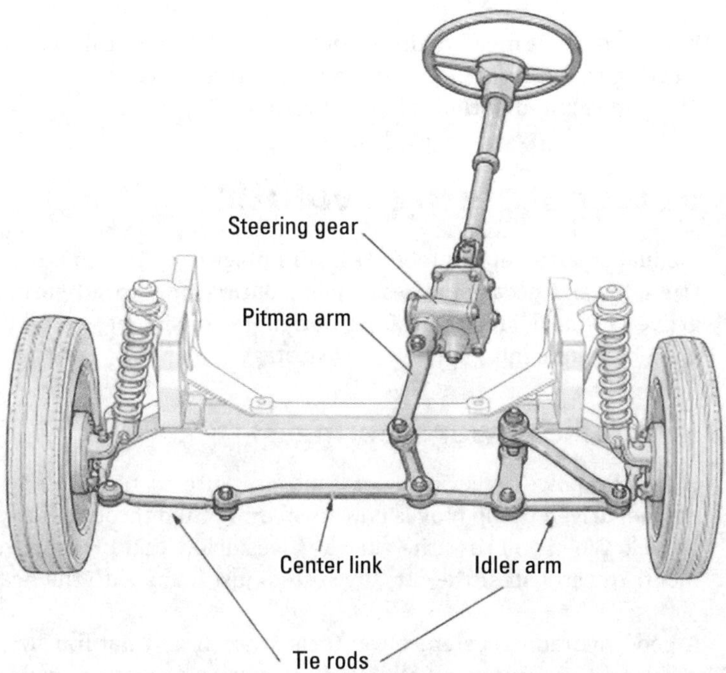

FIGURE 17-3: Old linkage steering.

Generated with AI using OpenAI

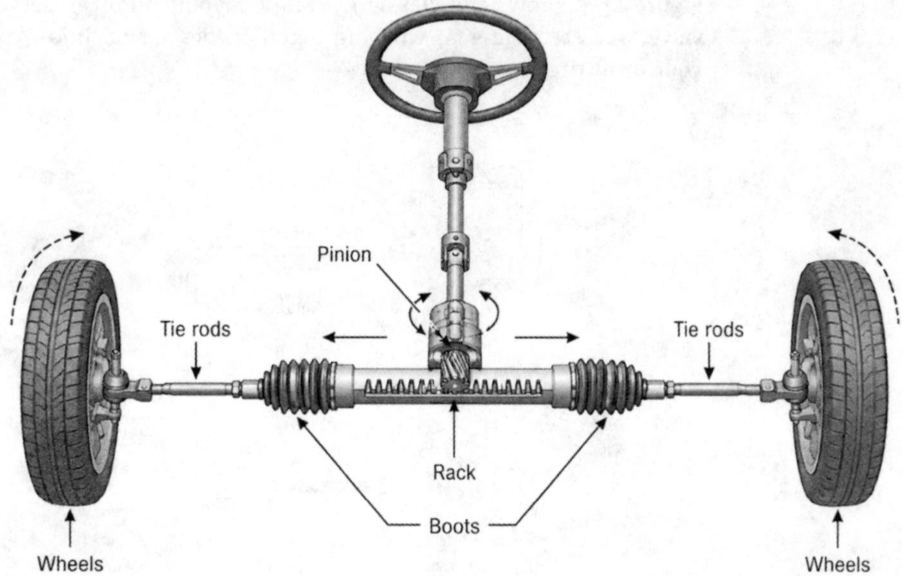

FIGURE 17-4: Modern rack-and-pinion steering.

Generated with AI using OpenAI

REMEMBER

Modern doesn't mean maintenance-proof. Tie rods still wear, boots still tear, and steering racks can still leak or develop internal play. The system may be simpler, but road salt and potholes haven't retired.

Power steering evolution

Manual steering absolutely worked in older cars. It also built character, forearm strength, and occasional resentment during low-speed parking. Power steering arrived to make steering lighter and more consistent — and it has since evolved from hydraulic muscle to electric strategy.

Hydraulic power steering

Hydraulic power steering uses fluid pressure to help you turn the wheels. An engine-driven pump moves power-steering fluid through hoses to a steering gear or rack. When you turn the wheel, valves direct that pressure to assist the movement. You still steer the car; the system just helps with the heavy lifting.

A good hydraulic system often feels smooth and natural. Its main downside is efficiency: The pump usually works whenever the engine runs, even when you're just cruising straight ahead.

Figure 17-5 shows the classic hydraulic layout: pump, reservoir, hoses, control valve, and steering gear working together like a tiny fluid gym membership for your front tires.

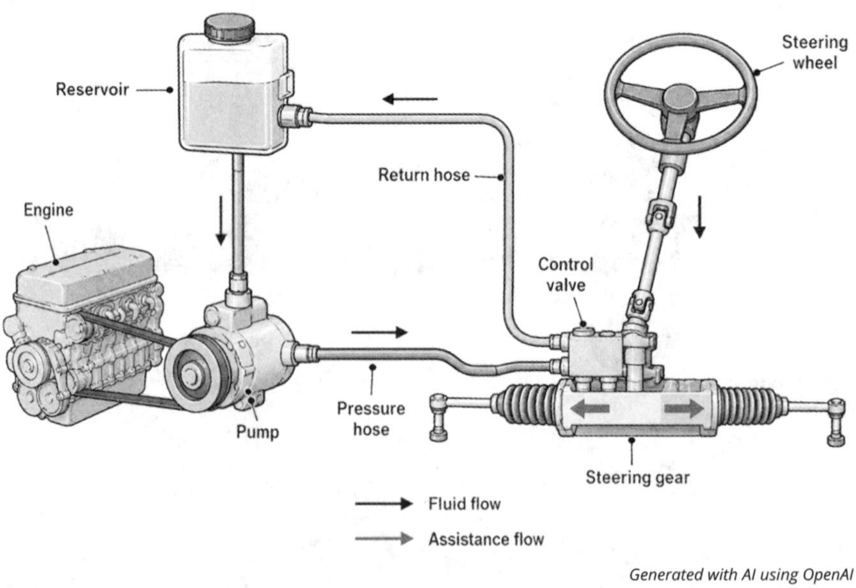

FIGURE 17-5: Hydraulic power steering layout.

Common hydraulic-system trouble clues include

- » A whining noise while turning, especially at low speed
- » Fluid leaks from hoses, seals, or the steering rack area
- » Steering that feels heavy, jerky, or inconsistent
- » Foamy or low fluid in the reservoir, which can mean air or leaks are involved

Electric power steering (EPS)

Electric power steering, usually called EPS, replaces most of that fluid-based assist with an electric motor, sensors, and a control module. Instead of engine power constantly spinning a pump, the system provides assist only when needed. That strategy saves fuel or energy, reduces plumbing, and makes the system easier to integrate with modern driver-assist features.

EPS can use a motor on the steering column or at the rack itself. The system watches steering effort, steering angle, and vehicle speed and then decides how much assist to add.

Figure 17-6 shows the basic EPS idea: Sensors notice what you're asking, the control unit decides how much assist makes sense, and the motor adds help without bathing the whole process in hydraulic fluid.

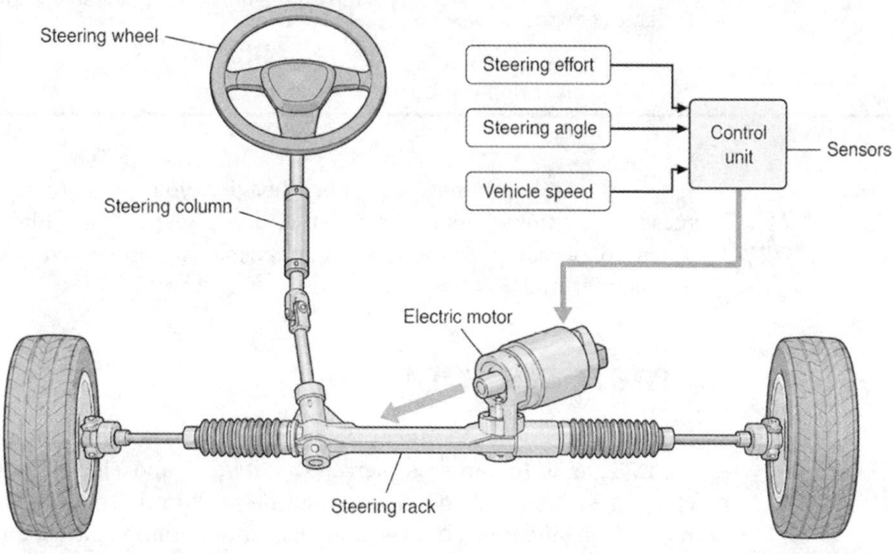

FIGURE 17-6: Electric power steering basics.

TIP

EPS is one reason modern cars can feel very light in a parking lot but nicely weighted on the highway. The computer changes the amount of assist with speed. It's trying to give you easy parking without making highway steering feel like a video-game controller.

Pros and cons of each

Neither hydraulic steering nor EPS is perfect. They're just different answers to the same question: How do we make steering light enough to live with and accurate enough to trust? Table 17-1 highlights the pros and cons of each system.

TABLE 17-1 Hydraulic versus EPS

Type	Pros	Cons
Hydraulic power steering	Often natural steering feel Proven design Strong assist on heavier vehicles	Leaks Hoses Fluid service Pump noise Small efficiency penalty (pump is usually always working)
EPS	No fluid Better efficiency Easier packaging Fewer leak points Easy integration with lane keep assist and self-parking	Can be expensive when electronics fail Can feel numb on some vehicles Often needs scan-tool diagnostics instead of the old "top off the fluid and squint at it" approach

WARNING

If steering suddenly becomes much heavier, you get a steering-system warning message, or the wheel binds or jerks, don't keep driving like nothing happened. A loss of assist is sometimes manageable at low speed, but a steering fault isn't something you "see how it feels by next week."

Smart steering

Modern steering is no longer just a simple "turn the wheel, point the car" arrangement. Thanks to cameras, sensors, software, and electric power steering, your steering system has gone from quiet helper to mildly opinionated copilot. It can now watch lane lines, help you squeeze into parking spaces, and generally act like it took one semester of driver's ed and came back very confident.

The good news is that these features can make driving easier and safer. The even better news is that the car still expects you to be the grown-up in the relationship.

Lane keep assist

Lane keep assist uses a camera — and sometimes other sensors — to watch lane markings. If the vehicle starts drifting without a turn signal, the system may vibrate the wheel, flash a warning, or gently nudge the steering to guide the car back toward the center of the lane.

The key word here is gently. Lane keep assist helps with unintentional drift; it's not a substitute for your hands, eyes, or judgment. Poor lane markings, snow, or grime can limit how well it works.

Figure 17-7 shows the basic logic: Camera sees lines, software interprets the lane, and the EPS system adds a small steering correction, if needed.

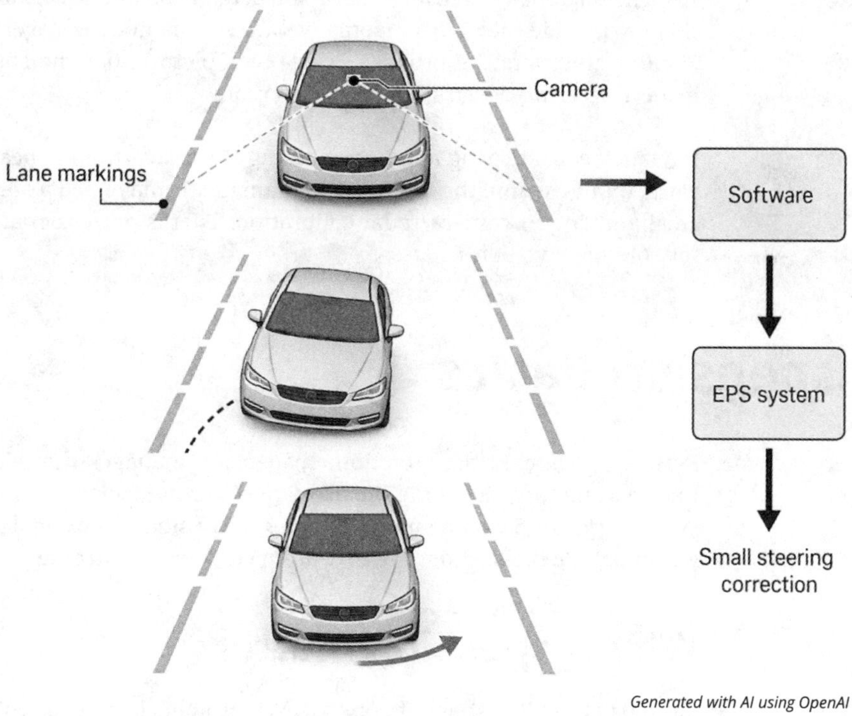

FIGURE 17-7: Lane keep assist flow.

Self-parking systems

Self-parking systems take that same electric steering hardware used in lane keep assist and put it to work during low-speed maneuvers. The vehicle looks for a space using sensors or cameras, calculates a path, and then turns the steering wheel automatically while you control some combination of brake, gear selection, and throttle — depending on the system.

The first time self-parking takes over, it can feel like the steering wheel has developed free will. Really, it is just automating the same steering motions an experienced driver would make. You still supervise and stay ready to stop.

ADAS integration

Modern steering is deeply tied into ADAS — Advanced Driver Assistance Systems. Steering-angle sensors, yaw sensors, wheel-speed data, forward cameras, radar, and stability-control modules all compare notes. If one piece of that data ecosystem is wrong, the car may throw warning messages or disable features until things are recalibrated.

This dependence on accurate steering and sensor data matters after alignments, suspension repairs, crashes, curb impacts, windshield replacement, or even a change in ride height on some vehicles. Chapter 18 covers alignment, and Chapter 20 covers the broader safety-tech picture, but the short version is that modern steering doesn't live alone anymore.

WARNING

If a lane keep, steering assist, or parking-assist warning appears after front-end work, don't assume the car is being dramatic. It may need a steering-angle reset, an alignment, or camera/radar calibration. That is professional-equipment territory on many vehicles.

Suspension Basics

If steering chooses the direction, suspension manages the relationship between the tires and the road while the body moves around above them. Without suspension, every bump would launch the tires into a small emotional crisis, and your car would handle like a shopping cart dropped down a staircase.

Why suspension matters

Suspension isn't just about comfort. Yes, it helps keep your coffee inside the cup and your spine on speaking terms with the seat. But its bigger job is keeping the tires in contact with the road as consistently as possible. Tire contact equals grip, and grip is what makes acceleration, braking, and steering work.

A healthy suspension helps with:

- Ride comfort over bumps, joints, potholes, and expansion seams
- Body control during braking, cornering, and acceleration
- Stable tire contact for steering, braking, and traction
- Predictable tire wear instead of weird edge wear that looks like your car has hobbies

Figure 17-8 shows the suspension's core mission in one image: Let the wheel move over a bump while keeping the body under control and the tire planted.

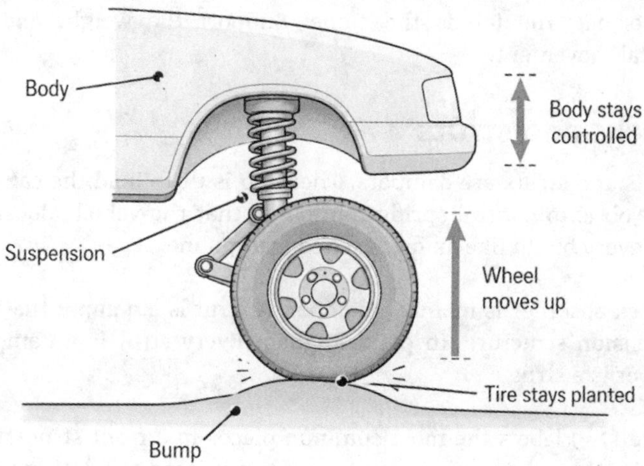

FIGURE 17-8: Suspension job overview.

Generated with AI using OpenAI

Ride comfort versus handling

Suspension tuning is a compromise. Too soft, and the car can feel floaty in corners and under braking. Too firm, and rough pavement can make the ride harsh and unsettled.

That fine line is why suspension tuning is about compromise. Springs support the vehicle and absorb big weight shifts. *Dampers* — the shocks or struts — control how quickly that spring motion happens. Together, they decide whether the car feels calm, bouncy, harsh, sporty, or like a couch that discovered caffeine.

REMEMBER

A comfortable ride isn't automatically a healthy ride. Worn shocks can feel soft, but soft because the car is underdamped isn't a luxury feature — it's a control problem wearing pajamas.

Major suspension components

Suspension looks complicated because many parts are doing small jobs at once. The easiest way to understand the suspension system is to meet the main players one at a time.

Springs

Springs hold the vehicle up, set the basic ride height, and absorb the major energy from bumps and weight transfer. Without springs, every bump force would go straight into the body, and your dentist would start sending thank-you cards.

Springs come in different forms — coil springs, leaf springs, torsion bars on some vehicles, and air springs in certain luxury or load-leveling setups. No matter the format, the job is the same: Support the weight and allow controlled vertical movement.

Shocks and struts

Shocks and struts are dampers. Their job isn't to hold the car up by themselves; their job is to control spring motion so that the vehicle doesn't keep bouncing after every bump like an overexcited trampoline.

A shock absorber is mainly a damper. A strut is a damper that is also part of the suspension structure. In plain English: Every strut is a damper, but not every damper is a strut.

Figure 17-9 labels the most common pieces in a front strut-style suspension so that the terms have a home in your brain instead of floating around like random vocabulary confetti.

Control arms

Control arms connect the wheel assembly to the body or subframe and guide how the wheel moves up and down. They help keep the tire in the right place while allowing controlled suspension travel.

Many control arms use ball joints and bushings at their connection points. If a control arm is bent from a curb strike or pothole hit, alignment can go out of range, and the car may pull, wander, or wear tires unevenly.

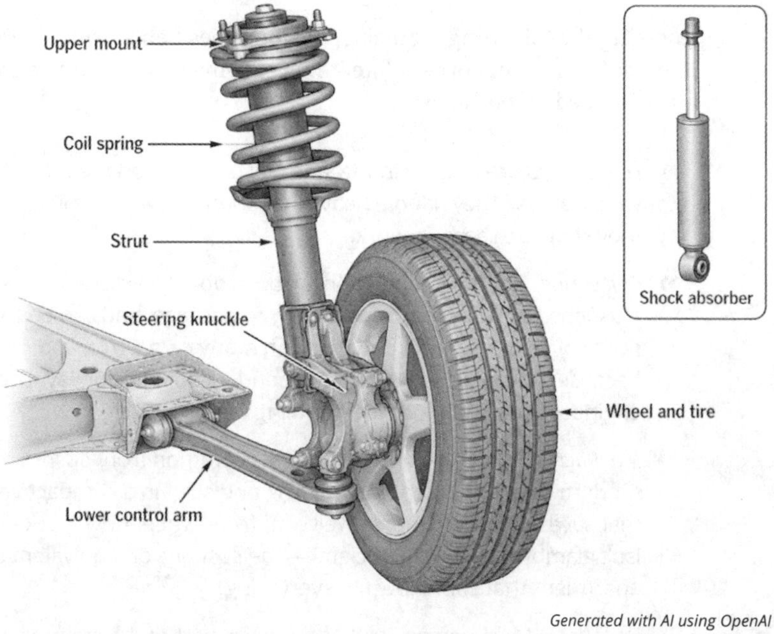

FIGURE 17-9: Common front suspension parts.

Bushings

Bushings are the rubber or elastomer cushions that sit between many suspension and steering parts. They allow a little movement, absorb vibration, and prevent metal parts from clanking directly into each other every time the road gets rude.

As bushings age, they can crack, soften, separate, or simply stop doing their quiet little job. The result can be clunks, vague steering, wandering under braking, extra vibration, or a feeling that the car has become oddly loose without anything obviously broken.

TIP

People often say shocks "support the car." Springs support the car. Shocks and struts control the motion. Mixing up those jobs is one of the most common beginner mistakes, right up there with calling every warning light the engine light.

Suspension types

Suspension systems all do the same basic job: Keep the tires planted, keep the body from bouncing around like a shopping cart with big dreams, and keep your spine from filing a formal complaint. They just go about that job in different ways. Some are built like work boots, some like running shoes, and some like luxury hotel pillows with a control module.

Knowing the following main suspension types helps explain why one vehicle rides like a sofa, another corners like it had too much coffee, and a third seems personally offended by potholes:

- *Leaf springs* are tough, simple, and still common on the rear axle of trucks and vans because they handle heavy loads well. They're not luxury champions, but they show up ready to work.
- *Coil springs* are the curled springs you probably picture when someone says "suspension." They're compact, easy to package, and can be tuned for a wide range of vehicles. You'll find them on many cars, SUVs, and crossovers because they play nicely with independent suspension layouts and let engineers chase a good ride-handling compromise.
- *MacPherson struts* are one of the most common front suspension layouts in modern cars. They combine a spring and strut in a compact vertical assembly that saves space and works well with front-wheel-drive packaging. The setup isn't glamorous, but it's efficient — the suspension equivalent of a small apartment that somehow fits everything.

  Because a MacPherson strut assembly is part of the steering and suspension structure, worn strut mounts, bearings, or dampers can affect both ride and steering feel. That is one reason front-end noises can be annoyingly good at impersonating each other.
- *Air suspension* uses inflatable air springs, plus a compressor, valves, and height sensors. It can give excellent ride quality and load leveling, but it also adds more parts that can leak or fail. If a vehicle with air suspension sags after sitting, runs the compressor constantly, or shows a suspension warning message, that is not "just how these are." It usually means a leak, sensor issue, or compressor problem is occurring somewhere in the system.
- *Magnetic ride* and other adaptive damping systems change shock firmness on the fly. The goal is simple: Stay comfortable on rough roads and firm up quickly when the vehicle is cornering hard.

Figure 17-10 compares the common suspension types at a glance so that you can keep the personalities straight: truck-tough leaf springs, everyday coil springs and struts, fancy air systems, and adaptive dampers with a graduate degree in reacting quickly.

TECHNICAL STUFF

Independent suspension means the left and right wheels can move somewhat separately instead of being tied together by one solid axle. Independent suspension usually helps ride and handling, though a solid axle still makes sense in some trucks and heavy-duty uses.

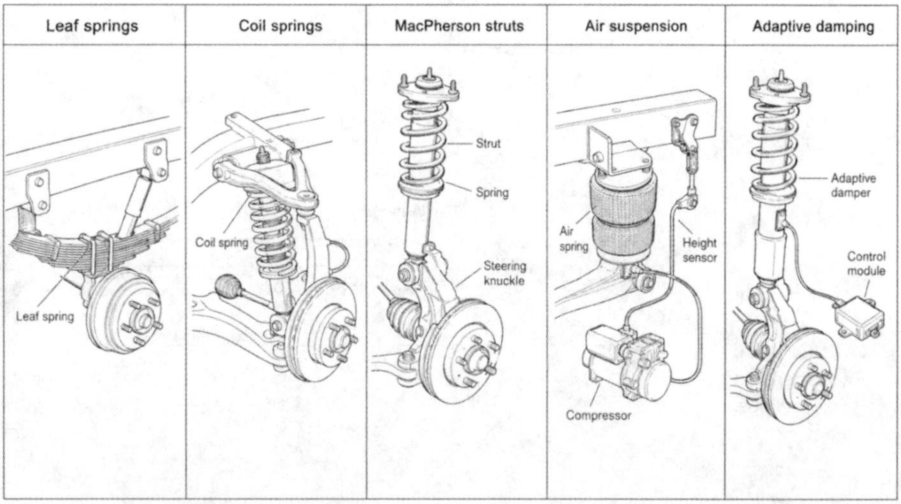

FIGURE 17-10: Suspension types at a glance.

Generated with AI using OpenAI

EV and hybrid suspension considerations

Electrified vehicles still use very normal suspension parts: springs, dampers, bushings, control arms, and so on. The interesting difference is what those parts have to deal with. Batteries add mass, electric motors add instant torque, and the quiet cabin makes noises that used to hide behind engine sound suddenly feel like a headline.

Battery packs are heavy, but they're usually mounted low in the vehicle. That low placement can help handling, even while the extra mass asks more from tires, bushings, bearings, and dampers.

Manufacturers often tune EV and hybrid suspensions differently to handle that extra weight, instant motor torque, and the lack of engine noise. Spring rates, damping, bushing stiffness, and even tire construction may be chosen specifically to deal with the vehicle's mass and quietness.

Figure 17-11 shows the basic idea: Battery weight changes the load picture, but it also gives engineers a low-mounted mass to work with. That's why some EVs feel heavy over broken pavement yet surprisingly composed in turns.

TIP

If an EV or hybrid seems to chew through tires quickly, don't blame the electric motor alone. Tire pressure, alignment, driving style, and suspension condition still matter a lot. Chapter 18 is where that story continues.

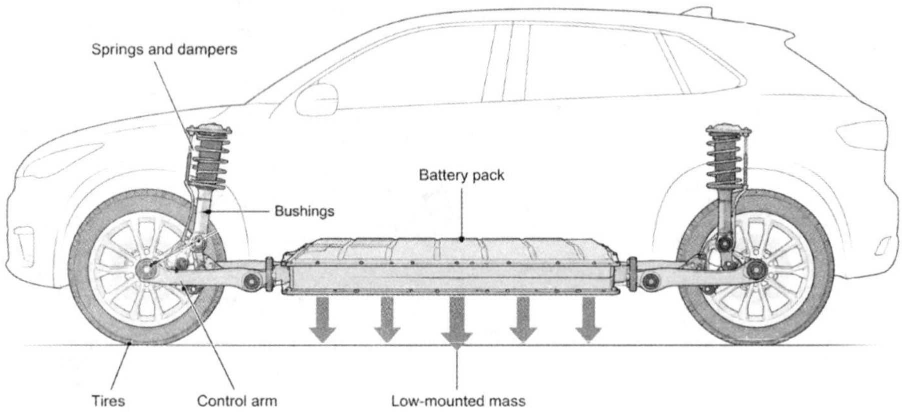

FIGURE 17-11: EV suspension realities.

Generated with AI using OpenAI

Common Steering and Suspension Problems

Steering and suspension problems rarely send a formal invitation. They show up as clues: looseness, noises, uneven tire wear, fluid leaks, wandering, vibrations, and ride behavior that just feels off. Your job isn't to diagnose every detail from the driver's seat. Your job is to notice patterns and know when a symptom deserves attention.

Loose steering

Loose steering can feel like the car takes a moment to respond after you turn the wheel, or like you're making constant tiny corrections on the highway. The wheel may have extra play around center, the car may wander in its lane, or the steering may simply feel less precise than it used to.

Possible causes include worn tie-rod ends, worn steering rack components, steering linkage wear on older systems, alignment problems, or low hydraulic fluid on a hydraulic system. Sometimes, the vehicle isn't truly loose so much as poorly aligned — which is why Chapter 18 and this chapter are best friends.

Clunks and vibrations

Clunks and vibrations can come from many places. A clunk over bumps may be a sway-bar link, bushing, strut mount, or control-arm issue. A vibration at speed may be tires, wheels, alignment, or worn front-end parts.

Still, the pattern matters. Try to notice when the symptom happens:

- **Over small bumps at low speed:** Think links, bushings, mounts, or other looseness in the suspension.
- **Mostly while braking:** Think brake or front-end movement issues — Chapters 16 and 21 help separate those clues.
- **Mostly at highway speed:** Tires, wheels, alignment, or worn suspension parts move higher on the suspect list.
- **Only during turns:** Steering joints, mounts, or other loaded front-end parts deserve attention.

Figure 17-12 is a symptom map, not a magic answer sheet. It helps you sort "what I am feeling" into a smarter starting point so that you're not replacing parts by horoscope.

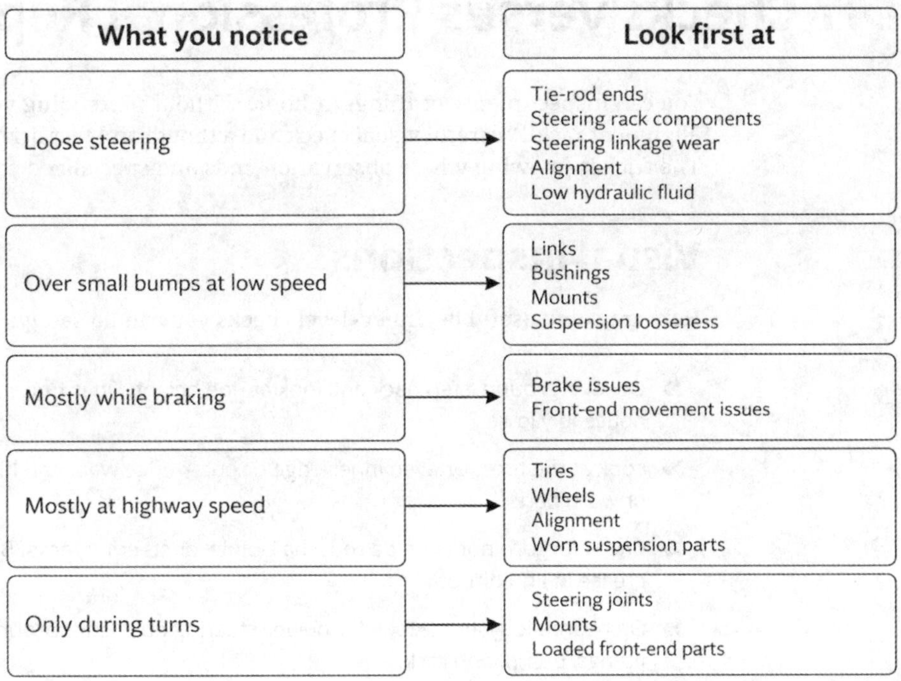

FIGURE 17-12: Steering/ suspension symptom map.

Generated with AI using OpenAI

REMEMBER

Tires can imitate suspension problems, and suspension problems can destroy tires. If a symptom feels vague, check tire condition and pressure before assuming the worst. The road only knows the tire is there.

Leaking struts

A strut or shock that is wet with oil may be leaking internally. The fluid inside the damper is what controls motion, so when it leaks out, the vehicle may bounce more, nose-dive more under braking, squat more on acceleration, or feel unsettled after bumps instead of calming down right away.

A light film isn't always a disaster, but obvious wetness, dirt stuck to oily residue, repeated bouncing, or uneven tire wear are good reasons to investigate. Dampers wear gradually, so many people don't realize how tired the suspension has become until it's fixed.

WARNING

Don't disassemble a loaded strut or coil spring assembly without the right tools and training. Compressed springs store a serious amount of energy. This job is one of those where overconfidence can rapidly become a cautionary tale.

DIY Checks versus Professional Repairs

You can inspect plenty of things at home without pretending your driveway is an alignment rack. A careful visual check and a thoughtful test drive can tell you a lot. The trick is knowing where observation ends and specialized equipment begins.

Visual inspections

Here are some useful beginner-level checks you can do safely:

- On level ground, step back and look at ride height. Does one corner sit noticeably lower?
- Look at the tires. Uneven inner-edge or outer-edge wear can hint at alignment or worn parts.
- Check for torn boots on tie rods, ball joints, or steering racks. Boots keep grease in and dirt out.
- On hydraulic systems, look for power-steering fluid leaks around hoses, fittings, pump, and rack.
- Look for oily struts or shocks, cracked bushings, broken spring coils, or shiny metal where parts have been rubbing.

- Listen during a slow parking-lot turn and over small bumps with the windows down. Front-end noises are often easier to hear at low speed.
- Notice how the car settles after a bump. One controlled rebound is normal; repeated bouncing is a clue.

TIP

Write down what you feel: when it happens, which side it seems to come from, what speed you were at, whether braking or turning changes it, and whether it happens hot, cold, loaded, or unloaded. Shops love good clues. Shops do not love "It made a sound once last Tuesday, maybe."

When to seek a shop

Some steering and suspension work is perfectly reasonable for an experienced DIYer. But a lot of it crosses into "You need proper equipment, torque specs, alignment tools, or enough spring-compressor experience to value your face." There is no shame in drawing that line early.

Involve a shop when:

- The steering feels unsafe, binds, or suddenly gets much heavier.
- You suspect worn ball joints, tie rods, control-arm joints, or steering-rack problems but can't confirm them safely.
- The job requires a wheel alignment afterward — tie rods, many control arms, and strut work all live here.
- An EPS warning, steering-angle issue, or ADAS calibration need shows up.
- Air suspension is sagging, adaptive dampers are faulting, or electronic modules are involved.
- The repair involves compressed springs, major front-end disassembly, or anything that makes you say, "This feels like a bad YouTube decision."

WARNING

Steering and suspension are safety systems. If the vehicle wanders badly, clunks like crazy, has a wheel sitting at a strange angle, or feels unstable at speed, don't keep driving and hope for clarity. Clarity sometimes arrives in the form of a tow bill — which is still cheaper than an accident.

IN THIS CHAPTER

» Decoding sidewall sizes, ratings, and date codes

» Choosing the right tire type

» Checking pressure, adding air, rotating on schedule

» Mastering alignment basics

Chapter 18
Smooth Moves: Tires, Balance, and Alignment

Tires are easy to ignore because they sit down there quietly doing their jobs while the flashy systems get all the attention. Nobody posts glamorous vacation photos of their sidewalls. But tires matter all the time, and when they're wrong — the wrong size, the wrong pressure, the wrong wear pattern, the wrong type for the weather — the whole car feels it.

This chapter is your plain-English guide to what tires do, how to read the information molded into them, how balance and alignment fit into the story, and how to spot trouble before it becomes an expensive rubber-eating hobby.

Why Tires Are More than Just Rubber

A tire is part spring, part grip device, part weather negotiator, and part shock absorber. It has to carry the vehicle's weight, survive heat, cold, potholes, and curbs, stay flexible enough to grip, stiff enough to steer accurately, and polite enough not to roar like an angry shopping cart on every highway trip.

Tires affect safety, comfort, and efficiency

If you change nothing on a car except the tires, you can dramatically change how it stops, turns, rides, and sounds. Good tires can make an ordinary car feel more stable and confidence-inspiring. Bad tires can make a very good car feel nervous, noisy, and one rainstorm away from a lecture in life choices.

Safety is the obvious part: Tires help determine braking grip, cornering grip, hydroplaning resistance, and straight-line stability. Comfort comes from how the sidewall and tread absorb little impacts and road texture. Efficiency shows up because rolling resistance affects how much energy it takes to keep the car moving — which means fuel economy on gas vehicles and range on EVs.

A healthy tire also helps the car feel consistent. Consistency is a bigger deal than many people realize. Predictability is what lets you brake, steer, and correct with confidence instead of wondering whether the car is about to improvise.

REMEMBER

The engine may make the drama, but the tires decide how much of that drama actually reaches the road. Every accelerate, brake, and steer command has to go through four patches of rubber roughly the size of postcards.

Only contact with the road

People repeat the saying for a reason: The tires are the only parts of the car meant to touch the road. Not the brakes. Not the suspension. Not your optimism. Just the tires.

That simple fact is why tire condition connects to almost every driving complaint. A pull may be alignment, but it can also be tire pressure or tire construction. A vibration may be a bent wheel or a balance issue. A loose-feeling front end may actually be worn tires with lousy grip.

Chapter 17 covers steering and suspension; this chapter explains why those systems are always in a group project with the tires.

Tire Construction and Modern Materials

Modern tires look simple from the outside, but inside they're layered little engineering projects. Their shape, internal structure, and rubber chemistry all affect grip, heat resistance, ride quality, wear, and efficiency.

Radial construction

Most modern passenger-vehicle tires are radial tires. In *radial tires,* the body plies inside the tire run roughly straight across from bead to bead, while steel belts under the tread help stabilize the footprint. In everyday language: The sidewall can flex, while the tread stays more controlled where it meets the road. Figure 18-1 shows the different parts of a tire.

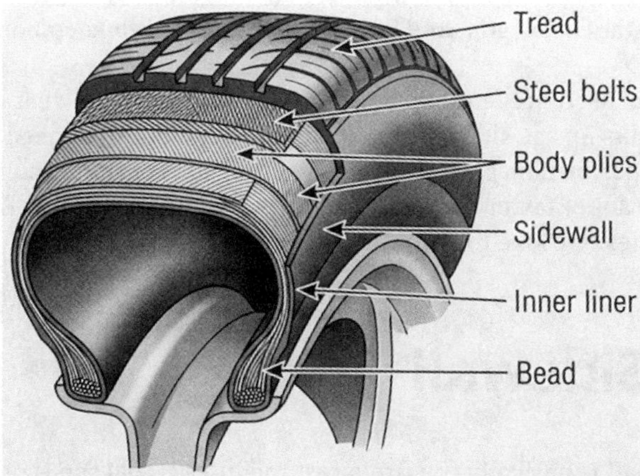

FIGURE 18-1: Basic tire anatomy.

Generated with AI using OpenAI

REMEMBER

The *tread* is the outer rubber that touches the road. The sidewall flexes and absorbs movement. The *bead* is the reinforced edge that seals against the wheel. Under the tread sit reinforcing belts that help the footprint stay stable under load.

Radial construction gives a very good mix of ride comfort, tread life, and stable handling. Older bias-ply designs still exist in specialty or historical applications, but for normal cars, trucks, and crossovers, radial tires are the standard. They won the popularity contest decades ago and never gave the trophy back.

Silica compounds

Rubber is not just rubber anymore. Tire makers blend natural and synthetic rubbers with fillers, oils, and additives to change how the tire behaves. One common modern ingredient is silica, which helps improve wet grip and can reduce rolling resistance when used well.

The basic idea is that the compound matters just as much as the shape of the tread. Two tires can look similar from across a parking lot and behave very differently in cold rain, summer heat, or long highway drives. Those performance differences are why buying the cheapest thing with the right size printed on it can be a false economy.

Reinforced EV tires

Electric vehicles ask a lot from tires. EVs are often heavier than similar gas vehicles, they deliver torque instantly, and their quiet cabins make road noise much more noticeable. Many EV-focused tires use stronger internal construction, lower rolling resistance designs, and tread patterns tuned to keep noise down.

Those EV-focused tire features don't mean every EV must wear a magical tire with lightning bolts on the sidewall. It means replacement tires need to match the load, speed, and performance needs of the vehicle. Ignore that, and you may get more noise, less range, faster wear, or handling that feels a little off — like the car is wearing shoes one size too enthusiastic.

Reading the Sidewall

TIP

A tire sidewall is basically the tire's resume. It tells you the size, type, load capacity, speed capability, age code, and a few other useful clues. At first glance, it looks like someone hid a spreadsheet in rubber. Once you know what to look for, deciphering the information on the sidewall gets much easier.

Tire size codes

A common tire size might look something like 225/45R17. Read left to right, that code usually means the tire is about 225 millimeters wide, the sidewall height is 45 percent of that width, the R means radial construction, and the tire fits a 17-inch wheel.

That middle number — the aspect ratio — is the part many beginners overlook. A lower number usually means a shorter sidewall, which often sharpens steering feel but can make the ride firmer and the wheel more vulnerable to pothole damage. A taller sidewall often rides softer and tolerates ugly roads better, but it can feel less crisp in quick transitions.

Figure 18-2 breaks down the code into plain English so that you don't have to decode it with squinting and guesswork.

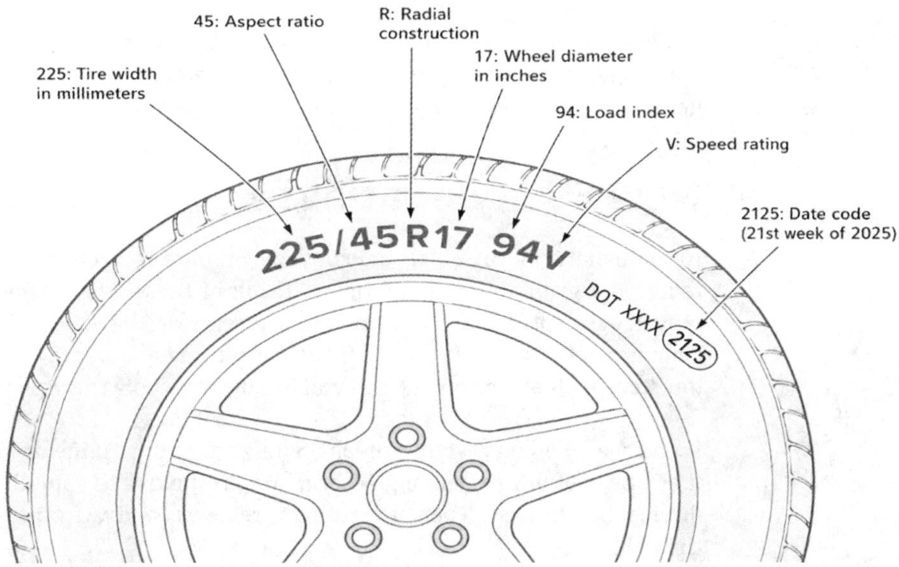

FIGURE 18-2: Sidewall code decoder.

Generated with AI using OpenAI

Speed and load ratings

After the main size, many tires list a load index and speed rating, such as 94V. The *load index* corresponds to how much weight the tire can carry. The *speed letter* reflects the tire's designed capability at higher speeds under proper conditions. For most drivers, the practical rule is simple: Meet or exceed the vehicle manufacturer's requirements.

These ratings aren't just performance-car issues. Load capacity matters on family SUVs, vans, pickups, and EVs, too. Installing tires that physically fit but don't carry enough load is the tire equivalent of buying folding chairs for a grand piano.

DOT and date codes

The DOT code includes a tire identification number, and the last four digits tell you the week and year the tire was made. For example, 2125 means the 21st week of 2025. That number is handy when checking how fresh a "new" tire actually is or when deciding whether an old spare deserves trust.

Age matters because rubber changes over time, even if the tread looks decent. Heat, sunlight, storage conditions, and plain old aging all affect a tire. A tire's age alone doesn't mean you need to panic every time a tire has a birthday. It does mean that very old tires deserve extra scrutiny, especially if they show cracking, hardening, or suspicious enthusiasm for losing grip.

WARNING

Don't judge a tire only by tread depth. A tire with plenty of tread but obvious cracking, bulges, repeated air loss, impact damage, or advanced age isn't a bargain. It is a polite-looking problem.

New EU-style ratings

In some markets, tire labels help buyers compare categories, such as rolling resistance, wet grip, and external noise. Think of these labels as quick-glance shopping clues, not a complete personality test for the tire. A label can help you compare options, but it can't tell you everything about tread wear, winter behavior, steering feel, or how the tire will handle a pothole the size of municipal regret.

If you see an energy-style tire label while shopping online or internationally, use it as one useful input among several. Match the tire to your climate, vehicle, and driving habits first. Then use ratings, reviews, and warranty details to narrow the field.

Types of Tires

Tires are like shoes: One pair is great for jogging, another is built for hiking, and one looks impressive until you try to do anything practical in it. The right tire depends on climate, vehicle type, and the kind of driving that fills most of your week.

Table 18-1 gives you a quick cheat sheet of the different tire personalities.

TABLE 18-1 Tire Type Chooser

Tire type	Climate and weather	Comfort and ride quality	Best use case
All-season tires	Work for most everyday conditions, including light rain and light snow. Not meant for serious winter weather.	Usually smooth, quiet, and comfortable.	Daily commuting, family vehicles, and year-round use in moderate climates.
Summer/ performance tires	Best in warm weather and dry or wet roads. Not for cold temperatures, ice, or snow.	Sharper handling, but often a firmer and noisier ride.	Sporty driving, performance cars, and stronger cornering and braking grip.

Tire type	Climate and weather	Comfort and ride quality	Best use case
Truck/SUV tires	Built for heavier vehicles and rougher conditions; some handle mud, gravel, or light off-road use.	Often firmer, with larger tread blocks and more road noise.	Pickups, SUVs, towing, hauling, unpaved roads, and heavier loads.
EV-focused tires	Designed for electric vehicles; may emphasize range, efficiency, quietness, or performance.	Often tuned to reduce road noise and support a smooth ride.	EVs that need tires suited for extra weight, instant torque, and range efficiency.

TIP

Choose tires for the worst conditions you regularly face, not the best conditions you daydream about. A tire that is perfect on sunny Saturdays but miserable on your icy Monday commute isn't actually the perfect tire.

Specialized Tire Systems

Modern tires are no longer just rubber hoops full of air. They now come with sensors, special construction, and enough built-in technology to make a simple tire change feel like a group project.

Run-flats

Run-flat tires are designed to carry the vehicle for a limited distance after losing pressure, which can spare you the joy of changing a tire on the shoulder while traffic flies by pretending not to notice. That feature is especially useful on vehicles with no spare.

The catch is that run-flats usually cost more, ride firmer, and can limit your replacement options. If your vehicle came with them, make sure the wheel setup, suspension tuning, and spare-tire plan don't assume they'll always stay in the picture.

TPMS sensors

TPMS stands for *Tire Pressure Monitoring System*, which is a very formal name for the feature that lights up when one of your tires starts slacking off. Some vehicles use *direct TPMS*, with a pressure sensor inside each wheel. Others use *indirect TPMS*, which uses wheel-speed data to detect when a tire is low. One system measures. The other makes a well-informed accusation.

Figure 18-3 shows the difference between direct and indirect TPMS, along with the reset behavior that often confuses people right after tire service.

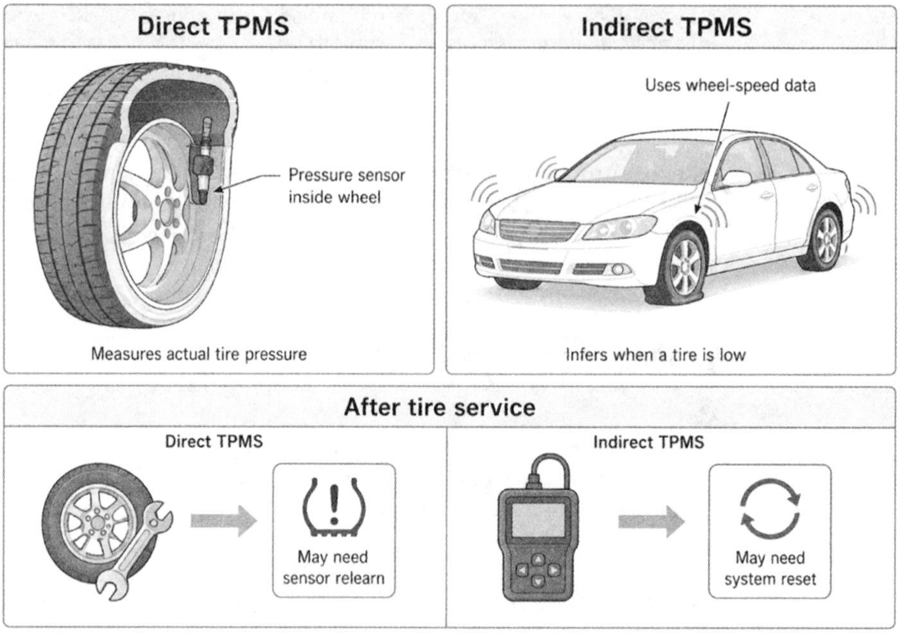

FIGURE 18-3: TPMS basics.

Generated with AI using OpenAI

REMEMBER

A TPMS light isn't decorative dashboard mood lighting. Check the tire pressure with a real gauge, inspect for damage, and add air or repair the tire as needed.

Smart tire technology

Some newer systems go beyond low-pressure warnings and track things like tread wear or tire temperature. That tracking helps with safety, efficiency, and maintenance planning, especially on high-end vehicles and fleets.

For everyday drivers, the main takeaway is simple: Tire service is getting more data-heavy. "Swap tires and hope for the best" is slowly being replaced by resets, relearns, and calibration checks.

Buying Tires

Shopping for tires is one of those jobs that feels simple until you open three browser tabs and suddenly have 47 choices, 12 unfamiliar terms, and a strong desire to fake your own disappearance. A little structure helps.

Dealer versus online buying

Buying from a dealer or local tire shop can be easier when you want one-stop service, quick advice, and someone to handle installation, balancing, and any warranty issues in person. The price may not always be the lowest on paper, but convenience has value — especially when the car is already there and you need it back without a spreadsheet summit.

Buying online can give you a wider selection and sometimes a better deal, especially for unusual sizes or specialty tires. The catch is that you still need a plan for installation, TPMS service, disposal fees, and possible warranty claims. A low online price can become less exciting once shipping and installation team up like tiny hidden pirates.

Warranty and registration

When you buy tires, pay attention to road-hazard coverage, treadwear warranty language, and any registration process. Registration matters because it helps manufacturers contact owners in the event of a recall. It isn't glamorous paperwork, but neither is discovering months later that your tires were trying to tell the government something important.

Also keep your invoice. Future warranty questions become much easier when you have purchase date, mileage, and rotation history instead of a vague memory that begins with "I think it was sometime after that one road trip."

Driving style and tire choice

Start with the basics: the correct size and ratings for your vehicle. Then think honestly about how you drive. Are you mostly highway commuting? Do you live in heavy rain? Do you tow? Do you spend winters scraping frost while muttering at the sky? The right tire choice follows the real pattern of your life, not the imaginary version where you're always on a racetrack or always conquering mountain trails.

Caring for Your Tires

Tire care is gloriously low drama compared with rebuilding an engine. A gauge, an inflator, a little attention, and a willingness to crouch near the wheels for a minute can save you real money and real trouble.

Checking pressure

REMEMBER

Check tire pressure when the tires are cold, meaning the car has been parked long enough that heat from driving has not raised the reading. Use the pressure listed on the vehicle's door-jamb sticker, not the maximum pressure molded into the tire sidewall. The sidewall number is a limit, not a daily recommendation.

Pressure affects more than tire life. Too little pressure can increase heat, worsen wear on the shoulders, reduce efficiency, and make the steering feel mushy. Too much pressure can reduce the size of the contact patch and make the ride harsher. In other words, tire pressure is the cheapest handling adjustment most drivers never think about.

Adding air

Adding air is simple: Remove the valve-cap, press the inflator onto the valve stem, add air in short bursts, and recheck with a gauge until you hit the door-jamb specification.

TIP

The trick is getting a good seal: Push the inflator on squarely and firmly. If you hear a loud hiss, it isn't seated; pull it off, line it up straight, and try again. If the inflator has a locking lever, press the chuck on first and then flip the lever to lock it. If you overshoot, bleed a little back out. This process isn't a soufflé. You're allowed to adjust.

If one tire keeps losing pressure, don't keep treating the compressor like a lifestyle. Slow leaks usually come from punctures, valve issues, wheel corrosion, or bead-seal problems. Top-ups are useful in the short term. Diagnosis is useful in the grown-up term.

Checking tire pressure is a simple routine, but the order matters. Start with cold tires, use the pressure listed on the door-jamb sticker, add air only as needed, and always recheck your work. The steps below walk you through the process without turning it into a garage drama.

Follow this basic tire-pressure routine:

1. **Check the tires cold.**

   Check before driving or wait at least three hours after the last drive. Use a reliable tire-pressure gauge.

2. **Compare the reading with the door-jamb sticker.**

   Find the recommended PSI on the sticker inside the driver's door area and then compare it with your gauge reading.

3. **Add air if the tire is low.**

   Remove the valve cap, press the inflator straight and firmly onto the valve stem, and add air in short bursts. If you hear a loud hiss, the inflator isn't seated well; pull it off, line it up straight, and try again.

4. **Recheck the pressure.**

   Use the gauge again after adding air. Add more air or bleed a little out until the tire matches the recommended PSI.

5. **Reinstall the valve cap.**

   Screw the cap back on snugly before it rolls away and disappears into the universe.

TIP

Keeping a quality gauge and a small inflator in the vehicle turns a low-pressure warning from a schedule-wrecking event into a five-minute maintenance chore.

Rotating at intervals

Rotation helps spread wear more evenly across the set, but the exact pattern and interval depend on the vehicle, tire type, and whether the tires are directional or staggered. The easy owner rule is to follow the owner's manual or tire maker guidance and rotate before one pair has a chance to become the overworked office department.

Rotation doesn't fix alignment problems, suspension wear, or repeated underinflation. It simply helps normal wear stay normal. If a tire shows a strange pattern, solve the cause instead of rotating the evidence to a different corner of the car.

If you plan to rotate the tires yourself, refer to the safe lifting and wheel-removal steps in Chapter 1 first and see Chapter 3 for torque-wrench basics. Then follow the rotation pattern and lug-nut torque specification in your owner's manual.

Balancing methods

Balancing is about correcting uneven mass in the tire-and-wheel assembly so that it spins smoothly. If an assembly is out of balance, you may feel vibration at certain speeds, often in the steering wheel or seat. A speed-related vibration isn't the car "getting older." The shake is physics filing a complaint.

Standard dynamic balancing is common during tire installation. Some shops also use road-force balancing, which can help identify stiff spots, wheel issues, or problem assemblies on sensitive vehicles. The important beginner point is that balance and alignment aren't the same thing. Balance fixes spin-related shake. Alignment fixes wheel-angle geometry.

Alignment Matters More than Ever

Wheel alignment sounds abstract until you see what bad alignment does to a fresh set of tires. Then suddenly, geometry becomes very personal. Modern vehicles also tie alignment into cameras, steering-angle sensors, and other driver-assistance systems, so this topic has more consequences than it used to.

Wheel alignment basics

An alignment isn't really about making the steering wheel look emotionally centered, though that is nice, too. It's about setting wheel angles so that the tires roll in the intended direction and meet the road correctly. The three terms you hear most are toe, camber, and caster:

- *Toe* describes whether the fronts of the tires point slightly toward each other or away from each other when viewed from above.
- *Camber* describes whether the top of the tire leans inward or outward when viewed from the front.
- *Caster* describes the tilt of the steering axis, which affects straight-line stability and steering feel.

You don't need to become alignment royalty to grasp the outcome. Wrong toe can scrub rubber away surprisingly fast. Wrong camber can wear one edge of the tread. Caster mostly affects steering stability and return-to-center feel. Figure 18-4 puts the angles into a friendlier picture so that they stop sounding like geometry villains.

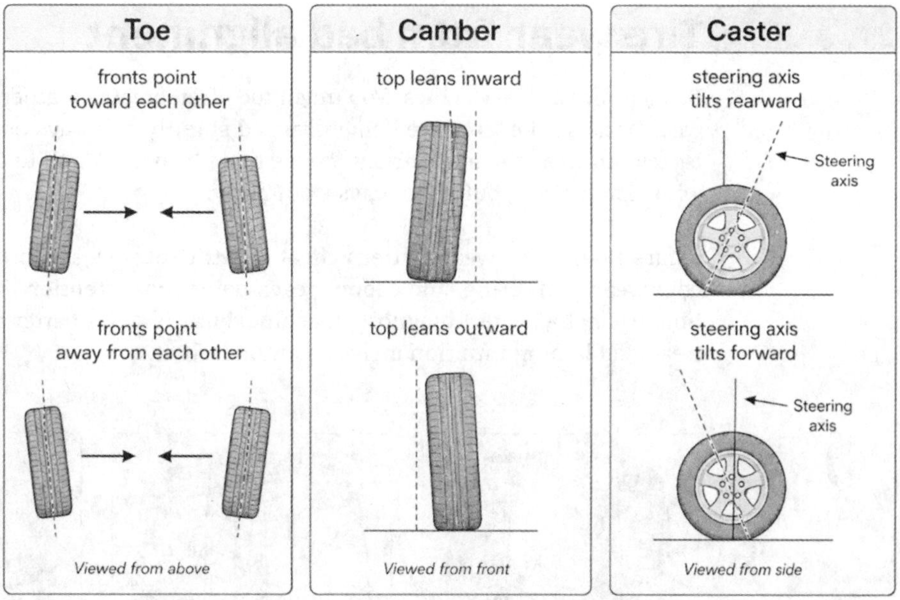

FIGURE 18-4: Alignment basics in plain English.

Generated with AI using OpenAI

ADAS calibration

On many modern vehicles, alignment work is no longer just a mechanical adjustment. Cameras, radar units, steering-angle sensors, and stability-control systems may depend on the car knowing exactly where straight ahead is and how the wheels are positioned relative to the body.

That straight-ahead and wheel-position information matters after alignments, suspension repairs, curb hits, collisions, windshield replacement, and sometimes changes in ride height or wheel-and-tire setup. Chapter 17 introduces this idea from the steering side; here is the tire-side truth: If the vehicle's driver-assistance features seem unhappy after front-end work, the car may be asking for calibration, not attention.

WARNING

If lane-keeping, steering-assist, stability, or parking-assist warnings show up after tire, suspension, or alignment work, don't assume the car is just being moody. Many vehicles need scan-tool procedures or camera/radar calibration that belong to a properly equipped shop.

Tire wear from bad alignment

Bad alignment leaves clues. Too much toe often creates feathered tread and rapid wear because the tires are being dragged slightly sideways as they roll. Camber issues can wear the inner or outer edge more heavily. A pull to one side may come with visible wear, but not always right away.

Figure 18-5 is the wear-pattern cheat sheet: Center wear, both-edge wear, one-edge wear, feathering, and cupping each point your attention in a different direction. It's not a perfect diagnosis machine, but it's miles better than staring at the tread and hoping intuition arrives by thunderbolt.

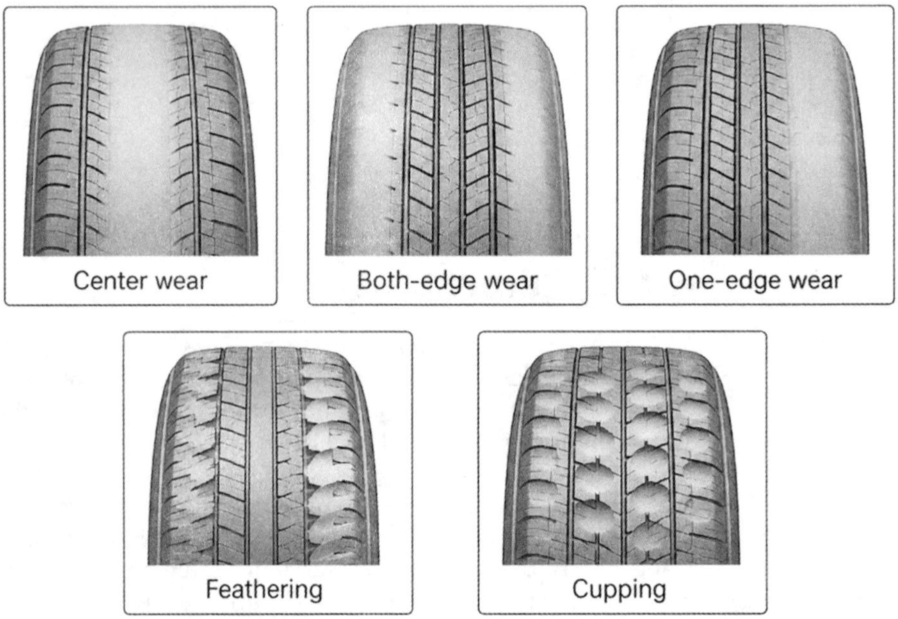

FIGURE 18-5: Tire wear pattern guide.

Generated with AI using OpenAI

Checking for Wear

A quick tread inspection tells you a lot about tire health. You're not just asking, "Is there enough rubber left?" You're also asking, "Is it wearing evenly, and is the tire telling me something about pressure, balance, or alignment?"

Tread depth tools

A tread-depth gauge is cheap, simple, and far more reliable than guessing by vibes. Measure in more than one spot across the width of the tire and around the circumference. Measuring helps you catch uneven wear instead of flattering yourself with the best-looking groove you could find.

If you don't have a tread-depth gauge, there are old coin tricks and built-in indicators, but a real gauge is clearer. This tiny tool earns its drawer space immediately.

Wear bars

Most tires include wear bars molded into the grooves. When the tread wears down close to those bars, the tire is telling you that replacement time is no longer a philosophical question. Wet and snow performance usually decline well before a tire is completely bald, so waiting until the tire looks like a slick racing tire isn't a clever economy move.

REMEMBER

Even if the tread-depth number technically clears a legal minimum in some places, you still need to think about your conditions. Heavy rain, winter weather, highway speeds, and towing all make healthy tread more valuable. Legal minimum and smart minimum aren't always twins.

Uneven wear patterns

Uneven wear is where tires become gossipy. They start telling you about inflation habits, alignment angles, worn shocks, weak bushings, or a balance problem that has been living rent-free for too long. Here are the most common uneven wear patterns and what they usually point to:

- **Center worn more than the edges:** Suspect overinflation.
- **Both shoulders worn:** Suspect underinflation.
- **One edge worn much more than the other:** Suspect alignment, especially camber or toe issues.
- **Feathered tread blocks:** Suspect toe misalignment or parts that let the wheel steer slightly as it rolls.
- **Cupping or scalloping:** Suspect worn dampers, imbalance, or suspension problems.

REMEMBER

A tire can wear out because the tire is old, but it can also wear out because something else on the car is wrong. Replacing tires without fixing the cause is like buying a new rug to hide a roof leak.

Eco Tire Tech

Tires are getting greener, which is good news because most people like breathing and also prefer not to leave behind mountains of worn-out rubber. This shift toward greener tires does not mean every eco-focused tire is perfect for every vehicle, but it does mean tire makers are trying to cut waste, improve efficiency, and use materials more responsibly without turning your car into a wobbly shopping cart.

Recycling old tires

Old tires can be recycled into things like playground surfaces, rubberized asphalt, mats, and other useful products. Recycling is a lot better than letting them sit in piles collecting water and looking like the opening scene of a mosquito documentary.

When you buy new tires, the disposal or recycling fee usually helps cover what happens to the old ones. It's worth asking the installer where your take-offs go. This small question tells you whether your old tires are getting a second act or just being shoved out of sight like embarrassing garage clutter.

Eco-friendly compounds

Manufacturers are also working on tire compounds that lower rolling resistance, last longer, and use more sustainable ingredients where possible. Of course, tire design is always a balancing act. Better efficiency sounds wonderful right up until it shows up wearing a clever disguise and quietly gives away wet-road grip.

The best eco-focused tires try to improve efficiency without making the ride noisy, the handling weird, or the tread life disappointing. The sweet spot is a tire that helps the planet a bit without making your Tuesday commute feel like a science experiment.

Sustainable manufacturing

The environmental story isn't just about the tire itself. It also includes how the tire is made, how much energy and water the factory uses, how materials are sourced, and how long the tire lasts in the real world. A tire that wears evenly, lasts well, and helps efficiency is usually better for both your wallet and the bigger resource picture.

TECHNICAL STUFF

Rolling resistance is the energy a tire loses as it flexes where it meets the road. Lower rolling resistance can improve fuel economy or EV range, but engineers still have to balance that goal against grip, tread wear, ride quality, and noise.

If you remember only one thing from this chapter, make it this: Tires aren't just rubber. They affect safety, comfort, handling, and efficiency all at once. Keep them inflated correctly, inspect them regularly, rotate them on time, and don't ignore weird wear patterns just because the car is otherwise acting innocent.

IN THIS CHAPTER

» Seeing what the drivetrain does between engine drama and wheels

» Following power flow through manuals, automatics, DCTs, CVTs, and electrified setups

» Sorting out AWD, 4WD, transfer cases, and torque vectoring

» Spotting transmission trouble before "we'll see if it goes away" gets expensive

» Understanding fluids, heat, and why lifetime fluid can be wishful thinking

Chapter 19

Shift Happens: Transmissions and Drivetrains

Engines and motors make power. Wheels turn that power into motion. The drivetrain is everything in the middle that has to translate one into the other without turning the whole trip into a loud, expensive tantrum. When it works, you barely think about it. When it doesn't, you suddenly become very interested in words like "slip," "shudder," and "why is it revving like that?"

This chapter is your down-to-earth guide to what transmissions and drivetrains do, how the main types differ, what modern AWD and hybrid systems are up to, and which symptoms are "keep an eye on it" versus "stop cooking that gearbox and call a grown-up." We're keeping the explanations plain, the humor legal, and the jargon on a short leash.

What the Drivetrain Does

The *drivetrain* is the chain of parts that carries power from the engine or electric motor to the drive wheels. Depending on the vehicle, that chain may include the transmission, clutch or torque converter, driveshaft, differential, transfer case, axle shafts, and a few control modules quietly making decisions behind the curtain.

Role of the drivetrain

In simple terms, the drivetrain gives the power source leverage choices. Your engine doesn't want to crawl up a hill, launch away from a stoplight, and cruise at highway speed using exactly the same gear ratio. Electric motors are more flexible, but they still need reduction gearing and a way to split power to the wheels. The drivetrain is what makes the vehicle feel usable instead of hilariously wrong for half its life.

Figure 19-1 is the big-picture map: Power starts at the engine or motor, gets shaped by the transmission or reduction gear, and then travels through shafts and differentials until the wheels finally do the part everyone notices.

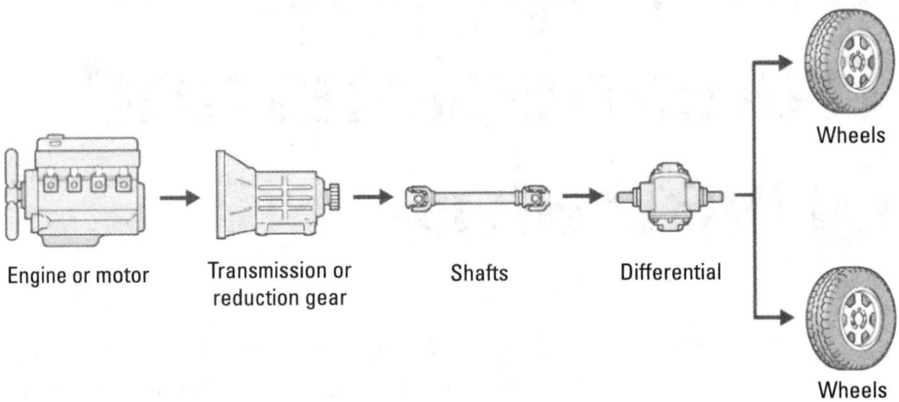

FIGURE 19-1: Drivetrain at a glance.

Generated with AI using OpenAI

REMEMBER

The engine makes power, but the drivetrain decides how that power shows up at the road. A strong engine with a sick transmission is like a great singer with a broken microphone: technically talented, practically disappointing.

Power delivery importance

Good power delivery isn't just about going faster. It affects smooth takeoffs, towing behavior, passing confidence, fuel economy, noise, and how relaxed the vehicle feels at speed. A drivetrain that delivers power cleanly makes a car feel polished. A drivetrain that hesitates, flares, bangs, or hunts around for a ratio makes even a nice vehicle feel like it woke up on the wrong side of the parking lot.

The need for clean, mission-appropriate power delivery is also why drivetrains are so different from one vehicle to the next. A work truck, a sports coupe, a family crossover, a hybrid taxi, and an EV commuter all want different things from the hardware. No one best transmission exists, only the one that fits the mission without annoying the owner too much.

How Power Flows

If you understand the path power takes, the whole chapter gets less mysterious. Think of power flow as a relay race with greasy shoes. One component passes torque to the next, and each handoff changes speed, leverage, direction, or which wheels get the job.

How engine power reaches the wheels

On a typical gasoline vehicle, the crankshaft sends rotation into either a clutch and manual transmission or a torque converter and automatic transmission. Inside the transmission, different gear ratios change how much torque multiplication you get and how fast the output spins relative to engine speed. From there, power goes to a differential, which lets the left and right drive wheels turn at slightly different speeds in a corner because physics is needy like that.

On rear-wheel-drive vehicles, power often leaves the transmission through a long driveshaft that runs to the rear differential.

On front-wheel-drive vehicles, the transmission and differential are usually packaged together in a transaxle, which keeps things compact and helps with packaging.

In AWD and 4WD systems, things get more social: Now you may have a transfer case, an electronically controlled coupling, or multiple differentials helping spread torque around.

Different drivetrain layouts

The main drivetrain layouts are front-wheel drive (FWD), rear-wheel drive (RWD), all-wheel drive (AWD), and four-wheel drive (4WD). FWD is common because it packages efficiently and usually behaves predictably in daily driving. RWD often feels more balanced under acceleration and towing. AWD aims for extra traction and stability by sending power to all four wheels as needed or all the time. Traditional 4WD is the truck-and-trail version, built more for loose surfaces and off-road use.

Figure 19-2 compares the common layouts so the names stop sounding like alphabet soup and start sounding like actual hardware choices.

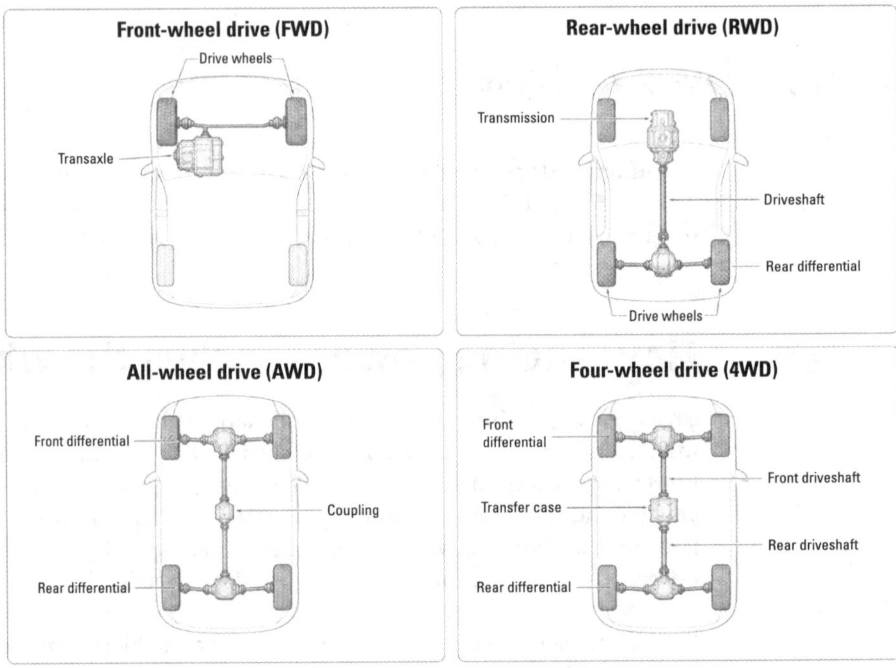

FIGURE 19-2: Common drivetrain layouts.

Generated with AI using OpenAI

TIP

If you can never remember what drivetrain your vehicle has, look in the owner's manual, the window sticker, or the model badge. Guessing wrong matters when you buy tires, tow the vehicle, or tell a shop what all four corners are doing.

Manual Transmissions

Manual transmissions are the old-school crowd favorite: simple in concept, satisfying when done well, and fully capable of making you look like a hero or a stall-happy menace depending on how your left foot is feeling.

Gears, synchros, clutches

A manual transmission is basically a box of selectable leverage. You use the clutch pedal to disconnect the engine from the gearbox long enough to choose a different gear ratio. Inside the transmission are gear pairs for the different ratios, shift collars that lock the chosen gear to a shaft, and *synchronizers* — usually called synchros — that help match speeds so that the shift goes in smoothly instead of sounding like you dropped a fork disposal unit into a blender.

The clutch itself is a friction sandwich. A clutch disc gets squeezed between the flywheel and pressure plate so that engine torque flows into the transmission input shaft. Press the pedal, the disc is released, and the engine can spin separately from the gearbox. Release the pedal smoothly, and the connection comes back in a controlled way. Release it like you're starting a lawnmower with feelings, and the car lets everyone nearby know.

Figure 19-3 shows the basic manual path from clutch to selected gear to output shaft. Once that map clicks, manual-transmission talk stops sounding like garage wizardry.

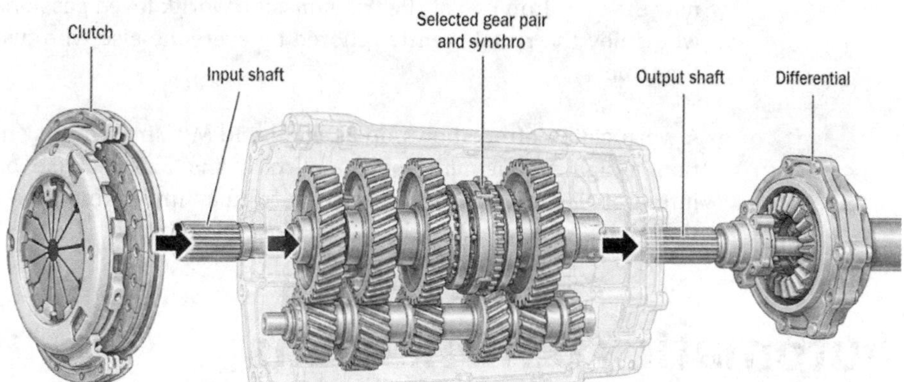

FIGURE 19-3: Manual transmission basics.

Generated with AI using OpenAI

TECHNICAL STUFF

Gear ratio is leverage. A low gear multiplies torque more but spins the output more slowly. A high gear gives less multiplication but lets the vehicle cruise at lower engine RPM for the same road speed.

Why enthusiasts love manuals

People who love manuals usually love the sense of involvement. You choose the gear, you decide when to shift, and the car feels a little more like a tool you operate instead of an appliance that politely handles everything for you. Done well, a manual can feel playful, connected, and weirdly satisfying for something that is basically you negotiating with a clutch disc.

Manuals also tend to be mechanically straightforward compared with modern multispeed automatics. Straightforward doesn't mean they're cheap to ignore, but the layout is easier to understand. Clutches wear. Synchros can wear. Bearings and seals can fail. Still, the system makes intuitive sense once you know what each part does.

Decline in modern market

Manuals have become rare in the modern market for one big reason: Most people would rather let the car shift for itself, especially in traffic. Automatics have also become faster, more efficient, and smarter, which removed many of the old reasons to defend a stick shift like it's a constitutional right.

That decline doesn't make manuals bad. It just makes them more niche. They're now the cast-iron pan of the transmission world: loved passionately by the people who enjoy the ritual, gently ignored by everyone else who just wants dinner on the table.

REMEMBER

A worn clutch often shows up as engine RPM rising without matching acceleration, a high engagement point, a burning smell after abuse, or difficulty getting into gear. That issue is very different from a "my engine is weak" problem, even though both can feel like the car has lost its ambition.

Automatic Transmissions

If manuals are about driver involvement, automatics are about doing a hundred little jobs for you quietly and, ideally, without drama. Modern automatics are remarkably good at that. They can launch smoothly, keep the engine in a happy range, adapt to hills and throttle habits, and still cruise efficiently at highway speed. It's a lot of choreography for something most drivers treat like a toaster with ambitions.

Traditional torque converter automatics

The classic automatic uses a torque converter instead of a manual clutch pedal. The *torque converter* is a fluid coupling that lets the engine keep running while the vehicle is stopped, and it also helps multiply torque during takeoff. Behind the torque converter sit planetary gearsets, clutches, and brakes that combine in different ways to create the various forward gears and reverse.

A good everyday description is that the engine spins the converter, hydraulic pressure and electronic controls decide which internal clutch packs apply, and the transmission chooses a ratio that fits the moment. The old automatic stereotype was soft, slushy shifts and a big fuel-economy penalty. Modern automatics heard those insults, got very defensive, and improved a lot.

Figure 19-4 gives you the broad idea: torque converter up front, gearsets and clutch packs inside, output going out to the differential.

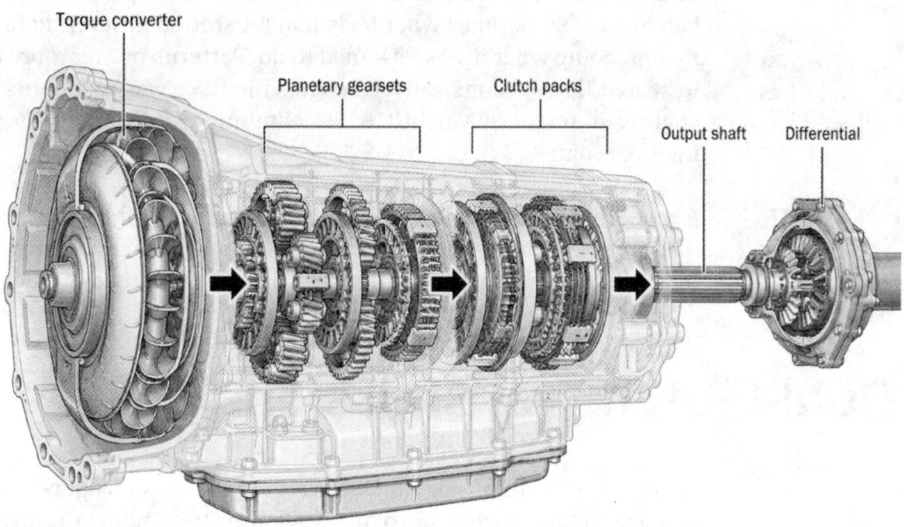

FIGURE 19-4: Automatic transmission basics.

Generated with AI using OpenAI

Modern six to ten speed

Many modern automatics have six, eight, nine, or even ten speeds. More gears let engineers keep the engine closer to its sweet spots for acceleration, fuel economy, and emissions. First gear can be nice and short for brisk takeoffs, while the top gears can be tall enough to let the engine loaf along on the highway instead of buzzing like it drank three espressos.

Of course, more gears also mean more possible shifts. Done well, you barely notice them. Done poorly, the transmission can feel busy, indecisive, or weirdly committed to the wrong gear. The good news is that modern control software is usually smart enough to avoid turning your commute into a shift-based interpretive dance.

Adaptive shifting

Adaptive shifting means the transmission control module watches how you drive and adjusts shift timing, firmness, and gear choice. If you drive gently, it may upshift sooner for efficiency. If you drive like every freeway merge is a personal challenge, it may hold gears longer and downshift more readily.

That adaptability is helpful, but it can also make people think the transmission has moods. Sometimes what feels like "it shifted differently today" is exactly the system doing what it was designed to do. Patterns matter more than one odd shift. Repeated flares, bangs, delayed engagement, or warning lights are real clues. One slightly dramatic downshift while climbing a hill is usually just the car reading the room.

TIP

A modern automatic that shifts a little differently right after the battery has been disconnected may need a short relearn period, which is normal. A modern automatic that keeps slamming into gear like it's settling old grudges is not.

Dual-Clutch Transmissions

A *dual-clutch transmission*, or DCT, is the transmission equivalent of trying to have your cake and launch-control it, too. It aims to combine the direct feel of a manual with the convenience and speed of an automatic.

How DCTs work

A DCT uses two separate clutches: One handles the odd gears, and the other handles the even gears. While one gear is being used, the next likely gear can already be preselected on the other shaft. Then the clutches trade jobs. That setup is how DCTs can shift so quickly — the next ratio is already standing backstage in full costume.

Some DCTs use wet clutches bathed in fluid, while others use dry clutches. The details vary, but the core idea is the same: computer-controlled clutch operation, very fast ratio changes, and less torque-converter mush than a traditional automatic.

Figure 19-5 shows the twin-path logic: one clutch for odd gears, one for even gears, with the next shift waiting impatiently in the wings.

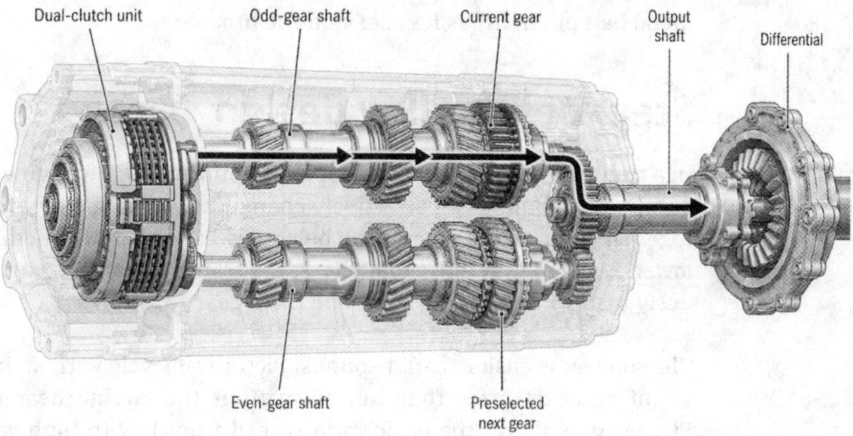

FIGURE 19-5: Dual-clutch transmission layout.

Generated with AI using OpenAI

Pros and cons of DCTs

The big selling point of DCTs is speed. DCTs can shift quickly and efficiently, which is why they show up in performance cars and some fuel-conscious applications. They can feel crisp, direct, and impressively alert when the software is well tuned. On the right road, a good DCT feels like the transmission finished your sentence before you did.

The downside is that some DCTs can feel awkward at very low speeds because they still have to manage clutch engagement. Parking-lot creeping, stop-and-go traffic, and gentle takeoffs can sometimes feel more like a slightly confused manual than a silky old-school automatic. Owners describe it with words like shudder, hesitation, or "why is this acting like I hired a new intern to drive it?"

Reliability also varies a lot by design and manufacturer. Some have done well. Some have developed a reputation that follows them around like a bad yearbook photo. The takeaway for beginners isn't all DCTs are trouble. It's fast and clever doesn't always mean simple or forgiving.

WARNING

Don't assume every low-speed DCT quirk means failure, but also don't ignore persistent shuddering, warning messages, delayed engagement, or overheating behavior. Clutch wear and software issues aren't fixed by optimistic thoughts.

CVT

A *continuously variable transmission*, or CVT, skips the usual stepped gears and instead changes ratio more smoothly across a range. That description sounds futuristic, which is helpful, because "two variable pulleys and a very important metal belt or chain" is less sexy on the brochure.

Steel belt/pulley design

In a common belt-type CVT, one pulley connects to the engine and another to the output. Each pulley can effectively change its working diameter. Move the halves together on one pulley, and the belt rides higher; move them apart, and it rides lower. By changing those diameters, the transmission can vary the ratio continuously instead of jumping from one fixed gear to another.

The concept is easier than it sounds. Picture a bicycle with an infinitely adjustable set of sprocket sizes that can always put the engine near the RPM it wants. Figure 19-6 shows the basic ratio spread from low to high without making you take a pop quiz on pulley geometry.

Fuel economy benefits

CVTs can help fuel economy because they let the engine spend more time in efficient operating ranges. They can also provide very smooth acceleration with no traditional shift shock. For everyday commuting, that trade-off can be perfectly sensible: fewer dramatic gear changes, better efficiency, and one less thing to think about.

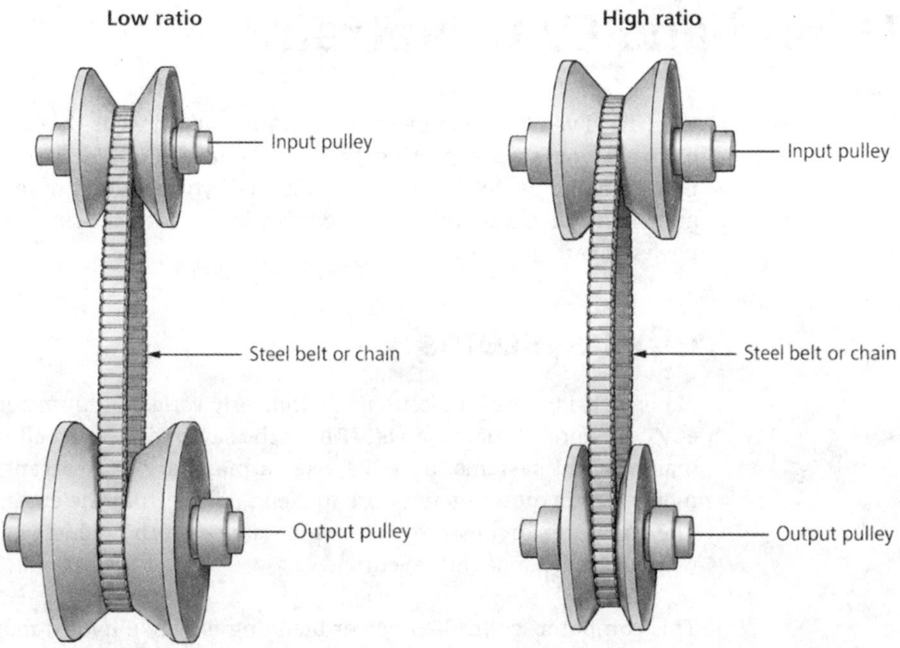

FIGURE 19-6: CVT ratio change.

Generated with AI using OpenAI

Driver feel concerns

The complaint some drivers have is feel. Because the ratio can change continuously, the engine may hold a steady RPM while the vehicle speed rises, which can sound strange if you grew up expecting the classic "rev, shift, rev, shift" rhythm. Some people describe that as rubber-band feel. Others describe it as "fine, actually, calm down."

Modern CVTs have improved a lot, and some even simulate stepped shifts to make drivers more comfortable. But the main beginner lesson is that unusual feel doesn't automatically mean failure on a CVT. Judder, slipping, overheating warnings, or persistent whining under load are more meaningful clues than "it did not shift like my uncle's pickup."

REMEMBER

CVT fluid isn't interchangeable with regular automatic-transmission fluid just because both are slippery and live near gears. Use the exact fluid the manufacturer specifies, or you may buy yourself a very expensive science experiment.

Hybrid and EV Drivetrains

Electrified vehicles change the drivetrain story in ways that are refreshingly logical once you stop expecting them to behave like old gasoline setups. Electric motors make useful torque immediately, hybrids blend multiple power sources, and many of these vehicles need far fewer ratios than a traditional engine-powered car.

eCVT systems

Many hybrids use an *electronic continuously variable transmission,* often called an eCVT. Despite the name, an eCVT isn't the same thing as a belt-and-pulley CVT. In many hybrid systems, an eCVT uses a planetary gear arrangement and one or more electric motor-generators to blend power from the engine and electric side. The computer orchestrates the whole dance so the vehicle can move efficiently without traditional shift events.

This computer-controlled power blending is why a hybrid may accelerate with a smooth, somewhat unusual sound profile. Nothing is necessarily slipping. The system is simply balancing engine speed, motor torque, battery state, and wheel demand in a way that would make an old three-speed automatic need a nap.

Single-speed gear reduction

Most EVs use a single-speed reduction gear. Electric motors can spin across a wide RPM range and make strong torque from very low speed, so they don't need a stack of gears just to feel competent leaving a stop. The reduction gear drops motor speed to something the axle can use, and then the differential handles the left-right wheel split.

For the driver, this setup is part of why EVs feel so smooth. No conventional upshifts interrupt acceleration. You press the pedal, torque shows up, and the car goes. It's delightfully drama-free in the way only instant torque can be.

Direct drive EV systems

EV drivetrains are much simpler than gasoline drivetrains. People often call them direct drive, but the term direct drive doesn't usually mean the motor is connected straight to the wheels with no gearing at all. Most EVs still use one fixed reduction gear and a differential. Think of this fixed-reduction setup as having one permanent gear instead of a transmission that keeps shifting through several of them.

This fixed-reduction setup works because an electric motor can deliver strong pulling power from a stop and keep working well across a wide range of speeds. In a gas-powered vehicle, the transmission has to keep changing gears to help the engine stay in its happy place. In many EVs, the motor doesn't need that kind of babysitting. Reverse is often just the motor spinning backward, which is much simpler than having a separate reverse gear.

Figure 19-7 shows the difference between a hybrid eCVT setup and a typical EV single-speed setup. The hybrid has to juggle engine and motor power, while the EV layout is usually much simpler: motor, reduction gear, and differential.

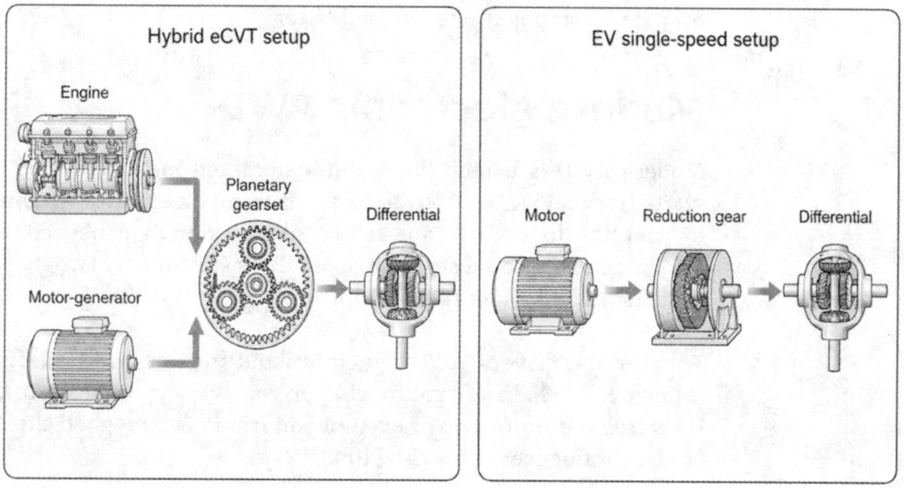

FIGURE 19-7: Electrified drivetrains.

Generated with AI using OpenAI

TIP

If you're used to feeling or hearing shifts, an EV can seem almost weirdly smooth at first. That sensation is normal. The car isn't forgetting to shift; it simply doesn't need to.

Four-wheel traction

The terms 4WD and AWD get used interchangeably in casual conversation, which is understandable and also how internet arguments begin. Both send power to all four wheels in some form. The difference is usually in how the system is built, how it's controlled, and what kind of use it's meant to handle.

Traditional transfer cases

Traditional four-wheel drive usually shows up on trucks and serious off-road vehicles. A transfer case sits behind the transmission and can route power to both front and rear axles. Some systems are part-time, meaning you shouldn't use certain modes on dry pavement because the front and rear axles are mechanically locked together with too little tolerance for turning differences. This locked front-and-rear axle setup is fantastic in mud or snow and less fantastic in a grocery-store parking lot.

Many truck systems also offer low range, which gives extra torque multiplication for crawling, steep grades, or hauling things up terrain that would make a cross-over start composing its farewell letter.

Modern electronic AWD

Modern AWD is usually more automated and more pavement-friendly. It often starts from a FWD or RWD base and uses an electronically controlled clutch pack or coupling to send torque to the other axle when needed. Some systems are always active to some degree, while others stay mostly two-wheel-drive until slip or demand tells them to wake up.

For everyday drivers, AWD is mainly about traction and stability in changing conditions. It can help you get moving on wet, snowy, or loose surfaces. What it can't do is create infinite grip or exempt you from needing good tires. AWD on bad tires is just confidence with a time limit.

Torque vectoring

Torque vectoring is a fancier way of distributing power side to side or axle to axle to improve traction and handling. Some AWD systems use torque vectoring to send more power to a particular wheel or axle during acceleration, cornering, or slippery conditions. Some modern 4WD systems can use similar brake-based or electronically controlled tricks, too, although traditional 4WD is usually more focused on rugged front-to-rear power delivery than on fine handling adjustments. Some systems use brakes to mimic the effect. Others use clutches or dedicated hardware to actively send more torque where it can help rotate the vehicle or reduce wheelspin.

Figure 19-8 is the clean comparison: traditional transfer-case 4WD for rugged duty, electronic AWD for everyday adaptability, and torque vectoring for extra traction and cornering polish.

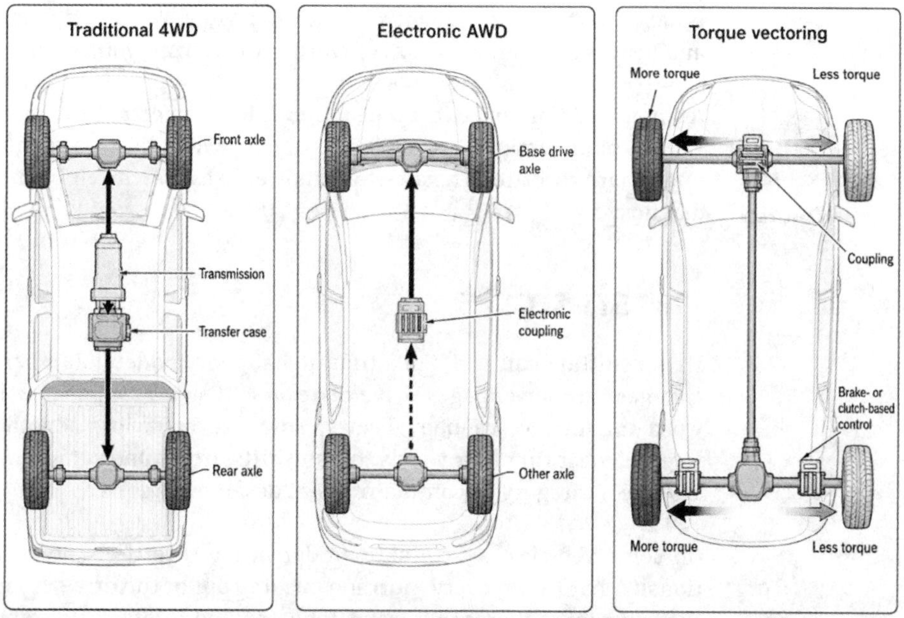

Generated with AI using OpenAI

FIGURE 19-8: 4WD versus AWD at a glance.

WARNING

Towing the wrong AWD, 4WD, hybrid, or EV vehicle with the wrong wheels on the ground can damage the drivetrain. Before the tow truck turns your transmission into a fundraiser, check the owner's manual for the exact procedure.

Diagnosing Trouble

Transmission and drivetrain problems often start with feelings: a flare, a bang, a hesitation, a vibration, a warning light, a new noise that was definitely not there yesterday. Your job as the owner isn't to become a gearbox surgeon in the driveway. Your job is to notice patterns early enough that the repair stays boring.

Slipping gears

Slipping usually means engine speed rises without matching vehicle acceleration. On a manual, slipping often points to a worn clutch. On an automatic or CVT, slipping can mean internal clutch-pack wear, hydraulic problems, belt or chain issues, overheating, or control problems. However it happens, slip creates heat, and heat is the transmission's favorite way to ruin your week.

REMEMBER

A single odd flare once in a blue moon is less important than a repeatable pattern. Does slipping happen only when cold? Only when hot? Only on the 2-3 shift? Only under hard throttle? Those details matter because "it felt weird" is a mood, not a diagnosis.

Harsh shifts

Harsh shifting can feel like a thump, bang, or sudden jolt when the transmission changes ratio or engages drive or reverse. Causes range from low or old fluid to worn mounts, valve-body issues, software behavior, adaptation problems, or internal wear. In other words, harsh shifts aren't one symptom with one answer. They're a category of complaints that deserves context.

REMEMBER

On some vehicles, a firm shift under heavy throttle is normal and even intentional. A hard slam every morning backing out of the driveway is less charming. If the behavior is increasing, repeatable, or tied to other symptoms, stop calling it personality.

Check-engine and transmission lights

Modern transmissions report their complaints electronically. A check-engine light, transmission warning, reduced-power message, or shift-related code can point you toward solenoid problems, speed-sensor issues, clutch performance concerns, overheating, or communication problems. The code isn't the whole story, but it's a very useful clue — kind of like the first witness in a messy neighborhood drama.

Table 19-1 gives you a transmission symptom guide. Warning lights, leaks, strange shifts, heat, and repeat symptoms help you decide whether to monitor the issue or get the vehicle checked right away.

REMEMBER

Repeated slipping, delayed engagement, or overheat warnings aren't "drive it a bit more and see." They're "every extra mile may be marinating the transmission in expensive regret."

TABLE 19-1 **Transmission Symptom Guide**

What you notice	Quick beginner check	What to note	What to do
Check-engine light, transmission warning, or reduced-power message	Scan for codes or have a shop scan it.	Did the light come on after a hard shift, overheating, towing, or highway driving?	Schedule diagnosis soon. The code is a clue, not the full answer.
Harsh shift, delayed shift, flare, or hunting between gears	Check for obvious leaks under the vehicle.	Does it happen cold, hot, uphill, at low speed, or during passing?	Get it checked. Repeated shift problems can get worse quickly.
Transmission slipping or engine revs without matching vehicle speed	Do not keep testing it hard.	Does the vehicle still move normally, or is it struggling to engage?	Shop now. Avoid driving if the vehicle feels unsafe or barely moves.
Burning smell, overheating warning, or transmission temperature warning	Pull over safely and let the vehicle cool.	Were you towing, climbing, stuck in traffic, or driving in heat?	Stop and seek help. Heat is hard on transmissions.
Fluid spots or puddles under the vehicle	Look for red, brown, or oily fluid, if visible.	Where is the leak, and how much fluid is showing?	Shop soon. Low fluid can cause major damage.
One odd event and then normal operation	Watch for repeat symptoms.	Write down speed, temperature, gear, road condition, and what the vehicle did.	Monitor briefly. If it repeats, get it diagnosed.
No movement, grinding, loud banging, or severe shuddering	Do not force the vehicle to move.	Note the symptom and warning messages.	Stop driving and arrange a tow.

Maintenance

Transmission maintenance is less glamorous than engine oil changes because it's harder to see and easier to ignore. Unfortunately, the transmission also notices when you ignore it. Fluid condition, the correct specification, and heat control matter a lot.

Fluid types: ATF, CVT fluid, DCT fluid

Automatic transmission fluid, or ATF, isn't just slippery red juice living its best life. It handles hydraulic control, lubrication, cooling, and friction behavior inside the unit. CVTs need their own specific fluid, and DCTs often use a fluid tailored to their clutch and gear design. The exact fluid matters because the transmission was engineered around it. Close enough isn't close enough.

Some older vehicles have dipsticks for checking transmission fluid. Many modern ones don't. They may use sealed designs with temperature-based fill procedures, special plugs, and scan-tool steps. These more precise checking and filling procedures are not manufacturers being dramatic. Fluid level and temperature really do matter that much.

Lifetime fluid myths

Ah, yes, lifetime fluid — one of the automotive world's most optimistic phrases. Sometimes it means "long service interval under ideal conditions." Sometimes it means "lifetime of the component as the warranty department defines life." It almost never means "this fluid will remain youthful and emotionally available forever."

Heat, towing, mountain driving, stop-and-go traffic, heavy loads, and just plain miles all age fluid. The smart move is to follow the owner's manual and pay attention to severe-service schedules when your driving actually qualifies. If the manufacturer gives a service interval, use it. If the fluid comes out dark, burnt-smelling, or glittery, the conversation has already gotten more serious.

Heat management

Heat is one of the biggest enemies of transmission life. Every slip event, hard launch, long tow, steep climb, or overloaded summer crawl adds thermal stress, which is why many vehicles use transmission coolers integrated into the radiator or mounted separately. Keeping fluid in the right temperature range helps preserve lubrication and friction behavior, which is a very unglamorous but extremely important way of avoiding repair invoices.

If you tow, haul, mountain-drive, or spend your life in traffic, heat management matters even more. Table 19-2 pulls together the maintenance logic: Use the right fluid, respect service intervals, and don't pretend heat is someone else's hobby.

WARNING

Don't top off or service a transmission with a random fluid because the bottle said "compatible with many applications." Transmissions are picky, expensive, and absolutely willing to punish improvisation.

TABLE 19-2 Transmission Maintenance Basics

Maintenance point	Why it matters	Beginner takeaway
Use the correct fluid.	ATF, CVT fluid, and DCT fluid are not interchangeable. Each transmission is designed around a specific fluid's friction, cooling, and hydraulic behavior.	Close enough is not close enough. Use the exact fluid specification listed for the vehicle.
Check fluid the right way.	Some vehicles have dipsticks, but many modern transmissions use temperature-based fill procedures, special plugs, or scan-tool steps.	Do not guess at the level. If the procedure is complicated, have a shop check it.
Follow the service interval.	Transmission fluid ages from heat, mileage, towing, stop-and-go driving, and heavy loads.	Follow the owner's manual, and use the severe-service schedule if your driving qualifies.
Be cautious with lifetime fluid.	"Lifetime" often means a long service interval under ideal conditions, not fluid that lasts forever.	Treat lifetime fluid as a reason to read the maintenance schedule, not as permission to ignore the transmission.
Watch fluid condition.	Dark, burnt-smelling, contaminated, or glittery fluid can point to overheating, wear, or internal damage.	Bad-looking fluid is not just dirty; it may be evidence of a bigger problem.
Control heat.	Heat is one of the biggest enemies of transmission life. Towing, mountain driving, hard launches, heavy loads, and traffic all add thermal stress.	If the vehicle works hard, heat management matters more. A cooler or proper service may be important.
Pay attention to symptoms.	Harsh shifts, slipping, delayed engagement, warning lights, or overheating messages can signal transmission trouble.	Do not keep driving hard and hoping the problem becomes shy. Note when it happens and get it checked.

When Repairs Get Serious

There is a big difference between a serviceable transmission concern and a transmission that is actively trying to become a plot twist. When the symptoms cross that line, restraint saves money.

Rebuild versus replace

A *rebuild* means the transmission is disassembled, inspected, and repaired internally with worn parts replaced. A *replacement* may mean a remanufactured unit, a used unit, or a factory replacement, depending on the vehicle and budget. Which route makes sense depends on cost, parts availability, the specific failure, vehicle value, and how long you plan to keep the car.

Used units can look cheaper up front but come with uncertainty. Rebuilt or remanufactured units can cost more but often bring better confidence if the source is reputable. There is no universal right answer. There is only the answer that matches the failure and doesn't make your wallet file a missing-person report.

When to see a transmission specialist

See a specialist when you have repeated slipping, delayed engagement, burnt fluid smell, metal debris, transmission overheat warnings, fluid leaks from the case or cooler lines, persistent shuddering, or codes pointing to internal performance faults. Also, see one when the fill procedure requires special tools or when the drivetrain layout is complicated enough that guessing could damage the unit, the transfer case, or both.

This advice is especially true on modern vehicles with adaptive controls, integrated electronics, hybrid systems, or manufacturer-specific service steps. Transmission specialists exist for a reason, and it's not because normal shops were bored. These units are complicated, expensive, and very good at getting worse when driven sick.

TIP

When you take the vehicle in, bring useful notes: when the symptom happens, hot or cold behavior, whether a warning light came on, whether towing or recent service preceded it, and whether the problem is getting worse. Good notes save diagnosis time, which can save real money.

REMEMBER

A healthy drivetrain should feel boring in the best way: smooth takeoffs, sensible shifts, predictable traction, and no mystery lights. If yours is slipping, banging, whining, or flaring, don't wait for it to develop a full Broadway number. Catch it early, service it correctly, and let the chapter title stay the joke instead of your repair bill.

5 Handling Car Crises and Choosing Help

IN THIS PART . . .

Stay calm and handle roadside emergencies safely.

Decode noises, leaks, and warning signs quickly.

Diagnose no-start problems without guessing.

Choose the right mechanic with confidence.

IN THIS CHAPTER

» Understanding airbags, seat belts, and child-safety hardware

» Making sense of cameras, sensors, and control systems

» Decoding ADAS, driver-monitoring, telematics, and EV safety in plain English

» Reading safety ratings

» Knowing what you can check yourself and when to call a pro

Chapter 20
Staying Calm in Emergencies

Modern vehicles are basically rolling paranoia machines, which is a compliment. They're built on the assumption that humans get distracted, weather gets rude, traffic gets weird, and occasionally somebody does something breathtakingly foolish three lanes over. The car tries to help in layers: structure, seat belts, airbags, brakes, stability control, cameras, radar, software, and on newer vehicles, even a system that watches whether you look sleepy enough to use a pillow as a personality trait.

This chapter is your guide to how those safety layers work, what they can and can't do, and how to stay calm when something goes wrong. We keep the explanations practical, the jargon on a leash, and the humor respectful of one important fact: In an emergency, the goal isn't to look cool. The goal is to go home with a story instead of a sequel.

Built to Protect

A safe car is not just one with lots of airbags. It's a whole strategy. Engineers think about avoiding crashes, surviving crashes, protecting people of different sizes, managing forces, warning the driver, and calling for help afterward. Safety isn't one heroic gadget. It's a team sport with very nervous, very capable equipment.

The basic safety philosophy is simple: First try to prevent the crash, then reduce injury if the crash still happens, and then make it easier to get help quickly. This philosophy is why a modern vehicle may brake for you, tighten a belt before impact, deploy airbags during impact, cut fuel or high voltage after impact, unlock doors, and place a crash call — all while you're still trying to remember where your coffee went.

Crash structures

The body structure is the first bodyguard. Modern vehicles use *crumple zones* to absorb energy in the front, rear, and sometimes sides, while trying to keep the passenger compartment as a stronger survival space. In a good crash design, the outer structure sacrifices itself in a controlled way so that the people inside don't have to volunteer as the crumple material. Metal folds. Energy gets managed. Occupants get a better chance.

Figure 20-1 is the big-picture map: Soft-ish zones up front and out back to absorb the hit, stronger side structures and a reinforced occupant cell in the middle, and restraint systems inside to manage whatever force still shows up at your seat.

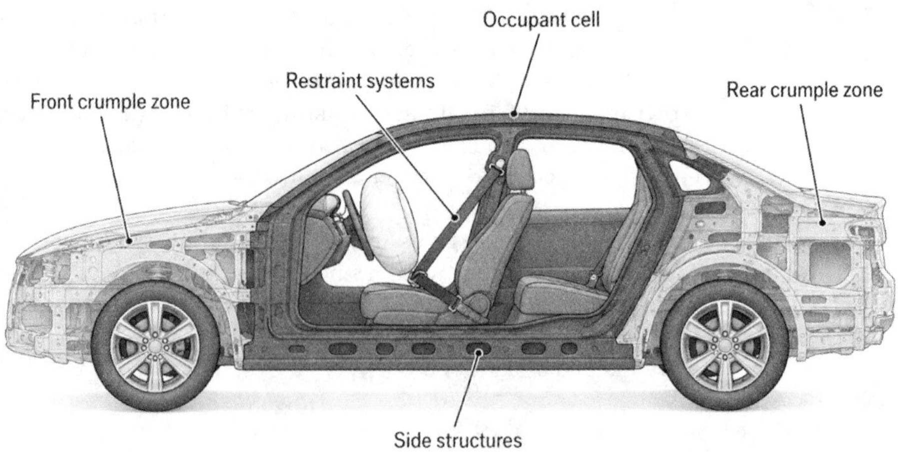

FIGURE 20-1: Safety structure at a glance.

Generated with AI using OpenAI

Integration of passive and active safety

People sometimes split safety into two buckets. *Passive safety* is the stuff that protects you in a crash: structure, seat belts, airbags, head restraints, child-seat anchors. *Active safety* is the stuff that tries to help you avoid the crash in the first place: ABS, traction control, stability control, headlights, cameras, sensors, and driver-assistance features. Modern vehicles blur those buckets together because the systems talk to one another constantly. The result is less one heroic part and more an anxious committee that never sleeps.

WARNING

No safety feature gives you permission to drive like physics signed a waiver. The systems improve your odds; they don't repeal momentum, ice, or human foolishness.

Airbags

Airbags are supplemental restraints. Supplemental is the key word. They're not magical cushions that replace seat belts. They're the fast, one-time emergency helpers that work with the belts to reduce how hard you hit the steering wheel, dash, door, pillar, or side glass.

Frontal airbags protect the head and chest in many front impacts. *Side airbags* usually protect the torso, and *curtain airbags* drop down from the roof area to help protect heads in side impacts and some rollovers.

TIP

Think of the airbag family as different relatives showing up for different kinds of bad news. Not every vehicle has every exact bag, and placement varies, but the mission is always the same: Spread out the forces and keep your body from meeting hard parts at impolite speed.

Figure 20-2 shows the common airbag lineup so that the names stop sounding abstract and start feeling like actual locations around you.

Many modern frontal airbags don't just have one dramatic personality. They may deploy with different force, depending on crash severity, seat-belt use, seat position, and other sensor inputs. A low-severity crash may call for less aggressive deployment than a severe crash. That difference matters because airbags work in milliseconds, and too much bag for the situation isn't the kind of enthusiasm anybody asked for.

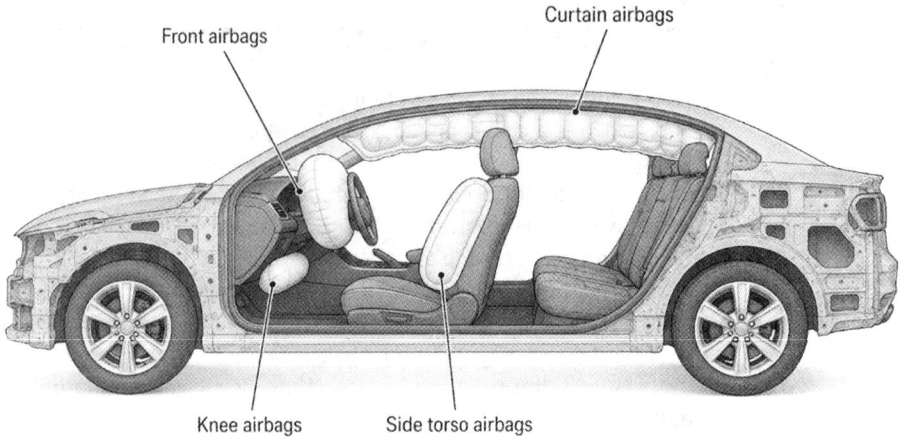

FIGURE 20-2: Common airbag zones.

Generated with AI using OpenAI

Occupant sensing

Occupant-sensing systems try to figure out who (or what) is in the seat. They may use weight sensors, seat-position data, and belt status to decide how the passenger airbag should behave, which is why you may see a passenger-airbag ON or OFF indicator. If the system thinks the seat is empty, lightly loaded, or occupied by a child restraint in a configuration the manufacturer expects, it may suppress the front passenger airbag. This sensing ability is also why piling a weird mountain of groceries, gym bags, and mystery life choices on the passenger seat can confuse things.

WARNING

Never put a rear-facing child seat in front of an active front airbag unless the vehicle manufacturer specifically allows and instructs for it. Airbags deploy with serious force, and babies don't negotiate.

Replacement after deployment

Airbags aren't reusable party supplies. Once deployed, they've done their job, and the system needs proper repair. Depending on the vehicle and the crash, that repair can mean replacing airbags, pretensioners, sensors, control modules, trim pieces, steering-wheel parts, dash components, headliner sections, and more. In plain English: If the airbags went off, you're entering professional repair territory, not "let me see what YouTube and optimism can do."

TECHNICAL STUFF

NHTSA notes that deployed airbags should be replaced right away and that proper repair may involve more than just the inflator module. On many vehicles, related sensors and control components are part of the repair as specified by the manufacturer.

Seat Belts and Child Safety

Seat belts are the least glamorous lifesavers on the vehicle. They don't beep because they're emotionally needy. They beep because being thrown around the cabin at crash speed is a terrible plan. A seat belt keeps you in position for the airbag to help, spreads crash forces across stronger parts of the body, and reduces the chance of striking the interior or leaving the vehicle entirely, which is the automotive equivalent of a plot twist nobody wants.

Modern belts do more than lock when you yank them. Many systems include *pretensioners* that tighten the belt early in a crash, plus *load limiters* that let the belt give a little in a controlled way so that the chest doesn't take an unnecessarily brutal hit. It's a clever combination: First hold you firmly and then manage the force. The belt is basically saying, "I've got you, but I'm not trying to crack your rib cage to prove it."

ISOFIX/LATCH systems

Child-seat anchor systems give you standardized lower anchors and a top tether point so you can install child restraints more securely and more consistently. In North America, the common term is LATCH — Lower Anchors and Tethers for Children. ISOFIX is the closely related term you'll hear in other markets. Same general idea: built-in anchor points so you're not inventing your own seat-mounting philosophy at 7:15 a.m. in a parking lot.

Figure 20-3 points out the lower anchors, top tether, and adult belt path because child-seat mistakes are common, and "close enough" is not the standard you want here.

Booster seat rules

Booster-seat rules vary by country, state, province, and the child seat itself, so the owner's manual, the child-seat manual, and your local law all matter. The general beginner rule is to keep using the appropriate child restraint until the adult belt fits correctly: lap belt low over the hips, shoulder belt across the middle of the chest and shoulder, not across the neck, face, or stomach. If the kid sits like a folded lawn chair, slouches under the belt, or keeps putting the shoulder belt behind the back because it's annoying, the fit isn't solved yet.

TIP

If child-seat instructions make you feel like you are assembling a moon lander, find a certified child-passenger-safety technician or local inspection event. A five-minute correction can matter more than the brand of seat.

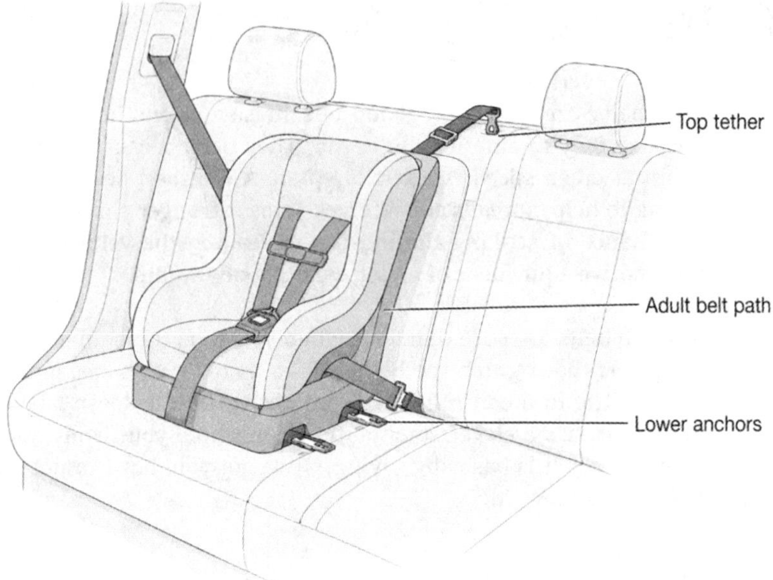

FIGURE 20-3: Child-seat basics.

Generated with AI using OpenAI

Cameras and Sensors

Modern safety systems need eyes and ears, and the vehicle gets them from cameras, ultrasonic sensors, radar, and sometimes *lidar,* a laser-based sensor that helps measure distance and shape. These helpers are great at noticing certain things quickly and repeatedly. They're less great at snow crust, mud, glare, stickers, and the universal human habit of assuming the computer saw what you forgot to look at.

Backup cameras (mandatory)

In the United States, all new light vehicles have backup cameras. These cameras are a genuinely useful safety upgrade, especially for seeing behind tall trunks, high tailgates, and the sort of small bike or toy that used to hide perfectly in the danger zone.

WARNING

A camera isn't a force field. It still has blind spots, distortion, weather limits, and a shocking inability to swivel itself because you refused to turn your head.

Parking sensors

Parking sensors are the beeping little narrators of low-speed maneuvering. They use ultrasonic sensors to judge how close you are to an object and then communicate that information using tones, graphics, or both. They're excellent at helping you avoid nudging a wall, pole, or shopping-cart corral. They're not excellent at interpreting every weird shape, every soft object, or every greasy blob coating the bumper sensor.

Blind-spot monitoring

Blind-spot monitoring usually watches the lanes beside and slightly behind you and then lights an indicator if another vehicle is lurking where mirrors are least helpful. Some systems will also beep or flash more aggressively if you signal into an occupied lane.

Helpful? Yes. Permission to quit shoulder-checking? Absolutely not. Figure 20-4 shows the typical awareness zones so you can see why these systems are assistants, not replacement eyeballs.

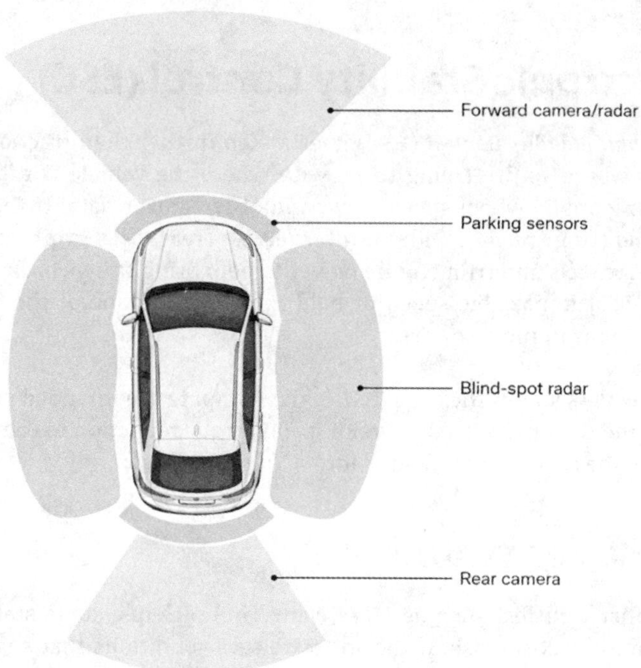

FIGURE 20-4: Common sensor coverage zones.

Generated with AI using OpenAI

REMEMBER

A safety system covered in road salt is like hiring a lifeguard and then handing them a blindfold. Clean the lenses and sensor faces with water, mild car-wash soap, and a soft microfiber cloth. Rinse away grit first. Avoid abrasive pads, harsh chemicals, and wax and don't blast the sensors up close with a pressure washer.

Control Systems

Some of the most important safety tech is invisible because it works in the background. You may notice it only as a flickering light on the dash, a brief reduction in engine power, or a moment where the car feels smarter than your right foot.

Traction control

Traction control tries to keep the drive wheels from spinning excessively when grip is poor. If one wheel starts turning much faster than the others on snow, rain, gravel, or a too ambitious launch, the system can reduce engine power and/or break the spinning wheel. Traction control is basically the part of the car that says, "Congratulations on your enthusiasm. Now let's try that with less chaos."

Electronic Stability Control (ESC)

Electronic Stability Control (ESC) goes a step further than traction control. It compares where you're trying to go with where the vehicle is actually going, using steering angle, wheel speed, yaw, and other sensor data. If the car starts *understeering* (front pushes wide) or *oversteering* (rear loses grip), ESC can brake individual wheels and trim engine power to help bring things back under control. ESC can't beat impossible speed or bald tires, but it's one of the biggest real-world safety wins in modern cars.

Figure 20-5 shows the basic ESC logic: Compare the intended path with the actual path and then use selective braking and torque reduction to calm the vehicle down before the situation graduates into a YouTube lesson.

Rollover stability

On taller vehicles, such as SUVs, vans, and pickups, some stability systems also watch for rollover risk. If the software sees conditions that suggest the vehicle is leaning into a bad decision, it may brake specific wheels and cut power to reduce the chance of a rollover. The system helps, but it doesn't turn a tall vehicle into a physics-neutral hovercraft. Load, speed, tires, and sudden steering still matter a lot.

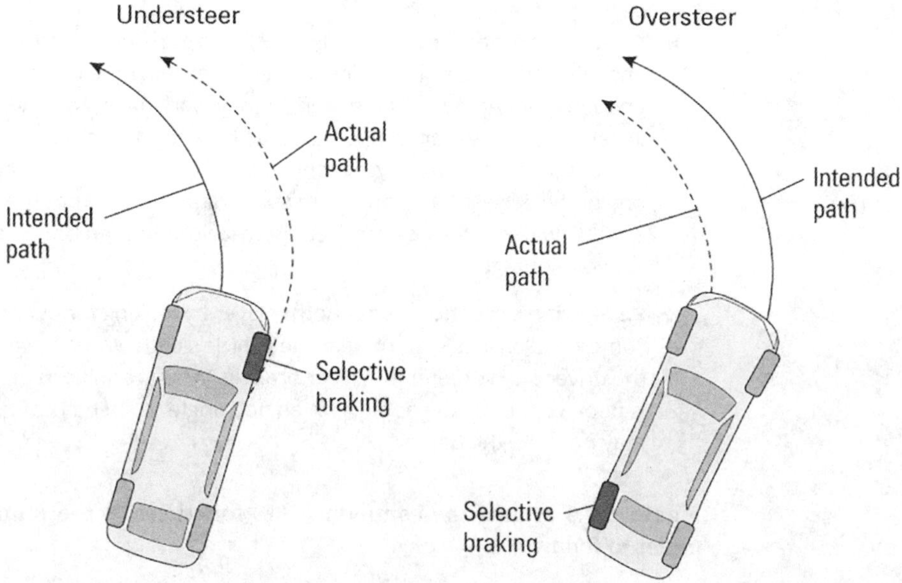

FIGURE 20-5: ESC in plain English.

Generated with AI using OpenAI

Advanced Driver Assistance Systems (ADAS)

ADAS stands for *Advanced Driver Assistance Systems*, which is a fancy way of saying "the car now has opinions." These systems can reduce workload and sometimes prevent or lessen crashes, but they're not self-driving miracles. They're more like a very alert coworker who is useful when supervised and deeply unqualified to take over your whole job.

Common systems include:

- **Adaptive cruise control** uses radar, cameras, or both to maintain a set speed and also adjust for slower traffic ahead. On many vehicles, it can gently brake and accelerate to maintain a chosen following gap. It's wonderful on long highway drives, unless you misunderstand it as permission to stop paying attention, in which case it becomes an expensive trust exercise.
- **Lane keep assist (LKA)** watches lane markings and may warn you or apply a small steering correction if the vehicle drifts without a turn signal. The key word is small. It's a nudge, not a chauffeur. Faded lane lines, snow, construction zones, glare, and messy weather can all limit how well it works, which is why keeping your hands on the wheel remains a wildly good idea.

- **Automatic emergency braking** (AEB) tries to recognize an imminent crash and apply the brakes if the driver doesn't react in time or doesn't brake hard enough. Depending on the system, it may work mainly at city speeds, across a wider speed range, or with extra capabilities for pedestrians and cyclists. It's one of the most impressive safety technologies in modern vehicles and also one of the easiest for people to misunderstand. AEB is not there so that you can text with confidence. It's there in case your human brain has a brief software outage.
- **Pedestrian detection** adds another layer by looking for people — and sometimes cyclists — in or near the vehicle's path. When it works, it can warn the driver and sometimes trigger braking. When conditions are bad, visibility is poor, or the person appears in an odd angle or speed profile, the system may not save the day.

Figure 20-6 groups the common ADAS functions so the family resemblance is easier to follow.

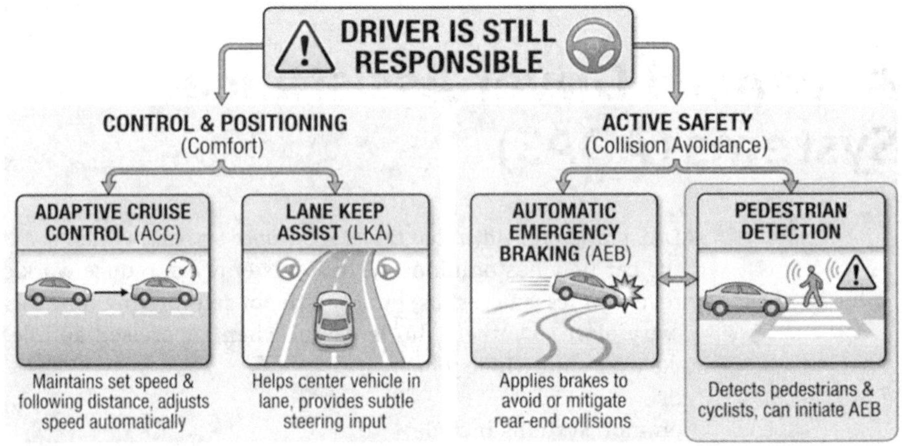

FIGURE 20-6: ADAS helper map.

Generated with AI using OpenAI

WARNING

If an ADAS feature stops working after a windshield replacement, bumper repair, alignment, collision, suspension work, or even a hard curb strike, don't assume the car is being dramatic. Cameras and radar often need calibration, which is professional-equipment territory.

Driver Monitoring

Some newer vehicles watch the driver as much as they watch the road. Usually, this monitoring means a camera or sensor system looking for signs of distraction, inattention, or drowsiness: eye movement, head position, steering behavior, lane wandering, or a combination of clues. The goal isn't to judge your life. The goal is to notice when your brain has quietly clocked out.

A driver-monitoring camera can tell whether you're looking at the road, looking at a screen, or staring into the middle distance like you just remembered something embarrassing from 2009. Some systems work only when assistance features are active; others monitor more generally. They vary a lot by brand, but the theme is the same: If the system thinks the driver isn't meaningfully engaged, it starts escalating warnings.

Drowsiness alerts may begin with a chime, message, or coffee-cup icon and escalate if the behavior keeps looking sleepy, distracted, or unresponsive. Some systems will tighten the safety net by increasing driver-assistance sensitivity or encouraging a stop.

WARNING

Driver-monitoring systems are helpful, but they're not a substitute for sleep. No camera in the world can make four hours of bad rest turn into good judgment.

Electric Vehicle Safety

Electric vehicles (EVs) bring a different safety conversation because they add a high-voltage battery pack, powerful electronics, and special crash-management needs. The good news is that modern EVs are designed around those realities from the beginning. The even better news is that most of the scary-looking orange stuff is protected by layers of hardware and software that are trying very hard to keep everybody alive and boring.

That safety plan usually comes down to three main areas:

- **Battery crash protection:** Battery packs are usually mounted low and protected within reinforced structures, shields, and carefully planned mounting zones. Engineers think hard about intrusion, coolant routing, isolation, and how to keep damaged cells from creating a much worse day after the initial impact. The battery is heavy, expensive, and absolutely not treated like loose luggage under the floor.

- **Automatic disconnects:** Hybrids and EVs use contactors and interlock logic to disconnect high voltage when a crash or serious fault is detected. In plain English, if the car thinks something bad happened, it tries to separate the battery from the rest of the high-voltage system very quickly to help reduce shock and fire risk for occupants, first responders, and technicians.
- **Thermal safety:** Battery thermal safety is about keeping cells in the right temperature range during driving, charging, parking, and — in rare fault cases — damage management, so EVs often have dedicated cooling systems, temperature sensors, software limits, and warnings. Most owners will never deal with anything dramatic. But if an EV has severe underbody damage, high-voltage warnings, smoke, or an unusual sweet/chemical smell after an impact, it's not a "drive it home and vibe-check it later" situation.

WARNING

Do not probe, cut, tow incorrectly, or improvise around orange high-voltage cables or damaged battery hardware. Post-crash EV evaluation belongs to trained professionals using manufacturer procedures.

Telematics

Telematics is the umbrella term for vehicle systems that use wireless communication to send or receive information, such as crash alerts, vehicle location, diagnostics, and software updates.

Safety doesn't stop at the crash itself anymore. Many vehicles can connect to a call center, emergency services, or a smartphone app to report a crash, send location information, or notify the owner about warnings. Your car has gone from machine to machine that may tattletale for your own good.

These telematic features include:

- **Connected safety:** Connected safety features may include crash alerts to your phone, stolen-vehicle tracking, roadside assistance buttons, remote diagnostics, or vehicle-health reports. Useful? Very. Also slightly humbling, because the car can now tell you it has a problem before you have finished pretending you did not notice the warning light.
- **Crash notification (eCall):** Some systems can automatically place an emergency call after a serious crash. In Europe, eCall is the best-known example. In other markets, automakers may route crash notification through their own connected-services platforms or subscription systems. However it is branded, the basic idea is simple: if you cannot call for help, the car might do it for you. That is an excellent feature and a weirdly comforting one.

» **Over-the-air updates:** Over-the-air updates can refresh software for infotainment, battery management, and sometimes driver-assistance behavior. Those updates can mean bug fixes, security patches, and feature improvements without a shop visit. Over-the-air updates don't mean that your car downloaded invincibility overnight. Always read update notices and if a manufacturer says a calibration or recall repair still requires a visit, it's not optional just because the Wi-Fi was feeling confident.

Safety Ratings

Safety ratings give shoppers a way to compare how well vehicles protect occupants and how effectively certain crash-avoidance features work. They are useful, but only if you read them with context instead of treating one star count like the entire biography of the vehicle.

In the United States, the National Highway Traffic Safety Administration (NHTSA) uses a star system for crash tests. The Insurance Institute for Highway Safety (IIHS) evaluates crashworthiness and crash avoidance/mitigation and also gives award designations for top performers. In Europe, the European New Car Assessment Programme (Euro NCAP) uses a star system that combines several categories, including adult occupant protection, child occupant protection, vulnerable road users, and safety assist. Same big mission, different testing programs and scoring methods.

Ratings do more than help shoppers, though. They pressure manufacturers to improve structures, restraints, headlights, and crash-avoidance systems because nobody wants to explain why their shiny new crossover folds like a lawn chair or can't see a pedestrian in time.

REMEMBER

One important nuance: Ratings are most useful when you compare vehicles from the same era, because the tests and scoring standards evolve. A five-star result from one period doesn't always mean the exact same thing years later.

TIP

Use ratings as a comparison tool, not a superstition. Check the latest results from the organization that tested the exact model and year you're considering and read beyond the headline score if safety is a buying priority.

DIY versus Professional

This whole chapter is about making you more informed, not turning you into a driveway airbag technician. Some safety checks are smart owner habits. Others are absolutely shop work. The trick is knowing the difference before confidence becomes performance art.

Owner checks (seat belts, warning lights)

You can and should do a few simple checks yourself:

- Make sure every seat belt latches securely, retracts smoothly, and isn't frayed, cut, twisted, or chewed up by years of abuse.
- Watch for warning lights related to airbags, ABS, ESC, TPMS, or driver-assistance systems. A warning light isn't dashboard decoration.
- Keep cameras, radar covers, and parking sensors clean. Mud, snow, stickers, cracked trim, and road salt can make smart systems act very dumb.
- Inspect child-seat anchor points and tether locations for obvious damage and confirm child seats stay installed tightly.
- After any crash, even a small one, pay attention to new warning lights, belt behavior, alignment changes, and unusual noises.

ADAS recalibration requires pros

Recalibration is where modern safety gets very unromantic. After windshield replacement, bumper work, suspension repairs, alignments, ride-height changes, some battery disconnect events, and many collisions, cameras and radar may need precise aiming and software procedures. Proper ADAS recalibration usually means targets, scan tools, measured distances, and a level shop environment — in other words, not your driveway, not your cousin's parking lot, and definitely not "I eyeballed it, and it seemed chill."

REMEMBER

The best safety system in the car is still the combination of a belted, attentive driver in a properly maintained vehicle. Let the technology help. Just don't ask it to raise your kids, read your mind, or repeal consequences.

If this chapter leaves you with one lasting habit, let it be this one: Take safety warnings seriously early. A belt problem, airbag light, cracked radar cover, dead backup camera, or post-repair ADAS fault is much cheaper to fix before it joins a crisis and starts freelancing.

IN THIS CHAPTER

» Translating weird clues before you buy parts out of frustration

» Reading smells, smoke, and puddles like a driveway detective

» Figuring out what pulls, shakes, and wandering steering mean

» Taking warning lights seriously without turning into a panic goblin

Chapter 21

Decoding Leaks, Squeaks, and Strange Sensations

Cars almost never fail politely. They squeak, smell odd, drip on the driveway, vibrate through the steering wheel, and light up the dash like a tiny casino. Rude? Yes. Useful? Also, yes.

This chapter is your translator. The goal isn't to make you psychic. The goal is to connect the clue with the pattern: what happens, when it happens, where it comes from, and what changes it. That habit saves money because it keeps you from replacing innocent parts just because they were nearby.

Why Strange Noises and Smells Matter

Most expensive failures send little RSVP cards first: a faint squeal before a grind, a sweet smell before an overheat, a small seep before a puddle. Catching the annoying phase is how you avoid the tow truck phase.

REMEMBER

One clue is a clue. Three matching clues are a case. A smell plus a puddle plus a warning light tells a much better story than any single symptom trying to perform solo.

When something weird shows up, ask five quick questions before your wallet starts ordering random parts:

- **What exactly is it?** Noise, smell, leak, warning light, vibration, or the deluxe combo platter?
- **When does it happen?** Cold start, hot engine, braking, turning, bumps, highway speed, or only after sitting?
- **Where does it seem to come from?** One wheel, under the hood, the exhaust, the middle of the car, or the cabin?
- **What changes it?** Speed, brake pressure, steering angle, acceleration, A/C use, or outside temperature?
- **What changed recently?** Pothole, fuel-up, battery swap, tire work, or a repair?

Noises

Noises are your car's passive-aggressive text messages. The important part isn't just the sound; it's what the sound cares about. Speed? Braking? Turning? Bumps? Engine load? Here are a few common car noises and the first places to look when they show up:

- **Brake squeals:** If the noise shows up mostly when you press the brake pedal, suspect brakes first. A light squeal can mean pad wear indicators, rusty rotors after rain, or pad hardware complaints. Scraping or grinding is a more serious mood and often means metal-to-metal contact. Chapters 15 and 16 are the full brake detective kit.

- **Suspension clunks:** Clunks over bumps or driveway entrances usually point toward steering and suspension parts, such as links, bushings, struts, or loose hardware. Clicking in turns can also point to a CV joint. And yes, once in a while the "front-end noise" is loose junk in the trunk doing community theater.
- **Engine knocking:** Engine noises care about rpm and load. A light tick can be valvetrain, injector, or even exhaust-leak noise. A deep knock that gets worse under load, especially with low oil pressure, rough running, or lost power, deserves immediate respect. That sound isn't a "let me monitor it until payday" sound.
- **EV inverter whine:** EVs and hybrids have their own soundtrack: Motor whir, inverter tone, brake-pump buzz, and cooling-fan noise can all be normal. What isn't normal is a brand-new shriek, grind, or warning message paired with reduced power. "Futuristic" is fine. "Sounds expensive and angry" is not.

TIP

Record the sound safely if you can. "Cold start, 35 mph, turning right, noise changes when braking" is gold. "It made a sound sometime this week" is fog.

Smells

Smells are chemistry sending you a memo. You don't need a superhero nose. You just need to notice whether the smell is oily, sweet, fuel-like, moldy, or hot in a way that makes your eyebrows suspicious. Be aware of the following smells:

- **Burning oil:** A burning-oil smell often means oil is leaking onto something hot, such as the exhaust. Valve-cover leaks are classic for this odor. A hot-brake or slipping-clutch smell is different, but the bigger clue is the same: Something is getting hotter than it should.
- **Coolant leaks:** Coolant often smells sweet. Under the hood, a sweet odor can point to hoses, radiator seams, pumps, or tanks. Inside the cabin, especially with foggy windows or damp carpet, it can point to the heater core. Chapter 13 is where you go once the sweet smell introduces itself.
- **Fuel odor:** A brief fuel smell right after refueling may be a loose cap or a splash. A persistent raw-fuel smell while driving, idling, or sitting in the cabin is different. Treat that as a fix-soon clue, not a charming quirk. Gasoline is many things, but forgiving is not one of them.
- **HVAC moldy smell:** If the vents smell like a wet gym bag when the A/C first comes on, the engine is probably innocent. That smell usually points to moisture and mildew in the HVAC system or a neglected cabin filter. Gross? Yes. Catastrophic? Usually no.

WARNING

A strong raw-fuel smell, especially with a visible leak or after an impact, is a stop-now clue — no smoking, no spark-making heroics, no "I will just drive it home."

Smoke Signals

Exhaust color is old-school diagnostics, and it still works. The key is to separate normal condensation from actual smoke and to notice whether the plume is brief, persistent, or paired with smell, rough running, or fluid loss. The color of exhaust smoke can give you a quick clue about what's happening inside the engine. Table 21-1 helps you identify the various exhaust colors.

TABLE 21-1 Exhaust Decoder

Smoke shade	Likely cause	What you might notice	What it may mean	When to worry
White	Condensation or coolant	Cold-start vapor that clears quickly; thick white smoke that stays after warm-up.	Brief startup vapor is usually condensation. Thick white smoke with a sweet smell or low coolant may mean a coolant leak.	Worry if the smoke stays after warm-up, smells sweet, or the coolant level keeps dropping.
Blue or blue-gray	Burning oil	Smoke may appear at startup, while accelerating, or after idling.	Oil is burning, often from worn seals, rings, turbo trouble, or poor oil control.	Worry if oil level drops, smoke keeps coming back, or the engine starts running poorly.
Black	Too much fuel, not enough air, or both	Dark, sooty smoke from the tailpipe.	Gas engines: too much fuel, injector/sensor trouble, or misfire. Diesels: airflow or boost trouble.	A steady soot show isn't normal, especially if it comes with poor mileage, rough running, or warning lights.
Diesel regen smoke	Diesel particulate filter regeneration	Hotter exhaust smell, idle changes, or fan running more than usual.	Diesels may burn off soot during regen; that alone isn't usually a problem.	Worry if smoke is heavy, warnings repeat, or regen happens too often.

WARNING

Condensation should fade as the exhaust warms. Persistent smoke after warm-up is the part that earns your attention.

Leaks

Leaks are your car autographing the driveway. Sometimes, the autograph is harmless A/C water. Sometimes, it's the first clue that an important fluid is escaping and taking your money with it. Start with location, color, feel, and smell. Dried residue matters, too. Table 21-2 helps you identify the main puddle suspects.

TABLE 21-2 Puddle Decoder

Puddle shade	Likely fluid	Feel	Smell	Common location
Usually amber, brown, or black	Engine oil	Slippery	Burnt smell	Often shows up under the engine area and leaves a dark stain
Red, amber, or brown, depending on type and age	Transmission fluid (ATF)	Slippery and thinner than engine oil	Slightly sweet, or burnt if overheated	Near the transmission or cooler lines under the car
Green, orange, pink, blue, yellow, or "surprise flavor"	Coolant (antifreeze)	More watery than oil and may dry into crusty residue	Often smells sweet	Typically leaks around the radiator, hoses, water pump, or heater core area
Usually clear to amber	Brake fluid	Slick, but thinner than oil	Mild chemical smell, or burnt if overheated	Near the master cylinder, brake lines, or around the wheels
Amber or light brown	Power steering fluid	Slippery, like light oil	Faint oily smell	Near power steering pump, reservoir, or fluid lines
Amber to dark brown	Differential fluid (gear oil)	Thicker	Smells unforgettable in the worst possible way	In the differential or rear of the car
Blue (sometimes green or orange)	Windshield washer fluid	Watery	Mild detergent smell	Near the washer fluid reservoir
Clear	AC condensation	Watery	No smell	Under passenger side after running the AC

TIP

If brake fluid is leaking, treat that as a stopping-problem clue, not a cosmetic one.

Modern vehicles make fluid ID trickier because CVT fluid isn't ordinary ATF, DCT fluid can be its own thing, and hybrids or EVs may use specific coolants for battery, motor, or inverter loops. Color can help, but the correct specification matters more.

REMEMBER

Color helps, but location and behavior help more. A clear puddle after the A/C runs is one thing. A slick leak near a brake line or wheel is another.

Strange Sensations

Cars also communicate through your hands, feet, and the seat of your pants, sometimes with all the subtlety of a marching band. The trick is noticing when the sensation happens and where you feel it most. Here are a few common driving sensations and what they may be trying to tell you:

- **Pulling while braking:** If the car pulls to one side when you brake, think brakes, tires, or front-end geometry. A sticking caliper, uneven tire grip, bad alignment, or worn suspension parts can all do it. Road crown can fool you a little; a strong, repeatable pull is the clue that matters.
- **Vibrations at speed:** A vibration at a certain speed often points to tires, wheel balance, bent wheels, wheel bearings, or driveline issues. Steering-wheel shake usually makes the front end more suspicious. Seat or floor shake often points farther back. If the vibration happens only while braking, move brakes way up the suspect list.
- **Steering wander:** *Wander* means the car never quite settles into a straight line. Low tire pressure, poor alignment, worn steering parts, tired shocks or struts, and some tire designs can all contribute. Crosswinds and road grooves can exaggerate steering wander, but they shouldn't make a healthy car feel like a canoe.

TIP

Write down where you feel the weirdness: steering wheel, brake pedal, seat, floor, or the whole car. That detail saves a shocking amount of time.

Dashboard Warnings

Warning lights are the car switching from hints to subtitles. They're not all equal, but they are all worth understanding. The following list shows the basic monitor soon warning versus stop-and-reassess warnings:

- **Check engine:** A steady check-engine light usually means the computer stored a clue and wants diagnosis soon. A flashing check-engine light is a different mood entirely; on many vehicles, it points to an active misfire serious enough to threaten the catalytic converter.

- **Brake warnings:** Brake-related warnings deserve respect. A red brake light can mean the parking brake is on, fluid is low, or the system sees a problem. An ABS light often means base brakes may still work, but anti-lock and possibly stability functions may not.
- **TPMS alerts:** A TPMS light usually means one or more tires are low. Low pressure affects grip, heat, wear, steering feel, and braking. On many systems, a flashing-then-steady TPMS light can point to a sensor or system fault instead of just low pressure.

WARNING

A red brake warning with a bad pedal, an overheating warning, an oil-pressure warning, or a hybrid/EV "stop safely" message is not a monitor-it-for-a-week situation.

Hybrid and EV Quirks

Electrified vehicles are still cars, but they have a few extra ways to sound mysterious. While some of these quirks are normal, others are the beginning of an expensive conversation. Here are a few hybrid and EV behaviors that may be normal — and a few that deserve professional attention:

- **Coolant for batteries:** Many hybrids and EVs have dedicated coolant loops for the battery, inverter, and motor. If coolant keeps disappearing, a battery or inverter cooling issue deserves real diagnosis, and these systems are usually picky about fluid type.
- **Regenerative braking feel:** Regen can make the car slow when you lift off the accelerator, and the feel can change with battery charge, temperature, drive mode, and traction. That changing brake feel can be normal. A pull, grind, harsh pulsation, or red brake warning isn't "just regen being quirky."
- **High-voltage insulation issues:** If a hybrid or EV throws a high-voltage warning, insulation-fault warning, or "stop safely" message, admire the orange cables from a respectful distance. Looking is fine. Poking is not.

TECHNICAL STUFF

Hybrid and EV braking may blend regenerative braking, friction braking, ABS, and stability control, so pedal feel can vary more than on an older hydraulic-only car.

DIY versus Professional

You don't need to fix everything yourself to be good at car ownership. Sometimes, the smartest DIY move is gathering clean clues and handing the shop a much better story than "it was making a noise."

These owner-level checks usually make sense before you book an appointment:

- Check fluid levels safely and correctly where accessible.
- Look for fresh leaks, wet spots, crusty residue, and obvious hose or belt problems.
- Check tire pressures and do a quick tire walk-around for damage or weird wear.
- Empty loose junk from the trunk so that it stops impersonating suspension damage.
- Write down the pattern: speed, temperature, turns, braking, bumps, startup, and warning lights.
- Record the sound or read codes.

TIP

Bring in a pro quickly for fuel smell, brake trouble, steering instability, overheating, heavy knocking, big fluid loss, thick persistent smoke, a flashing check-engine light, or any hybrid/EV high-voltage warning. These warning signs aren't "maybe later" clues.

The good news is that you don't need to walk into a shop empty-handed. If you can describe what it does, when it does it, and what changes it, you have already made the repair process faster and smarter.

IN THIS CHAPTER

» Separating "won't crank" from "cranks but won't start"

» Checking batteries, cables, fobs, and gear-selector drama without replacing half the car

» Jump-starting safely and using quick code clues like a calm roadside detective

» Knowing when DIY makes sense and when to call for help before your day files a complaint

Chapter 22
What to Do If Your Car Drops Dead or Won't Start

When a car suddenly drops dead, it feels personal. One minute you have transportation; the next minute you have a decorative driveway monument with cupholders. The good news is that no-start problems usually fall into a few predictable buckets.

This chapter helps you sort the failure, do the safe checks, and know when to stop improvising and call for backup. Think of this chapter as a roadside triage for cars.

First Things First

When a car suddenly goes silent, refuses to start, or decides that forward motion is now a personal boundary, the temptation is to panic first and think later. Do the opposite. Handle the situation in two steps: Get yourself safe and then figure out whether the problem is something simple, something serious, or something that requires a tow truck and a long, disappointed stare.

If the engine quits while you're moving, use whatever momentum you still have to get out of traffic. Turn on the hazard flashers, avoid hard steering inputs, and remember that steering and brake assist may feel heavier than usual once the engine stops. Chapter 20 covers the full roadside-safety mindset; this chapter covers the detective work after the adrenaline stops tap-dancing on your spine.

Before you diagnose anything, make the scene boring. Boring is good. Set the parking brake if you're safely stopped, stay clear of traffic, and use reflective gear or warning triangles if conditions call for it. If you smell fuel, see smoke, or get a hybrid/EV "stop safely" warning, step away from the DIY fantasy.

WARNING

Do not stand in traffic to become a better mechanic. A car can be fixed later. You, ideally, should remain unflattened.

No-Start Conditions

Not all "my car won't start" problems are the same, even though they all produce the same facial expression and the same urgent search for someone to blame. Before you start poking parts, separate the symptom into one of three buckets. This one step saves time, money, and a shocking number of unnecessary battery purchases.

- **The engine does not crank at all.** If you turn the key or press Start and the engine doesn't spin, you have a no-crank problem. That usually points toward the 12-volt battery, bad battery connections, a starter-control issue, a Park/Neutral or clutch-switch problem, or a key/immobilizer tantrum. Listen for clues: Total silence, one heavy click, or frantic rapid clicking all tell different stories. Flip to Chapter 5 for a deeper dive into your car's electrical system.
- **The engine cranks but never starts.** If the engine spins normally but never starts, the starter is probably doing its job. Now think fuel, spark, air, timing, or computer permission. In modern cars, cranking but not starting can mean

anything from a weak fuel pump to a crankshaft sensor that has decided it's retired and not taking questions. Chapter 5 explains the starting system, and Chapters 7 and 8 cover fuel-system mischief in more detail.

- **The engine starts only when the moon is in a cooperative mood.** Intermittent no-starts are sneaky. The car starts perfectly until it's hot, cold, wet, or late for something important. Loose battery terminals, failing crank sensors, heat-soaked starters, weak fob batteries, and parasitic drains all love that act. Write down when it happens. Part 2 includes a few chapters on no-start conditions and their causes.

REMEMBER

Sort the symptom before you sort the parts. No crank, cranks but won't start, and starts then dies are three different mysteries wearing the same trench coat.

Battery and Electrical

Before blaming the starter, fuel pump, or a conspiracy involving "all these computers," start with the electrical basics. Modern vehicles depend on clean, steady voltage, and when the 12-volt system gets weak, the whole car can act like it forgot how to be a car. Many no-start problems turn out to be battery, connection, charging, or drain issues dressed up in more dramatic costumes. Here's what you need to know:

- **Dead batteries:** A weak 12-volt battery is still the reigning champion of no-start complaints. Dim lights, slow cranking, repeated clicking, and electronics acting haunted all point that way. On newer vehicles, low voltage can make healthy modules behave very stupidly. Chapter 6 is the full battery-and-charging deep dive. On average, a car battery lasts about three to five years, but conditions like extreme heat or heavy electrical demand can shorten that timespan.
- **AGM, lithium, and smart charging issues:** Modern cars are picky about batteries. If the vehicle came with an AGM or lithium 12-volt battery, replacing it with the wrong type can create charging weirdness, fault messages, or short life. Some vehicles also need battery registration or relearn procedures after replacement, and smart charging can make normal voltage look suspicious.
- **Parasitic drains:** If the car starts fine every day but dies after sitting, suspect a drain. Maybe a light stayed on, a module never went to sleep, or an accessory kept nibbling electrons. A dead-after-sitting pattern is a giant clue, so note how long it sat and what was plugged in.

TIP Keep a jump pack charged and in the car. It's the adult version of bringing snacks: You hope you won't need it, but when you do, you look like a genius.

Fuel, Ignition, Starter, and Key-Fob Shenanigans

Once the battery basics look reasonably innocent, the suspects widen dramatically. Now you're dealing with the systems that actually make the engine crank, deliver fuel, fire the spark, and decide whether the car recognizes you as its rightful human. The next stage of no-start diagnosis is where a simple no-start can turn into a soap opera starring the starter, alternator, fuel system, ignition system, and a key fob with trust issues. Start with these common suspects:

- **Starter and alternator suspects:** A single heavy click with no crank often means a weak battery, poor cable connection, or a starter/solenoid problem. If the car starts after a jump and soon dies again, or the battery light was on first, the charging system joins the suspect list. Chapter 6 covers the testing strategy.
- **Fuel and ignition problems:** If the engine cranks briskly but never catches, think fuel, spark, or missing timing information from the crankshaft or camshaft sensors. Chapter 5 helps with starting logic, and Chapters 7 and 8 cover the fuel side. Guessing by vibes is expensive.
- **Immobilizers and push-button quirks:** Modern anti-theft systems can stop a start even when the battery is fine. A dead key-fob battery, missing transponder signal, unpressed brake pedal, or transmission not fully in Park can all imitate catastrophe. Try the spare key if you have one, and on some push-button cars hold the fob close to the start button or backup sensing spot.

Hybrid/EV and Overheating Twists

Electrified vehicles bring a few extra plot twists to the no-start drama. A hybrid or EV can look completely dead for reasons that have nothing to do with the big traction battery, and overheating can shut down a vehicle in ways that make the problem seem weirder than it is. The main rule here is simple: Treat these cars as familiar in some ways, different in some very important ones, and never let curiosity drag you into high-voltage nonsense.

REMEMBER

Hybrids and EVs add one important plot twist: Even with a big traction battery onboard, a weak 12-volt battery can still leave the whole vehicle looking dead. If the computers can't wake up and close the contactors, nothing interesting happens. Chapter 10 covers the bigger electrified-vehicle picture.

If a hybrid or EV shows a high-voltage isolation fault, "stop safely" message, or other serious propulsion warning, do not go exploring around orange cables. High voltage is professional territory.

WARNING

Also, remember that many electrified vehicles have specific towing rules; some can't be dragged with the drive wheels on the ground without causing expensive heartbreak. If the engine died hot, or refuses to restart after overheating, stop treating it like an ordinary no-start. Severe overheating can trigger protective shutdowns and can damage major components. Hybrids and EVs add extra cooling loops, so an overheating message may not be about the radiator alone. Chapters 12 and 13 are the cooling-system command center.

WARNING

Never try to jump-start the high-voltage battery in an EV or hybrid. The 12-volt system may be jump-started on some models, but the high-voltage pack isn't a DIY booster-cable activity.

Jump-Starting without Summoning Regret

If the 12-volt battery is too weak to crank the engine or wake up the computers, a careful jump-start may get you going. For a conventional gas vehicle, use the safe connection order shown in Figure 22-1:

1. **Park the donor vehicle, turn everything off, and keep the clamps from touching each other.**
2. **Connect the red clamp to the dead vehicle's positive (+) terminal.**
3. **Connect the other red clamp to the donor battery's positive (+) terminal.**
4. **Connect the black clamp to the donor battery's negative (–) terminal.**
5. **Connect the last black clamp to the dead vehicle's approved ground point, not just any random metal part.**
6. **Start the donor vehicle.**

   It may take a few minutes of charging before the dead vehicle will start.
7. **Remove the clamps in the reverse order once the vehicle starts.**

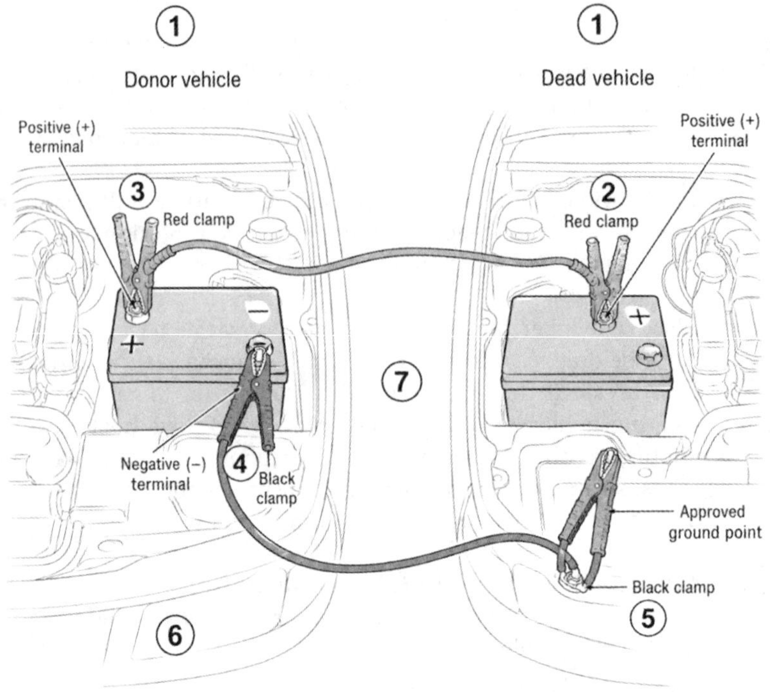

FIGURE 22-1: Safe 12-volt jump-start sequence and connection points.

Generated with AI using OpenAI

For hybrids and EVs, use only the designated 12-volt jump points listed in the owner's manual. Never try to jump-start the high-voltage battery.

TIP

Portable jump packs are great because they eliminate the second-car dance and reduce the odds of your helper freelancing the procedure. If the vehicle needs repeated jump-starts, the problem isn't bad luck. It's a battery, charging, drain, connection, or control issue that still needs diagnosis. For the deeper battery-and-charging story, see Chapter 6.

OBD-II and Warning Lights

If a warning light is on or if the engine cranks but won't start or starts and dies, a cheap OBD-II scanner or Bluetooth dongle can help you read trouble codes and narrow down which system to check next — especially if the engine cranks but won't start or starts and dies. You're not trying to become a code poet; you're just narrowing the search. Chapter 3 covers useful scan tools, and Chapters 5, 6, 7, 8, and 21 help interpret the clues.

TIP

Take a photo of the warning lights and stored codes before disconnecting the battery or clearing anything. Cars have a remarkable talent for forgetting evidence the moment you are finally ready to be responsible.

DIY versus Help

Not every no-start problem deserves a full driveway detective drama. Some checks are sensible, quick, and safe for an owner to do, while others are an excellent way to turn a manageable problem into a larger, smokier, more expensive one. The goal isn't to prove you and a flashlight can defeat modern automotive engineering through force of personality; the goal is to rule out the obvious, avoid making things worse, and know when it's time to call for backup.

Safe checks

These are reasonable owner-level checks before you call in the cavalry:

- Confirm the tank contains fuel. The fuel gauge is usually honest, but not always morally strong.
- Make sure the transmission is fully in Park or Neutral or press the clutch fully on manual-transmission vehicles.
- Check battery terminals for looseness or corrosion and look for obviously damaged cables.
- Try the spare key or replace the key-fob battery if the immobilizer seems grumpy.
- Scan for codes if you have a reader and write down exactly what the car does instead of summarizing it as "nothing."

When to call roadside or a shop

Call for help promptly if the vehicle died in traffic, smells like fuel, shows smoke, overheated badly, keeps killing batteries, grinds the starter, or throws hybrid/EV high-voltage alerts. Also, call if you simply can't do the checks safely where the car is sitting.

The best outcome isn't proving you can fix everything with a flashlight and stubbornness. The best outcome is getting the right clue, making the safe call, and getting the car running again without upgrading the problem.

IN THIS CHAPTER

» Matching the repair to the right kind of shop

» Using reviews, photos, and written estimates without getting snowed by shiny words

» Understanding labor rates, diagnostic fees, warranties, and consumer protections

» Building a solid long-term shop relationship

Chapter 23 Picking the Right Mechanic

Choosing a mechanic can feel like a leap of faith, but instead of butterflies, you get warning lights, mystery noises, and a bill with words like module and actuator on it. The good news is that you don't need to know how to rebuild an engine or decode every service acronym to choose wisely. You just need a practical way to match the problem to the right shop, ask a few smart questions, and notice whether the place feels competent or merely talented at sounding expensive.

This chapter helps you accomplish that decision-making process. You find out what different shops are actually good at, which certifications mean something, how to read the signs of a trustworthy operation, and how to keep your cool when estimates, warranties, or disagreements show up. The goal is simple: Help you feel comfortable, confident, and much less likely to be bamboozled by a waiting-room coffee machine and a confident shrug.

Why Choosing the Right Mechanic Matters

A good mechanic does more than fix parts. A good mechanic diagnoses correctly, explains clearly, works safely, and treats your time and money like they matter. That combination isn't glamorous, but it's exactly what keeps a repair from turning into a sequel nobody asked for.

Some repairs are mostly about convenience. Others are about safety wearing casual clothes. Brakes, steering, suspension, tires, fuel leaks, and electrical faults can move from annoying to dangerous in a hurry. The right mechanic helps protect you from sloppy work, missed causes, and parts-cannon guessing.

Good service also saves money over time. Accurate diagnosis prevents repeat visits. Clear explanations help you approve the right work at the right moment. And a shop that tells you what can wait, what can't, and why is worth far more than one that simply slides a large number across the counter and hopes your face doesn't twitch.

REMEMBER

You're not hiring a magician. You're hiring a process. Competence, communication, and honesty beat mystery, swagger, and random parts replacement every time.

Service Facility Types Today

Not every repair facility is built for every job, and that is perfectly normal. Different shops have different strengths, equipment, training, and business models. Choosing well is less about finding the single best shop in the universe and more about finding the right fit for the job sitting in your driveway.

Your options include:

- **Dealerships:** Dealership service departments are usually the best choice for factory recalls, warranty repairs, software updates, and complicated brand-specific issues. They have factory information, branded tools, and regular exposure to the quirks of one manufacturer. If your car needs a recall completed or a module programmed, a dealership is often the cleanest path from problem to solution.
- **Independents:** Independent shops are often the sweet spot for routine maintenance and a huge range of everyday repairs. The best ones combine experience, lower overhead than many dealerships, and a strong interest in keeping customers for the long haul. If you want practical advice, solid

communication, and a place that handles normal car life without making every oil seep sound like the end of civilization, a good independent is hard to beat.

- **Specialty EV/hybrid shops:** Electrified vehicles add high-voltage safety procedures, battery cooling systems, charging faults, and brand-specific software behavior. A true EV or hybrid specialist sees those patterns all day long. For battery, charging, isolation-fault, or hybrid-system problems, a specialist can save time, prevent guesswork, and reduce the odds of someone treating orange cables like regular weekend hardware.
- **Mobile mechanics:** Mobile mechanics can be wonderfully convenient for batteries, starter replacements, some brake work, basic diagnostics, pre-purchase inspections, and other jobs that do not require a full shop setup. They are less ideal when the repair needs a lift, alignment rack, tire machine, advanced programming, or a long diagnostic session involving smoke machines, oscilloscopes, or a technician muttering thoughtfully at live data.

TIP

When you call a shop, lead with the vehicle and the symptom: "2018 Honda Accord hybrid, warning light after charging" beats "My car is acting weird." Specifics help the right shop say yes, no, or not yet instead of booking you into a dead end.

Certifications

Certificates on the wall are not magic, but they're useful clues. They tell you where a shop or technician has invested time and training. Think of them as supporting evidence, not a personality test and definitely not a guarantee that the waiting-room fern is also trustworthy.

Here are a few key certifications and what they mean:

- **ASE:** ASE certification means a technician has passed exams in specific repair areas and usually has relevant hands-on experience. It suggests baseline knowledge and commitment to the trade. It doesn't mean every ASE tech is a genius, but it does mean the person has cleared a recognized standard instead of simply looking confident near a toolbox.
- **OEM certifications:** OEM, or original equipment manufacturer, certifications matter most when the repair depends on factory procedures, programming, or unusual systems. If the work involves advanced driver-assistance systems, software flashes, brand-specific diagnostics, or warranty decisions, factory-backed training becomes much more relevant.

- **EV-specific training:** For EVs and hybrids, ask about high-voltage safety training, battery service experience, charging-system diagnosis, and insulation or isolation-fault procedures. EV repair is not the time for cheerful improvisation. Electrified vehicles reward shops that know exactly where the risks are and exactly how to approach them.

Evaluating a Shop

You can learn a lot about a shop before handing over the keys. You're looking for signs that the place is organized, honest, and interested in solving the problem rather than just selling activity. You don't need perfection. You do need evidence that the adults are adulting. Look for:

- **Cleanliness:** A repair facility doesn't need to sparkle like a luxury hotel lobby. It does, however, need to feel orderly and reasonably safe. Tools should look managed rather than exploded. Customer areas, paperwork, and vehicles should not seem like they're one coffee spill away from archaeological status.
- **Communication:** Good shops ask useful questions, listen to your description, and explain next steps in plain language. They don't make you feel silly for noticing a smell, a vibration, or a dashboard light. They also don't hide behind jargon as if every repair were a secret wizard ritual.
- **Transparency:** Transparency means written estimates, clear approval steps, honest timelines, and explanations of what was tested and what was found. You should know whether the shop is diagnosing, repairing, waiting on parts, or simply waiting for your authorization while your car sits there contemplating its life choices.

Before you book, a quick phone screen can tell you a lot:

- Have you ever worked on this make, model, and powertrain?
- How do you handle diagnosis before recommending parts?
- What are your diagnostic fee and approval process?
- What warranty do you offer on parts and labor?

REMEMBER

Clear answers don't guarantee a perfect visit, but vague answers are useful too. They tell you to keep driving your search instead of your car.

Modern Tools of Trust

Modern cars generate useful data, and modern shops have better ways to share what they find. These tools are good news for customers because evidence beats vibes.

Photos and short videos can make a diagnosis far easier to understand. A leaking shock, cracked belt, worn brake pad, or corroded battery terminal is much less mysterious when you can actually see it. Good digital inspections create a record, support recommendations, and make it easier to separate real problems from theatrical adjectives.

Reviews are helpful when you read them like a detective, not like a panicked shopper at 11:47 p.m. Look for patterns: repeated praise for communication, accurate diagnosis, fair handling of comebacks, or the opposite. A single one-star novel about a man who "just knows" the alternator caused everything is less useful than ten calm reviews that describe what the shop did and how it handled follow-up.

Specialty Shops

Some repairs live in a narrow lane. When they do, specialization isn't fancy; it's efficient. The more unusual the system, the more valuable deep daily experience becomes, especially in the following areas:

- **EV battery service:** Battery-pack cooling issues, charging faults, high-voltage isolation problems, and battery-related warning messages are strong clues that you want a shop with dedicated EV equipment and training. This type of work is for people who already know the safety steps, not people who are excited to learn them on your car.
- **Hybrid drivetrains:** Hybrid drivetrains blend gasoline, electric, cooling, and control systems into one busy little ecosystem. A symptom that feels like a transmission issue may be a battery or motor-control issue, and a rough-engine complaint may have a hybrid-system twist. A specialist is often faster because the pattern is already familiar.
- **Performance tuning:** Modified vehicles often need shops that understand aftermarket parts, custom calibrations, drivability side effects, and the difference between "sporty" and "now it stalls at stoplights." If the vehicle is tuned or heavily modified, choose a shop that lives in that world rather than one that meets it once a month and sighs deeply.

Costs

Repair bills can feel personal because they rarely arrive with balloons. Still, most of the scary line items become much less scary when you understand what they're paying for and why.

A higher labor rate doesn't automatically mean a shop is greedy, and a lower one doesn't automatically mean it's a bargain. Rate reflects overhead, tools, information access, training, location, and the kind of work a shop is set up to do. A cheap labor rate attached to poor diagnosis is one of the most expensive bargains in car repair.

Diagnostic fees pay for time spent testing, measuring, scanning, confirming, and ruling things out. You're paying for expertise and process, not for the mechanic to gaze dramatically at the hood and whisper a lucky guess. When the problem is intermittent or electronic, good diagnosis is the repair before the repair.

Most shops normally mark up parts. The markup helps cover sourcing, warranty handling, stocking hassles, and the risk the shop assumes when it stands behind the repair. What matters isn't whether markup exists; what matters is whether the overall estimate is reasonable, clearly explained, and tied to the right fix.

TECHNICAL STUFF

Many shops use flat-rate labor guides rather than a stopwatch. If a job pays 2.0 hours and an experienced technician finishes sooner, the billed time may still be 2.0 hours. You're paying for the established labor operation and the skill it takes to do it efficiently.

Warranties and Protections

Good paperwork isn't glamorous, but it's the thing that turns confusion into clarity later. Estimates, approvals, invoices, and warranty terms matter most on the day something doesn't go according to plan.

Factory safety recalls are usually handled by authorized dealerships at no charge to the vehicle owner. A *factory safety recall* is when a vehicle manufacturer identifies a safety-related defect or noncompliance with standards, and they issue a formal notice to owners. This notice informs you that the manufacturer will fix the problem at no cost, ensuring the car is safe to operate. If you suspect a recall applies, check the vehicle identification number and get it addressed promptly.

Recalls are one area where the correct answer is often simple: Let the authorized shop handle the manufacturer's fix.

REMEMBER

If you have an extended warranty or service contract, say so before major diagnosis or teardown begins. Some contracts require prior approval, use specific parts rules, or limit where the repair can be done. Surprises are much less cute when they happen after the engine is already half disassembled.

In many places, customers have rights to written estimates, approval before added work, and detailed invoices. Some locations also regulate return of replaced parts or disclosures around used and rebuilt components. You don't need to memorize every rule, but you should expect paperwork that makes sense and a process that respects your authorization.

WARNING

Never authorize "whatever it needs" without limits. Set a dollar ceiling, ask for a call before additional work, and make sure the estimate clearly separates diagnosis, recommended repairs, and optional items.

Building Relationships

Finding a good mechanic is a lot like finding a good barber, dentist, or contractor: Once you have one, life gets easier. Familiarity improves communication, and a shared vehicle history makes future visits faster and less dramatic.

A shop that sees your vehicle regularly can spot patterns sooner. It knows what was done last time, what is overdue, what has already been ruled out, and whether the "new" noise is actually a returning guest with a familiar face.

Make sure you communicate clearly with your shop. Describe symptoms, not just theories. "It shudders at highway speed when I brake" is more helpful than "I think the rotors have trust issues." Good symptom descriptions help the shop test the right conditions and reduce the odds of expensive guessing.

Also, pay attention to service reminders, which can be genuinely useful when they're based on mileage, time, and the way you actually drive. They're less useful when every reminder reads like a panic attack in postcard form. Use them as prompts, not commandments, and ask the shop to help you prioritize what matters now versus soon.

Complaints and Resolutions

Even good shops can have communication misses, defective new parts, warranty comebacks, or honest mistakes. If something seems off, start with the shop promptly and give it a fair chance to inspect the issue. Calm, specific communication usually gets you farther than showing up ready to deliver a closing argument to the service counter.

If you leave an online review, be factual, specific, and proportional. Say what work was done, what was promised, what happened, and how the shop responded.

REMEMBER

Reviews are most useful when they inform other customers, not when they read like a revenge monologue written on three espressos and a parking-lot grudge.

If the dispute involves dealer warranty work, recall work, or a manufacturer-backed repair program, start with the service manager and then the manufacturer's customer-assistance channel. For larger payment disputes or unresolved complaints, consumer-protection agencies, credit-card dispute processes, or arbitration may be available depending on where you live and how you paid.

The goal is not to "win" a repair argument. The goal is to get the car fixed correctly, pay fairly for the work that was actually needed, and know who you can trust next time. Achieve that goal, and the whole process gets much less mysterious, much less stressful, and much less likely to make you consider buying a horse.

6
The Part of Tens

IN THIS PART . . .

Build habits that save money and prevent repairs.

Drive smarter to save fuel and energy.

IN THIS CHAPTER

» Giving your engine, tires, brakes, and battery the cheap attention they deserve

» Catching little problems before they turn into "well, there goes my weekend and my wallet" repairs

Chapter 24

Ten Car Care Habits That Save You Money

The cheapest repair is the one you never need. Most money-saving car habits aren't glamorous, which is rude because glamorous usually costs more and saves less. The real bestie move is the small, repeatable stuff: checking pressure, changing fluids on time, paying attention to warnings, and protecting the parts that age while you're busy having a life.

Small, boring habits beat heroic, expensive repairs every single time. In this chapter, we share ten car care habits that pay off in the long run.

Monitor Oil Life

Use the oil-life monitor and the exact oil spec your owner's manual calls for, especially if your car wants synthetic. The old 3,000-mile sticker isn't holy scripture anymore, but neither is wishful thinking. If you do lots of short trips, towing, or stop-and-go misery, your interval may need to be shorter. Fresh oil is cheap; worn bearings, timing hardware, and turbo drama are not. For a step-by-step guide on checking your oil, see Chapter 14.

Check Tire Pressure

Check tire pressure with a real gauge once a month, even if the TPMS light is staying quiet and acting innocent. Rotate on schedule and fix alignment if the wheel is crooked, the car pulls, or the tread is wearing like it lost a fight. Proper inflation saves fuel and keeps you from replacing a full set early. For more details on tire care, see Chapter 18.

REMEMBER

Use the pressure on the driver's-door sticker, not the maximum number molded into the tire sidewall. That sidewall number is the ceiling, not the goal, bestie.

Keep Your Filters Clean

Engine air filters, cabin air filters, and serviceable fuel filters all save money in their own deeply unglamorous ways. A clean engine filter helps performance and mileage. A clean cabin filter keeps the blower from working overtime and stops your vents from smelling like a damp gym bag. A fresh fuel filter, where applicable, protects pumps and injectors from dirt and water.

Check Your Fluids

Coolant, brake fluid, and transmission or CVT fluid are not fill-it-and-forget-it liquids. Low coolant can cook an engine, neglected brake fluid can corrode pricey parts, and ignored transmission fluid can turn a smooth gearbox into a very expensive personality problem. Use the correct fluid, watch for leaks, and follow the service schedule instead of waiting for symptoms to audition. For a deeper dive on fluid checks and types, head over to Chapter 14.

TECHNICAL STUFF

Brake fluid, coolant, ATF, and CVT fluid aren't mix-and-match bottles. Modern systems can be wildly picky, so match the exact spec before topping anything off.

Maintain Your Battery

Keep the 12-volt battery terminals clean, the hold-down tight, and the voltage checked before winter or a road trip. If the car sits, use a maintainer instead of hoping it feels cooperative next month. On hybrids and EVs, remember the tiny 12-volt battery can still leave you stranded, while the orange high-voltage stuff is firmly in the hands-off category. To find out more about battery care, see Chapter 6.

Pay Attention to Your Brakes

Pads and rotors are way cheaper than calipers, wheel bearings, or a tow truck after a metal-on-metal meltdown. Pay attention to squeals, grinding, pedal feel, and pulling under braking. If you drive a hybrid or EV, regen may save pad wear, but it can also let rust and sticky hardware sneak up on you because the friction brakes get used less often. For the full scoop on brake care, see Chapter 15.

Watch Your Alignment

A good alignment does more than keep the steering wheel straight. It protects tires, helps mileage, and keeps suspension parts from taking extra abuse. If the car wanders, bounces, clunks, or chews one edge of a tire faster than the rest, handle it early. Tires are too expensive to let bad geometry eat them for sport. For alignment details, see Chapter 18.

Pay Attention to the Check Engine Light

Don't ignore the check engine light until the car turns a small problem into a family event. A basic OBD-II reader is great for clues, especially for easy stuff like a loose gas cap, but it's not a crystal ball. Read the code, note the symptoms, and if the light is flashing or the car is running rough, stop pretending it can wait. For more on using OBD readers, see Chapter 3.

REMEMBER

A flashing check engine light usually means stop driving and prevent catalytic-converter damage, not swing by the parts store next weekend.

Protect Your Vehicle's Surface

Paint, trim, glass, and interior materials age whether you notice them or not. Regular washing, a decent ceramic spray or sealant, targeted paint-protection film in high-abuse areas, and simple interior protectants are cheaper than repainting panels, replacing sunbaked trim, or reconditioning a sad cabin before sale time. Looking cared-for also helps resale, which counts as saving money with extra steps.

Perform Scheduled Maintenance

Follow the maintenance schedule in your owner's manual, keep receipts, and write down what got done and when. Performing and keeping track of scheduled maintenance protects warranty coverage, makes diagnosis easier, and boosts resale because buyers love proof almost as much as they love a car with no weird surprises. You don't have to use the dealer for everything, but you do need the right parts, the right fluids, and records that show you did not just wing it.

TIP

A simple notes app, glove-box folder, or phone photo album of receipts still counts. Future you, your mechanic, and future buyers will all say thanks.

IN THIS CHAPTER

» Using Eco modes, tire pressure, and lighter loads to squeeze more from every mile

» Letting apps and basic maintenance save money

Chapter 25
Ten Ways to Save Fuel and Energy

Saving fuel and energy isn't about one magic trick. It's about stacking a bunch of small, sensible habits until your car quietly costs less to run. You don't need monk-like self-control or a spreadsheet called Car Feelings. You mostly need smoother driving, smarter trip planning, proper tire pressure, and the courage to remove the mystery junk living in your trunk.

The cheapest gallon of gas and the cheapest kilowatt-hour are the ones you never had to use in the first place. In this chapter, you discover tips that help you drive green and save money.

Drive Smoothly

Hard launches, late braking, and accordion-style speed changes burn extra fuel because every burst of speed has to be paid for twice: once to get moving and again when the brakes throw that motion away as heat. Pretend you have a full mug of coffee in the cupholder and would like it to stay there. Smoother throttle, calmer stops, and steadier cruising help gas cars, hybrids, and EVs alike.

Take Advantage of Eco Modes

Eco Mode isn't magic, but it is useful. On gas cars, it usually softens throttle response, changes shift timing, and calms the climate control a little. On hybrids and EVs, Eco mode may add gentler accelerator mapping or stronger lift-off regenerative braking, also known as regen. (For more on regenerative braking, see Chapter 10.) Use it when you want easy efficiency, but don't treat the button like it exempts you from common sense, traffic, or maintenance.

REMEMBER

Eco mode helps most when you help it back. If your right foot is doing launch-control cosplay (pretending you're on a racetrack), that little green leaf on the dash is just there for emotional support.

Make Smart Trips

Short cold starts, backtracking across town, and sitting in peak traffic all waste fuel or range without giving you anything fun in return. Batch errands so that one warm trip does the work of three cold ones, leave earlier when traffic is in one of its moods, and use route-planning or charging apps so you're not wandering around hunting for a plug like it personally insulted you.

Check Tire Pressure

Underinflated tires waste energy every minute they roll. Check pressures with a real gauge, pay attention to TPMS, and use the number on the driver's-door sticker, not the dramatic maximum printed on the tire sidewall. When replacement time comes, low-rolling-resistance tires can help mileage or range, but still buy enough traction for your climate so that you don't save pennies and lose grip like a fool. For more detailed tire guidance, see Chapter 18.

TECHNICAL STUFF

Rolling resistance is basically the energy a tire burns by flexing as it rolls. Less flex usually means better efficiency, which is why pressure and tire design matter more than most people think.

Unload

If your trunk is carrying a gym bag from 2022, three mystery totes, emergency shoes, and a bag of "I'll deal with it later," congratulations: You're hauling extra weight for no reason. More mass means more energy to get moving, especially in stop-and-go traffic. Clean out the junk, pull off racks you're not using, and stop making your poor car commute with your clutter. Even small items add up, especially in stop-and-go driving.

Be Mindful of Aerodynamics

At city speeds, extra drag is annoying. At highway speeds, it's a full-time thief. Empty roof racks, cargo boxes, open windows, and big upright gear punch the air like a parachute, which is why they quietly crush mileage on road trips. If you need to carry stuff, a hitch carrier is often kinder to efficiency than a roof box, and the most aerodynamic accessory is still the one not currently bolted to your car.

Use Regen Braking

On hybrids and EVs, regen pays you back a little every time you slow down, but only if you leave enough room to use it. Lift early, brake smoothly, and let the car harvest energy instead of sprinting to the red light and panic-stopping at the last second. Just don't get weirdly competitive about maxing regen when the battery is full or cold, because the car will limit it anyway. (For more on regenerative braking, see Chapter 10.)

Practice Smart Charging

Charging habits matter almost as much as driving habits. Precondition an EV while it's still plugged in so battery heating or cabin cooling uses wall power instead of driving range. Use off-peak rates when your utility offers them and treat DC fast charging like airport food: super useful on trips, not always the cheapest everyday lifestyle. Your battery doesn't need you flexing at every fast charger in town.

REMEMBER

Fast charging is a tool, not a personality. Road-trip hero? Absolutely. Daily habit when Level 2 at home or work would do? That is usually just paying more for the same electricity with extra battery heat on the side.

Use Good Apps

A good app can turn efficiency from vague guilt into useful feedback. Eco-driving apps and built-in telematics can show trip efficiency, idle time, charging cost, tire pressures, and route planning that cuts wasted miles. Use the data to spot patterns, not to become a dashboard goblin obsessing over every decimal. The goal is cheaper driving, not a new anxiety hobby.

Practice Preventive Maintenance

A neglected car burns more fuel and energy because it is working harder to do the same job. Dirty filters, low or wrong fluids, dragging brakes, old spark plugs where applicable, and bad wheel alignment all make efficiency worse in boring little ways that add up. Keep maintenance current, fix warning lights, and handle alignment when the car pulls or the steering wheel sits crooked. Simple habits, my friend — that's the whole trick!

TIP

If you want one easy rule to remember, it is this: Smooth inputs, proper tire pressure, less junk, and current maintenance beat almost every efficiency gadget sold in a flashy package.

Appendix

Monthly Maintenance Checklist

Keep this car wellness checklist on your phone and treat it like brushing your teeth: quick, easy, and worth it!

Under the Hood

- ❑ **Battery:** Check for corrosion, clean and tighten terminals
- ❑ **Engine oil:** Check dipstick or digital level display
- ❑ **Coolant reservoir:** Level between MIN/MAX when cold
- ❑ **Brake fluid:** Check level near MAX line
- ❑ **Serpentine belt:** Look for glazing, cracks, missing ribs
- ❑ **Engine air filter:** Hold to light, replace if dirty
- ❑ **Cabin air filter:** Check condition and airflow direction
- ❑ **Hoses:** Check for swelling, soft spots, cracks, crusty clamps

Fluids

- ❑ **Power steering fluid:** If hydraulic system is equipped, check level in reservoir

- ❑ **Transmission fluid:** Only if dipstick is accessible, check level
- ❑ **Washer fluid:** Fill with all-season formula

Tires and TPMS

- ❑ **Tire pressures:** Set to door jamb spec when cold
- ❑ **Tread depth:** Measure three spots across tire, check wear bars
- ❑ **Wear pattern:** Check for center, edge, and feathering wear
- ❑ **TPMS:** Confirm the system is functioning properly

Wipers and Washers

- ❑ **Wiper blades:** Check for chatter, streaks, and skips
- ❑ **Washer spray:** Test spray pattern
- ❑ **ADAS cameras and sensors:** Wipe clean gently

Tech Checks

- ❑ **Dashboard:** Review any warning lights
- ❑ **OBD-II scan:** If check engine light is on
- ❑ **Vehicle health app:** Review maintenance reminders

EV and Hybrid Extras

- ❑ **Charging cable:** Inspect pins, latch, and jacket
- ❑ **Inverter/battery coolant:** Do a visual check when cold (don't touch orange cables)

Index

Numerics

A

B

C

D

E

F

G

I

N

O

P

Q

R

T

U

V

W

Z

About the Authors

Desiree White: Desiree White, widely known as The SheMechanic®, is a self-taught mechanic, engine builder, and owner of Crown's Corner Mechanics in Conyers, Georgia. A former nurse and single mother, she began buying, repairing, and reselling vehicles while searching for a way to earn extra income. She later launched her mobile mechanic business, traveling throughout Metro Atlanta and quickly becoming the No. 1 mobile mechanic in five counties. That momentum allowed her to expand into a 9,000-square-foot shop in Conyers, where she built Crown's Corner Mechanics into a leading local repair business and a platform for mentorship, advocacy, and education.

White's work has earned wide attention for both her automotive skill and her entrepreneurial story. She has been featured by TikTok in its U.S. small-business spotlight and by outlets including FOX 5 Atlanta and The Associated Press. She has also brought her experience to broader conversations about women's leadership and small-business growth, including appearing as a speaker at the National Foundation for Women Legislators in a session focused on how TikTok helps scale women-owned small businesses.

Beyond the shop, White is a passionate advocate for women in the skilled trades, youth workforce development, and small-business opportunity. Through the ProTech Pathway Foundation and its hands-on internship program at Crown's Corner Mechanics, she is helping create a direct pathway into the automotive industry for aspiring technicians, career changers, and young people who need real-world training in a real working shop. She has also participated in Skills Jam programming connected to the SkillsUSA National Leadership & Skills Conference, using her platform to encourage the next generation to see the trades as respected, life-changing careers.

At the heart of her work is a simple mission: to break barriers, build confidence, and show people that these skills can be learned. Through her shop, her public platform, and her teaching, White is committed to making automotive knowledge feel more approachable, more empowering, and more accessible for everyone.

Deanna Sclar: Deanna Sclar is also the internationally best-selling author of *Buying a Car For Dummies*, a money-saving guide to every aspect of car ownership, including buying, selling, financing, auto insurance and claims, and more. A former contributing editor to *Family Circle*, *Boys' Life*, *Exploring*, and the *Los Angeles Times*, her articles have appeared in *Redbook*, *New Woman*, and other national magazines.

As an automotive expert and consumer spokesperson, Deanna has appeared on more than 800 radio and TV shows, including her own segment on *NBC Nightly*

News with Tom Brokaw; Good Morning America, Today; the Lifetime, CNN, and National Public Radio networks; and local shows in 30 major cities. Her *Auto Repair For Dummies* video was a National Home Video Awards finalist. She's cohosted *Outrageous Women*, a weekly TV talk show, and has produced, written, hosted, and edited several documentaries. Her "Auto Repair For Dummies" course at California State University, Northridge, drew the largest crowds ever in their continuing education program.

A lifelong environmental activist, Deanna led the group that threw the first Earth Day celebration in New York City and convinced Mayor Lindsay to start the first urban recycling program. The former "Thumbs Sclar" has restored two classic cars, a truck, and three homes. An inveterate gypsy and bluewater sailor, she has crewed her way across the Pacific and Polynesia, sailed and dived in Hawaii and the Great Barrier Reef, trekked alone for nine months through southeast Asia and five months through Brazil, and crossed the Atlantic in a small sailboat with a companion and a cat.

"My goal is to prove that we have control over our lives," she says. "Whether you are working on a car or making a lifelong dream come true, it's a do-it-yourself world. Knowing this has turned my life into a great adventure, and I want to pass the good news on to everybody else!"

Desiree's Dedication

To my children:

You didn't just watch me build a business — you watched me build a life.

From a carport to a thriving shop, every step was taken with you in mind.

Let this be your reminder: You don't have to wait for opportunity. You can create it.

— Desiree White

Desiree's Acknowledgments

Writing this book has been one of the biggest honors of my life, and there is no way I could have done it alone.

First, I want to thank Tracy Boggier, Executive Editor, and Nina Hook, Editorial Assistant, at Wiley, for reaching out to me in the first place and giving me this opportunity. Thank you for believing that my story, my experience, and my voice deserved a place in this book.

To Nicole Sholly, Development Editor, at Wiley, thank you for showing me the ropes and helping prepare me for what it really takes to write a book. You helped make this process feel possible.

And to Kelly Ewing, Development Editor, thank you for being with me through this entire journey. You have edited this book, guided me, encouraged me, and truly held my hand every step of the way. Your patience, care, and support meant more than I can put into words. Thank you for sticking with me through all of it.

To my husband, Laertes "DoRight" White, thank you for being that creepy, persistent man who kept showing up at my door with vintage cars for me to work on when I thought I wasn't ready. You showed me I was ready, and then you showed me how I was supposed to be loved. Thank you for encouraging me, supporting every decision I have made on this journey, and always seeing more in me than I could see in myself. We aren't done yet, baby.

To my son, Dakota Curry, you were just a young teenager when I suddenly started tearing apart cars in the carport. We cried together during that first transmission swap we did, and yes, it took us three times, but you stayed right there by my side learning with me. Look how far we have come, son. I am so proud of you.

To my daughter, Sophia Hill, you blow me away with everything you soak up just by being present. First you were there in the carport, then handing me tools on my mobile jobs, and now installing pistons in motors by yourself at ten years old. No matter what you do in life, you are going to be astonishing.

To John Clark, my right hand in the shop, you unknowingly became my mentor over the years. Thank you for always explaining, always creating, and never wanting to take a darn vacation or day off. You are the shop, and I am beyond grateful for all that you are.

To Jeremiah Durden, my longest employee, my son's best friend, and my second son, you didn't even know how to do an oil change when you started working with me. Now you are one of our top technicians, helping train and guide everyone around you. By training you while I was still training myself, you taught me patience and reminded me that no question is ever dumb. Thank you for showing me that I could be a teacher as well as a leader.

I also want to acknowledge Jennifer Keen. You are the reason I have my shop. Thank you for believing in me so much that you wrote me a check and pushed me to get a brick-and-mortar location. You saw something in me after just a few mobile repairs to your RV that I still thought was only a dream. You helped make it real, and I will never forget that.

To my team, my customers, my supporters, and everyone who has followed this journey, encouraged me, trusted me, and cheered me on, thank you. So much of what I have built has been built in public, and your support has carried me through more than you know.

This book would not exist without the people who believed in me before I fully believed in myself. Thank you all for helping me build this life, this business, and now this book.

Publisher's Acknowledgments

Executive Editor: Tracy Boggier
Development Editor: Kelly Ewing
Copy Editor: Kelly Ewing

Senior Managing Editor: Kristie Pyles
Production Editor: Tamilmani Varadharaj
Cover Image: Glenda Powers/stock.adobe.com